BREAKING
FREE

Bob,

You have been involved with ADI
for a while now & I thought
you might appreciate this.
It is really the history according
to Ken Harris but still is an
ok summary.

[signature]
11/1/00.

BREAKING FREE

FREE

Transforming Australia's Defence Industry

Chris Coulthard-Clark

Australian Scholarly Publishing

© Chris Coulthard-Clark 1999
First published 1999 by Australian Scholarly Publishing Pty Ltd
PO Box 299, Kew, Victoria 3101
Suite 102, 282 Collins Street, Melbourne, Victoria 3000
Tel: (03) 9817 5208 Fax: (03) 9817 6431
Email: aspic@ozemail.com.au

National Library of Australia cataloguing-in-publication data:

Coulthard-Clark. C. D. (Christopher David). 1951-.
Breaking free: transformation of Australia's defence industries.

Bibliography.
Includes Index.
ISBN 1 875606 68 8.

1. Defense industries – Australia – History.
2. Australia – Industries.
3. Australia – Armed Forces – Procurement.
I. Australian Defence Industries. II. Title.

355.260994

Design by Green Poles Design
Printed in Australia by Imprenta

CONTENTS

PREFACE

Since before the First World War, Australia had operated a group of facilities providing equipment and support for its armed services. In 1988 the government decided to take what remained of these, which until then had been part of the Department of Defence, and form them into a separate government-owned company – Australian Defence Industries Pty Ltd, or ADI as it quickly became known. This step, which became effective in May 1989, was a response to major problems which had long beset this area of state activity. As detailed in the chapters which follow, the defence factories had been a perpetual drain on the public purse. Here is told the story of how the creation of ADI turned around a major loss-making government business enterprise (GBE) into one returning profits to its owners, the Australian people, and how ownership of these assets was eventually turned over to private enterprise with a further sizeable return to the public coffers.

The writing of this book was directly commissioned by ADI. Recognising that it had received custody of a significant part of Australia's industrial heritage, in 1991 the company engaged two academics, Professor Roy MacLeod and Dr Andrew Ross, to carry out a pilot survey of the wealth of historical material which ADI had inherited – primarily to recommend a strategy for managing its preservation or disposal, as appropriate. A further objective was to make an assessment of documentary records which might support the writing of a history of munitions supply and organisation in Australia, from the earliest times up to the present.

The principal finding produced from this report in March 1992 was that two histories should be written: one dealing with the transitional and contemporary history of ADI from around 1982 onwards, with a short introduction linking the early history of munitions with events of the 1980s; and a second, more extensive volume dealing with the entire history of munitions supply in this country. When this advice was weighed, a decision was made within ADI to commission a single volume covering the period from 1889. This project would be carried out by an historian working to the company as a consultant, but not employee. The brief provided to the author stipulated only that some two-thirds of the work should address the issues of transition in the period of the 1980s and beyond.

This background is provided to explain to the reader both my relationship with the company and the freedom I enjoyed to explore those aspects and issues which seemed, in my judgement alone, to be important in an historical context. It should be understood that no pressure was placed on me to shape this book in any particular way or to serve any special purpose. What was asked for was a 'warts and all' history recording the company's origins and progress. So committed was ADI to this principle that the managing director insisted that those executives who were interviewed for the project were not to attempt to rephrase or polish their words when they later saw themselves quoted in the draft text – in effect requiring that they live with the views and opinions they gave at the time, however inelegantly expressed.

On the other hand, this book is not an attempt to provide a definitive account of the history of defence production in Australia. While the century between the creation of the Colonial Ammunition Company in 1889 and the advent of ADI in 1989 is dealt with in a fair amount of detail, this effort was undertaken primarily to show the motives, course and degree of success involved in this area of government activity. It specifically aims to highlight the problem which the creation of ADI was intended to fix, and then examine what the outcome has been and how that was achieved.

For the many thousands of people who over the years have worked in one or other of the defence factories mentioned in this book, there may be some disappointment to find so little of the day-to-day detail of what it was like to work there. Clearly that was a task beyond the scope of a single volume of this sort. Indeed, considering the long histories of several of the factories – some of which have now closed – a strong case exists for these facilities to have individual studies written about them. It has been a conscious decision to make this volume a study of a problem and its solution, rather than of people and establishments.

Despite this deliberately narrowed focus, I have tried to convey a close feel for the role, personalities and motives of the people whose story this is. In particular, I have made sure that much of the narrative of what was done and why comes from the mouths of the participants in these events. Part of the reason for this approach stemmed from the recognition that here was, in fact, a marvellous opportunity to write about an event of historical importance while nearly all the key players in that drama were still accessible. That a few have already passed on was an additional factor behind the company's desire to get the rest on record.

By reason of its size, complexity, and the strategic significance of the activity which it embodied, the corporatisation of ADI can be viewed as of national importance. At the time of the company's formation, the eleven facilities within its structure were employing 6500 people in three States, and turning out production worth nearly half a billion dollars every year. As one of the first and largest undertakings of its kind in Australia, the ADI experience deserves to be regarded as something of a case study.

There is, moreover, a wider significance to the company's advent, deriving from international events taking place in the same timeframe. In Britain, the Conservative Party, led by Margaret Thatcher (elected to office in May 1979), was transforming that country's social, economic and industrial scene. The Thatcher government's efforts were directed towards reducing the extent of regulatory controls and reversing the historical trend towards public sector involvement in areas of commercial activity. There, too, enterprises were being taken out of the bureaucracy and corporatised as statutory authorities and companies; many state-owned enterprises were also returned by sale to the ownership of the private sector, or privatised.

The purpose behind these reforms was, as Thatcher's Secretary of State for Environment (Michael Heseltine) explained in 1995, two-fold:

> ... first, to improve the efficiency of State industries and to stem the losses they were making, and second, to widen the share ownership of these companies, among employees and the general public.

According to Heseltine, the Conservatives' program was outstandingly successful:

> The efficiency of the companies has increased beyond recognition. The customer receives better and faster services than before – and in many cases cheaper ones! And on share ownership we have ... [expanded] the number of shareholders from 3 million in 1979 to more than 10 million today ...

> Since the privatisation process began in the UK, 48 major businesses have been sold and some £60 billion raised for the UK taxpayer. Instead of costing the taxpayer £50 million each week in 1978–79, the privatised companies are paying the Exchequer some £55 million each week.[1]

The Thatcher government's apparently ground-breaking policies were watched with interest around the world. The changes made to the management of Britain's state industries were widely emulated, including in the matter of ownership. The July 1994 report of the World Bank estimated that 15,000 separate state-owned enterprises have been privatised, most of them since 1990.[2] In her retirement these days, Lady Thatcher proudly reflects on the fact that now 'almost universal lip service is paid to the case for privatization'.[3]

While it is undoubtedly true that privatisation has become the political creed of the 1990s, dissenting voices from the new orthodoxy are frequently and loudly heard. Indeed, in Britain dissatisfaction at pricing policies adopted and high executive salaries paid by authorities newly-freed from government control produced a strong public backlash. Many observers were predicting that pursuit of privatisation – described by one Australian writer as 'a system of grand larceny, legitimised by the hocus-pocus of economic theory'[4] – would see Thatcher's Conservative successor, John Major, ejected from office, long before that outcome eventually materialised on 1 May 1997.

As some commentators point out, however, the wrong conclusions should not be drawn from the Major government's defeat. Writing before the Labour Party under Tony Blair swept into power, one respected British journal stressed that the manner and lengths to which privatisation had been pursued in Britain was not a fair reflection of its worth as a policy:

> [It] may be the government that is discrediting privatisation, rather than vice versa ... This dislike seems to have little to do with the merits of privatisation, which are genuine and considerable ... Remember that privatisation's enduring unpopularity did not prevent the Tories from winning the last four general elections.[5]

Another comments that Blair's victory also could not be construed as a repudiation of Thatcher's legacy, since there was little inclination to wind back her reforms:

> The Conservatives were certainly defeated, decisively so, but this was a rejection of their performance, not their basic ideas ... And by the time of its victory, New Labour had embraced Thatcherism, although a remake of Thatcherism heavily leavened with 'compassion' and 'inclusiveness'. The return of the Labour Party to power after almost two bleak decades in the wilderness represented not a defeat for Margaret Thatcher but a consolidation of her revolution.[6]

The debate goes on. Argument often revolves around whether selling off is really essential to lift GBE performance or whether corporatisation alone will suffice. Some claim that the only requirement for achieving greater efficiency is exposure to competition, and replacing the public service outlook with a commercial culture.[7]

Despite the benefits of privatisation, the Labor government in power at the federal level in Australia from 1983–96 was more cautious about viewing it as a panacea. Although plans were developed to sell off a range of government assets,

this local program by no means represented a total departure from the principle of
public ownership of enterprises. Nor has it been implemented willy-nilly, resisting
the enormous attraction of finding quick money-spinners to help balance budget
deficits in difficult times.

To some minds the approach adopted in Australia seems timid, and indicative
that government commitment to genuine economic reform is only half-hearted.
An example frequently cited by these critics is that of Australia's near-neighbour,
New Zealand. Here, five years after the Tory victory in Britain, the Labour government of David Lange was elected in July 1984. Under the guidance of the
finance minister, Roger Douglas, it set about implementing a program of radical
change aimed at creating a more competitive economy, resorting to both corporatisation and privatisation and a dramatic shift towards deregulation.

By 1992 the rewards of reform were being reaped across the Tasman.
Privatisation of the Rural Bank, Post Bank, Air New Zealand, NZ Telecom,
Petrocorp and the Government Printing Office had each reportedly been followed
by significant gains in productivity and the development of new and better services. The privatised Post Bank turned an expected $50 million loss into a $30 million profit; NZ Telecom increased its profits by 300 per cent while cutting the real
cost of phone services by 20 per cent, waiting time for a phone connection from
six weeks to three days, and for directory assistance from up to 20 minutes to
20–30 seconds. Other corporate bodies, such as those supplying electricity and
coal, similarly achieved huge profit improvements or turned around losses while
reducing prices to customers.[8]

Such results prompted one Australian newspaper columnist to observe in 1994
that:

> By managing its economy much more effectively than we have since 1983, by
> undertaking courageous steps towards the reform and opening up of its econ-
> omy to the world, and by dealing roughly, though at some considerable cost,
> with the cosy institutions of the past, it [New Zealand] shows every sign of
> being on the brink of overtaking Australia, perhaps before the centenary of
> federation in terms of living standards and economic performance.[9]

The significance and relevance of the New Zealand experience to Australia's
circumstances, however, remains – like Britain's – open to debate. One local writer
attempted to point up the similarities:

> New Zealand['s] institutions and its culture are like Australia's. What is more,
> the two nations are tackling their respective economic problems in broadly the
> same ways. Indeed, the generic policy options are limited.[10]

Another remarked:

But it is quite another thing to suggest that we would have been better off in this country if we had not stuck with our more gradualist economic and industry reform process.[11]

Most commentators agree that New Zealand's economic woes were more acute than Australia's, and that the pressures and need for change were not only greater but that the New Zealand economy had further to come to reach a comparable state. Buttressing the case that there is nothing to suggest that Australia would have been better off following the New Zealand path is evidence that the latter's overall economic performance has, in fact, fallen 'disastrously behind' Australia's since about 1987, and that gains through restructuring in Australia were achieved without anything like the severe adjustment costs of the New Zealand program.[12]

There is, nonetheless, something rather strange about arguments as to whether or not Australia has been tardy in embracing fresh and innovative ideas from overseas, and whether or not New Zealand rather than Britain would have served as an appropriate model to follow. Few of those entering the debate recognise that many features of the 'new' reforms are not only not new at all, but embraced measures actually pioneered in Australia in the nineteenth century. Notions of removing business activities from direct departmental control had a history in this country dating back to the 1880s, when the colony of Victoria placed its railways under a board of commissioners. Such an approach seemed so radical at the time that British experts later studied the Australian 'model'.[13] Many readers of this book may be surprised, too, to discover that munitions supply in this country had its origins in the private sector rather than as a government organisation.

While vast changes separated the Australia of the 1980s from a century earlier, the irony of a return to trying what was initially a home-grown cure (though now packaged in very different form) is obvious. As shown by this study of how and why Australia's defence factories came to take shape as a government company, there is much about the processes entailed which have about them an element of 're-inventing the wheel'. This fact, however, only reinforces the point that a study of the advent of ADI is both timely and valuable in providing understanding in a major area of public policy.

Perhaps the first tribute that should be paid, therefore, is to the foresight of the ADI management who decided that the best time to act in commissioning a history had already arrived. I regard it as very much my good fortune to have been given the opportunity to work in this little-explored field, in Australia, of industrial history.

A debt of gratitude must be expressed to the many people who have given their time and assistance to be interviewed for this book. This included many who still have an association with the company, and others whose knowledge or connection with the subject were less direct. All were ready to help flesh out my knowledge and understanding of events which are still so recent that it will probably be a decade or so before the majority of scholarly researchers discover the period. I am particularly thankful to those who read the draft manuscript, in whole or part; their comments resulted in many improvements to both style and content.

Further thanks are due to a number of bodies and individuals who met specific requests for assistance. Among them I would mention Allom Lovell & Associates, conservation architects of Melbourne, for help in tracking down source material relating to the early history of ammunition production at Footscray; Virginia Macleod of the Local History Resource Unit, Pittwater Council, for assistance with information regarding the Von Bieren powderworks at Elanora Heights, Narrabeen; Mr B.L. Hayhow, sales manager for Explosives Division of Imperial Chemical Industries, Auckland, New Zealand, for assistance with information about the history of the Colonial Ammunition Company; Professor Roger Wettenhall, for enabling me to 'audit' his Masters degree course on Public Enterprise at the University of Canberra; and Wing Commander Graham Walton, of Central Photographic Establishment, RAAF Base Williams, Laverton, Victoria, for assistance in photographically copying the portrait of John Whitney, then held at ADI Footscray.

A salute goes to Dr Ross Babbage, now Corporate Executive Strategic Analysis at ADI's headquarters, who co-ordinated and administered the project during its initial two-year life as well as during its subsequent extension from late 1997 to update and revise the manuscript for publication. I am grateful for his steady support and willing assistance whenever required. Leigh Funston, Angela Bennett and Sheridan Chapman, from the Corporate Relations side of headquarters, were also always ready to meet my requests for material.

Finally, to my former wife and business partner, Tina, I am full of thanks. This book would not have been completed on time without her effort in the role of research assistant. Although we have moved on, I know we both miss the long conversations to which this project gave rise as we explored the connection and implications of parts of the story with which we were dealing.

CHRIS COULTHARD-CLARK
Canberra
June 1999

ABBREVIATIONS

AA	anti-aircraft
AAO	Australian Audit Office (title subsequently changed to Australian National Audit Office)
ACTU	Australian Council of Trade Unions
ADF	Australian Defence Force
ADI	Australian Defence Industries
AEW	Aircraft Engineering Workshop (Pooraka, SA)
AGCF	Australian Government Clothing Factory
AGEW	Australian Government Engine Works (Melbourne)
AIDC	Australian Industry Development Corporation
AIF	Australian Imperial Force
ALP	Australian Labor Party
AMASS	Australian Minesweeping and Surveillance System
APG	Australian Property Group
ASC	Australian Submarine Corporation
ASEAN	Association of South East Asian Nations
ASTA	Aerospace Technologies of Australia
AVO	Australian Valuation Office
AWM	Australian War Memorial, Canberra
BHP	Broken Hill Proprietary Co. Ltd.
CAC	Colonial Ammunition Company/Commonwealth Aircraft Corporation
CAD	computer aided design
CAM	computer aided manufacture

CDP	Chief of Defence Production
CEO	Chief Executive Officer
CGM	Chief General Manager
CIWS	close-in weapons system
CSIRO	Commonwealth Scientific and Industrial Research Organisation
CSP	commercial support program
CSS	Commonwealth Superannuation Scheme
DAS	Department of Administrative Services
DDS	Department of Defence Support
DFDC	Defence Force Development Committee
DHA	Defence Housing Authority
DRSC	defence required support capability
DSTO	Defence Science and Technology Organisation
EWCAPSS	electronic warfare command and processing sub-system
GAF	Government Aircraft Factory (later Factories)
GBE	government business enterprise
CGEW	Commonwealth Government Engine Works (see AGEW)
GE	General Electric Co. (United States)
GGM	Group General Manager
GM	General Manager
GRP	glassfibre reinforced plastic
GST	government sales team
GWESF	Guided Weapons and Electronics Support Facility (St. Marys, NSW)
HDH	Hawker de Havilland Co.
HMAS	Her Majesty's Australian Ship
HMS	Her Majesty's Ship
IAC	Industries Assistance Commission
ICI	Imperial Chemical Industries
IDD	Industrial Decontamination Division
IHI	Ishikawajima-Harima Heavy Industries Ltd. (Japan)
MGS	Mason, Gray & Strange
MSB	Munitions Supply Board
MSD	Munitions Supply Division
MSL	Munitions Supply Laboratories
NAB	National Australia Bank
NATO	North Atlantic Treaty Organisation
NED	Naval Engineering Division
NLA	National Library of Australia, Canberra
NSRB	National Security Resources Board
ODP	Office of Defence Production
OTC	Overseas Telecommunications Commission

PDF	Production Development Facility (Salisbury, SA)
PNG	Papua New Guinea
PSOC	Principal Supply Officers Committee
RAAF	Royal Australian Air Force
RAF	Royal Air Force
RAN	Royal Australian Navy
RCM	reserve capacity maintenance
RDX	cyclonite explosive
REFA	Review of Explosive Factories of Australia
RES	regional environmental study
RFP	Resources, Finance & Plans Division
RMA	revolution in military affairs
RN	Royal Navy
RNZAF	Royal New Zealand Air Force
SAA	small arms ammunition
SAF	Small Arms Factory (Lithgow, NSW)
SARP	small arms replacement program
SECA	Systems Engineering Consortium of Australia
SLR	self-loading rifle
SMLE	short magazine Lee-Enfield rifle
TDS	Transfield Defence Systems
TNT	trinitrotoluene
UDS	Universal Defence Systems
UK	United Kingdom (Britain)
US/USA	United States/United States of America
WED	Weapons & Engineering Division

1

A STRATEGIC NEED

Production in Australia of munitions and other warlike stores and equipment needed for defence purposes had its origins, in a haphazard way, during the nineteenth century. From the mid-1830s, for example, vessels built in local shipyards for colonial government service were often armed for a secondary defence role.[1] In 1855, at the time of the Crimean War, a 60-ton ketch called *Spitfire* was built as a gunboat at Cuthbert's yard at Millers Point, Sydney.[2] During the Maori wars across the Tasman in the early 1860s, two gunboats were built at P.N. Russell's Sydney ironworks for the New Zealand government and another by the Australian Steam Navigation Company; also used by British forces in the Waikato War were several brass mortars fabricated at Cockatoo Island by Captain Gother Mann, the engineer-in-chief and superintendent of convicts at the dockyard there.[3] In 1872–73 four armed schooners were constructed in Sydney for the Royal Navy squadron which was based in Australian waters from 1859.[4]

Until the 1870s the Australian colonies had generally flourished in a regional environment as tranquil as implied by their Pacific Ocean setting. In September 1870, however, the last British garrison troops had been withdrawn from Sydney, and the colonists were left with the prime responsibility for their own defence. Over the next decade the spillover effects were felt of rising tension in Europe, especially the extension of European conflicts and ambitions into the South Pacific. Attempts by foreign powers to acquire island empires in the region gave rise to concerns which, combined with disputes with Britain over issues of commerce and immigration, focussed attention on defence matters as never before.[5] Colonial governments responded by raising small military forces, composed mainly of volunteer citizen soldiers but trained and administered by cadres of permanent staff, and by establishing fixed defences at their principal ports.

Proposal for a federal arsenal

In February 1881 the New South Wales government appointed a commission to inquire into all aspects of the organisation and administration of that colony's defence forces. This body comprised four colonels from the military forces of New South Wales, Victoria and South Australia, under the chairmanship of Colonel (later Major-General Sir) Peter Scratchley, a visiting British officer who had been appointed consulting engineer to all the Australian colonies except Western Australia, and to New Zealand as well. Among the recommendations contained in the commission's report was a suggestion that steps should be taken to set up a small arms ammunition plant.[6]

The justification for this proposal was an argument that the colony needed to lessen its dependence on England, which in times of need could not meet its own demands, or did so through buying from private firms at greatly increased costs. From the outset, therefore, the case justifying the possession of local sources of supply for defence materiel was based on both strategic and economic grounds: having a local defence industry represented what might well be the crucial or strategic edge in any emergency which arose.

It was purely coincidental that in 1884 a factory to manufacture gunpowder was built at Narrabeen, north of Sydney, initially as a private enterprise. The project encountered financial difficulties, however, and the works closed without any gunpowder ever being produced, leaving the substantial stone premises as the sole monument to this failed undertaking.[7]

Follow-up to the commission's findings was, paradoxically, more pronounced in neighbouring Victoria than it was in New South Wales. The southern colony had been the first in Australia to create a local navy, following the passing of a British act of parliament authorising such forces in 1865. In that same year a select committee of the Victorian parliament dealing with defence issues had urged that 'it has become the duty of the Government to take prompt steps to establish a powder manufactory' in the colony, though no action was taken at the time.[8] During the decade of the 1880s Victoria also embarked on a program which caused spending on defence to rise from under £80,000 in 1880 to £350,000 ten years later.[9]

On 27 January 1882 Frederick Sargood, a major in Victoria's volunteer forces and a former parliamentarian, wrote to the War Office to inquire about the machinery required for manufacturing cartridges for the Martini-Henry .45-inch army rifle.[10] At that time he was in London as special delegate to the Imperial Commission for the protection of British possessions abroad, and also a member of the Board of Advice to the colony's Agent-General.[11] He was supplied with the plans and specifications before returning to Melbourne later that year and regaining a seat in the Legislative Council, but nothing immediately came of this initiative.

Significantly, in November 1883 the government set about establishing a separate department of state to control and manage the affairs of Victoria's large and growing military structure. Sargood became the first Minister for Defence appointed in Australian history, a portfolio he retained until 1886.[12] In this capacity he presided over the vigorous program to build up Victoria's forces, which included local fortifications and armament supplies. This was an effort which took on particular importance following the possibility which arose during March–May 1885 of war breaking out between Britain and Russia over the Pendjeh crisis (the Russian occupation of northern Afghanistan).

With a sense of urgency, on 11 June 1885 Sargood asked the Victorian agent-general in London, Sir Graham Berry, to make inquiries about the costs of establishing a factory for manufacturing 6-inch fortress guns and field guns. In this instance the minister was probably acting at the suggestion of his new secretary to the defence department, Major-General M.F. Downes, who had taken up appointment in Melbourne in April.[13] As Downes was an artillery officer, with experience in local fixed defences during his previous position as commander of South Australia's military forces, it would have been understandable that he had an interest in such an area.

A reply to this request was not received for a year, when Berry passed on a report written by Captain Edward Palliser to Canada's minister for militia and defence regarding the arsenal then proposed for construction at the west-coast naval base at Esquimalt, British Columbia. Accompanying this correspondence were quotations for machinery and tools necessary for a gun factory, with the cost of a plant estimated at over £12,300.[14] Obviously, the munitions business was going to be a very expensive enterprise for colonial governments to enter.

The agent-general was also able to enclose an interesting newspaper item by Palliser regarding Canada's contribution to imperial defence. This pointed out that, at a time when Australia was 'worried and harassed' by annexations of islands in the Pacific, the base at Esquimalt would dominate 'the rear of any ring fence of islands others may set up round Eastern Australia'. While Canada was thus filling 'a great strategic want', Palliser argued that 'it would be well [for Australia] to follow Canada's example and establish a central arsenal, say at Melbourne'.[15]

Underlying this exploration of the costs associated with implementing practical measures were concerns at a declining security situation in Australia's near-region. In April 1883 the Queensland government, with the approval and support of other colonies, attempted to forestall reported German plans to annex the eastern half of New Guinea by itself taking possession of the territory on behalf of the British empire. The failure of London to endorse this action led to the convening of an inter-colonial convention in Sydney during November–December of that year.

This meeting clearly recognised that Australian interests might sometimes diverge from England's – or at least that it was not wise to depend entirely on the British shield. Great unease was already felt within Australia over French aims in the New Hebrides, so that when Germany subsequently went ahead and annexed the north-eastern part of New Guinea in 1884, colonial administrations drew a clear lesson as to the futility of attempting to influence the policies of a remote and unsympathetic government in London.

The 1883 convention resolved to set up a Federal Council of Australasia, which would be authorised to act with respect to 'the relations of Australasia with the islands of the Pacific'.[16] New South Wales and South Australia (with New Zealand) abstained from membership of the Council, which in consequence functioned as little more than 'a debating society'.[17] Nonetheless, in subsequent years the Council was responsible for the first joint efforts by the governments represented to fortify key places such as the coaling station at Thursday Island, off North Queensland, and King George's Sound in Western Australia.

At the first session of the Federal Council of Australasia, meeting in Hobart in January–February 1886, the Tasmanian premier, Adye Douglas, proposed the establishment of 'an Arsenal on the mainland of Australia for the purpose of manufacturing and supplying munitions of war for Australasia'.[18] Douglas' motive had little to do with contributing to imperial defence, since to Council members he predicted a 'United States of Australasia … independent of the little island in the Northern Hemisphere'; when called to order for his remarks he recalled the toasts of 40 years earlier to an 'Australian Republic'.[19] The proposal having been coloured with such connotations, discussion of the merits of an arsenal was inconclusive and the motion withdrawn.

Later that same year Major-General Downes, in his capacity as secretary of the Victorian defence department, wrote to the new premier, Duncan Gillies, pointing out the need for a plant for manufacturing small arms ammunition along the lines proposed by the 1881 royal commission. Downes had been a member of that body, and he had attempted to convince his colleagues on the commission of the need for a 'central arsenal for all the Colonies' which was mentioned in its report.[20]

A key element in Downes' thinking was that:

[It] would be more advantageous for a factory to be started by a private company having at their command experienced managers and foremen, than to incur the outlay of constructing one and obtaining technical and foremen staff at high salaries.[21]

Implicit in his approach was a belief that direct government involvement or managerial control in such a venture was not essential for its success. If private enterprise could meet the need which had been identified, it should be encouraged to do so. Here was a further example of a view which had emerged in the 1880s – most noticeably in Victoria of all the Australian colonies – that business enterprises, even where reflecting an important role of government (such as railways), were best run at arm's length from government control.[22]

Another important aspect of Downes' proposal was that the other Australian premiers should be approached about joining in the setting up of one central factory, although – as already seen – the disposition towards joint action at this time was hardly strong. Approaches were made to colonial governments around Australia, and New Zealand and Fiji as well, asking that they indicate whether they would encourage the project by a joint subsidy or guarantee. These would promise nothing more, however, than to make purchases of ammunition – if quality and price were equal to that obtainable through importation from Britain.[23]

The Colonial Ammunition Company

In an effort to initiate an enterprise along the lines sketched by Downes, the Victorian premier used the Budget speech in July 1886 to declare his government's willingness to reward any company which manufactured locally a certain amount of ball cartridges of approved quality with a bonus of £2500, to offset the capital expenditure involved. In addition, the government offered a free grant of land for the erection of a factory.[24] This initiative led to considerable correspondence with interested companies in Australia and elsewhere, especially England.

Among the responses received was one from Captain John Whitney, a 50-year-old former British Army officer who was already engaged in producing cartridges for small arms and sporting rifles at a plant in New Zealand. Whitney had migrated to Auckland with his family of three sons and three daughters late in 1884, just in time to become caught up in the war fever created by the Pendjeh crisis the following year. He had immediately joined the local volunteers, taking command of an artillery battery at Auckland, and was subsequently appointed assistant aide-de-camp to the colonial commander, Major-General Sir George Whitmore.[25]

Whitney was thus in a position to see the dramatic effects which the crisis over Afghanistan had engendered for New Zealand, and indeed all of Britain's colonies. Lacking an ammunition reserve, London had been forced to retain all ammunition manufactured in British works and suspend exports, causing a shortage throughout the empire. The New Zealand Minister for Defence, John Ballance, tried to find a local manufacturer as a matter of urgency. Seizing this opportunity, Whitney formed a partnership with an Auckland gunsmith, W.H. Hazard. Their initial attempt to manufacture .577 Snider cartridges failed dismally; Hazard quit the partnership, leaving Whitney £600 in debt to his bank.[26]

Forming a private company, Messrs Whitney and Sons, Whitney persisted with the scheme. Despite delays in obtaining powder propellant, unsuitable materials and a government stipulation that all machinery had to be made in New Zealand, a satisfactory cartridge round was produced. By the end of 1886 some 150,000 rounds had been delivered to government authorities, and the company was preparing to embark on the manufacture of shotgun shells. The latter proved immensely popular and saw total production grow to about two million rounds by the end of 1887.[27] The revenue generated by these orders enabled Whitney to expand his Mount Eden premises.

Whitney realised that further opportunities existed on the Australian mainland when he journeyed to England to purchase more modern machinery. On 21 May 1887 he wrote to the Victorian agent-general in London mentioning his intention to form a company which would comprise his existing firm in conjunction with several British ammunition manufacturers and others, including T.S. Hall and W.K. D'Arcy, two prominent figures with mining interests in Queensland.[28] In effect, Whitney was transforming his private business into a limited liability company in order to finance the expansion he was planning.

Following up his initial expression of interest, on 21 July Whitney wrote again, this time directly to Sir James Lorimer (Sargood's successor as defence minister, then also in London for the 1887 Colonial Conference). He explained that he had now formed 'a small private company in the production of small arms ammunition & possibly, later on, of war stores generally'. The new firm – the Colonial Ammunition Company (CAC) as it was duly registered on 30 January 1888 – was, he indicated, prepared to start a factory in Victoria if the government would provide a subsidy of not less than £5000; a site in a position which was suitable, from a military point of view, to meet the needs of all the Australian colonies; favourable terms on importing the necessary plant and material; and a ten-year contract.[29]

Negotiations with Whitney were pursued following his return to New Zealand, and in February 1888 the Victorian government accepted the CAC proposal. At this point an attempt was made to persuade New South Wales to join in the project, leading to an exchange of correspondence between colonial governments over the question of siting the proposed factory. In a letter dated 14 May 1888 the New South Wales premier, Sir Henry Parkes, stated that he would seek parliamentary approval to share the costs of establishing a federal factory 'if ... the locality could be chosen at the conterminous point of the three colonies of South Australia, Victoria and New South Wales, or, if this is not practicable, at some eligible place – Albury or Echuca, for example – on the River Murray'. CAC agreed to consider an inland location, provided it was paid a bonus of £20,000 instead of the £5000 previously sought. When Victoria asked New South Wales to contribute half this cost, the latter refused, with the result that Melbourne went ahead on its own.[30]

By 28 May an agreement between the government and CAC was formalised which required the company to produce three million rounds per year for 25 years, to meet the annual training requirements of the military forces in several colonies as well as provide stocks against a future emergency. A site for a factory was selected on the Saltwater (now Maribyrnong) River at Footscray, on the western outskirts of Melbourne, adjacent to a government gunpowder magazine opened ten years earlier. The lease over this site was incorporated in an act of parliament – the first time this had happened in Australia.[31] Production commenced the following year, at which time Whitney handed over to his eldest son, Asa, who continued as general manager until 1898. The first deliveries of ammunition were made to the Victorian militia in July 1890. A century later, the Footscray site was among those inherited on the creation of Australian Defence Industries Ltd.

Apart from the notable step achieved with the advent of the CAC works, for several years there was no increased movement towards achieving uniformity of organisation and armament between the forces of the Australian colonies. Even the calls of such respected British figures as Major-General J. Bevan Edwards, the newly-appointed commander of British troops in China, who visited Australia to inspect defence arrangements in 1889 and whose recommendations are generally thought to have prompted Parkes' pro-Federation speech at Tenterfield, made little difference. Among the suggestions which Edwards offered for creating a truly federal defence force were a small arms manufacturing plant serving all the colonies, a wharf capable of landing and handling heavy guns, and an ordnance store.[32]

Other events were also taking place which limited the utility of the modest step which had taken place in Australia. Even as CAC began local production, new weapon and ammunition types were being introduced into the British services. Development of cordite as a more powerful and smokeless propellant to replace black powder meant it was possible to reduce the size of military rounds to .303 inch. At the same time, a new type of rifle barrel designed by Metford was introduced which utilised brass-based cartridges. Martini-Henry rifles were now converted to Martini-Metford weapons, or later, to accommodate a further improvement, to Martini-Enfield rifles. In 1888 a bolt action rifle, the Lee-Metford, which used the same calibre bullet, was adopted by the imperial army.[33]

In Australia, the military forces attempted to grapple with both new technological developments and pressures for uniformity engendered by moves towards federation of the colonies. An inter-colonial conference of military commandants from New South Wales, Victoria, South Australia and Queensland met in Sydney during January 1896. In the wake of the Sino-Japanese War of 1894–95, this body considered a range of matters of mutual concern. Among the recommendations made – at Queensland's request – was adoption of the .303 Lee-Metford as a standard magazine rifle for Australian forces; also considered, but rejected, was a proposal for establishing small arms and ammunition factories.[34]

No sooner had the colonies decided on a weapon of modern standard than the British services adopted the Lee-Enfield bolt-action rifle later that same year. The

Colonial Defence Committee in London suggested, however, that, in view of the cost involved, it was unnecessary for colonial forces to follow with a large-scale conversion to the new pattern. Nonetheless, by 1900 CAC had switched to manufacturing .303 Lee-Enfield bullets, after reaching an agreement with colonial premiers in 1898 for the supply of four million rounds annually.[35]

In one important respect, the benefits provided by the CAC factory were questionable. As was pointed out at the time, having the means to produce ammunition counted for very little unless it was matched by the ability to produce locally the essential ingredient – propellant. The reality was that the Footscray operation was still totally dependent on imported gunpowder. A contemporary press article extolling the safety of the new factory to nervous nearby residents incidentally explained this situation quite clearly:

> Each day's supply of powder will be obtained from the magazine, about two thirds of a mile away, and there will never be more than a day's supply, amounting to 100 lbs. [45.4 kg] collected in the factory at any time … . [It] is positively stated that the explosion of the whole 100 lb. would probably not even break the double glass of the skylights.[36]

That this claim regarding the safety of the whole operation was actually wrong was vividly demonstrated by an explosion in September 1897, which killed three female workers and destroyed part of the factory.

The author of an 1897 defence polemic, George Craig of Sydney, sharply observed that:

> This business is simply equal to having no powder factories in Australia at all. The defence, danger, and ammunition supply remain the same if no powder factory exists to make powder within Australia.[37]

Equally bad in Craig's view was the fact that local ammunition production utilised black powder at all, considering the advances which had been made with smokeless propellant such as cordite. This raised the spectre of Australian troops being placed at significant tactical disadvantage in any operations involving them.

It was, Craig thundered, little short of scandalous that in 1893 the New South Wales premier, Sir George Dibbs, had committed his colony by signing a contract for the supply of black powder until 1900. He went on to declare:

> I hope that Parliament in its wisdom will smash the contract up, and then leave some private company to relieve the Treasury by establishing a powder factory near Sydney. The old powder factory near Narrabeen is central, most suitable, is easily worked, is well built, and economic in the distribution of manufactured powder for the several points of defence and fortification, on land or

sea, in the Austral-Pacific. A syndicate should buy it at once, to make the best and most modern smokeless powder.[38]

In this question it seems that Craig was reflecting rather than leading debate, since the matter of a cordite factory being established in Sydney was already under official consideration, having been discussed at the conference of military commandants in 1896. When CAC learnt of this possibility, Asa Whitney quickly voiced his opposition to the idea. Supplying his factory with smokeless powder from such a source seemed 'hardly feasible' to him, while the prospect of an additional ammunition plant being established in New South Wales to utilise locally-produced cordite was alarming on business grounds; '… there is not room for one Ammunition Factory in these colonies let alone two'.[39]

Though CAC responded to the threat to its interests by offering in April 1897 to include the manufacture of cordite as part of its existing operation, matters did not go entirely its way. A new agreement was negotiated with the Victorian government which provided for cordite-propelled cartridges to be included in the company's contract from 1 July 1898, but the cordite was to be supplied by the government.[40] Supplies of this propellant came from the Nobel company's factory at Deer Park, also in Melbourne's western suburbs, acquired in 1897 through the purchase of the Australian Explosives and Chemical Co. Ltd. which made nitroglycerine required for blasting in the mining and quarry industries.[41]

Matching the attention given to military developments in the last two decades of the nineteenth century, equally important events of a naval character were taking place. Coinciding with the raising of the Royal Navy station in the Pacific based on Sydney into an admiral's command in 1885, a major program of construction was undertaken to upgrade the facilities available at Sydney for the support of the local British squadron. The main set of buildings which still stand today at Garden Island were all completed in the decade 1886–96.[42] These provided a permanent home in Australian waters not just for the Royal Navy squadron but, from October 1891, the auxiliary squadron of cruisers and gunboats which (under the terms of the 1887 Colonial Conference) the colonies paid for to maintain local protection.

Creation of government-owned factories

Following the federation of the Australian colonies in 1901, calls were periodically heard for gaps in the new nation's defence capacities to be closed. When the new Commonwealth government set about taking stock of the defence forces it had acquired, a committee of inquiry was established to look into the extent and condition of the ordnance and warlike stores taken over. Reporting early in 1902, this body found that in the case of rifle ammunition there were alarming shortages.

Instead of the stock level recommended in 1899 of 500 rounds for each rifle in the inventory, there was on average about 200 rounds held for each .303 weapon and 300 for the now quite obsolete .45 Martinis. In Victoria this figure was only 17, and 28 in Western Australia.[43]

It was hardly surprising that in April 1902 Major-General Sir Edward Hutton, the newly-arrived British commander of the Australian military forces, prepared at government request a minute which outlined the main factors and issues which he considered should constitute the basis of a national defence policy. This again referred to the desirability of creating an arsenal to undertake the manufacture of guns as well as small arms,[44] but once more circumstances showed that this suggestion was in advance of its time.

Nonetheless pressures were building. After the British Army adopted the .303 Short Magazine Lee-Enfield (SMLE) rifle as general issue in September 1903, the dominions and colonies were asked to standardise on the same weapon by submitting orders to the imperial authorities. Already, in February that year, enterprising citizens in Lithgow, New South Wales, had lobbied Joseph Cook, their member in the House of Representatives, urging their town – already the site of a fledgling iron and steel industry – as suitable for an arsenal in preference to importing weapons from Britain.[45]

Over the next few years the attention of Australian defence authorities was focussed on rationalising and unifying the forces along national lines. These efforts received a boost from Japan's victory in its war with Russia of 1904–05, which led to increased awareness of security issues in Australia. During 1905 the newly-instituted Military Board, which administered the Army, set about examining the production capacity of CAC's Footscray factory, noting that it could produce eighteen million rounds of small arms ammunition annually. After negotiations with the company, a reserve of ammunition components was established to ensure some continuity of supply during an emergency.[46]

Attention began to be given to other aspects of the military forces' needs. An ammunition reserve was established for field and garrison artillery, and action begun to investigate manufacture in Australia of harnesses, saddlery and ammunition wagons. Where possible, orders were placed with local suppliers to provide sufficient camp equipment for the Commonwealth's entire force, and also medical equipment such as transport wagons and ambulances. It became a deliberate policy of the Military Board to pursue local supply of war *matériel*, with the aim of encouraging development of Australia's defence infrastructure and, as noted in the Inspector-General's report for 1907, 'eventually render the Commonwealth independent of overseas supplies for the whole of its Warlike Stores, including guns and ammunition'.[47]

By this stage the government of Prime Minister Alfred Deakin was ready to consider the establishment of local small arms and cordite factories, with the avowed intention of building up Australia's defence capability. At the 1907 Colonial

Conference in London, Deakin had rejected British proposals for the War Office to organise the supply of war *matériel* for the colonies. Here he argued that:

> Our position at the other side of the globe, surrounded by alien races to whom we cannot look for aid or assistance in this matter, and far from any sources of supply of arms and material of war is very different [from other members of the Empire, such as Canada] and we feel its urgency.

Deakin pointed out that the War Office had failed to provide a satisfactory supply of small arms in the past, causing the Secretary of State, Lord Haldane, to interject that this had probably been because of the excessive demand for such weapons during the Boer War. To this Deakin responded, 'Exactly, you are always ready to execute orders when neither of us is under pressure', and charged that the War Office 'looks after itself before it looks after us'. He then announced that consideration was being given to the building or leasing of an ammunition factory in Australia 'to make us independent' for 'any of the reasonable requirements of war'. He left the conference determined to develop Australian defence along national lines.[48]

In a major speech to parliament in December 1907, the Prime Minister made plain his government's determination and goals in this regard. The program he outlined provided for a massive enlargement of the local forces involving the creation of a National Guard numbering (after eight years) 200,000 men in the event of a defence emergency. The cornerstone of this scheme was to be the introduction of compulsory military training; as he remarked, the government was attaching 'great importance to the creation of the utmost power of resistance locally, both as to war materials and men'.[49]

The intention revealed by Deakin was that this new force would be equipped and supplied from Australian sources. Explaining that each year 20,000 new rifles would have to be purchased for the Guard, he declared that these weapons would be made locally, not imported:

> We have satisfied ourselves, after careful inquiry, that they can be made here cheaper than they can be purchased abroad. Every rifleman will have a bandolier equipment. It will consist of a sling, water-bottle and straps, great coat, blanket, waterproof sheet, mess tin and haversack. All these will be made locally.

Deakin went on to outline the position with the field artillery, where waggons and limbers were already being manufactured within the Commonwealth. But gun carriages for the 6.7-inch guns were also to be produced locally, and an ammunition factory established. This meant that a cordite factory would be needed too, producing percussion caps and fulminates (used as detonators) in the same works.

The economics of establishing the latter factory would, he noted, be greatly assisted if 'we can obtain orders for the supply of the Imperial Squadron in Australian waters'. The government also had under consideration investing in a rolling mill for the manufacture of ammunition cases. Proving the seriousness of the government's intent in this area, during his speech Deakin tabled a report on the feasibility of the proposed cordite factory prepared by C. Napier Hake, Victoria's chief inspector of explosives, based on a recent visit to England to investigate the latest developments taking place in the industry there and elsewhere.

Deakin's government fell before this ambitious scheme could be implemented, but nonetheless much of it came to pass soon afterwards through the efforts of the Labor government headed by Andrew Fisher. In June 1908 a naval engineer officer, Commander William Clarkson, embarked on a similar investigation to Hake in England, Europe and America regarding the possibilities of manufacturing rifles.

By March 1909 tenders closed for equipping a small arms factory to produce 15,000 rifles a year, with bids coming from three British firms and the Pratt & Whitney Company of Hartford, Connecticut, in the United States. The latter was by far the lowest (just over £68,000), and was accepted. A site for the new works was chosen at Lithgow, already favoured with a coal mine for power and a steel works, and contracts were let in 1910 for the construction of the necessary buildings. The factory commenced production in February 1912 and was officially opened the following June.[50]

Emphasising the national significance of the process under way with the various defence factories was the fact that the Lithgow facility was the first in Australia to use 'repetition manufacture', or what is more commonly known these days as mass production. At a time when the labour content of the SMLE produced by the Royal Small Arms Factory at Enfield in Britain was 72 hours, Pratt & Whitney had contracted to make the same rifle in 28 hours. Moreover, the deal concluded with Pratt & Whitney was an innovative package (the company undertaking to supply all equipment such as tools, gauges, jigs and fixtures, along with a complete plant for maintaining and reproducing them) which attracted worldwide interest.[51] Thus the defence factories should be understood for their role as an important medium in pioneering the introduction of new technology and manufacturing processes in Australia.

By the time Lithgow was in production, other defence facilities were already opened. In August 1911 a factory for producing harnesses and leather goods such as saddlery accoutrements was begun in the Melbourne suburb of Clifton Hill, while in January 1912 another for the production of uniforms and other items of service clothing such as headgear commenced operating in South Melbourne. The latter, the Commonwealth Clothing Factory, had been established as a result of a 1909 inquiry by the Department of Defence and the Postmaster General's Department regarding the best means of supplying the requirements of both. In the same month that the Small Arms Factory (SAF) was opened, the planned cordite works produced its first batch of propellant at a site at Maribyrnong, Melbourne. This milestone was only reached after an earlier attempt had to be suspended when the locally-made metal vats leaked as soon as the first nitric acid was put in them.[52] By 1914 a woollen cloth factory was under construction at North Geelong, Victoria.[53]

The program embarked upon was expensive. A return presented to the Senate in 1912 showed that over £252,000 (about $13 million at current values) had been invested so far in buildings, plant and equipment, while goods valued at little more than £60,000 had been produced. And as one account later noted, these figures 'related principally to the clothing and harness factories, as the cordite factory had not yet produced anything, and the small arms factory was credited with production to the value of only £362'.[54]

There were also some problems associated with getting the factories up and running. In the case of the clothing factory, considerable opposition was encountered from the civilian competitors in the trade. This feeling manifested itself at the opening of the Commonwealth works, when many of the competent hands engaged as operators failed to appear through having been made better offers by private employers. The factory manager was consequently obliged to hire workers without experience in the tasks required, and put to the expense of training them.[55]

Not the least of the voices raised against the factory program were those of political opponents. For example, in June 1915 Joseph Cook strongly criticised the Fisher government for having set up the factories without properly securing the approval of parliament. Regardless of opportunism on Cook's part, there was validity in his charge that:

> Instead of calling in private enterprise in a *bona fide* way to help them in the supply of war material, the Government ... have aimed all through at setting up a Government institution for the production of munitions of war ... I venture to say that the less we have to do with the cultivation of social experiments ... when the fate of the Empire is at stake, the better it will be for all concerned.[56]

There is little doubt that the Labor Party under Fisher was purposely pursuing 'self-containment' in defence. Making this principle a matter of policy meant, though, that commercial alternatives to meeting the nation's needs in the field of defence production were not considered. While it may well have been true that other practical approaches to achieving the required ends were not viable, there is no evidence extant to show that such were even explored. The role of publicly-owned enterprises as a 'development stimulator' has a recognised and time-honoured place in Australian history. In newly developing countries it is hardly surprising that governments take the lead 'to plug gaps likely to result from the abdication of private enterprise or to provide services for which the nation would otherwise go begging'.[57]

Adding to the size and diversity of the defence edifice which the Commonwealth was in the process of erecting, were developments of a naval character. The formal adoption of compulsory universal military training in July 1911 was followed in October by the creation of a Royal Australian Navy (RAN) as a fleet unit of the Royal Navy. Moves towards this end had been initiated in 1909, when the Fisher government placed an initial order for three torpedo boat destroyers from England. A feature of this arrangement was that one of these 700-ton vessels was to be assembled in Australia, at the state-run dockyard at Cockatoo Island in Sydney Harbour.

The destroyer planned for local assembly, *Warrego*, was launched in April 1911, by which time another major step towards local construction had already been settled upon. In March that year negotiations had been commenced for construction at Cockatoo Island of a light cruiser (5400 tons) and a further three destroyers. An order for these vessels was formally placed in October the same year, with the keels of two of the destroyers being laid down on 25 January 1913.[58]

In addition to a squadron of fast and modern ships (cruisers, destroyers and submarines, with a battlecruiser as flagship), the RAN also acquired a substantial shore establishment. On 1 July 1913 the (Imperial) Australia Station ceased to exist, with the ships of the British squadron at Sydney moving to Auckland to form a New Zealand Division of the Royal Navy.[59] The various establishments of the Sydney naval base (Garden Island, Admiralty House, the Royal Edward Victualling Yard, Spectacle Island and Tresco) were taken over by the Australian Naval Board, while other assets (such as the survey ship HMS *Penguin* and sundry small vessels, and the Admiralty's coal stocks) were purchased. Ownership of nearby Cockatoo Island had already been transferred to the Commonwealth in February 1913 at a cost of £876,716.[60]

Industry and the Great War

Considering the size of the defence burden which the Commonwealth had taken on by this time, it was fortunate that justification for the policy pursued became available almost immediately through the outbreak of the First World War in August 1914. Thus, while it was admitted in 1917 that the various factories had cost over £2.5 million (more than $126 million in today's prices) to operate during the first three years of the war, this was offset by an almost exactly equal value of goods produced.[61]

More importantly, however, it could be argued that having the factories in production, or well-advanced, enabled a great many demands arising from the war effort to be met in timely fashion, in some cases at all. The official war history considered that it would have been 'very difficult if not impossible' in 1914 to efficiently fit out the Australian Imperial Force (in which 417,000 men enlisted by 1918) without them. As wartime defence minister Senator George Pearce was fond of saying, 'You cannot make an army by merely clapping your hands'.[62]

Naturally, greatly increased demands were made upon the factories in terms of output, which could only be met by expanding them. At Lithgow, for example, the installation of additional machinery during the war years necessitated the doubling of the factory's floorspace. Moves were made in September 1914 to extend working hours of personnel by 20 hours, to a total of 68 per week. Additional men were also recruited, and from July 1915 a second shift was begun, to work the factory's machinery throughout the night. Whereas 250 men had been employed at the factory in 1912, at its peak staffing level (reached during 1917) there were 1378 men and boys. Despite periodic industrial disputes, rifle production at the factory was double the monthly rate originally expected.[63]

The story was much the same at the other works. At the harness factory at Clifton Hill, staff levels tripled to reach 441 in 1916. An increase of such magnitude predictably led to pressure on workspace. A new building was erected and extensions made, while additional accommodation came in the form of the loan of a portion of a civilian firm's premises – along with 28 of its employees.[64] At the clothing factory, extensions were already in hand at the time war was declared, though they were only those planned for the factory's intended workforce of 300. Staff numbers actually rose during 1915 to 714; hours had also increased to nearly 80 a week, although these soon returned to normal once additional work was spread among private firms in several States to ameliorate 'general distress in the clothing trade'.[65]

The cordite factory at Maribyrnong, similarly, more than doubled its 80-man workforce during the war years, after authority was given to quadruple production. Alterations and extensions to plant and buildings were also put in hand soon after the outbreak of war. Among the new structures completed in 1915 were buildings for the manufacture of cannon cordite, such as used by big naval guns. From 1915 the factory also began supplying cordite to New Zealand.[66]

In the case of the woollen cloth factory at Geelong, this was still in the course of construction when war began. The first process of manufacture was not commenced until September 1915, and the factory did not come into full production until the following April by which time nearly 250 operators were employed. The chief benefit derived from the operation was that the various grades of cloth required for service uniforms were soon being provided at costs 10–20 per cent cheaper than paid to commercial mills.[67]

Even for the non-government works of the Colonial Ammunition Company at Footscray, the war brought great changes. Expansion of the factory during 1910–14 proved particularly timely and involved the construction of rolling mills, a foundry and factory for making brass percussion caps. These new works were on a leased site adjoining the original CAC factory, located on the bluff overlooking the river flats. By 1917 a staff of over 2000 was employed at Footscray, producing two million rounds a week to meet the ammunition needs of Australia's hugely increased military forces.

With its original lease from the Victorian government expiring in 1914, the company looked for a new agreement with the Commonwealth but found this initially delayed while the latter looked at the option of establishing a factory of its own. Eventually a new agreement was reached covering a five-year period from 1 July 1917, which committed the federal government to purchasing a minimum quantity of 40 million rounds annually. This draft arrangement itself underwent protracted scrutiny within the Defence Department, finally resulting in a three-year contract being signed with effect from 1 July 1919.[68] Delays in resolving such questions clearly showed the uncertainties for companies having the Defence Department as a customer.

Associated with the increased need for ammunition came a rising requirement for supplies of propellant, and in turn for acetone – a necessary ingredient in the manufacture of cordite. This commodity became harder to obtain from Canada, the usual supplier, and the locally-sourced material was expensive because of the relatively small quantities produced. Accordingly, a decision was made in 1916 to undertake production of acetate of lime (from which acetone was derived) by a process of fermentation from waste molasses. A plant was designed and constructed in the Brisbane suburb of Bulimba, located here because of proximity to the Queensland canefields which were a vast and ready source of molasses.[69] This factory began operating in October 1918, as a subsidiary of the cordite factory.[70]

Apart from their own production, the factories were an important means for encouraging private industry in taking up defence-related work. Even after private firms had been organised to meet extra defence needs, the clothing factory in particular played a useful role through providing samples and patterns to commercial contractors. The factory thereby enabled a standard of quality for supplies to be fixed, made expert comparisons of products, and gave advice in settling disputes between outside contractors and the department. At the same time, it carried out experiments and produced designs for new uniform clothing.[71]

A further feature of the defence factories concerned the employment opportunities which they offered to women in a national industrial workforce which was predominantly male. At their peak wartime level (in June 1916), almost 30 per cent of the factories' 2727-strong work force were women.[72] Since Lithgow, the largest factory, exclusively employed men and boys, there is a significant distortion implied in this figure. Several of the factories – notably the clothing and woollen cloth works – at that time had a much higher proportion of female staff (84 and 50 per cent respectively).

While the government's own factories appeared to give satisfactory performance in the course of the war, there were some significant diseconomies in its

Built as a commercial venture in 1884, this gunpowder factory at Narrabeen, New South Wales closed amid controversy the following year without ever coming into production. A decade later calls were made for the plant to be acquired and turned to manufacturing smokeless powder for defence purposes. (Mr P.E. Kindred)

In 1882 Frederick Sargood (1834–1903), a Victorian parliamentarian and militia officer, made enquiries about establishing a local ammunition factory. Appointed the next year as Victoria's first Minister for Defence, he explored options for setting up a factory to manufacture artillery in 1885. (NLA)

John Whitney can rightly be regarded as the father of the Australian defence industry. While serving in New Zealand's militia forces in the 1880s (from which he ultimately retired with the rank of major), he established an ammunition factory at Mount Eden, Auckland. He later set up the Colonial Ammunition Factory and opened the plant at Footscray, Victoria, in 1889.

This 1890s view shows the Colonial Ammunition Company's factory beside the Saltwater (Maribyrnong) River at Footscray, Victoria. An explosion in 1897 destroyed part of the factory, and several times the plant was engulfed by floodwaters, but it continued in operation until the close of the Second World War.

Inside the cordite cut-off machine room (for loading .303-inch rounds) at CAC's factory, about 1906.

This undated view inside CAC's Footscray works is probably from the early 1900s, and shows that conditions for the largely female workforce were almost Dickensian in their awfulness.

Manufacturing saddles at the government factory opened at Clifton Hill, Melbourne in 1911. The first of the factories established by the Department of Defence in the years leading up to the First World War, this workshop also produced harnesses and other leather goods required by the armed forces.

The small arms factory established in the New South Wales rural town of Lithgow in 1912 was the first in Australia to employ mass production methods. Thus defence facilities were often an important medium for introducing new production techniques and processes into civil industry.

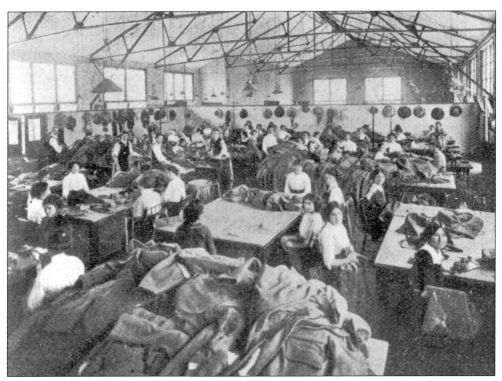

The government clothing factory in South Melbourne made uniforms and headgear for the services from January 1912, despite some opposition from the civilian trade. During the war years which soon followed, over 80 per cent of the factory's 700-strong workforce were women.

A program of local warship construction began in 1910, when one of the RAN's first three English-built destroyers was brought to Sydney for assembly at the state-run dockyard at Cockatoo Island. Later vessels were fully constructed in Australia, including the light cruiser Brisbane, shown here at its launch in 1915. (AWM neg.#P0444/214/136)

Immediately before World War I, CAC's facility at Footscray was expanded with the addition of rolling mills, a foundry and cap factory. These works, shown here in 1916, occupied a leased site facing Gordon Street about a kilometre west of the original riverside factory.

This workshop at Stirling, Western Australia, was one of a number of factories specially established in 1915–16 to undertake the manufacture of 18-pounder artillery shells for the Western Front. This short-lived experiment proved that local industry was capable of producing munitions, but cost the taxpayer dearly. (AWM neg. #H1991)

After 1918, technical defence industry skills were boosted by the experience gained by some 3000 trades-men sent to work in Britain's wartime factories. This group is shown inside the general service shed at the Andover aerodrome, Salisbury. (AWM neg. #D101)

Situated on a bend in the Maribyrnong River, the Cordite Factory produced its first batch of propellant in June 1912. In the 1920s it became a fully-fledged explosives factory, producing TNT and filling a range of gun rounds and bombs.

A view of the lower ammunition factory on the original site at Footscray shortly before the Commonwealth bought out CAC's interest. By July 1927 the company had wound up its Australian operation.

The members of the Munitions Supply Board in 1936: (from left) A.E. Leighton, CMG, Controller–General of Munitions Supply; M.M. Maguire, OBE, ISO, Assistant Secretary, Department of Defence; J.K. Jensen, Secretary MSB; and Colonel T.J. Thomas, OBE, Finance Secretary, Department of Finance.

From the late 1930s Essington Lewis, chief general manager of BHP Ltd., played a leading role in preparing the nation's civil industry for war. Appointed Director-General of Munitions in 1940, in 1942 he became Director-General of Aircraft Production as well, which virtually made him Australia's 'industrial dictator'. (AWM neg. #077691)

The manufacture of 2-pounder anti-tank guns was carried out at the General Motors plant in the Adelaide suburb of Woodville. A large amount of wartime production came from nearly 250 annexes established alongside existing factories.

The delivery end of the AFV (armoured fighting vehicle) production line established in the NSW railways workshops at Chullora. At right is an AC.1 cruiser tank armed with a 2-pounder gun; 66 were built before the program was cancelled in 1943.

Workers inspecting rounds of .303 ammunition at Footscray. By 1943 nearly 40 per cent of the 80,000 Australians working in the nation's munitions factories were women. Often compulsorily called up, they usually found themselves in low-paid, repetitive, uninteresting and sometimes dangerous jobs. (AWM neg.#7728)

The first production lots leave the ammunition factory at Rocklea, Queensland, in February 1942, following the completion of service tests. Ammunition-making spread to all Australian States in the course of the Second World War.

A worker at the Maribyrnong ordnance factory removes an 8-inch naval shell from a lathe, October 1939. (AWM neg.#22/8)

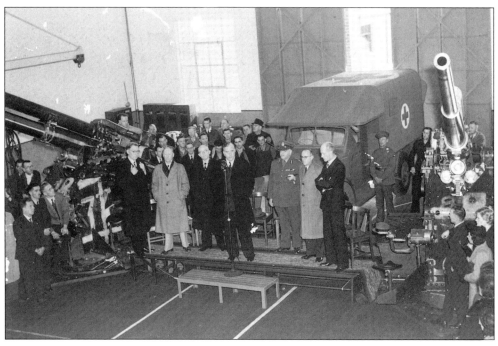

Prime Minister R.G. Menzies speaks during the presentation of a Fighting Services Ambulance by staff and workers at Ordnance Factory Maribyrnong, 7 June 1941. This factory alone was employing over 8000 people by the following year, as output increased in response to wartime requirements.

The ordnance factory established at Echuca, Victoria in 1943 specialised in manufacturing ball-bearings. This shows part of the production line using oscillating raceway grinders.

Eleanor Roosevelt, wife of the American president, on a tour of the Footscray ammunition factory in September 1943. On her right (obscured) is the factory manager, R.H. Doyle. The female workers are engaged in visual inspection work.

The scene at the Commonwealth Aircraft Factory at Fishermen's Bend, Victoria in May 1941, with CA–6 Wackett Trainers under construction in the foreground and Wirraways behind them. Begun only in 1938, Australia's military aircraft industry employed some 44,000 workers during the Second World War. (AWM neg.#7278/12)

Construction of the Captain Cook graving dock at Garden Island, Sydney during the Second World War was at the time the greatest engineering feat undertaken in Australia. Begun in 1940, the dock was opened early in 1945. (AWM neg.#065439A)

A 'Miles of Munitions' parade is pictured making its way down Collins Street, Melbourne on 29 October 1943. Held to promote the government's fourth war loan, this display of weapons – as one newspaper noted – was proof of 'the amazing strides that have been made in their production in this country' and that taxpayers were receiving good value for money.

A general view inside the ammunition factory at Mildura, Victoria in February 1944. This factory had a life of only two years, commencing production in January 1943 and ceasing in January 1945, even before the Pacific War was concluded.

The factory complex established at Penfield (Salisbury) and Finsbury in South Australia comprised over 1000 buildings. After the Second World War ended, these were sold or leased to civil industry. In 1977 the Adelaide branch of the CSIRO's National Measurement Laboratory was located in the two-storey administrative building (in centre of picture).

The main entrance of the Defence Standards Laboratories at Maribyrnong, previously known (from 1948) as Defence Research Laboratories. Before that, the buildings were called the Munitions Supply Laboratories – the name which appears on the wall of the main building, above the windows.

In the 1950s Australia's aircraft industry was bolstered by a steady flow of defence orders. The Commonwealth Aircraft Corporation's plant at Fishermen's Bend made Sabre fighters for the RAAF, powered by Avon jet engines, which it also manufactured.

attempts to gear up civil industry in support of the war effort. One area which later came in for considerable criticism was the undertaking to manufacture ammunition for 18-pounder quick-firing field guns. At the start of the war the Australian government was interested in the prospect of making these weapons, along with the fused shells to fire from them, as part of its self-containment policy. Inquiries directed to London in September 1914 seeking 'full details of manufacture' received little encouragement, however, because the War Office could spare no-one for the time-consuming task of assembling the mass of specifications and other data entailed.[73]

Inquiries were next made with British manufacturers about purchasing the complete plant (less power supply) for such a factory, but this course led nowhere.[74] In the meantime, the question of shell manufacture had taken on a different dimension following reports of serious ammunition shortages being experienced in France, due to the inability of British industry to cope with unanticipated rates of expenditure. Agitation had begun in the press during May 1915, claiming that Australian firms were able and willing to help meet the shortfall in production.[75]

In response, offers of assistance were cabled to London by the Australian government, and in June a departmental committee formed earlier to deal with the question of shell manufacture was expanded into a Federal Munitions Committee. Added to representatives of various areas in the defence organisation were a number of consulting members drawn from science, manufacturing and commerce. This body's role was limited to assisting in the development of civil industry to handle munitions manufacture. It had no authority to place orders, or to enter into financial agreements on the government's behalf. In time the committee would come into conflict with the government over matters concerning the defence factories, only to be reminded by the Minister for Defence that these works were a departmental responsibility. It should not interfere in their operation, but concentrate purely on organising private enterprise.[76]

When advice was finally received in July that the British Ministry of Munitions could 'take practically unlimited supplies' of 18-pounder shells, and drawings and specifications arrived the next month, the process began of letting tenders. The challenge thus offered to Australian industry was eagerly taken up by 25 firms who went to considerable effort and expense, some forming new non-profit companies and erecting new factories specially for the task.[77] A cable received from London in February 1916 added a new twist to the situation, stating that the position in Britain had improved and a requirement no longer existed for supply of 18-pounder shell from Australia beyond the current contracts. Despite this clear warning, government authorities were slow to appreciate its implications and pressed on with exploring the possibility of manufacturing 6-inch and 4.5-inch high explosive shells instead.[78]

In June 1916 advice received via the high commissioner's office in London made clear that continuance of any form of shell manufacture was completely futile, and a halt was finally called. By this time some 15,700 rounds worth about £17,300 at the agreed rate had been produced, and these were paid for by the UK Ministry of Munitions. The Australian government met the cost of the remaining output which suppliers delivered, meaning that taxpayers picked up the balance of the whole experiment – over £100,000, which included claims for compensation for disruption of production, reorganisation of factories and special machinery, which the Minister for Defence considered it fair to entertain.[79]

The whole episode of producing artillery ammunition from local resources had cost the country dearly. More than this, however, the official history of Australia's part in the war suggests that the effort was essentially misguided, since it flew in the face of distance and the rapidity of technological development.[80] It was a clear case where departmental enthusiasms had become carried away in ignorance of actual requirements. A far more sensible form of assistance to Britain's munitions effort was the supply of steel bars (for producing shell bodies) from the newly-completed steelworks at Newcastle, New South Wales. Almost 18,000 tons of munition steel were supplied from these works during the course of the war.

Other efforts at weapons production also led nowhere. Preliminary plans for a factory to manufacture machineguns were dropped, while attempts by the New South Wales government to produce such weapons at Walsh Island dockyards, Newcastle, failed to produce results. More success attended the production of hand grenades. A local inventor, Harold Berry, designed a new type of projectile called the Welch-Berry, which incorporated an explosive specially developed by R.J. Lewis, chief inspector of explosives in Victoria. Fifteen thousand of these bombs were manufactured and shipped to England, but the War Office decided not to adopt the type – in the interests of standardisation – and they were used only for instructional purposes.[81]

While nothing came of attempts to make weapons larger than small arms, as opposed to the ammunition for them, artillery needs were at least partially met through local resources. A contract placed in June 1911 with the Cockatoo Island dockyard for mountings and pedestals for 6-inch breech-loading fortress guns was fulfilled, albeit after considerable delay in obtaining cast-steel of the necessary quality. Eventually, two of the five sets ordered were completed after more urgent war requirements had been met. Other orders for ammunition wagons and limbers for 18-pounder field guns were filled by a civilian firm, as they had been before the war.[82]

Another potentially costly mistake almost arose over persistence by Australian authorities with the notion of creating one large central arsenal at Tuggeranong, in the Australian Capital Territory. Within this facility was intended to be focussed the manufacture of all peacetime defence needs:

> … field artillery guns, carriages, wagons, ammunition, &c., together with their constituent parts, such as shells, cartridges, fuzes, high explosives, &c.; machine

guns, small arms, aeroplanes and all other stores peculiar to the Military Forces.

Under the concept developed for this establishment, it was envisaged that the arsenal would serve as:

> ... a centre for the privately-owned factories of the Commonwealth, so that their foremen and leading hands could go there from time to time and so be familiarized with the processes of manufacture of munitions, with the view that, in the event of war, the whole manufacturing resources of Australia would be available for these purposes.[83]

At an estimated cost of almost £1.5 million, the arsenal was an expensive undertaking, especially when another £650,000 was required for a complete new town to house workers and their families.[84] Careful planning was required, too, if disruption of the existing contribution of the nation's industries to the war effort was to be avoided. By 1917, however, it was realised that wartime experience in Britain had caused the doctrine of centralising defence production to become outdated.

In November, grave misgivings were expressed by Arthur Leighton, the 44-year-old former manager of the cordite factory. Though appointed general manager of the arsenal project in 1916, he had remained in England after being co-opted as a technical adviser on explosives to the Ministry of Munitions. From his vantage point in London, he recognised that Australia was on the verge of committing a colossal blunder and wrote to attack the whole concept behind the scheme. He pointed out that the trend was actually towards dispersing defence production to major population centres where labour and supporting services were more readily available, and it was possible to better utilise commercial industry.[85] On the basis of advice from him and others, the scheme faltered and eventually, in mid-1919, was formally abandoned.[86]

Before the arsenal idea met its demise, two benefits to Australia were reaped. The first of these was a scheme to send Australians to England to join in the industrial effort taking place there. After about 100 chemists and some draftsmen arrived between the end of 1915 and October 1916, Leighton suggested that the government take the opportunity to send the men selected as the future heads of its munitions supply staff, to gain wider experience. Advice from another Australian expert in London suggested that both Britain and the arsenal scheme would be well-served by sending as many workers as possible.[87]

As a consequence of these urgings, further contingents of workers followed; by the end of the war more than 3000 tradesmen had arrived in England to relieve the need for skilled workers, not just in munitions and ordnance factories but such places as aircraft production workshops as well. A later appeal by Britain for unskilled labourers saw the further dispatch of some 2200 navvies, mostly recruited from state railway departments around Australia.[88] Even though the arsenal project did not go ahead, a large proportion of the men sent as munitions workers proved to be an asset in furthering the growth and development of Australian commercial industry in the postwar period.

At the end of the war a second benefit arose from Australia's arsenal scheme. This concerned the opportunity to buy machine tools and equipment put up for disposal in Britain as wartime factories were dismantled. Purchases were begun by Leighton in December 1918, involving laboratory equipment and plant of use in the establishment of fuze and filling factories. After he was recalled to Australia in February 1919, the process was continued by his successor, John Jensen – a former accountant at the Lithgow works who had risen during the war to Chief Clerk in the defence department's central office in Melbourne – although government approval for this activity was not formally obtained until early in 1920.[89] Plant with a reported 'book value' of £1.5 million was obtained at scrap rates of a mere £167,000 and shipped back to Australia, with the intention of reassembly in the new arsenal facility.[90] This shrewd acquisition would ultimately provide the basis for the next expansion phase of the nation's defence industry.

By the closing stages of the Great War, Australia was thus in possession of a defence industrial capacity which was quite remarkable for a nation with a population of about five million. For the first time in its history, the country had been required to harness the effort of civil industry to engage in large-scale defence work. This undertaking had involved not just goods of military utility apart from arms and ammunition, but previously untried and complex areas of skill such as shell-making. More importantly, a range of factories had been brought into existence and rapidly built up specifically to meet the needs of the armed forces in peace, while serving as a focal core for wartime manufacturing.

A notable feature of the edifice which was now in place was that, while founded mainly on factories which the government itself owned and controlled, the continued operation of the Colonial Ammunition Company's works at Footscray meant that a situation existed of mixed private and public enterprise in this area of prime strategic importance. Though pursuit by pre-war governments of a policy of defence self-reliance (to the extent possible) had created this situation, the experience of the war had apparently justified the wisdom of this course, confirming that this was an area in which national government had to be prepared to carry the main burden. The principle of direct government involvement, not just control, oversight and encouragement, had now become entrenched.

2

CHANGING FORTUNES OF DEFENCE INDUSTRY

The capitulation of Germany in November 1918 was not an event long foreseen and anticipated. Only after the last great enemy offensive in March of that year had been met and turned back by the Allies was the Great War's outcome confidently in sight, although as late as June fighting was fully expected to continue at least into the next year and possibly even 1920.[1] Because of such expectations, there had been little time in which to begin slowing down the mass of manufactured items produced in Britain, or Australia. When the German collapse came, the brakes on industry had to be applied suddenly and sharply.

Compounding the situation were stockpiled holdings of war goods which were now surplus. At the same time as Australia began steps in 1919 to dispose of its excess stores of clothing and other items, large quantities of supplies were received from the British government as an 'imperial gift' – including, for example, enough combat aircraft to form Australia's own air force in 1921. These factors, combined with a pressing need for the Australian government to institute stringent economy measures, meant that the considerations entailed by the policy of defence self-sufficiency were now significantly altered.[2]

The impact of these changed conditions was initially uneven in its effect. Output and employment levels at the cordite and harness factories were reduced sharply during 1919. The acetate factory in Brisbane also waned in importance following the end of hostilities, especially as a new technique had been developed for making cordite which did not require acetone. Although acetone production continued until 1922, the factory turned increasingly to supplying methylated spirits and power alcohol for motor vehicles, while operating with fewer employees.[3]

At Lithgow instructions were received in March 1919 to cut back rifle production to 20,000 a year, and 125 men were retrenched. Once conditional approval was given for work to be undertaken for other government departments and commercial firms, however, employment levels went back up slightly in 1920–21. Similarly, at the clothing factory, military requirements declined but output was maintained by accepting orders from other government departments and instrumentalities, such as the Victorian police department and the railways and tram authorities. The woollen factory, too, was initially unaffected, principally because of the need to begin making tweed cloth for use in civilian garments required by returning soldiers of the AIF.[4]

At the government's naval establishments at Sydney, Cockatoo Island and Garden Island, the situation was similar. Both had been kept busy throughout the war with repairing and refitting vessels of the Royal Australian Navy, and were each employing about 3000 men by the time peace returned. But while Garden Island began laying off men in large numbers, Cockatoo Island was still heavily engaged with construction of the cruiser *Adelaide* and a fleet oiler, *Biloela*. The workforce at the latter dockyard accordingly stayed high, reaching a peak of nearly 3500 in 1920.[5]

Policy of the Munitions Supply Board

Following Leighton's return from England in April 1919, he was called upon to assist in formulating a policy on which to develop defence production in the postwar period. In a report dated 27 May, he elaborated on his vision for the sort of arsenal which he believed a nation like Australia should have. This did not shun entirely the notion of concentration, though he shied away from isolating defence production in a remote locality like Canberra. Instead, he argued the merits of spreading his arsenal to place it alongside commercial industry in major population centres. In the scheme offered by him, development of munitions supply was to be focused mainly on Maribyrnong.[6]

The government prevaricated for much of the next two years. Although construction of new buildings to house research laboratories at Maribyrnong was authorised, this was no indication that Leighton's plan had been accepted by the government since £25,000 for these structures had already been placed on the 1919–20 parliamentary estimates. This authorisation was, moreover, probably dictated by pressures on space within the Army's Victoria Barracks on St. Kilda Road, which the laboratories had been occupying since the war. The quantity of laboratory equipment arriving from England and now piling up in Melbourne threatened, it has been suggested, to become a political embarrassment unless accommodation was prepared to allow for its utilisation.[7]

The lack of government direction on this subject was made plain in April 1920 after the Defence Council (the principal advisory body in defence matters) recommended expenditure of £8.25 million on defence, £800,000 of which was earmarked for munitions construction. When the Prime Minister, W.M. Hughes, spoke in parliament the following month, he emphasised the continuing requirement for an arsenal but failed to commit his government on the crucial question of its location.[8] In these circumstances it was as much as Leighton could achieve to persuade the government in September to transfer the functions of the departmental branch responsible for planning associated with the now defunct Tuggeranong scheme to a Board of Factory Administration, with himself as chairman.[9]

Despite the frustrating pace, the plan for a single comprehensive supply organisation was slowly coming together. A major step towards this end came in January 1921, when the Commonwealth took over the Colonial Ammunition Company's small arms ammunition factory at Footscray on a seven-year lease. The company had made approaches the previous year arising from its acute financial position and, since the options of acquiring the factory or establishing new and separate works were considered impracticable at the time, there seemed little alternative to meeting the CAC's request for altering the terms of its existing agreement.[10]

Subsequently, negotiations to finalise the leasing agreement gave rise to a major dispute over responsibility for the company's liabilities under existing agreements, prompting litigation which went as far as the High Court before being resolved in the Commonwealth's favour.[11] This aspect aside, the incorporation of Footscray into the fold of the government factories marked the end of a unique arrangement in the defence production field, as CAC had been the only private firm with a direct peacetime role in such a military-oriented activity. Among some within the defence department, though, the outcome was exactly what had been desired in any event. As Jensen admitted to Leighton not long after the takeover:

> ... I am glad that at last we are controlling this factory. It has been my ambition ever since the war broke out for the Department to get its clutches on the place, so I am pleased it has come off at last.[12]

In March 1921 Leighton also put to the Minister for Defence the case for forming a munitions supply branch within the department. He pointed out that this would effectively constitute an embryo ministry of munitions which, in the event of a war, could be taken out of Defence whenever supply problems reached a scale which warranted such separation. Acceptance of this scheme led on to the creation of a Munitions Supply Board (MSB) to replace the Board of Factory Administration on 13 August 1921. This new body was a statutory body under the chairmanship of Leighton, who now became Controller-General of Munitions Supply.[13]

Within the new organisation was vested responsibility for all matters concerning the supply of goods to the defence forces. This involved the MSB in purchasing, research and design, inspection and the administration and development of defence factories. The grand objective was to help Australia achieve self-sufficiency in munitions production, through keeping alive core skills which were not normally available in commercial industry but were essential for expansion in war, and through developing wartime plans for the organisation of the whole of the nation's industry. Towards this end, the MSB was also conscious of a need to assist in developing secondary industry, to ensure that processed raw materials needed for defence products were available from within Australia rather than requiring importation from overseas.[14]

After obtaining government approval in late 1921 for a modest three-year development program of munitions capabilities, the MSB initially planned to implement the scheme Leighton had first outlined in May 1919. Under this arrangement, the munitions factories — small arms, ammunition and cordite — would revert to late-1914 production levels, thus accounting for about two-thirds of the program's expected annual cost of £1.2 million. Leighton, however, recognised the extent to which later conditions had changed the basis for such calculations. Both the amount of imperial gift stores available and naval limitation talks then under way in Washington made it unlikely that the government would countenance expenditure at the level required for this plan.[15]

In December, therefore, Leighton drew up a new scheme aimed at saving about £800,000 from annual costs by reducing production in all the existing factories to a nucleus basis only. The balance would be used to fund the maintenance bill and to support a more modest program of development to be spread over six years instead of three. Of course, under this plan, each new capability would have to be established on a nucleus-only basis, since orders from the services were not expected to be forthcoming to make the enterprises viable. Despite the heavy element of subsidisation thus involved, by such means it would be possible to continue to bring into existence the range of desired production capabilities. After winning support of his colleagues on the MSB, and of the Army, Leighton took his scheme to the Minister for Defence, Walter Massy-Greene, in January 1922.[16]

Within the post-war Hughes government, defence policy had become centred on the need to plan for the contingency of possible raids by an enemy, rather than major attack or invasion. On this basis, the emphasis within Australia's forces had been placed on the navy, operating in conjunction with the Royal Navy, as the arm most needed to prevent an opponent obtaining a position from which to strike. One recent historian has, however, pointed to this policy as being dictated by economic practicality, rather than subservience to British strategic doctrine as usually portrayed.[17]

The reality, according to this line of argument, was that Australia simply could not afford the large ground and air forces needed to cope with invasion — if this was to be accepted as a credible scenario on which to predicate planning. There was, though, a degree of concern and reserve as to the reliance which might be placed on assurances from London regarding the levels of British support which would be forthcoming in circumstances of major attack or invasion. Australian governments during the 1920s and 1930s accordingly preferred to retain a measure of insurance by building up the nation's defence industrial capacity, not least because this was an affordable option.

On this basis it is understandable that the government agreed to Leighton's scheme, with Prime Minister Hughes announcing endorsement of such an approach during a parliamentary statement on defence policy in May 1922. Under the guidance received from the government, the MSB could plan on having an annual amount of £500,000 available for its purposes from the 1922–23 financial year. After £350,000 of this was used for maintaining existing capabilities, the remainder could be put towards adding new areas of manufacturing such as the production of field guns and gun ammunition, machine guns and pistols.[18]

The major area of activity missing from the revised MSB program, when compared with the original 1919 scheme, was that of aircraft manufacture and engine production. Not just financial limitations had forced its deletion, but also a belief by the government –as it transpired, erroneous – that commercial industry would move to fill this void if given encouragement through tariff protection and subsidies.[19] The aim of avoiding competition by government instrumentalities with commercial industry remained an important tenet of philosophy for the ministries headed by Hughes and, from February 1923, by S.M. Bruce.

Concern that government enterprises should not harm or undermine private firms was, by this time, having an effect on several of the defence factories. During 1921 the woollen mill at Geelong had been granted permission to accept trade orders, following curtailment of service needs for its product. In July of the next year, defence minister Massy-Greene decided that this factory should be closed as a government institution, announcing in parliament that its sale was seen as 'the best alternative' to allowing it to operate in 'competition against private trade'. This decision was promptly challenged by the Labor opposition, led by James Scullin. In line with his party's objective of nationalising the country's principal industries, Scullin argued that the factory ought to continue to supply goods not just to meet the needs of Commonwealth departments but for sale to the public as well.[20]

The government specifically rejected retention on this basis, contending that 'the legitimate functions of government' would be exceeded. As the Commonwealth's total annual requirement for cloth only amounted to about 80,000 yards, there was no justification for maintaining a complete factory with plant capable of producing more than seven times this quantity each year. Following the defeat of Opposition motions in both houses of parliament, the factory was advertised for sale in July 1922. Although tenders had to be called a second time in December before an acceptable price was realised, eventually the factory was transferred in June 1923 to the ownership of the Federal Woollen Mills Pty. Ltd.[21]

During 1923 the Bruce government made it a matter of policy to dispense with any factory not strictly necessary to meeting service requirements. As a result of this decision the harness factory – already suffering from a severe drop in defence orders for leather goods – similarly ceased production and closed down in March of that year, after the section producing canvas goods was first transferred to the clothing works.[22] Although the clothing factory was also experiencing a downturn in demand, with the number of employees falling to 222 in 1924, the fact that it operated on a self-supporting basis spared it from reductions due to cuts in treasury funding.

Within the defence group of establishments, the acetate factory was fortunate to escape closure at this time. By 1925, though, the cost of producing power alcohol (principally for the Postmaster-General's Department and the Royal Australian Air Force) had risen to uneconomical levels and the factory ceased operations. The plant was placed into maintenance with only four men remaining as caretakers, this number being reduced to just two in 1932. It remained in this condition until 1934 when the decision was taken that it no longer warranted the cost of maintenance. The factory's plant was dismantled, and buildings and land transferred to the Department of Interior for disposal.[23]

In line with the strategy adopted by the MSB for the factories in the munitions group, the small arms works at Lithgow felt the chill wind of retrenchment in 1922 as its staff was cut to barely 300. A delegation to the defence minister requesting that the factory be allowed to undertake work from alternative sources was told that the government's policy precluded making goods in competition with private industry; only items not manufactured in Australia could be considered. The minister gave assurances that rifle production would continue, though at the greatly reduced level of only 3000 per year.[24]

Within a couple of years the Lithgow plant received a mild boost to offset these reductions with the construction of extensions to enable the installation of some of the 1656 items of machinery purchased in England at the end of the war. These additions allowed the factory to advance its skills in interchangeable mass production, the technology which enabled rifle components to be swapped without detriment to any one weapon's operation. This was the most modern form of manufacturing, requiring levels of precision that were far higher than encountered in the rest of Australian secondary industry, and meant that Lithgow became the local centre of excellence in this technique.[25] After a new machine shop was erected along the western boundary of the factory site, the manufacture of parts for the Vickers sustained-fire machine gun was commenced in 1924, followed by production of the complete weapon from 1928.[26]

At Maribyrnong, too, the picture was not entirely bleak. In March 1922 the buildings to house the central research laboratories – later known as the Munitions

Supply Laboratories – were opened, providing facilities for testing for modification and development purposes. In mid-year the cordite works, employing only a nucleus staff, were converted to the production of TNT and other explosives. Now known as the Explosives Factory, these works were also expanded from 1924 to undertake the filling of gun rounds and bombs, along with producing paints, lacquers, aircraft dopes and general chemicals required by the services.[27] Very quickly this factory, too, became the local leader in complex chemical engineering.

In July 1922 a field artillery depot that had developed in the Maribyrnong area during the war years was taken over by the MSB and progressively turned into an ordnance factory which was the best equipped engineering shop in the country. Commencing with a woodshop operating in two converted buildings in 1923, the next year a toolroom was established in a former horse-stable. By 1925 an experimental shell shop was in operation (in another stable conversion), machining 18-pounder shell bodies from solid bar. In the same year, a gun and carriage shop was constructed for manufacturing the 18-pounder gun, followed by a forge shop in 1927–28. Again, much of the plant and equipment for this establishment was from British factories dismantled at the end of the war, though other machinery came from stock purchased by the government from Australian firms which had engaged in shell-making in 1915–16.[28]

At nearby Footscray, matters were also moving in interesting ways. The range of production here was expanded in 1925 after a new gun ammunition factory was constructed, as a separate establishment, alongside the CAC works on Gordon Street (away from the river flats). Under arrangements negotiated during 1916, an agreement was now reached for the purchase of CAC's interest in its factory by the Commonwealth. Finally deciding to exercise this option, the government took possession from midnight on 31 December 1926 and merged the CAC factory with its own. The company's Australian operation was voluntarily wound up in July the following year, bringing to a close this unique example of direct private participation in defence production.[29]

Competing with commercial enterprise

By 1929 the first munitions development program was nearly completed, despite difficulties confronting its implementation. Notwithstanding that the amount expended during the early 1920s on Australia's munitions factories and laboratories was far greater than that of all other British dominions combined for the same period,[30] the local program had been consistently under funded. Soon after 1922 the government had abandoned its undertaking to provide an annual sum of £500,000 for this purpose, and despite a further statement in 1925 by the then defence minister, Sir Neville Howse, assuring that the program's thrust would be continued, the shortfall of money was never made up.[31]

By 1928–29 the situation had reached a stage where the organisation so painfully brought into being and nurtured by the MSB faced the prospect of mutilation, if not extinction. The declining level of funds available was presenting the MSB not simply with the spectre of creeping obsolescence of its capabilities; the funds allocated were insufficient even to maintain the various factories. On this basis the munitions structure simply could not survive.

The only hope seen by Leighton for his organisation was to increase the amount of income generated by the various works and thereby offset the reduction in funding provided for maintenance. If this effort failed to achieve such an outcome, reducing expenditure was the only alternative. Since the munitions group was already operating on a nucleus basis, the scope for economy by this means was slender indeed and could only be achieved by closing down one or more of the factories. The problem faced in avoiding the necessity for such drastic measures was that the amount of work coming from orders placed by the three services (and from other federal or state agencies) was stagnant or shrinking. The more critical impediment remained, however, that of government policy, which prevented defence factories from competing with private enterprise.[32]

Faced with this dilemma, in June 1929 Leighton discussed with his colleagues on the Board the option of closing the small arms factory. Shutting down one of either the ordnance, explosives or ammunition works must vitally effect the other facilities within this group. The loss of Lithgow would, it was judged, cause least damage to the munitions supply structure as a whole. Fortunately, the need to adopt this course was removed by election of the Scullin Labor government in October 1929, although the workforce at Lithgow was further cut to around 250 by mid-1930.[33]

Labor's arrival in office was followed almost immediately by dramatic events overseas that heralded the onset of a world depression, thereby causing even further constriction of public spending. However, the new ministry was not ideologically opposed to allowing government instrumentalities to engage in commercial trading. When the MSB sought the government's policy on this matter, the Prime Minister responded that open competition with private enterprise was not approved 'at present'. The factories were, though, free to supply goods in circumstances where their capabilities were not duplicating the capacity of commercial firms – and without restriction to items which were not yet manufactured in Australia.[34]

Over the next few years, the defence facilities began producing a range of commercial products in addition to their small outputs of defence requirements. Within the Maribyrnong-Footscray complex, the ammunition factory supplied industry with rolled brass and nickel sheets and strip along with thousands of brass lipstick containers; the ordnance factory made automotive spare parts; and the explosives factory produced commercial paints, lacquers and industrial chemicals, such as oil of mirbane (nitrobenzene) which was used in shoe polish, while also filling an order for cordite from New Zealand.[35]

The small arms factory at Lithgow manufactured an even more diverse array of goods. After rifle production had ceased in 1929, the facility turned to making mining equipment, airframe components, iron-heads for golf clubs, police hand-cuffs, centre punches, nail punches and spanners, pencil sharpeners, bottle openers and resealers, door closers, sewing machines and refrigerator compressors. One particularly notable item produced was Western Electric cinema sound projectors, the first of which was installed in the State Theatre in Sydney in 1930. In all, 110 projectors were made, and eventually most cinemas around Australia used machines from Lithgow.[36] Even more important, and controversial, was the manufacture of combs, cutters and sheep shearing hand pieces, until then imported at exorbitant prices.

In an exercise in reverse engineering, by 1931 the Lithgow factory was able to duplicate parts that were truly interchangeable with existing shearing equipment, hence breaking the foreign monopoly and achieving a 20 per cent saving to local wool producers.[37]

Under the new policy guidelines, the value of the defence factories' output (exclusive of the clothing factory) remained static at around £150,000 annually, but the proportion of this total comprising commercial work trebled to 9 per cent in 1929–30, then leapt to 24 per cent the following year. In 1931–32 the value of production rose to £227,000, of which commercial work accounted for 27 per cent.[38]

Allowing the government factories to accept, let alone actively seek, opportunities of a purely commercial kind was understandably resented by private companies. For firms confronted with competition for scarce business during the worst of the Depression, whether the defence factories should be allowed to function outside their intended sphere involved issues of survival, not just political ideology. To the businesses effected, it seemed that their government competitors were unfairly advantaged; since the cost structures of the latter were underwritten by public money, it was alleged that this allowed them to tender for work at unrealistically low prices.

When, for example, the ordnance factory ventured into manufacturing car parts in 1930, complaints followed from several quarters. The factory had been approached by the General Motors Corporation about producing a trial batch of axles to be sold as replacement parts; these items were normally imported as it was not economical for the company to make them locally. By one account, unauthorised Australian manufacturers had been producing inferior copies of the parts and selling them as genuine spares, thereby bringing the company into disrepute. After establishing that the Maribyrnong product was of satisfactory quality, in October General Motors decided to place an order for axles with the factory, along with another for timber bodies to be fitted to motor trucks (a special requirement which the company could not undertake in its own plant at Woodville, South Australia).[39]

Meanwhile, in August, a strongly worded complaint was made by the Victorian Chamber of Manufactures regarding the ordnance factory's acceptance of orders of this nature. The reply sent to this representation emphasised the government's policy of substituting local manufacture for goods which were imported. The case was argued nonetheless that it was 'wasteful and indefensible' for the large amount of government capital invested in munitions factories to 'lie idle', just because these could not be fully utilised in munitions production; moreover, work needed to be found for existing employees. Accordingly, it might happen that:

> ... occasionally the Munitions Factories will be doing work which might be done in commercial workshops. It is hoped, however, that those cases will be limited, and only dictated by the necessity just outlined.

While every endeavour would be made to ensure that the manufacturing capabilities developed in government works 'compete as little as possible with established Australian manufactures', the letter concluded by expressly declining to give an undertaking 'that any class of order will be refused'.[40]

Further complaints were received from the Master Body-Builders Association of South Australia and another body building business in that State, and also the Victorian Motor-Body Building Association, regarding the timber truck bodies. The objections voiced by these organisations were answered with the claim that:

> ... it is understood that, if this Department did not accept the orders for these accessories, the Company concerned would not place them elsewhere in Australia.

Allegations that such jobs were accepted at loss-making rates were rejected with an invitation to inspect 'the very exact system of costing' observed by defence instrumentalities. This offer to open the accounts and costing system of the ordnance factory was taken up in late January 1931 by three members of the motor body trade. Nothing further was heard following this visit, apart from an indirect report that the representatives had been convinced that the system found was equal to anything used by commercial businesses.[41]

At the elections in December 1931 Labor lost power to a conservative government led by J.A. Lyons. The new ministry curtailed to an extent, but did not totally reverse, the practice of allowing the defence factories to accept non-government work. Commercial work might still be accepted if the defence minister was satisfied that orders could not be filled elsewhere in Australia to the extent or satisfactory standard of quality required. Since existing business contracts were legally binding, these had to be continued but were to be reviewed as opportunity allowed.[12] In effect, the government recognised the facilities as an important expansion base for defence capability at a time when financial pressures were forcing a contraction of the armed services themselves. In any event, these institutions had to be kept economically viable if the investment they represented was not to be lost.

Where state-owned enterprises did not have recourse to commercial work their future became bleak indeed, providing little alternative to closure or sale, as the case of Cockatoo Island dockyard well illustrated. In June 1921 the organisation, management and activities of this establishment, along with Garden Island naval depot, had been the subject of a royal commission which noted that Cockatoo Island was 'the only naval establishment of its kind in the Commonwealth' and recommended that it be maintained 'for the purpose of effecting whatever repairs and fittings may be necessary for ships of war'. The commissioners particularly commented that the unfortunate idea 'seems to be prevalent in the public mind that the Dockyard at Cockatoo is an unnecessary establishment', rather than 'an important undertaking and a necessary factor to the naval defence of Australia'.[43]

As a result of this inquiry, Cockatoo Island was transferred to the Prime Minister's Department, where it came under a newly-created Shipbuilding Board of Control. Among the first acts of the Control Board was the sacking of 1600 workers, which still left a large workforce to carry on existing contracts. From September 1923 the management of Cockatoo Island passed to a statutory Australian Commonwealth Shipping Board. However, when this body attempted to improve the financial viability of its dockyard by seeking outside business, it found itself blocked. In 1926 the Commonwealth attorney-general successfully sued the Shipping Board in the High Court to void its participation in a contract for construction of the Bunnerong power house.[44]

By 1928, with the construction of a seaplane tender (*Albatross*) for the RAN due for completion, the lack of further shipbuilding orders made the dockyard a considerable embarrassment. The next year tenders were called for the sale or lease of the yard to private enterprise. However, despite some interest from overseas, no acceptable bids were forthcoming. This temporarily forced the abandonment of moves for disposal, although further labour cuts followed which reduced the workforce to 200–300 – barely enough to maintain buildings and plant. In January 1933 Prime Minister Lyons announced the decision to lease the yard to a newly-formed Australian private company for a 21-year period.[45]

The public statement issued by the Prime Minister made clear how much the action taken over Cockatoo Island owed to the attitude of the Bruce government in the 1920s. Lyons recounted that 'for some time' the dockyard had incurred for the government 'very heavy losses', notwithstanding the retrenchments carried out, before declaring that:

Moreover the judgement of the High Court, known as 'The Bunnerong Judgement', has made it difficult, if not impossible, for the Dockyard to accept any work other than Government work. Activities in recent years, consequently, have been restricted. The position has become so acute that it was necessary for some definite action to be taken ... Without the conclusion of this lease, the Government would have had no alternative but to close down the establishment, and thus throw out of employment a large number of men.[46]

Perhaps buoyed by the precedent that had been set, within a couple of years the Commonwealth found itself confronted with further opposition to the commercial activities of one of its instrumentalities. In 1935 the Victorian attorney-general challenged in the High Court the operations of the clothing factory, on the basis that the Commonwealth did not have the authority to produce clothing other than purely for defence purposes. The Court ruled, however, that it was constitutionally valid for the factory to produce a diversified range of clothing for sale to bodies outside the regular naval and military forces, provided its primary role was for defence purposes. This essentially left the question of which areas of trade the factories should engage in as a matter for the discretion of the governor-general and responsible ministers.[47]

Rearmament years

Despite the favourable outcome to this case, by the mid-1930s the need for the government factories to rely heavily on a volume of non-defence work had begun to pass. The value of such work as a proportion of total output of the munitions group was already declining, from a high of 30 per cent in 1932–33 and 1933–34, to 27.5 per cent in 1934–35 and 23.6 per cent in 1935–36.[48] The reason for this was the commencement of a steady process of rearmament, gradual at first but increasing, in the years leading up to the Second World War.

The first phase of this revival of the nation's defence production capabilities came in 1933 under the Lyons government's defence minister, Sir George Pearce, who also held this portfolio throughout the First World War. During 1932 Pearce made attempts to secure overseas business for the MSB facilities, particularly in supplying Britain's forces in the Far East. These approaches succeeded in gaining some orders from New Zealand, but not from the British who, despite the rhetoric of empire co-operation, followed more nationalistic impulses when it came to foregoing opportunities for their own industry.[49]

Notwithstanding the failure to secure large orders, the increase in business obtained was enough to encourage Pearce to press on with rejuvenating the MSB facilities. Though Australia was still experiencing tough economic times, his seniority and authority in Cabinet allowed him to secure funding in the financial year beginning 1 July 1934 for a modest boost to the defence forces. The RAN received the largest share in the form of some additional ships, but the Army also gained coastal and anti-aircraft (AA) guns to assist in the protection of major ports, and the RAAF several new squadrons.

Included in the package were sufficient orders for each factory in the munitions group to return to nucleus production in their special sphere. The ordnance factory was to make the Army's first AA guns, and the small arms factory was enabled to resume rifle production. The ammunition factory, which had been facing closure as recently as July 1932 due to a lack of work,[50] now had orders for gun and small arms ammunition – which meant that the explosives factory also benefited. The latter gained a facility to produce solventless cordite for naval gun rounds. As a result of this program, not only did the factories escape the pressure for one or more of them to close down, but capital development worth £405,000 for their refurbishment was approved.[51]

Following hard on the heels of this initiative came further programs which modified and expanded the scale of growth within the various facilities. In October 1934 Pearce was succeeded by R.A. Parkhill, who promptly instituted another three-year scheme which overlapped his predecessor's. This, too, was superseded after the 1937 Imperial Conference in London, when Parkhill (now Sir Archdale) and Lyons gained fresh insight into the gravity of the prospects for war. A revised program was consequently announced in August 1937 which was planned to continue into 1939–40. Under this scheme, the MSB was to receive new capital development worth £1.4 million to enable manufacture to be undertaken of new high performance 3.7-inch AA guns at the ordnance factory, the ammunition for these weapons at the ammunition factory, and the .303-inch Bren light machine gun (which had been chosen by the Army to replace the Lewis gun) at the small arms factory.

In March 1938 the treasurer in Lyons' ministry, R.G. Casey, pushed a further rearmament program to specifically improve the front-line effectiveness of the RAAF and the Army. The MSB received a new capital allotment of £700,000 to expand production at the ammunition and explosives factories, along with sufficient orders to put behind it the need to engage in non-defence work. Although the value of munitions production in 1938–39 doubled, this did not mean that the factories were swamped with orders; rather, their capacity for producing most types of munitions was now being utilised, but still at levels far below their maximum rate.

Even this was not the last word in what was becoming a rush to develop Australia's defensive capacity. The Munich crisis in September 1938 highlighted the likelihood of war in Europe and resulted in uncertainty about the position of Japan in such a conflict. The government, in response, announced a further program that was additional to both the Casey and Parkhill plans already being implemented. As a result of these various schemes, over £54 million had now been committed towards rearmament in the seven financial years extending from 1934–41. The annual value of production coming out of the defence factories in 1939–40 was nearly £3 million – almost ten times what it had been in 1934–35.[52]

The impact of these greatly changed conditions was plainly seen at the various facilities. The Lithgow factory, for instance, had to be largely reorganised in preparation for manufacture of the Bren gun, and new facilities erected. Additional construction, extensions and modernisations were carried out in 1938–39 to provide for increased production of .303 rifles and Vickers machine guns, and new plant was also procured to bring the factory's capabilities up to modern standards. Due to the loss of some machinery at sea, and the need to manufacture other equipment in Australia under licence, the Bren project was to suffer considerable delay. The first trial weapon was not finally completed until January 1941, when full-scale production finally started.[53]

At the ordnance factory at Maribyrnong, service orders also triggered a spate of construction and machinery installation to provide new production capabilities. Among the additional machinery bought were lathes for turning projectiles and a second shell-forging plant which, on advice from the War Office in London, was ordered from a German firm. These items were paid for through a form of barter-trading in Australian wool, which a British intermediary arranged. The last of the ordered items was shipped from Holland on the first day of war in Europe, in September 1939.[54]

Among the important steps taken in this pre-war period was the setting up in 1933 of a Principal Supply Officers Committee (PSOC) within the Defence Department. This body, which included in its membership a representative of each of the three services, mirrored similar committees in Britain and other dominions. Its purpose was to develop the means for organising private industry to undertake munitions production in the event of war. Among its functions were responsibility for monitoring national stock levels of raw materials needed for defence production, developing plans for the supply of critical items in the event of a defence emergency, and maintaining a register of contractors whose machinery could be diverted to war work if required.[55]

The chairman of the PSOC was Leighton, who had long resisted its establishment in the belief – correct as it happened – that this was a ploy by the services to bring the MSB under their direct control.[56] The committee was kept inactive for most of its first few years in existence, waiting for government direction on the extent of its task. Serious conflict developed later, especially after the Defence Committee directed in September 1935 that the investigative work of the PSOC was to be at an advanced stage by the end of 1939, when it was thought probable that war would break out in Europe.[57]

In April 1936 Lieutenant-Colonel L.E. Beavis, the Army's former liaison officer in London, was appointed to head the Supply Board (subsequently renamed the Defence Resources Board), the co-ordinating body which served as the

PSOC's executive. Imbued with a sense of urgency, as well as great personal energy and determination, he was soon at odds with Leighton over when the effort of organising commercial industry for war should actually commence. Beavis wanted this work begun immediately, whereas Leighton – mindful of the cost likely to be involved and the financial limitations still faced by the government – considered that available funds were best utilised in first developing the defence factories. After a year of disputation, Beavis was removed and returned to the Army, and the PSOC reorganised so that it functioned without the Defence Resources Board.[58]

Despite this outcome, the plan already developed by the PSOC represented a valuable blueprint for action. It envisaged a scheme of placing 'educational orders' with individual private companies or non-defence instrumentalities, both as a means of training them and to test their ability to respond as required. Those facilities which managed orders satisfactorily were to become the site for 28 special armament annexes, to be constructed alongside and operated by them on behalf of the government. To gain the co-operation of industry and enable its resources to be drawn upon fully, the PSOC plan also proposed establishing an Advisory Panel on Industrial Organisation composed of leading industrialists. This recommendation was promptly adopted by the government, and in March 1938 the Prime Minister announced the panel's creation under the chairmanship of Essington Lewis, chief general manager of Broken Hill Proprietary (BHP) Co. Ltd. and one of the country's most able and respected industrial leaders.[59]

The role of Lewis in assisting in the mobilisation of industry was to prove of unparalleled importance. Not only was BHP under his leadership among the first companies to become host to an armament annex, he had already played a key personal part in establishing for Australia a viable aircraft industry. Some manufacture of complete aircraft had taken place locally, including the production of six metal-framed Moth trainers for the RAAF at the ordnance factory in 1933, but development in this field had been mainly confined to production of components, repairs or assembly of imported parts. In 1935, however, Lewis had taken the lead in acting on a suggestion by the government for the creation of such a capability. The enterprise which Lewis initiated – with others – was essentially a private one, undertaken by a consortium of companies which formed the Commonwealth Aircraft Corporation (CAC) in October of that year, with its works at Fishermens Bend, Melbourne.[60]

The corporation brought itself into being by buying up the shares of the Tugan Aircraft Company and taking control of this existing company as a nucleus. Tugan, with its works alongside Mascot aerodrome at Sydney, was already engaged in making Gannet passenger aircraft for the RAAF, among other buyers. A machine of this type, delivered to the RAAF in February 1938 for use in a communications role, was the first aircraft produced by CAC after it moved the former Tugan plant and equipment to Melbourne in October 1937.[61]

The absorption of Tugan Aircraft was a device meant not only to secure for

CAC a production base, but also to obtain the services of the existing company's manager, L.J. Wackett, a former airforce officer with experience in experimental aircraft design and manufacture dating back to 1924. Wackett was now appointed CAC's manager and chief engineer; his first task was to lead a mission to study aircraft production overseas and to recommend a type that would be suitable for manufacture in Australia. After visiting Italy, France, Germany, Czechoslovakia, Holland, England and the United States, Wackett's team made its selection of a type considered to best meet the requirement of the Royal Australian Air Force for an advanced trainer. This was the NA-16 design of the North American Aviation Company, later amended to an updated version of this type, the NA-33.[62]

The recommendation was adopted by the government and an order placed with CAC in May 1938 for an initial 40 of these aircraft, the number being increased later that year to 100. This was despite strong protests from London that Australia was departing from its traditional supplier and thus weakening the defence bonds of the British Empire. Had the government heeded such arguments, either delaying or abandoning the selection of what became the 'Wirraway' in Australian production, it is clear that the nation's air defence would have been without even the benefit of the first of these machines, which came into service at the outbreak of war.[63]

Nonetheless, as a reaction to the alarm created within imperial circles, the British and Australian governments concluded an agreement in 1939 under which British-designed Beaufort bombers were to be built for both the RAAF and the RAF in a factory alongside CAC at Fishermens Bend.[64] In Sydney, the De Havilland company also began work at its Bankstown works on production of the Tiger Moth trainer, powered by Gipsy aero engines manufactured in Australia.[65] As a consequence of these separate measures, in the last few years prior to the Second World War, an industry geared to the production of military aircraft was taking shape in Australia. Although a crucial start had been made, orders had to be placed in the United States for further aircraft.[66] Nonetheless, it is clear that Australia would have been in a far worse position had its fledgling aircraft industry not been established.

In this period of rapid expansion of effort, the government administrative machinery needed to control it became more complex and warranted division into separate administrative entities. Apart from six years from 1915 when the Navy enjoyed a separate existence, the defence function had reposed within a single departmental entity. Now many of the functions which it controlled assumed separate departmental status. In 1938 Civil Aviation was established, followed by Information the next year. In June 1939 a Department of Supply and Development was formed, while in November of that year came the major split, with the three services – Army, Navy and Airforce – gaining autonomy as departments, while the rump of the old organisation became Defence Co-ordination (reverting to the title of simply Defence in 1942). Under these arrangements, the

Munitions Supply Board (renamed the Factory Board) went into Supply and Development, along with the Contracts Board and the PSOC (now called the Defence Supply Planning Committee).[67]

Expansion in the Second World War

Once hostilities began in September 1939, the production of munitions became a major preoccupation of the government. This was heightened by the fall and occupation of France by Germany in 1940, which produced a crisis situation for Britain whereby Australia effectively lost its access to British sources of supply. In June 1940, Essington Lewis was appointed director-general of munitions. All Commonwealth factories connected with munitions and aircraft production came under a new Department of Munitions which he controlled. Left behind in Supply and Development (with the clothing factory) was the responsibility for procurement of all stores and material other than munitions and including foodstuffs until 1943.[68]

Clothed with wide executive powers, Lewis has been described as 'virtually an industrial dictator'.[69] Initially, the department he headed remained under the same minister as Supply and Development, and it was not until June 1941 that Munitions acquired fully separate status. At this time Munitions lost aircraft production, which was divided off into a new department of that name, although as a remarkable compliment to Lewis he was made director-general of this activity too.[70]

In the months following June 1940, the production of munitions expanded enormously. By the time this effort reached its peak in May 1943, the Commonwealth government had built 39 factories in addition to 213 annexes or extensions to existing privately-owned factories or state instrumentalities, such as railway workshops; by the end of the war a total of 47 factories had been authorised, although two of these – at Swan Hill (Vic.) and Katoomba (NSW) – were never completely equipped, and the number of annexes established totalled 244.[71] Much of the equipment produced in these improvised facilities had not been manufactured in Australia previously, with machine tools and some types of electrical and optical apparatus being entirely new to local industry.

An example of the processes at work is illustrated in the development of the Lithgow factory. At the outbreak of war the manufacture of all small arms was concentrated at this one facility. Following the virtual destruction of the fighting power of the British Expeditionary Force on the beaches of Dunkirk in 1940, Australia was asked by London to make available as many rifles as could be spared. Some 30,000 weapons were promptly despatched from stocks, although this severely reduced the resources of the Australian Army and created an urgent need to expand rifle production in this country.[72]

Accordingly, a new factory was erected at Bathurst, some 65 kilometres west of Lithgow, and commenced production in September 1941. While there had been no previous industrial experience in this locality, within a short period 2000 sets of rifle components were being produced here weekly, although all barrel manufacture and assembly operations were still carried out in the parent factory.[73] Almost as the Bathurst factory was opened, the Army sought an increase in production to 4000 rifles per week. It was decided to duplicate the Bathurst installation at Orange, some 65 kilometres further west, where again only unskilled labour was available. Commencing production in March 1942, this plant was further improved by the addition of barrel manufacture, leaving only the assembly of the rifles to be retained at Lithgow, which was then free to concentrate on producing Bren and Vickers machine guns.[74]

Continuing the process of tapping previously unused resources in country areas, in early 1942 the decision was taken to continue decentralising production to towns in the central west of New South Wales. This activity continued throughout 1942–43, with feeder factories for producing machine gun components established at Forbes, Wellington, Mudgee, Cowra, Young, Parkes, Dubbo and Portland – all within 240 kilometres of Lithgow. Another such facility was prepared at Katoomba but remained uncommissioned when the need for these factories began to decline from 1944.[75]

At its peak level in 1943, the system of decentralising production saw 5731 workers employed in multiple shifts at the parent works at Lithgow, 1600 at Bathurst, 2491 at Orange and a further 2264 in the feeder factories. This total of just over 12,000 was a far cry from the 536 engaged on small arms manufacture in 1939. A further feature of the position at Lithgow was that women were first engaged in production from March 1942, and by mid-1943 fully 35 per cent of the factory's workforce was female. By this means the required weekly production rate of 4000 rifles was achieved, along with 150 Bren guns, 70 Vickers guns and large quantities of spare parts.[76]

The experience of the other original munitions factories was similar. The ammunition factory at Footscray expanded until it reached a peak of over 9300 workers in 1942. Concerns expressed by defence commentators since 1938 that the small arms ammunition requirements of Australia were dependent on this one facility finally led to action to establish a duplicate factory, subsequently sited at Hendon in South Australia. Footscray was called upon to train large numbers of workers for employment in its sister factory and in additional ammunition factories (some intended as feeders) established at Mildura (Vic.); Albury, Broken Hill, Goulburn, Rutherford, Tamworth, Hay and Wagga Wagga (NSW); Rocklea (Queensland); Finsbury, Clare, Kapunda, Moonta, Mount Gambier, Murray Bridge and Port Pirie (SA); Welshpool and Kalgoorlie (WA); and Derwent Park (Tas.). The Finsbury plant was itself employing over 5300 workers in 1942.[77]

Expansion to meet the services' needs also effected the explosives factory at

Maribyrnong, which became a large and versatile filling facility handling shells, bombs, mines, grenades and depth charges. The number of personnel employed here reached over 8100 in 1942, and expertise developed was utilised to extend explosives-related manufacturing operations to new sites and annexes established during the war years. Again, the capability of this factory was duplicated in a new facility at Penfield (Salisbury) in South Australia. Begun in November 1940, the new plant produced its first batch of TNT just over a year later. The factory was, however, not completed as designed until January 1943, but within six months was employing 5000 workers.[78]

Other explosives facilities brought into existence were a gunpaper plant at Ballarat in Victoria (September 1940), located on the Adelaide–Melbourne rail-line to enable it to feed both the main Victorian and South Australian plants; and two filling factories at St. Marys and Villawood, both on the western outskirts of Sydney. The St. Marys facility, established in July 1941, was employing over 2000 workers by mid-1944. Another factory for the manufacture of American-type smokeless powder was established in 1943 at Mulwala, near Yarrawonga on the Murray River. During 1939 the Australian and New Zealand subsidiary of Imperial Chemical Industries (ICIANZ) – which had bought the Nobel factory in 1928 – had also approached the government about setting up an additional TNT factory at Deer Park (Albion). This was financed by the Commonwealth as an 'armaments annexe' and produced both TNT and cordite.[79]

At the ordnance factory, the workforce engaged in making guns and shell, along with a diverse range of other items, had risen to nearly 6000 in mid-1943. Here was also developed a ball-bearing manufacturing capability, which in 1943 was transferred to Echuca, one of five Victorian country centres where additional ordnance factories had been located. The other of these new works were at Bendigo, Horsham, Stawell and Hamilton, the most important of which was Bendigo. Established in 1942 and employing nearly 1200 people by mid-1943, this plant provided additional capacity to undertake the heavier types of ordnance. The most important work done here was the manufacture of 4-inch gun mountings of the type used to arm merchant ships, and relining of large-calibre guns – in particular 6-inch and 8-inch naval types for both the RAN and the RN. In addition a wide variety of equipment was produced for the Army.[80]

Supporting this growth in the production effort was the work of the Munitions Supply Laboratories. The staff of this establishment, which existed to ensure quality control of materials used in and produced by the munitions factories, numbered about 80 in 1938. By mid-1943 more than 1150 personnel were employed at MSL, and branches had been established in other States. In addition to providing vital metrology and calibration services, some 500 of the staff were engaged in making gas masks, about a million of which were produced for the services during the war.[81]

At the clothing factory, war needs gave rise to increased levels of production in a much wider range of items. Although the factory was expanded and the number of employees increased from 484 in 1939 to 604 by 1945, the resources of private industry had to be enlisted to meet demand. Even so, difficulties encountered in obtaining supplies of artillery textiles such as cartridge bags, and also special canvas goods, led to the setting up of a second government clothing factory at Carlton in 1941 to produce these items.[82]

The start made in 1938–39 to create a local aircraft industry also received a boost and underwent rapid expansion during the early stages of the war. After France fell to invading German forces in June 1940, Britain stopped the export of equipment and parts for the Beaufort project in Australia. Although the embargo was lifted within a few months, enabling the first locally-made bomber to be delivered by August 1941, this occurrence graphically illustrated the critical need for self-reliance in the manufacture of defence equipment to the maximum extent possible.

The value of the local source of supply was steadily and impressively demonstrated as some 700 Beauforts were delivered by August 1944. The manufacture of additional types was also undertaken in Australia's three aircraft production outlets – CAC, the Beaufort Division, and the De Havilland Aircraft Company – and these were eventually employing some 44,000 workers between them. By the end of the war about 3500 machines of nine different kinds had been produced, along with nearly 3000 engines of three types.[83]

Within the Department of Aircraft Production, set up in 1941, was a Maintenance Division, which organised the manufacture of aircraft parts and the servicing of RAAF machines, as well as aircraft of American airforce units, the RAF and RNZAF. This division comprised an aircraft engine factory at Lidcombe near Sydney, and airframe repair workshops at Parafield airfield, near Salisbury (SA); the latter facility also had machine tool workshops located at Northfield. Manufacturing was carried out by various annexes in South Australia under contract to the Airframe Repair Workshops.[84]

On the naval side, Australia faced requirements for naval support far greater than that experienced in the First World War. During the Second World War the south-west Pacific was a major theatre of operations, and from 1942 the RAN and allied navies needed facilities to repair damaged warships. Cockatoo Island was the only large shipbuilding and engineering works available in Australia, but it was still leased to a private concern, the Cockatoo Docks & Engineering Company. Under a special wartime agreement, the company continued to operate the yard in return for an annual management fee based on turnover.[85] On this basis, the yard carried out conversion and modification tasks, along with refit, maintenance and repair jobs needed by the services.

During the 1930s Australia's merchant shipbuilding industry was moribund. Although shipyards had existed at Adelaide, Newcastle and Maryborough, these had become uneconomic after 1924 and been closed – in some cases dismantled.

Cockatoo Island was now to play a key role in reviving a shipbuilding capability vital to the war effort through helping to disseminate the technical skills needed to bring these former centres, and new ones at Brisbane and Whyalla (SA), to full capacity. Thus, when a decision was made early in the war to embark on a program to locally construct corvettes (ocean-going minesweepers suitable for escort work), of which 60 were ultimately built, only eight of these small ships were produced at Cockatoo. Similarly, when a program for frigates was begun in late 1942, all but two of the fourteen vessels produced were built in yards other than Cockatoo, though to the latter went the distinction of constructing three destroyers of the Tribal class for the RAN.[86]

Among the naval facilities which received new or special emphasis as a result of the war was the naval depot at Garden Island. This fulfilled functions which might be expected of it in converting and fitting out civilian vessels for wartime purposes, and also carried out work involving the construction of mountings for 4-inch naval guns. In May 1940 the Prime Minister, R.G. Menzies, announced the government's decision to construct there a naval graving dock expected to cost nearly £3 million and take three years to build. Until then, only two dockyards in Australia (Cockatoo Island and Mort's Dock, Sydney) operated dry docks able to accommodate large warships of cruiser size. Possession of this additional dock would, Menzies said, 'make Australia a fit base for a powerful fleet' and remove the necessity, in certain contingencies, for ships needing refit or repair to use facilities at Singapore.[87]

At the peak of the construction work, reached in July 1943, the project employed over 4100 men. When they had finished, Garden Island was an island no longer but an appendage to the Sydney suburb of Potts Point. The dock, named in honour of eighteenth century naval explorer, Captain James Cook, was officially opened in March 1945. Within its first year of operation it had handled six British capital ships (the largest, HMS *Anson*, displacing more than 45,000 tons) in addition to two RN aircraft carriers. A second but smaller graving dock was also built at Brisbane in 1942, at a time when that more northern centre was closer to the scene of naval operations.

In 1942 the Commonwealth also took over the dockyard formerly owned by the Victorian government at Williamstown, turning it into a naval facility. At Port Melbourne the navy was also acquiring another support facility in the form of a marine engine works. A government decision in 1941 to improve the nation's capacity to build merchant ships had created a subsequent need for additional engine building capacity. Two factories were built to operate under the control of the Shipbuilding Board, the first of which was to be at Melbourne. Begun in a temporary workshop in March 1942, this facility commenced the manufacture of equipment for Fairmile launches used by the RAN. In July the erection of a substantial new facility was started, with the main building completed in March 1943. This new factory was equipped to build large steam reciprocating engines, and after the main propelling machinery for two merchant vessels was finished in 1944–45, work began on two frigate engines for the RAN. The second engine workshop was built at Rocklea, near Brisbane.[88]

By the time the Second World War ended in 1945, the industrial landscape of Australia had been transformed. Whereas primary industry had dominated the nation's economy since Federation, in the course of the war years secondary industry had finally overtaken it in terms of value of production and the proportion of the workforce employed. Moreover, secondary industry was now much more capable and skilled as a result of meeting the many challenges which the war had presented. As the official history observed, 'Developments that might otherwise have been spread over 25 years were compressed into little more than five years'.[89]

In all of this, the defence factories had played a crucial part. Having survived the 'lean years' of the Depression, these facilities had served as the prime means for transmitting the specialist technical skills and standards required in munitions production into commercial industry, thereby enabling the latter to take up the burden of war production on a national scale. But the very success of this process of making industry more capable of meeting defence needs meant that the post-war role of the defence facilities was certain to change. With industry now able to meet so many of the support requirements of the peacetime forces – indeed, having left behind the defence factories in all but a few specialised areas of capability – the part the facilities would play in the future would increasingly require re-evaluation.

3

THE PRICE OF DEPARTMENTAL CONTROL

Unlike the period of the First World War, when Germany's collapse came suddenly and defence production continued at full speed until the conflict's last days, the outcome of the Second World War was anticipated long before the Japanese surrender in August 1945. Australia's industrial output had begun declining from early 1943, when the government decided to transfer as much as possible of the national effort to producing food. Consideration also began to focus on what to do with the numerous munitions factories, since only a few of these would be needed for peacetime defence purposes.[1]

Accordingly, in the small arms group, the various feeder factories commenced disbanding from January 1944 and had all been closed by March 1945. In the ammunition group, feeder factories began closing from October 1943 and were transferred to other departments or uses, followed by many of the main factories during the first months of 1945. In the ordnance group the rural feeder factories began closing from late 1943, while in the explosives group the complex at Villawood was put onto a care and maintenance basis from November 1944.[2]

The end of the war brought the closure of further establishments and an inevitable wind-down of those which remained. The heavy curtailment of small arms output during 1945–46 caused the closure of the other main factories at Bathurst and Orange, such production as continued being re-established at Lithgow. The making of Vickers and Bren guns was terminated, although the making of .303 SMLEs continued until 1956. Once more, the bulk of Lithgow's post-war production became of a commercial nature, including .22 sporting rifles and .410-inch shotguns, refrigerator parts and sewing machines.[3]

The ordnance factory at Maribyrnong, along with the wartime plant at Bendigo which had been retained, also faced severe reductions in service orders. Both turned to commercial work from 1946 in line with a government policy of 'assisting in the re-establishment of industry and of fitting ex-servicemen for trained jobs'.[4]

Production slowed down, too, at Footscray, which by June 1946 was again the sole manufacturer of small arms ammunition (even though the rolling mill section at the Finsbury factory was kept in operation until early 1952 to assist commercial development in South Australia). Here non-defence orders also became a significant part of the factory's output, including plastic goods such as telephone cases, deodorant blocks, and cardboard boxes. The original ammunition works on the river flats, referred to as No.1 SAA Factory after a new facility (No.2 SAA) had been constructed about a kilometre away in the opening stages of the war, was leased to Myer Emporium Ltd in 1945 for use as a bulk furniture store.[5]

The position was much the same in the non-munitions defence establishments. The No.2 Clothing Factory at Carlton was closed down in March 1947, and the manufacture of artillery textiles which had been carried on there from 1941 returned to the original clothing establishment in South Melbourne. Continuing large orders from government departments other than Defence – such as the Postmaster-General's – ensured, however, that the future of the main works was not in question.[6]

In the aircraft factories, production was also cut back to a mere trickle, with only contracts for Mustang fighters and Lincoln bombers allowed to continue – though at a very low level. The industry here was saved, however, by fresh orders placed in August 1946 with the de Havilland company for 50 – later increased to 80 – Vampire jet fighters, and by the decision of CAC to diversify to meet heightened post-war demand for housing and household goods. At about the same time CAC also received an order to commence full local manufacture of the Nene engine powering these aircraft.[7]

Post-war rationalisation

In the meantime the government moved to recoup some of its huge wartime expenditure. According to the volume of the official history on *The Role of Science and Industry*, the Department of Munitions and its agencies had spent at least £300 million – much of this on expendable items such as guns and ammunition, tanks and aeroplanes, 'which in the economic sense represented so much waste'.[8] A later historian broadly endorses this estimate, but suggests that figure includes the £285 million worth of munitions actually produced – the vast amount of which was chargeable to other departments (mainly the three services) or foreign governments such as the UK.[9]

What was not accounted for in this way were additional capital costs of £84.5 million spent on factory buildings and works, plant and machine tools, and residual costs of £20.5 million for things like training. Such expenditure could be partly offset by selling buildings and plant to state governments and commercial industry. By July 1949 nearly £32.5 million of the Commonwealth's investment had been regained through directly liquidating assets, and perhaps as much as another £16 million still remained virtually intact at the end of the war for use in industrial development.[10]

Locating munition factories in regional towns, where untapped labour resources could be utilised while also effecting a strategic dispersal of vital production, now provided an opportunity to achieve other goals when it came to stimulating development of the nation's peacetime secondary industry. The sale of wartime factories became a key element in a government program of 'industrial decentralisation'. Across Australia, more than 4300 buildings were available for disposal – and this figure did not include some 200 annexes attached to existing private factories, or food dehydration factories, power alcohol distilleries, flax mills, aircraft production establishments and a great number of storage buildings.[11]

By the end of July 1946 some 120 enterprises had bought or leased space in former munition factories, and this figure rose to 293 by August 1949. Factories in rural towns were usually taken over for use by single businesses. Despite the earnest rhetoric of industrial decentralisation, the majority of the development which occurred under this government program inevitably still took place on the fringes of capital cities, since this was where the vast conglomerations of buildings up for disposal were located. For example, over 1000 buildings were available at Salisbury-Finsbury, on the northern outskirts of Adelaide, while at St. Marys, on Sydney's western edge, were another 900. At these sites were created community industrial estates which accounted for 217 of the firms which by 1949 were utilising former munitions factories.[12]

Organisationally, there was an administrative contraction to match the shedding of unwanted facilities. In November 1946 the Department of Supply and Shipping reabsorbed Aircraft Production, including the Beaufort Division (by this time called the Government Aircraft Factory, GAF), the aero-engine factory at Lidcombe, and the airframe repair workshops at Parafield (with a machine shop annexe at Northfield).[13] In April 1948 this entity relinquished some functions to a new Department of Shipping and Fuel and reverted to its earlier name of Supply and Development, which it retained until March 1950 when it became simply Supply.

In addition to taking back the remaining factories from the now abolished Department of Munitions, the revamped Supply organisation absorbed the Munitions Supply Laboratories (renamed the Defence Research Laboratories, and later still the Defence Standards Laboratories). It also exercised responsibility for shipbuilding (until 1951), long range guided weapons research and development, and control of materials used in producing atomic energy. Since 1947 the Long Range Weapons Establishment (later called the Weapons Research Establishment) had its headquarters in part of the wartime factory site at Penfield (Salisbury).[14]

By the time the process of post-war rationalisation was completed in 1950, Australia's defence establishment still possessed an industrial base for its direct support which was much larger than that existing before the war. Now, in addition to the original four munitions establishments (small arms, ammunition, explosives, ordnance) and the clothing factory, there were aircraft factories at Fishermens Bend, additional ordnance works at Bendigo and Echuca, a marine engine works at Port Melbourne, and an explosives factory at Mulwala. As well, part of the wartime factory at Penfield had been retained on a maintenance basis, providing reserve capacity should expansion be required to meet a future conflict, and four synthetic ammonia plants were in operation producing ammonium sulphate, ammonium nitrate, methanol and nitric acid.[15] There were now also naval dockyards at Garden Island and Williamstown directly available to serve the RAN's needs, in addition to a number a commercial shipyards.

This situation had no sooner been reached than a new climate of uncertainty associated with international affairs provided a boost to defence production which arrested and reversed the process of decline. On 25 June 1950 the smouldering antagonisms of the Cold War found an outlet in Korea, when the communist republic in the north of the peninsula suddenly invaded its southern neighbour. Australian defence forces were immediately committed to this struggle.

The Prime Minister, R.G. Menzies, was on an overseas visit when this crisis broke, but on his return in August his government interpreted events in Asia as signifying the onset of a period of heightened tension which might well lead to major conflict between the superpowers. In a series of radio broadcasts during September, Menzies issued a dramatic 'Defence Call to the Nation'. The sense of urgency thus conveyed persisted into the next year as well, with it being widely reported that in March 1951 Menzies had warned a conference of State premiers that Australia should be ready to face a new world war within the next three years.[16]

Acting on its assessment of the need to raise the level of defence preparedness, the government decided on an increase in spending to provide for compulsory national service training, expanded citizen and permanent forces, and a program to stockpile strategic and defence-related materials. In December 1950 a National Security Resources Board (NSRB) was established to undertake the planning necessary to balance the civil and military aspects of the national economy. The effort initiated at this time was to continue until 1954, when it was scaled down for strategic and economic reasons.[17]

In July 1951 parliament passed a Defence Preparations Act which gave the government extraordinary new powers. The primary objective of the legislation was to expand the capacity of the Australian economy to produce or manufacture goods for defence purposes. The NSRB was charged with implementing measures to divert and control resources needed for defence production, adjust the national economy to meet war needs, and maintain and sustain the population of Australia and its allies while preparations for war continued.[18]

The implications of these events for the defence factories were enormous. Not only did expansion of the existing Australian forces carry a direct requirement for extra quantities of a range of goods, but planning was also conducted for a possible need to despatch an expeditionary force of three divisions to the Middle East. In addition, Australia expected to play a wider supporting role in allied strategy, not just as a food arsenal but as a supplier of munitions and other military items to allied forces operating in regions where it was the nearest-placed major source.[19] The forms such 'mutual assistance' might take were expressly canvassed during a visit to Australia by a representative of Britain's Joint War Production Committee during May 1951.[20]

Giving expression to the heightened emphasis on defence arrangements at this juncture, the munitions and aircraft production activities of the Supply organisation were once again formed into a separate Department of Defence Production in May 1951.[21] By the end of 1951 the Menzies government had decided the size of the forces it would mobilise in the event of war, and settled on supply and munitions programs. In the event, the immense strain placed on Australia's economy by early 1952 would cause some modification to these plans. Most importantly, an initial preference for the goal of self-sufficiency through local production had to be abandoned in favour of making some large purchases of heavier and more complex combat equipment from overseas.[22]

Nonetheless, under the stimulus thus provided the defence facilities found themselves enjoying a resurgence of orders. Substantial demand was generated, for instance, by the Navy's expansion program, which entailed the construction of Battle and Daring class destroyers, two inshore minesweepers, a fleet tanker, and a boom-working vessel; also included was the conversion and modernisation of another seventeen ships. Apart from work placed with the naval dockyards, the ordnance establishment at Maribyrnong produced guns and anti-submarine mortars for the new ships while the works at Bendigo manufactured the gun mountings and turbine gear cases (complete with gearing) required.[23]

A similar build-up of the RAAF and the RAN's fleet air arm saw 540 aircraft ordered during the three years from June 1950, in addition to some 150 already approved at that date. Just as local production accounted for 122 of the latter, the bulk of the new orders was also to be made in Australia. The GAF received an order in 1950 for 48 Canberra medium jet bombers, while CAC gained an order in May 1951 for 72 (later increased to 112) Sabre jet fighters; both these major projects were on the point of beginning production by 1953. The Avon jet engine used by both these types was also to be manufactured locally, with production shared between CAC and the engine annex at Lidcombe.[24]

The introduction of high-speed aircraft powered by turbo-jet engines caused the abandonment of the test flight field operated at Fishermens Bend, since this area was becoming increasing enclosed by industrial development. In 1953 a new airfield was established at Avalon, 50 kilometres south-west of Melbourne towards Geelong, complete with a 7000-foot runway and appropriate buildings and services. Final assembly for flight testing of all jet-engined aircraft manufactured or overhauled in Victoria was conducted from that site, as well as servicing and modification of these machines.[25]

Further aircraft orders followed, with CAC contracted in late 1951 to make 62 Winjeel basic trainers, while an order was placed with de Havilland at the same time for 41 (later 109) Vampire advanced trainers. Throughout this period, GAF was engaged in developing a subsonic target drone called Jindivik. Begun in 1948, this project moved into production in 1952 and continued for the next four decades, with exports to the United States, Britain and Sweden. Also notable at this time was the development, again by GAF, of a heavy anti-tank guided missile to meet a UK requirement; after test firings in 1956, 826 of these weapons, known as Malkara, were delivered to Britain from July 1958. With a steady stream of work, the level of employment within the industry rose from a post-war low of 6600 in mid-1948 to 12,300 by mid-1955.[26]

The clothing factory (which had stayed behind with the Department of Supply) also enjoyed increased orders, with the value of production trebling from £346,000 in 1948 to nearly £1.3 million in 1952. Increased volumes brought pressure on workspace at the South Melbourne premises, however, and forced the transfer of the Caps and Canvas Section to a new factory in Brunswick during the Christmas vacation period of 1952. In part of the area thus vacated was begun the production of gold bullion badges of rank and embroidery for caps of senior officers, insignia, and flags and regimental colours, while the canvas section completed a large order of marquee tents for the Army. Adding to the workload of the clothing facilities in this period were orders for uniforms and bunting placed in connection with the royal visit in 1954 – the first to Australia by a reigning British monarch – worth more than £2 million.[27] ·

The new strategic concerns also found expression when, in 1953, the North Atlantic Treaty Organisation (NATO) adopted 7.62 mm (.30-inch) as the standard ammunition size for infantry small arms in the armies of member nations, replacing the variety of calibres then in use (including .303 of the Lee-Enfield). Although Australia was not a party to the NATO alliance, late the following year it joined Britain and Canada in adopting the 7.62 mm L1A1 self-loading rifle (SLR) as a common infantry weapon.

The SLR was basically the same as the rifle made by the Belgian company Fabrique Nationale d'Armes de Guerre, S.A., of Herstal-lez-Liege, for Belgium, Germany and other NATO countries. By arrangement between the three Commonwealth partners, the L1A1 was to be manufactured locally in each country, using basic drawings which ensured that parts from their separate production centres were interchangeable.[28]

Planning for production at Lithgow began early in 1955 when a sample weapon was received. Activity intensified as basic specification drawings and other information became available, in preparation for concurrent manufacture to be undertaken. Complete reorganisation of the Lithgow works was carried out from 1956, with new buildings erected and more modern machine tools purchased. By the time this program was finished the factory bore almost no resemblance to the way it looked as recently as the beginning of the Second World War, when overhead shafting and belting was still in use. Even with this upgrade of the factory, the manufacture of a proportion of SLR components had to be subcontracted out to commercial suppliers around Australia.[29]

Adoption of the SLR by the Australian services also brought with it the need to convert the ammunition factory at Footscray to 7.62 mm production. New plant imported from France was installed and by 1958 the first batches of the new rounds produced.[30] To assist in the establishment of 7.62 mm production in New Zealand, which was also adopting the L1A1 rifle, seven new machines were loaned from Footscray, and technical information, drawings and tooling were supplied as well.[31]

The demands of the defence program even breathed life back into several former facilities which had been closed after 1945. The explosives facility at Deer Park was re-opened in 1954, becoming known as the Commonwealth Explosives Factory Albion, and plant for the manufacture of RDX (cyclonite explosive) was added there three years later.[32] Pressure on the explosives factory at Maribyrnong also prompted the reactivation of the factory at St. Marys, to undertake the filling of explosive devices up to the size of 1000-pound aircraft bombs. Since all except the pyrotechnics section of the wartime complex had been turned over to civil use, in September 1954 the government decided to build a new factory adjacent to the original works rather than repossess the old one. Construction began a year later and the new St. Marys filling factory opened in December 1957.[33]

Uncertain workloads

By the late 1950s, however, the tide was turning once more and Australia's defence industry faced a renewed bout of contraction. In April 1958 the Department of Defence Production was merged into Supply again, signifying that the priority accorded this area of activity at the start of the decade had well and truly passed. In 1959 the ordnance factory at Echuca making ball-bearings was sold as a going concern to a group of foreign manufacturers, and by September of the same year two of the synthetic ammonia plants were also sold and a third one closed.[34] From this juncture, the dearth of major new service orders made it difficult for the facilities to provide worthwhile production levels and employment for their labour forces, and increasingly caused them to revert to seeking non-defence work.

Illustrating this trend, the ordnance factory at Maribyrnong began making power plant for the Victorian State Electricity Commission's stations at Yallourn and Newport, and also ice-making plant for commercial use (some of which was exported to communist China). By 1963 the range of products coming from this factory included cement kilns, mechanisms for carpet-making machines, gates and gate frame hoist and control systems for the Snowy Mountains scheme, cranes for BHP's steel works, and tooling for Australian carmakers.[35]

At the same time, major business from the civilian sector was won by the Bendigo ordnance establishment. During the early 1960s this factory undertook the manufacture of trolley frames for three ladle cranes (with lifting capacity of 300 tons, 75 tons and 15 tons respectively) to be installed at BHP's Newcastle works. It also made the main structure of the first of two 550-ton cranes ordered from Adamson-Alliance Company for the Port Kembla works of Australian Iron and Steel Pty. Ltd. Other work came from the Snowy Mountains Hydro-electric Authority, for items such as a lifting cylinder.[36]

Notwithstanding the important element which commercial production was coming to represent, throughout this period the two remaining ordnance factories still had to remain responsive to Defence needs for new and highly specialised capabilities. In 1963, for instance, Maribyrnong began making motors for guided missiles, 'a precision engineering task which required the development of difficult manufacturing techniques'; such was the importance of this new area that in 1967 a Guided Weapons & Electronics Support Facility was added to the other activities conducted at St. Marys. In 1964 considerable funds were approved to provide additional plant at Maribyrnong to make medium calibre forged shells, to meet the services' possible war needs. In addition a program was embarked on to modernise plant at the factory, leading to about 8 per cent of wartime plant being replaced.[37]

By the mid-1960s the pendulum had swung again, following the commencement of Australian participation in the Vietnam War and the introduction of national service for the Army. Beginning with Army advisers in 1962, by 1965 Australia's defence commitment had grown to include ground combat troops as well as RAAF and RAN contingents. Before Australian forces began reducing in 1970, leading to a complete withdrawal in 1972, the presence had reached a peak of over 8000 personnel. Supporting the enlarged forces and the commitment in Vietnam entailed the stepping up of production levels at the various defence factories back in Australia.

At Maribyrnong, for example, the ordnance factory found itself in 1968 engaged in 'urgent action ... to manufacture canister shot and 20-pounder high explosive shell for the Centurion tanks sent to Vietnam'. Requirements also arose for a wide range of other products, including such items as a lightweight telephone suitable for use by Army engineers in searching narrow tunnels dug by enemy forces.[38]

Following the end of Australia's involvement in the Vietnam conflict, the old problem of sustaining the flow of work at the factories returned. With defence orders down yet again, the need to actively pursue commercial work returned, simply to maintain viability. For its part, Maribyrnong secured contracts in 1974 for the manufacture of spare parts for the automotive industry, for forging and machining heavy engineering equipment, fabricating an overhead crane, and the manufacture of office furniture.

A continuation of the situation in which funding levels were limited and defence orders were down led to a reduction in the workforce at Maribyrnong through the practice of not replacing 'wastage'. By 1977 the number of employees at the ordnance factory stood at just under 850, already down from 870 the previous year. As one account has noted, this policy caused major difficulties because several of the retirees not replaced were highly skilled tradesmen, while the acceptance of a large number of small projects (such as the manufacture of wooden furniture for federal and state government departments) also created 'some programming difficulties'.[39]

By 1982 the number of employees had again risen, to just over 1000 (337 'salaried staff' and 670 'wages personnel'), but the Maribyrnong works was still carrying out some commercial work to fill in gaps between the workload generated by defence orders.[40] Not until late 1984 did the factory receive its first major ordnance contract in more than a decade, when the Australian army ordered 105 mm L118 and L119 Light Guns (howitzers) to replace aging field guns under what was dubbed 'Project Hamel'.[41]

Although the ordnance facilities have been the main example cited to illustrate the fluctuating workloads experienced in the period from the 1950s to the 1980s, the story was much the same at other of the defence facilities. As previously described, Lithgow was heavily committed from the mid-1950s producing the L1A1 rifle with which the Australian forces were re-equipped. From the time the first of these weapons was delivered to the Army in March 1959, over 200,000 of this type had been made in Australia up to May 1972.[42] Adding to the SLR production run at Lithgow were orders received from 25 other countries, including New Zealand and Malaysia.

An additional requirement existed for variants of the same weapon. In June 1962 production commenced of a heavy-barrelled bipod-mounted automatic version (L2A1) developed by Canadian Arsenal, followed by a shorter one known as the L1A1-F1. From 1963 Lithgow also began tooling up to manufacture a 9 mm submachine gun called the F1, a modernised version of the wartime Owen machine carbine. Of 172 parts comprising this weapon, 130 were produced at the small arms factory while civil industry supplied the rest.[43]

In more recent years other orders came to Lithgow for production of a range of military items, from tracks of M113 Armoured Personnel Carriers to links connecting the rounds in belts of 30 mm cannon shells.[44] Despite these various defence requirements, the small arms factory still found that it needed to obtain commercial work to supplement its output – just as had happened during the depressed 1930s. From 1970 onwards, a wide diversity of non-defence items was manufactured in increasing quantities, including some of the items made before the war such as shearing handsets, handcuffs, golf irons and door closers.[45]

A similar trend was evident in the defence aviation industry, where the employment level in the aircraft factories had been falling during the late-1950s. By mid-1961 the number of workers had reached 6500, but at this juncture a major boost was received from several new orders, the most important of which was placed at the end of 1960. GAF became the prime contractor for 30 French Mirage jet fighters; CAC made the Atar engines which powered them, and became the subcontractor for the aircraft wings and fins. This project was later increased to 116 machines, including 16 two-seat trainer versions, and ran until January 1974 when the last Mirage was delivered to the RAAF.[46]

Adding to activity in the aircraft factories from 1960 were orders for an advanced ship borne anti-submarine guided missile known as Ikara. Wholly designed and developed in Australia, some 700 of these weapons were manufactured for the RAN and the navies of Britain and Brazil. Another order followed in 1965, for 75 (later 97) Italian Macchi jet trainers, providing work which also continued until 1972. This time CAC was the prime contractor for the airframe as well as the British Viper engine powering it, but the de Havilland company – now Hawker de Havilland (HDH) – was brought in as sub-contractor for wings and sub-sections of the fuselage.[47]

The importance of the Mirage and Macchi projects for the local industry was demonstrated in the increased number of workers employed within the factories, which reached 9000 in mid-1966. Not all areas of the existing establishment benefited from the new work, however; the Airframe Repair Workshop at Parafield – whose main role covered repair of the older Dakota, Canberra and Winjeel types – was closed down in mid-1969, except for its annexe in what had become the northern Adelaide suburb of Pooraka. The latter became an independent establishment, in July 1974 being renamed the Aircraft Engineering Workshop.[48]

As with other defence facilities, a problem now emerged with a lack of worthwhile orders. In 1969 GAF commenced development work on a recoverable target drone called Turana in response to a RAN requirement, but there were no new major aircraft projects for more than a decade after the Mirage and Macchi orders were placed. An attempt to enter into local manufacture of helicopters was made in 1971, but this proved a costly mistake. Under an agreement reached between the government and the American Bell Corporation, 75 Kiowa OH-58A light observation helicopters were to be purchased for the Army. After an initial twelve machines had been imported, the next 43 were to be jointly built with an increasing level of Australian content. By the fifty-eighth machine, Australian-produced rotor heads would be incorporated, for which purpose special high technology gear-cutting machinery was imported and installed by CAC.

In addition to the batch of military machines to be purchased, the arrangement provided for the building of another 125 civil versions of the same machine (the Type 206 Jet Ranger), which the Bell company would purchase for commercial sale in Australia and overseas. This program was never achieved, as in June 1974 the government announced a cutback which terminated the program at only 56 aircraft – before the point had been reached where significant Australian construction was to be achieved. No locally-cut gear assemblies were ever installed, so that the special machinery imported for the task remained unused. One account records:

> Furthermore, it has been claimed that the compensation paid for the cancellation of the order was very close to the actual savings made by not proceeding with the full plan. ... [The episode] did little for the image of Australia as a reliable contractor for offset orders.[49]

With little work available, the aircraft factories were obliged to look for non-defence stopgaps. It was in this context that GAF became involved from 1970 in a project to design, develop and manufacture a twin-engined turbo-prop general purpose aircraft suitable for civil as well as military use. The type, called Nomad, was in production from 1972 until closure of the assembly line in 1984 (by which time a total of 170 machines had been built). Throughout this period, however, the venture was conducted purely on a 'stop-go' basis, and its chief significance was that it enabled the factory to hold together its skilled labour force at a time when no other work was available.[50]

Of special significance in this period was consideration given by an interdepartmental committee in mid-1977 to proposals to form GAF into a statutory corporation on a full commercial basis. Although both CAC and HDH supported such a move, the committee itself did not. While it accepted that GAF should enjoy increased operational freedom and a separate identity within a departmental framework, it saw little need for autonomy in programming and management which were the arguments which normally justified the statutory corporation form of organisation. Deciding that no clear case for such a move could be demonstrated, the government did not adopt the proposal.[51]

Even while the defence facilities as a whole actively sought any work which became available, their plight had reached serious proportions by the mid-1970s. The extent of the problem confronting them can be gauged from the fact that the workload within the munitions group alone had fallen from 4.6 million man hours in 1969/70 to 2.6 million in 1972/73 and to just 1.3 million in 1976/77, a total decline of over 70 per cent in seven years.[52] This merely highlighted the unique position of these factories, and the special problems they faced through the requirement to be always responsive to the Defence department as their primary client, even though that customer might not have a constant need for their output.

Management problems

Quite apart from the fluctuations which occurred periodically in the work loads of government factories, other deficiencies existed within the management arrangements under which they operated. As already narrated, for most of the period after the Second World War the defence factories were administered as part of the Department of Supply, apart from the years 1951–58 when a separate Department of Defence Production was in existence. Following reabsorption of the latter, Supply was a large organisation with responsibility not just for defence production but also weapons research and development activities, laboratories, procurement, and stores and transport. In September 1959 it was employing 17,800 people, 9200 of whom were in the factories.[53]

Although spread around all the Australian States, and with an overseas staff as well, by the mid-1960s Supply was one of the few government departments – if not the only remaining one – which did not completely separate its head office and regional functions. Until June 1967, the department's branch in Melbourne carried out both central office and Victorian regional activities 'without any clear distinction or identification of the separate functions', although regional organisations had been established in other States.[54]

The Department of Defence had begun progressively transferring its offices to Canberra from Melbourne in 1958, so that by the early 1960s the bulk of its staff was located at the seat of government. Not until 1967, however, was the decision taken by Supply to establish a head office in the national capital, in anticipation of which the opportunity was 'taken to examine the department's functions ... to evolve organisations for Canberra and Victoria which reflect the changing emphasis in ... operating groups'. As a result of this process, a structure was developed which provided for the creation of five divisions at Central Office; two of these – titled 'Aircraft, Guided Weapons and Electronics Supply', and 'Munitions Supply' – were concerned with production activities.[55]

The move to Canberra began in 1968, with the secretariat and the main elements of three divisions moving in January of that year to new office accommodation in the Anzac Park West Building on Constitution Avenue. The two production divisions, with an assortment of branches from the divisions already moved, did not follow until early in 1969.[56] As a result of this change, and following the creation of a separate regional office for North Queensland (based on Townsville) in 1968, the size of Supply continued to grow. By 1971 the department was employing 22,000 people, and within the whole of the federal bureaucracy only the Postmaster-General's Department had a bigger payroll.[57]

These arrangements for controlling the activities of the defence factories had a significant shortcoming, a fact expressly recognised in a report called for by the government into the reorganisation of the Defence group of departments. This document, presented in 1973, was written by Sir Arthur Tange, then the secretary of the Defence department and one of Australia's most senior and seasoned bureaucrats. Tange commented on the uncertainties under which factory managers laboured due to the lack of a defence program which extended over a period of years, and also the enlargement of the problem which arose through a separation of factory planning from the existing machinery for deciding expenditure under the Defence program.[58]

If Tange's comments were intended to provide a case for more closely integrating the production activities carried on by Supply with the departmental activities of Defence itself, this was not the outcome which resulted. Instead, the defence factories stayed outside the ambit of the department they were mainly designed to serve. Even though Supply was abolished in June 1974, its roles and responsibilities in this regard were transferred to a new Department of Manufacturing Industry.

This departmental entity proved short-lived, giving way to the Department of Industry and Commerce barely eighteen months later, in December 1975. After less than a year, in November 1976, the Department of Productivity replaced Industry and Commerce, only for the latter to be revived four years later. To cynical observers in the factories effected by these constant changes, it appeared to be a case of the prime minister of the day looking for a portfolio with which to reward or promote a favoured member of his party in parliament.[59]

That placing the defence factories under new or other government departments made little difference to the problem of administering them was made plain from time to time in public statements from whichever ministry held the responsibility. In 1977, for instance, the annual report of the Department of Productivity observed in respect of the ordnance facility at Maribyrnong that 'long-term defence projects [were] needed to give the factory stability'.[60] Not until 1979–80, after new guidelines covering defence spending had been formulated by the government, was there any expectation that more money would be provided for substantial upgrading of capital facilities.[61]

It is salutary, however, to realise that it was not a case that the defence factories were facing a crisis of economic viability and survival while commercial industry was not. Although government ownership insulated them to a degree from ordinary requirements of strict profitability, they were actually in better shape than many of their civil counterparts and competitors. The problems facing defence industry were, in many respects, merely a reflection of a far wider situation.

A 1975 green paper written by a committee appointed by the government to advise on appropriate policies for Australian manufacturing industry pointed out that:

> [This area] is in acute financial crisis. Unemployment is high. Factories are running below capacity. Many firms have borrowed to the hilt, with capacity under trust deeds and credit standing eroded. Their profit and prospects make it hard to raise equity. But their need for cash increases, to finance stocks that are slow to sell and that cost more because of inflation. Such firms are in serious financial trouble; some are closing …
>
> In part, manufacturing's problems are manifestations of the world economic crisis in which all countries, including Australia, are enmeshed. But in Australian manufacturing there is a deep-seated and long-standing malaise. That malaise has sharpened the impact on industry of the current economic crisis. When it passes, the malaise of manufacturing will still be there.[62]

Compared to many of their civil counterparts, therefore, the problems of the defence factories were nothing that another major war would not fix. Creation of the various departments administering the facilities from the mid-1970s had achieved little in solving many of the worst structural problems besetting those establishments. Regarding the naval dockyards, for example, Tange had commented in 1973 on the problem which these facilities had become in trying to best locate administrative responsibility for them within the bureaucracy:

> In planning and executing their work, they have the difficult problems of management to which shipyards are notoriously exposed, including complex industrial relations. These problems are magnified in naval dockyards by operational priorities, safety requirements, equipment secrecy, unpredictable workloads and industrial differences between seamen artificers and the multiplicity of civilian trade groups.

In Tange's view, creation of a more satisfactory balance was needed 'among those who express the operational priorities for dockyard work … those responsible for planning work programmes, the dockyard management and the central Defence machinery'.[63]

Emphasising the accuracy of Tange's description of the difficulties, the level of industrial disputation reached new heights at Garden Island in 1974–75 and at Williamstown a year later. This situation, coinciding with a general decline in Australian shipbuilding generally and a prolonged absence of orders for new naval vessels, produced a climate of sustained inefficiency which prompted a series of government-commissioned reports into the best means of achieving stability.

The first of these post-Tange inquiries into dockyard industrial relations was carried out on Garden Island in 1974 by W.B. Wilson the Deputy Public Service Arbitrator. In a submission put to Wilson's committee by unions, it was argued that the position of dockyard general manager at Garden Island should be filled by a civilian administrator rather than a naval officer, as had been done at Williamstown some years earlier. Although Wilson's report broadly endorsed this view by commenting on the 'reaction of hostility' which service officers induced among a section of yard employees, he did not actually recommend such a change.[64]

While both Garden Island and Williamstown yards carried out repair, refit, docking, modernisation and conversion of naval vessels, the latter was the principal site for construction of warships up to destroyer size. In August 1980 the Minister for Defence, D.J. Killen, announced an internal review of management procedures at the Victorian yard with the aim of recommending action which would promote the completion of work placed there within specified delivery times and budget estimates, and satisfactory standards of quality. The review team produced their final report in January 1981,[65] but by then other events had overtaken the reform process.

In a major statement to parliament the month after instigating this review, Killen announced the government's intention – subject to negotiations to be concluded – to undertake construction at Williamstown of two American-designed FFG-7 guided missile frigates for the RAN, with the option of another four of these ships later. In a statement during December, however, he made clear that there were conditions attached to this offer of new work for the ailing shipyard. 'We must assure ourselves that the management, operating and industrial arrangements at … Williamstown can cope effectively with such a programme', he said, adding that 'recent experience with the Dockyard has not been good'.[66] Accordingly, he had decided to appoint a committee to advise on changes which might be necessary to ensure that the frigate program, once begun, would proceed efficiently.

The committee formed to conduct this review was headed by Ross Hawke, a senior administrator from the BHP company with experience in the shipbuilding industry. Other members were Alan Sharpe, recently retired as the deputy chief scientist, and a serving naval officer, Commodore Nigel Berlyn. It recommended that Williamstown should operate as a commercial enterprise after major overhaul of the management structure. This was to be achieved by making the yard a statutory body, managed by a board responsible to the relevant minister but relieved as far as possible from Public Service restrictions concerning manpower. Additionally, the committee urged that attention be given to forging a new start in relations between the workforce and management, with the aim of achieving better understanding and promoting a new spirit of industriousness, co-operation and enthusiasm at all levels. On the basis of this review, the government decided to retain Williamstown, while prosecuting a program of reform including new management arrangements.[67]

Attempts at commercialisation

Apart from the lack of stability which affected the administration of the defence production area from the mid-1970s, the factories experienced other problems as they struggled to achieve some degree of viability and economic respectability in their operation. From the outset, factory managers were on the horns of a dilemma. Governments not unnaturally required a reasonable level of return from their output for the lowest possible outlay of public money to subsidise operations. Yet the establishments needed continual capital investment to keep abreast of advances of technology, and other updating just to maintain their capability to manufacture the types of defence equipment that may be required.

As a subcommittee of the joint parliamentary committee on foreign affairs and defence (set up under the chairmanship of Hon. D.J. Hamer to investigate industrial support for defence needs) reported in 1977, much of the plant in the government factories was already obsolete. Some machines had been in use for more than 50 years and were so worn they were unsuitable for performing tasks requiring close tolerances. Moreover, funds for replacement plant had steadily declined from over $5 million a year at the end of the 1960s to only $1.5 million for the years 1974–77.[68] It was hardly surprising that, coincidentally, the Defence White Paper published in 1976 had identified the need for a five-year program which would cost $2.3 billion for equipment (ships, aircraft and armoured vehicles) and plant alone.[69]

The battle against obsolescence aside, the factories faced other problems arising from government funding priorities. Critics believed that the sheltered position enjoyed by defence industry was a disincentive in rectifying the worst features of factory management regimes. These facilities were, however, never entirely free from pressures to maintain and improve standards and performance, and to eliminate the excesses of their operations – if only for the sake of public appearances.

As industrial enterprises, it was to be expected that the facilities would also need to adopt many of the proven features and practices commonly used by commercial businesses to improve competitiveness. As early as 1959 departmental publications emanating within Supply were extolling the virtues of methods engineering units then being set up within the factories to guide, develop and co-ordinate work practices, and organise training programs. Although predicated on an assumption that the 'scope and character of conventional organisation and methods work is not adequate to serve the needs of a Department with a strong emphasis on technical and scientific operations', here was nonetheless an attempt to introduce improved organisational methods to the activities of the factories.[70]

First applied at the small arms works, the methods engineering process had been directed towards improving production methods and factory layout, setting efficient standards of performance, and establishing management control systems.

The effort, it was claimed, had yielded 'considerable cost economies' at Lithgow.[71] This was principally through providing information which could be extended to provide the basis for a labour cost control system, thereby enabling management to more accurately forecast cost trends, labour requirements and production capacity. As a result of this experience similar systems had been, or were in the process of being, established throughout remaining Supply establishments.[72]

Undermining efforts to sharpen the efficiency of the factories were, however, a number of cosmetic shields which were effectively intended to excuse or explain away the fact that these establishments continued to operate – in commercial financial terms – as substantial loss-making enterprises. Describing the gap between the running cost of establishments and the return from the goods produced as 'reserve capacity maintenance' (RCM) was one attempt to put a positive face on diseconomy. In the view of one with experience of this period, the concept of RCM quickly became 'the balancing item between revenue and costs' and was employed to deliberately maintain an artificial sense of viability about the factories.[73]

The reality which such a term disguised in 1979/80 was that the munitions factories incurred costs of $100 million yet returned only $54 million in earnings from sales, with the difference being made up from what were termed 'government allocations' – effectively, taxpayer subsidy.[74] The gravity of the position is further underlined by figures from this same period which the Department of Productivity included in its publicity material. These disclose that only 44 per cent of output from the department's twelve establishments was for the Australian Defence Force (ADF); 19 per cent was for private industry, 11 per cent for government non-defence requirements, while about 9 per cent was for export. No attempt was made to explain the remaining 17 per cent.[75]

Another device employed which amounted to subterfuge was the concept of 'critical labour level' below which manpower at each facility could not be allowed to fall without incurring unacceptable diminution of its capacity to cope with changes in production which may be required of it. In theory, staffing at this level envisaged little more than core establishments, necessitating extensive retraining of personnel and the consequent foregoing of any capacity as an expansion base for either the government or private sectors in the event of major conflict.[76] The reality was that individual facilities remained grossly over staffed for their current (usually meagre) work loads.

Other deficiencies existed in accounting procedures utilised in the factories. An examination into the financial management at Lithgow, for example, carried out by departmental auditors between December 1981 and May 1983, had highlighted the serious need for fundamental reforms in the areas of inventory control, and production planning and control. Lithgow had been regarded at the time as the model factory in the area of costing, yet discrepancies were discovered in production quantities as counted compared with those that were supposed to exist based on factory cost records, and it was found that other financial records did not give a historically true and fair picture of trading.[77]

Although Lithgow had been the factory selected for this exercise, auditor criticism was not confined to this establishment. A report prepared in April 1982 pointed out that forward planning within the whole of the Munitions Supply Division (MSD) was defective. Figures produced which suggested that levels of production had been steadily increasing over recent years were misleading, since what they really stated were an increase in labour levels being applied to production. As the report noted:

> Most manufacturing organisations report achievement in terms of items produced, but not so with the MSD factories. This in itself would be regarded as a control weakness in that, generally, it is a technique used to camouflage from management what is actually happening … [78]

The truth of the matter was that productivity had been eroding at an annual rate of 5 per cent.[79]

These were shortcomings which reflected the malaise effecting the defence production area generally. As one of those involved in bringing to attention the audit deficiencies described later recalled, exertions on this score were not only unwelcome but greeted with active hostility. The practices exposed were crucial to the culture of self-deception which, while aimed at 'keeping the wolves of the Finance Department at bay', also sought to mask inefficiency and waste involving substantial sums of taxpayers' money.[80]

In addition to modest attempts to follow the lead of industry in certain management practices, there came the introduction of computer technology. Again, the small arms works at Lithgow was the first to feel the effects of this advance, when a Sirius computer was introduced in the early 1960s to assist in planning the factory's activities. This machine was utilised in developing the master factory program, together with section programs for the 7.62 mm rifle project. 'In collaboration with the Departmental committee on automatic data processing, the factory is directing its activities ultimately to cover all phases of production control, supply and personnel functions'.[81]

Computer technology was progressively extended to other facilities in the defence group. At the clothing factory, for example, which had led the local industry with the installation of modern plant such as the first automatic cloth cutter in Australia, a third generation computer controlled cutting machine was installed in 1984. Integrated with this machine were modern computer systems used for grading patterns to various sizes and plotting the laying-out of marker points. Sewing stations were also controlled, where possible, by microprocessors, while considerable effort was devoted to upgrading computer production information systems, including through the use of computer aided design (CAD) technology.

Computers also made their mark at the naval dockyards. In 1968 the RAN's flagship, the aircraft carrier HMAS *Melbourne*, underwent a major modernisation at Garden Island to equip it for operating recently-introduced A4G Skyhawk fighter bombers and S2E Tracker anti-submarine aircraft. In the course of this program other improvements were also made to aviation fuel systems, the steam catapult and arrester units, flying control arrangements, radar and communications, and the ship's power system; air conditioning was provided to many parts of the ship, and a liquid oxygen generation plant was installed to support flying operations. This was, at the time, by far the largest project ever attempted at the Garden Island yard and the first managed entirely using computerised network analysis.[82]

At both Garden Island and Williamstown considerable expense had been incurred by the early 1980s to establish systems to monitor project progress, yard productivity and ships' hull strength. Use was now being made of CAD and computer aided manufacture (CAM), and numerical control machine (NCM) technology, while plans were in hand to extend computer services to the areas of material control and financial administration.

Such innovations were critical to improving the image of both dockyards as efficient and profitable commercially-based enterprises. As promotional literature of the period explicitly recognised, economic pressures for a reasonable return on funds outlaid meant that the yards had to become more competitive and attract an increased share of the market for refit and repair work and associated services from commercial shipping companies. Achievement of this goal depended on establishing a record for excellence in performance, and reliability with regard to cost and time schedules.[83] Such improvements relied heavily on the effectiveness of management in dealing with the reputation of both yards as industrial relations quagmires.

A question of closures

Growing concern over the likely impact of reduced work loads for the defence factories ensured repeated efforts took place during the 1970s to identify the options for overcoming an expected shortfall of orders. The Minister for Supply, R.V. Garland, began this process in March 1972, when he proposed to his Defence counterpart that, in view of the declining demands placed by the armed services, an examination be conducted into the role and structure of the factories to determine a peacetime policy.

In response to the suggested guidelines for this examination advanced by Supply and Defence, in April 1973 the Defence (Industrial) Committee set up an interdepartmental committee chaired by Supply to establish probable service requirements for munitions over the next five years. This body was, however, initially unable to produce credible estimates of demand in this area, due to changes under study in stockholding policy, and could only point to a greatly reduced level of future ordering.

Shortly before the Department of Supply went out of existence, a further examination of the issues was made by the Munitions Supply Division (MSD) in a submission to the Defence (Industrial) Committee in December 1973. This recognised that:

> There is occurring ... such a considerable and general down-turn in the Services production required from Government Munitions Factories and such an implicit low threat situation that it is necessary and timely to re-assess the purposes of and the need for Government munitions factories.[84]

The MSD submission presented short-term proposals for urgently dealing with the situation, including for the establishment of a permanent interdepartmental committee to explore all possible sources of work for the factories. In the medium-term, however, a need was accepted to achieve 'an orderly rearrangement of and adjustment in the factories' scale of operations, including consideration of their redundancy'. As part of this process, suggestions were made for the transfer of much of the ordnance work performed at Maribyrnong to Bendigo and Lithgow, and for the concentration of propellant manufacture to Mulwala leading to the closure of the Maribyrnong explosives factory. Ultimately, even greater rationalisation was proposed through the establishment of an integrated explosives group of factories in the Albury-Wodonga region, close to the existing factory at Mulwala, which would enable the closure of the Albion explosives and St. Marys filling plants.[85]

Taking up the thrust of the MSD submission, a committee of inquiry was convened in June 1974 specifically to investigate the availability of suitable work to maintain the labour force of the factories which were now under the new Department of Manufacturing Industry. Among the conclusions this body reported in October was a recommendation for greater consideration to be given to 'maximising local production of defence stores, having regard to cost and other penalties', while private industry should also be further pursued as a source of work 'provided marketing and commercial production philosophies and skills are developed to cope with this area'.[86]

Although there was no immediate enthusiasm for the option of reducing the number of factories in operation, the pressures towards this course were considerable at times. The 1974 inquiry particularly noted the position of the explosives factory at Albion, which was expected to complete its current orders by the end of the year. Unless an order was forthcoming on the basis of stockpiling explosives, this facility would be without any work and faced being 'mothballed'. Though such a course was averted at this time, rationalisation of the explosives factories continued to be mooted, with the Maribyrnong facility coming under scrutiny during the first half of 1976.[87]

Examination of the vexed question of workloads continued over the next few years. An interdepartmental committee, formed in 1975 to consider funding appropriations to cover the premium entailed in local production of defence items which would otherwise be bought overseas on cost grounds, gave its findings in January 1976. Its report endorsed the notion of allowing staff at the factories to reduce to the 'critical labour level', and called for guidelines to be issued to purchasing acquisition areas within the Defence department to ensure that suitable orders were diverted from overseas or local private industry to the factories, without increase to the defence outlay.[88]

Where individual factories were unable to continue even a semblance of commercial viability, there seemed little alternative to closure or disposal. One of the facilities to feel the chill wind of this reality in the 1970s was the engine works at Port Melbourne, then a relatively small outfit of 180 employees with an annual wages and salaries bill nearing $1.3 million.[89] The AGEW mainly engaged in building large marine diesel engines for installation in Australian coastal ships, these being types designed and proven overseas.

Between 1949 and 1962 a total of sixteen such engines had been manufactured under licence from the British firm William Doxford & Sons, followed since 1961 by a further thirteen of the world best-selling type produced by the Swiss company Sulzer Bros. Other activities carried out by the works included the overhaul, repair and testing of marine diesel engines, including the Gray Marine engines in RAN ships, and the operation of a 24-hour consultant service for any ship experiencing engine troubles in Australasian and western Pacific waters.[90]

In May 1975 the Minister for Manufacturing Industry, K.E. Enderby, decided to explore the prospects of establishing a viable industry in large diesel engines within Australia. Under an agreement with Ishikawajima-Harima Heavy Industries Ltd. (IHI) of Japan, AGEW also carried out servicing of Pielstick engines and held stocks of spare parts for this type on consignment.[91] On the basis of this connexion, the minister invited IHI to conduct a feasibility study into manufacturing aspects of his plan, with Sulzer and the French company owning the Pielstick design making a study of marketing, sales and servicing.

The final report delivered by IHI in August made clear that it would be possible to manufacture engines in Australia by 1982 at a price competitive with the same engines produced elsewhere. This assumed, however, that AGEW was restructured in accordance with IHI advice and received favourable price treatment from the two ordnance factories which undertook forging and heavy machining of major components for the engine works. Under the scheme proposed, AGEW was to become a statutory authority in receipt of specified government assistance, but enjoying a high degree of independence in the business matters crucial for its commercial survival. Using AGEW's existing workforce and facilities – after reorganisation and upgrading – major improvements in productivity could realistically be achieved which would reduce the total cost of each engine by 25 per cent.[92]

The success of such a venture was, the IHI report found, heavily dependent on an initial level of government assistance well in excess of that which had been indicated as favoured, involving a loan of $5.2 million repayable from when the works began making a profit in 1980–81, along with subsidies and tariff protection. Moreover, the report judged as essential that AGEW secure the orders for seven diesel engines then or shortly to be required by Australian shipyards, a factor which raised the clear possibility that direct government intervention might be needed to ensure that these orders did not go elsewhere.

Even more importantly, though, the findings of the study had caused IHI to decide against taking up its previously expressed interest in participating with equity investment in a joint venture with AGEW. Involvement of Japanese capital would, IHI felt, conflict with nationalistic sentiment regarding local ownership and hinder co-operation between AGEW and other interested parties such as Sulzer. On the basis of these various considerations, the decision was taken by the Australian government not to proceed with the plan but to dispose of the plant. AGEW was subsequently put on the market for sale to private enterprise, but in the absence of a suitable buyer the decision was taken to close it down in July 1979.[93]

Over the years other facilities had come close to suffering a similar fate. In 1962, for example, a proposal to construct new premises for the clothing factory had instead precipitated an enquiry into its whole future. This facility operated on the basis of 'no profit/no loss', essentially seeking to merely recover the cost of production and overheads, although in practice prices were fixed to provide a slight profit margin to cover unforeseen contingencies.[94] Rather than the matter of the operation's viability, the question of continued government involvement in clothing manufacture now attracted attention.

This review, conducted in 1964 by Sir John Allison (chairman of the Defence Business Board) and Leslie Brewster (a company director and business adviser to the Department of Supply), argued in favour of continuing the existing arrangement. The Allison-Brewster report accepted that increased opportunities might be given to commercial companies to tender for defence work, but regarded the factory as providing an assured source of uniforms and other specialised items of clothing which private industry considered unattractive because of relatively short production runs. Moreover, keeping the factory in government control would ensure that it was responsive to defence needs.[95]

Accordingly, after the Parliamentary Standing Committee on Public Works endorsed the need for a new factory in October 1968, work on premises located in the Melbourne suburb of Coburg finally went ahead in November 1969. In that year the canvas factory at Brunswick was closed down, partly because of the limited volume of work in this field but also because of private industry eagerness to undertake this work. With building of the new Coburg facility completed in December 1970, the transfer of plant and machinery was carried out during the Christmas vacation period, enabling normal production to commence in mid-January 1971 and the official opening to take place three months later.[96]

The future of the clothing factory was again examined in an inquiry conducted in 1976 by the Industries Assistance Commission into Australia's clothing, footwear and textile industries. The IAC inquiry heard that there were no significant technical reasons why items from the government factory could not be made by private industry, and in fact there were even price penalties associated with some things produced at Coburg. It was asserted, though, that the factory continued to provide a guaranteed source of supply while maintaining production and design skills which would be important for expanding production by industry in any defence emergency.[97]

The Commission had accepted the proposition that the clothing factory was desirable, though considered that scope existed to achieve substantial cost savings. Low work levels subsequently experienced at Coburg reportedly acted to defeat efforts to implement reductions. Under-utilisation of the factory, combined with government employment policies which prevented surplus staff being retrenched, limited the option of adjusting staff levels to the available workload. Inefficiencies were admitted to have occurred, though it was claimed that these were overcome through a combination of increased orders and a changed employment policy. As will be seen in the next chapter, the future of the clothing factory continued to hang in the balance for the next few years.

In the case of Bendigo, there had also been periodic consideration given to the problems which that ordnance plant's continued operation posed in terms of productive return for costs incurred. In July 1960 a Department of Supply working party had investigated the option of selling the factory, but concluded that this course was 'unlikely to produce a worthwhile result for the Commonwealth'. Two years later a sub-committee of Supply's board of management for production also noted that retaining the Bendigo plant was not really justified by current service requirements, but opted for allowing it to continue 'at least cost to the Defence vote'.[98]

Despite the high cost of the factories, Australia's munitions industry continued to receive the broad support of parliamentary groups during this period, expressed in two reports by the parliament's Joint Committee on Foreign Affairs and Defence. As already noted, the first of these was the Hamer report, which considered industrial support for defence activities; submitted in interim form in June 1977, a further chapter was tabled the following October and the whole printed in final form early in 1978.[99] The second, the Katter report of 1979, considered defence procurement issues.[100]

In both parliamentary reports, endorsement was given to a policy of developing local defence industry capabilities in preference to overseas purchase, to smoothing out discontinuities in workloads, and achieving overseas sales to boost the profitability of local factories. Although these were principles with which most people agreed, even echoing existing government policy in some respects, there was little in such arguments that pointed the way to overcoming the grave practical deficiencies so long apparent in the facilities' operations. Yet matters plainly could not be allowed to continue as they had been. Something had to be done.

By the end of the 1970s, Australia's defence industry had degenerated from the relative high-point attained during the Second World War to a quite parlous state. Faced with persistent uncertainties regarding the levels of work likely to be available and thus hindered in their capacity to plan logically for the future, the facilities were nonetheless confronted with the continual need to maintain and develop the complex and costly capabilities involved in the production of defence equipment. This requirement remained, moreover, whether or not worthwhile orders were forthcoming from the armed services. All this had come about in a period of great changes affecting the face of manufacturing industry across Australia, and indeed the international scene.

The difficulties confronting many of the facilities was compounded by a nightmarish industrial situation, often fuelled by the weakness and inexperience of managers. Other problems underpinning the edifice were so structurally entrenched that the solutions tried – such as shifting the responsibility for administration between ever-changing departments, and introducing up-to-date technology and modern business practices in an effort to emulate the best features of private industry – all were without major or lasting effect. The reality was increasingly evident that government enterprises which operated according to public service ethos and procedures were intrinsically disadvantaged in an increasingly competitive commercial environment. The outlook too often encountered was embodied in a remark, possibly apocryphal, attributed to an unnamed senior defence bureaucrat who declared 'We are not here to be efficient; we are here to be audited'.[101] The scene was now set for a number of more radical solutions to be tried.

4

IN PURSUIT OF COMPETITIVENESS

Further substance to discussions over the future of Australia's defence industry was added during 1981 by Donald Eltringham, special adviser on defence production in the Department of Industry and Commerce. In November 1980 he was asked to produce a comprehensive report which would include how improvements could be achieved in the performance of the factories, the organisational structure to apply, the role of the factories *vis-a-vis* the private sector, priorities for future investment in capabilities, and – most importantly of all – the scope for rationalisation between factories and also with private industry.

The three volume study which Eltringham delivered in April 1981 presented a detailed blueprint for a total reshaping of the defence production area. It was, though, preceded by another report Eltringham wrote early in February of that year. This document offered a narrower view of the specific question of restructuring and sale of certain of the facilities, in response to a specific query put to him regarding the possibilities of pursuing such a course.

In his first report, Eltringham urged the government to seize the opportunity to restructure the facilities, consolidating these into a smaller number of factories. Ordnance work, he argued, should be centred at the Maribyrnong factory and the Bendigo plant sold. Explosives manufacture and rocket filling could be focused on Albion and the production of propellants carried out at Mulwala, allowing the Maribyrnong explosives factory to be sold. The aircraft engineering workshop at Pooraka should be sold, and the clothing factory either sold or leased to private enterprise.[1] In the subsequent main report he also added the suggestion that the government aircraft factories 'be leased, preferably with sale of some equity, or sold to private enterprise'.[2]

Although largely repeating and expanding on ideas which had been aired earlier, Eltringham's conclusions were injected into an atmosphere which was ripe for change. Even as he had been developing his proposals, an *ad hoc* committee of ministers (popularly dubbed 'the Razor Gang') had been reviewing the wider question of the many functions in which the Commonwealth was involved. Since this body was chaired by Sir Phillip Lynch, the Minister for Industry and Commerce, the advice contained in Eltringham's first report found receptive ears. The committee of ministers had already, in January 1981, identified the clothing factory as one area for possible disposal, but sought confirmation from an independent industry expert.

John Blood, chairman of the Textiles Council of Australia, was invited by the secretary of the Department of Industry and Commerce, Neil Currie, to carry out the necessary survey. His conclusions, given in a letter to Lynch on 19 February, indicated that the factory might not be saleable as a 'going concern'. Since private manufacturers disliked dealing with the cumbersome Defence tendering procedure and might decline to seek contracts for specialised items, the government could still have to retain the capacity to produce these. Moreover, the costs of garments would almost certainly rise to reflect charges which the facility did not have to meet under existing arrangements.[3]

Despite the qualifications which Blood attached to his conclusion that the clothing factory 'could, in fact, be closed and the majority of the supply required by the Armed Forces could in fact be manufactured by private enterprise', the government was now persuaded to press ahead with disposing both of that facility and the ordnance factory at Bendigo. In a statement to parliament on 30 April the Prime Minister, Malcolm Fraser, announced that Bendigo was to be offered to the private sector 'for sale as a going concern' while the clothing factory would be similarly offered for sale or lease.[4]

The basis for the government's decision to sell or lease the Coburg plant, along with that at Bendigo, was referred in September that year to a Senate select committee. In the report made the following year, the committee split along party lines in its recommendations over the clothing factory, with the two government representatives endorsing the option of attempting 'with maximum vigour' to achieve a sale, while the non-government senators argued equally strongly for retention in public ownership. The latter rejected the proposed government course as driven primarily by ideological considerations rather than sound practical reasons.[5]

Interestingly, however, even the proponents of selling noted that, if Coburg was retained by the government, the factory management should be given 'more autonomy to operate as a commercial enterprise'. Under such an arrangement 'notional' costs were expected to be taken more fully into account, thus providing the management with more incentive to pursue 'profitable purchasing and pricing policies'.

As this debate dragged on, in February 1983 Robert Millar, the chairman of the Production Board, was tasked with considering the likely effects on the Services of closing Coburg, along with its competitiveness in relation to the private sector and steps which could be taken quickly to improve its performance. In addition to listing the deleterious position in which closure would put the Services, Millar suggested that evidence that the factory was costing the government too much may well have been overstated. Eventually, in April 1983, the newly-elected Labor government headed by Bob Hawke announced that the factory would be retained in public ownership, its role unchanged.[6]

As in the case of the clothing factory, the Senate select committee diverged on clear party lines over the view taken of the situation at Bendigo. Government members of the committee noted that the ordnance factory was operating at less than half its capacity, and that half of what work load it did have was non-defence in nature. They concluded therefore that the facility was maintaining – at great cost to the taxpayer – skills which were hardly unique or essential to national defence, especially since its capabilities were largely duplicated at Maribyrnong which also had an excess of capacity. The non-government senators again argued for retention of Bendigo, which was a marginal seat, though under a radically changed policy which would enable it to operate as a more viable enterprise. They urged that the answer lay in giving the factory a greater defence load and more profitable commercial work.[7]

The Bendigo plant was advertised for sale or lease the following year, but only one response had been received by the closing date of 11 June 1982. This constituted no more than a proposed basis for a leasing arrangement, heavily hedged around with conditions, and in the opinion of the government's advisers had no legal status since it did not amount to an offer capable of conversion to a enforceable contract. After discussion in Cabinet the following month, it was publicly announced that the Bendigo facility also would be neither sold nor leased, but was to continue as a government factory.[8]

Problem of Defence Support

While nothing had come of this attempt at rationalising Coburg and Bendigo, other events were even then in train which were to effect the factories as a whole. In April 1981 the government had appointed a committee chaired by John Utz, the chief executive of Wormald International Ltd., to review the Defence organisation as part of the process initiated under Sir Phillip Lynch. Although the final findings of this Defence Review Committee were not presented until October 1982, a preliminary report was made available in the previous May at the request of Prime Minister Malcolm Fraser.

Tabled in parliament on 21 May, the interim report of the Utz committee proposed the establishment of a Department of Defence Support to draw together a range of activities then being handled by the departments of Defence, Industry and Commerce, and Administrative Services. Grouping defence-related activities in this fashion, the committee argued, would foster the development of the industrial capacity across the nation which was required to support defence operations, and thus further the government's goal of increased self-reliance. The Utz Committee also noted that the performance of the various factories was not as good as it should be, due to a number of detrimental factors.

Responding to the Utz report in advance of its publication, and in great haste, the government adopted the recommendation for a Department of Defence Support and formally brought it into being on 7 May. According to observers close to these events, this change had little to do with seriously tackling the problem posed by the factories. Instead it came about in the context of a major ministerial reshuffle in which the main losers were seen to be the defence minister, Jim Killen, who became vice-president of the Executive Council, and Ian Viner, who lost Industrial Relations to take up the more junior Defence Support portfolio.[9] Creation of the new department, it is held, was therefore primarily to provide an additional ministry required to achieve the Prime Minister's organisational agenda.[10]

Under the new arrangement not just the munitions, aircraft and clothing factories were drawn together under one administrative umbrella but so too, for the first time, were the shipbuilding facilities formerly run by the Navy itself. Apart from managing the dockyards at Williamstown and Garden Island (except for the fleet base activities at the latter), Defence Support was now also responsible for Cockatoo Island, although this continued to be leased from the Commonwealth by a private operator. While this change at least clearly acknowledged the linkage which lay at the heart of the facilities' role, it also ultimately failed to resolve the fundamental difficulties effecting them. As with previous attempts to improve their position by shifting ministerial responsibility, the high hopes held on the creation of the Department of Defence Support went unrealised.

For a start, the new organisation was no less unwieldy. In its central office and 27 establishments (not all of which were defence production facilities) there were 19,000 employees, which made it one of the largest departments in the public service.[11] Even though this staffing figure was down to about 15,000 by 1984, Defence Support still accounted for an expenditure of $598 million in that year, of which just $242 million (or 40 per cent) was recovered through sales to its customers.[12] Essentially, the facilities continued to survive only by virtue of a massive taxpayer subsidy.

When the Hawke Labor government took office in March 1983, the new Minister for Defence Support, Brian Howe, gave assurances that the incoming administration was committed to revitalising manufacturing industry in Australia. There followed fresh efforts to tackle the more obvious shortcomings in the factories' operations. Corporate planning – a recognised technique for focusing the

priorities and direction of management in commercial enterprises – was introduced during 1983–84.[13] In July 1984 boards of management (as recommended by
the Utz Committee) were also set up to oversee the operations of the munitions
and aerospace factory groups; a third board, for defence shipbuilding, was proposed
but not approved at this time. Comprising members drawn from industry, unions,
and the Public Service, these boards gave advice on implementing reforms aimed
at fostering a more commercial approach.[14]

Undoing much of the good in such initiatives were, however, attempts insti-
gated by Howe to increase worker participation in the running of the facilities. The
minister was from the Victorian branch of the Labor Party and, in the words of one
ministerial colleague, had the same 'woolly-minded commitment' of that State's
Labor government to building a workers' utopia on a foundation of power sharing with trade unions.[15] Beginning with an informal meeting with union representatives in Melbourne on 25 March, to seek co-operation 'in making the
Defence Support budget work for Australia',[16] he embarked on a well-meaning
initiative to secure industrial peace through greater consultation and communication.

The series of 'sweetheart' deals (consent agreements under Section 28 of the
Conciliation and Arbitration Act) which Howe struck with the unions was, it is
said by one ministerial colleague, reached without any Cabinet authority or the
knowledge of any other minister.[17] The outcome of these arrangements was, in
most instances, to complicate immeasurably the running of individual facilities. As
Howe's critic also tartly observed, they also had the effect of reducing the factories
even more to the status of sheltered workshops and of 'surrendering managerial
control to the unions – something which made factory disposal more necessary'.[18]

The concept which the Defence Support department embodied proved, however, to be even more fundamentally flawed. To some commentators there were
parallels between the new arrangement and that which had previously existed
when the Department of Supply operated more or less as a handmaiden to the
Defence organisation. A directive issued on 13 July 1982 by Prime Minister Fraser
had set out a far more complex relationship. Under this, the ministers for Defence
and Defence Support were required to 'work closely together', but with the latter
always constrained to operate within policies approved by his Defence colleague.
The defence minister was, therefore, clearly the more senior figure; indeed, until
May 1983 the Minister for Defence Support was even designated as Minister
Assisting the Minister for Defence.[19]

Other instructions contained in the directive provided that funding of the new
department was to be decided as part of the total Defence outlay, subject to the
same processes and degree of scrutiny as other elements of defence expenditure:

> For this purpose the Department of Defence Support will make available to
> the Department of Defence all relevant information and documentation and

the Department of Defence Support is to participate fully in the financial planning, programming and budget control processes of the Department of Defence.

Belatedly, the impracticality was discovered of attempting to make one minister and his department substantially subordinate to another within a legal and administrative framework which provided for the independence of both. Quite apart from duplication of effort, which meant that scarce resources were not being put to best use, there was often a wide separation of view between the two departments. Instead of harmonious working towards common goals, relations between Defence and Defence Support became strained and at times acrimonious.

The potential for such conflict had existed from the very beginning – as evidenced by the purposeful wording embodied in the directive from Fraser, who himself had experience as defence minister in 1969–71. Although always tricky, the relationship became more difficult in the first Hawke government because of the relative status between Howe and the defence minister, Gordon Scholes. The problem was that, while Howe was regarded as a 'factional apparatchnik' with considerable clout in his home State, Scholes – who also came from Victoria – had no power base at all but mainly owed his standing to having won a marginal seat. Scholes was therefore in an untenable position from the outset of his occupancy of the Defence portfolio.[20]

Perhaps inevitably, differences at the top were reflected at lower levels of contact between the two departments and extended into many of organs of the committee system operating within Defence. The Utz committee had recognised this system as the key to successfully integrating Defence Support into that organisation. The original prime ministerial directive had included the Minister for Defence Support and the secretary of his department as members of the Council of Defence.[21] After a further review, the secretary of the Defence Support department, Charles Halton, also joined the Defence Committee and the Defence Force Development Committee (DFDC).

While senior officers within Defence had been taken by surprise by the recommendations of the Utz committee, most had been prepared to work with the new arrangement.[22] This situation changed, however, as it became apparent that Defence Support was pursuing an agenda entirely its own. As departmental head, Halton in particular seemed intent on building Defence Support into a separate empire with little regard for what Defence, as its main customer, either wanted or actually required. Tension consequently began to develop over Defence's attempts to contain the cost of the facilities controlled by Defence Support, while the latter sought to create a new, more meaningful role for them which promised little in the way of savings. Indeed, following the formation of Defence Support, costs associated with its function had risen sharply – from $181 million in 1980/81 to nearly $341 million in 1982/83, and to just over $417 million in 1983–84.[23]

By May 1984 there were bitter battles raging over the decision by Defence to trim $52 million from the draft estimates submitted by Defence Support for its 1984/85 budget, leading Halton to send a terse letter to Sir William Cole, the secretary of Defence.[24] Details began surfacing in the Press, with one report that the Prime Minister had been called upon to settle what was 'yet another dispute' between the two departments.[25] Consideration of a defence policy for industry in that year also sparked poisonous wrangling in the Defence Committee, which was referred to Cabinet after Defence Support maintained its dissent.[26] Attempts were made at various times to resolve some of these differences and arrive at a better working arrangement. On one occasion the two ministers and their departmental heads met, at Howe's suggestion, over dinner at Parliament House. This did little good though, because the issues were talked around rather than addressed.[27]

In the DFDC, too, matters approached an unworkable stage. From the first meeting of this body which Cole chaired on taking over at Defence in February 1984, he was horrified at the level of disputation between representatives of the two departments. Describing the situation as 'dreadful', he recalls that even obtaining agreement on the minutes of previous meetings involved much painful time-wasting.[28] Other officials attending meetings of the DFDC at the time also remember discussion in this forum as having the farcical character of a 'Punch & Judy' show.[29]

The Office of Defence Production

In December 1984 – ten years and five identity changes after the demise of the Department of Supply – the factories finally returned to the Defence fold. In the second Hawke ministry announced after Labor's general election victory, the Department of Defence Support was amalgamated with Defence; Howe was promoted in Cabinet to the Social Security portfolio. Gordon Scholes was, as one press report put it, 'savagely demoted' to the minor post of Minister for Territories. The Defence portfolio was now filled by 35-year-old Kim Beazley, a former tutor in politics at the University of Western Australia who had previously held Aviation.[30]

Coincidentally, as this reshuffle was taking place, the Production Board chaired by Malcolm Buckham (Deputy Secretary of Defence Support) was meeting at the small arms factory in Lithgow. The board's members knew that the new ministry was being announced that day, though not the detail of the changes entailed. As the group flew back to Canberra, the light aircraft carrying them passed through a very heavy hail storm. In what was seen as 'an interesting omen', the plane's windscreen cracked and sheets of water landed in Buckham's lap.[31]

Under the new arrangements, the facilities remained grouped in an enlarged

Department of Defence as the Office of Defence Production (ODP). The new body was charged with managing, in a business-like way, the range of specialised capabilities it had inherited to provide an industrial base in support of the Australian Defence Force. Heading it was a senior executive of deputy secretary rank, known as the Chief of Defence Production (CDP).

The first CDP was Fred Bennett, although he was only acting in this appointment and returned to his permanent position as Chief of Capital Procurement in Defence after eleven months. While purely a transitional figure, Bennett, nonetheless, performed a crucial role in shaping the objectives of the new organisation and settling its top management structure. No less important, though, was the very necessary part he played in mending the rifts created during Defence Support's existence and restoring links between ODP and the central organs of the Defence organisation.

In appointing a successor to Bennett as CDP, Cole was keen to find someone with business manufacturing skills. He recognised that, in such a large department as he now headed, he could not himself devote a lot of time to closely monitoring the facilities' performance. Cole therefore particularly wanted a tough executive, one he could trust to do the job required and resist the temptation to 'empire-build'.

After advertisements for the position produced only one credible candidate from the private sector, he decided to compromise by obtaining instead a person with good management skills.[32]

The man selected was Lionel Woodward, a softly-spoken senior administrator from the Department of Immigration. Although he was known to and had worked with Cole on structural reform issues during the latter's period in charge of the Public Service Board, Woodward was a newcomer to the defence production field. In an interview with Cole, it was made clear to him that the secretary viewed his appointment as something of a gamble, especially since he lacked the engineering background which was almost traditional among his predecessors. What was expected of him was progress in reforming what Cole strongly suspected was a grossly inefficient as well as expensive area of departmental activity, while ensuring that the climate of conflict formerly experienced with Defence Support did not recur.[33]

In formulating an approach to his task, Woodward soon discovered that he had powerful support from the defence minister's office. Syd Hickman, then Beazley's senior adviser, recalls first meeting Woodward by accident outside Cole's office not long after his arrival in the department in November 1985:

> I stopped and said hello while we both waited for something or other, and we had a chat. I asked him 'What needs to be done to make this [ODP] efficient?' and he replied 'Everyone knows what needs to be done but its just too difficult – its not politically possible.' So I said, 'Well, let us worry about the

politics. Just figure it out and send it across the lake to us [in Parliament House], and we'll see whether its possible or not'.[34]

As Hickman well knew, his boss had been a close observer of the battles between Defence and Defence Support in his capacity as Assistant Defence Minister to Scholes. Beazley himself confirms his awareness of 'a clear sense of outrage within Defence that they should be effectively carrying an organisation with extraordinary industrial practices and such a poor record of delivery'.[35] While this observation was undoubtedly correct, it was also true that Defence itself bore a large measure of responsibility for the situation that had developed. In its role as client, the department had chosen to manage the manufacture of defence products in an extremely cumbersome and bureaucratic manner, with inappropriately skilled quality and engineering resources, so that it, too, had contributed to the record of high costs and appallingly bad performance.

Woodward was also to quickly find that he needed support at high level if he was going to make the sort of impact expected of him. The abolition of Defence Support had not wiped out at a stroke the culture which that entity had once represented, a situation which was largely inevitable considering that the majority of ODP's staff had been inherited from Defence Support and its predecessors. The entrenched attitudes within many parts of the organisation often meant that little more than lip service was paid to ODP's more commercial objectives. Recognition that ODP remained essentially unreconstructed had resulted in it being widely regarded as an 'outcast' within the Defence family.

During his time as CDP, Bennett had been careful to reassure Defence audiences to whom he spoke that his organisation was accepting of limitations on the scope of its activities, stressing that pursuit of 'commercialisation does *not* mean that ODP would be allowed to extend willy nilly into activities of low defence priority, or aggressively seek subsidised sales to other markets'.[36] He emphasised instead the need to 'move management thinking towards commercial aspects such as markets, products and prices rather than production aspects which have been dominant in the past'.[37]

Other public statements issued on behalf of the Office, however, still propounded the old line that the need to maintain an industrial capacity for strategic purposes meant that ODP 'cannot be run on fully commercial lines – a degree of excess capacity for current purposes is implicit in the requirement'.[38] Precisely that argument had bedevilled previous attempts to rectify the diseconomy of defence production in Australia.

The difficulty of changing what amounted to an established culture was confronted by Woodward during a first meeting with his general managers at ODP's Anzac Park West offices. As he gave them his preliminary views on the task before them all, he was surprised to read in the eyes of many of his listeners the hostile message coming back:

It was a whole series of things … a mixture of disdain; of me being a new kid on the block and what the hell would I know about it, not even being an engineer; the feeling that we've had these smart arses coming in here before and we'll wait it out and do him. Some made positive noises, but in its totality the reaction was extremely negative.

As discussion continued Woodward found himself assuming a shape-up-or-ship-out stance, which he asserts was totally uncharacteristic of his normal style since he had never experienced anything like it before:

There was a good deal of annoyance when, at the end of it, I said 'Well, if you're not with me then you had better start looking for a job somewhere else'. Only then I think a few of them realised I was truly serious. It was probably a turning point. Some of them turned out to be extremely good, very able people, but it was, coincidentally, also the start of an exodus.[39]

Within the organisation itself, Woodward found that a considerable amount of strategic planning for the future of the ODP facilities had already been carried out. In line with expectations that ODP would evolve into a more self-supporting, commercially-oriented organisation, work on developing a definitive ten-year corporate plan was in hand. A business plan for 1985/86 was also in place which sought to tackle the problem of stemming the drain on the Defence vote by reducing operating costs and lifting productivity levels.

This work was the product of Sandra Welsman, who had been brought in from CSR Ltd. by Bennett. Coming from outside the bureaucracy, she was untied to public service processes and had focused on issues in ways which others had not before. While much of her thinking seemed to Woodward very broadly-based and general in nature, needing to be translated into action which was realistic and achievable, nonetheless he acknowledges that she had made a valuable start in picking up on the same problems to which his instincts had alerted him. He was convinced that 'whichever way you looked at it, something had to be done; the whole thing was out of kilter'.[40]

In December 1985, three or four weeks after taking up the CDP post, Woodward had his first interview with Beazley at which he was asked to give his impressions. He recalls:

I said that the work I'd done confirmed that we were pretty inefficient. I had rumbling around in my head already questions over pricing. I also thought we were overstaffed for the job being done, that we were keeping the establishments open for the sake of keeping them open rather than actually to do a job of work. Productivity was, in my assessment, poor in many cases, as were industrial relations.

After probing further on some aspects of these findings, the Minister responded that Woodward's views matched what he had long suspected. Beazley told him to come up with some specific propositions about tackling these matters.[41]

Later that same month, the recommendation made earlier by Eltringham in respect of the Aircraft Engineering Workshop at Pooraka, South Australia, was finally implemented. This facility had long been facing uncertainty, having posted operating losses for the last five years due to the cessation of Nomad production. In December 1984 the Minister for Defence Support had told the 40 employees that the workshop had only a six-month period in which to turn this situation around, either by finding its role within South Australian industry or on the merits of its own efficiency. Beazley had subsequently confirmed this stance soon after Defence Support went out of existence.[42] Now, after further evidence that the establishment was not viable, the decision was finally taken to sell it to private interests. Bought by the Heavymech company for $525,000, the workshop was handed over to its new owner in February 1987.[43]

At the same time that the decision was taken to dispose of Pooraka, the closure of the explosives factory at Albion was announced, to become effective from September 1986. This was a step taken in accordance with a report into the explosives factories produced by Bill Pheasant in July 1985, which had been commissioned during 1984 by the then Minister for Defence Support.[44] Albion's functions in the manufacture of high explosives and propellants would be transferred to the existing factory at Mulwala over a six-year period under what was dubbed 'Project REFA'. Until improved and more efficient plant had been brought into commission at Mulwala, the Albion works would be retained on a 'care and maintenance' basis. Decontamination of the factory and removal of obsolete and surplus buildings would also be carried out in preparation for disposal of the site.[45]

While taking these decisions to dispose of a few facilities judged to be no longer economically viable or essential for defence purposes, Woodward turned his attention to more fundamental issues at the remaining establishments. By this stage it had been realised that the key to significant productivity gains lay in making the facilities cost-effective by matching their workforce to current and projected work loads. This involved overcoming inflexible employment practices, and changing the situation where the mix of skills and staffing levels had become distorted due to the combined effects of past government decisions and the willingness of managers to buy short-term industrial peace.[46]

Nowhere were such measures more necessary than at ODP's three largest establishments – Garden Island, Williamstown and the Government Aircraft Factories (GAF) – which between them employed 7681 people and shared a common feature in their excessively high running costs.[47] The situation which reportedly existed at GAF, where some 50 workers for whom no further useful employment could be found were placed in a shed and described as a 'think-tank', could not be allowed to continue any longer. Trimming the workforce at each of these places by some 1500 jobs was expected to produce large savings.

The government's intention to rationalise operations at the three facilities was not publicly announced by Defence Minister Beazley until 21 March 1986.[48] Woodward had, however, first discussed such a program with the managers of each during the previous December. When contacted by phone on Christmas Eve, the general manager at Garden Island was found to be fully supportive and enthusiastic about the plan. Rear Admiral Nigel Berlyn, a serving officer of the RAN, had many years' exposure to the culture of inefficiency which prevailed at that dockyard as a naval user of the facility, before finding himself placed in charge. He was therefore fully persuaded of the need for reform, and had been developing a program along similar lines which he hoped could save even more than the $10 million which Woodward was proposing – perhaps as much as $17–18 million annually.

After warning of the difficulties which would have to be surmounted, and seeking assurances of funding for the necessary redundancy packages, Berlyn pledged Woodward that everything possible would be done to ensure the plan was implemented.[49]

When it came to the other two establishments, Woodward could be less confident of the outcome. It began to seem to him necessary, or at least desirable, to have someone handling matters there as a project officer, preferably someone with commercial experience. As he recalls:

> I wasn't sure how much knowledge of real industry we had in the place. I felt it would be useful to have someone who could perform that sort of role, someone who I was quite sure that I could trust … [50]

The person who came to Woodward's mind was 44-year-old Ken Harris, who was a first assistant secretary whom he had known in the Immigration Department.

After starting out with Thomas Brown & Sons Ltd. in Brisbane, Harris had launched himself on a public service career in the Australian Bureau of Statistics, later becoming an adviser in the House of Representatives and Assistant Commissioner in the Trade Practices Commission in 1976. In January 1986 he had just completed a year on secondment to private enterprise, working with the Boral company in Sydney, and was contemplating his personal future direction. When contacted by Woodward, Harris knew nothing about ODP and was not particularly attracted to the idea. Woodward, however, arranged for him to meet with Cole. In Harris' words:

> He [Cole] gave me a lot of reasons why I should be interested, so eventually I went over there in the job of Special Adviser Production Development … to undertake this commercial activity.[51]

With Harris concentrating on the problems of GAF and Williamstown, other senior officers of ODP – Doug Powell and Ron Taylor – explored options for reductions in the munitions factories, while Berlyn pressed on with changes at Garden Island.

On 18 July 1986, following extensive consultations between the Defence Department and union bodies, Beazley announced staffing reductions were to take place at ODP's big three establishments. The target levels set envisaged 1063 jobs disappearing, roughly 350 from each place. While about 150 of these positions would go through 'natural wastage' (normal retirement and employee movement), with the general agreement of the Australian Council of Trade Unions (ACTU) a voluntary retrenchment package was also offered as an inducement to staff to produce the desired numbers. In the event, a somewhat better response than required was attained, with a total of 1189 workers leaving during the period up to the end of August 1986.[52]

Cutbacks on this scale were a new experience within the government bureaucracy, as Harris discovered when he began dealing with the Public Service Board. Approaching this authority for assistance and advice regarding the proper procedure to be followed in retrenching government employees, he was assured that the Board was practised and knowledgeable in this area. He later recalled:

> I remember them saying that they were just doing something similar for the Belconnen Mall Authority [in Canberra], and had a team in place for handling this sort of thing. I asked how many people did that exercise entail, and they said about six … it might have been ten or a dozen. Then they asked me how many I was looking at. When I told them, they just gulped and fell off their chairs. You've got to understand that when we started this, the idea of large-scale retrenchments was really an anathema to the Public Service.[53]

Selling the notion of redundancies at the facilities affected was, predictably, not easy either. Workers were naturally anxious about their future, as well as concerned to preserve the benefits and privileges wrung from conciliatory ministers in more halcyon days. Beazley himself took part in several meetings at which the department's proposals were explained to staff and union representatives as part of the consultative process, and his reception was less than warm. Harris recounts one such meeting which the minister addressed at the department's offices in Melbourne:

> I wasn't allowed to go to it, but I remember looking down into the courtyard from the Minister's office on the top floor. There were busses with big signs all over them, television cameras, the works … a real big demonstration. Beazley went into this, and I met him afterwards as he came out of the lift. He was really angry and commented 'That bastard Howe has a lot to answer for!' Later,

when we were having a talk about the meeting, he said, 'Ken, what we're doing here is de-Howeing this organisation'.[54]

Harris himself got a taste of the workers' feelings when he attended a later meeting at Garden Island to explain the retrenchment proposals:

I remember one burly Painter and Docker asked me in front of this big gathering whether I was going to retrench him and all his mates, and would he be paid all his sick leave. I said no, you don't get paid sick leave. I said – a big mistake on my part – 'What you should do is thank God you've had a healthy life'. He looked at me and said, 'Well, Mr. Harris, you better make certain you've got plenty of sick leave, because you'll need it before all this is finished'. Those were stirring days all right.[55]

Significantly, resistance to change was not a universal or simple knee-jerk reaction. Vital leadership in the negotiations came from the ACTU, which could plainly see the ultimate outcome if a sensible accommodation was not reached which included a large number of retrenchments. Defence officials were therefore a little surprised when the key issue of workforce size was scarcely contested by the unions, and 'many useful points on structural and management issues' raised instead. Although union representatives undoubtedly wished the whole question would go away, and unrealistically hoped that the process might be delayed or even reversed, a mood of ultimate acceptance prevailed.[56]

Hiving-off of facilities

Despite the success of this first bout of retrenchments, the intractable problem of changing work practices still remained. Because of their size, the three main ODP establishments remained the most pressing areas which had to be addressed, yet each posed individual problems. In the words of Syd Hickman, the facilities were very different entities: 'Williamstown was maliciously and deliberately inefficient. GAF was ideologically weird, a real social experiment. Garden Island was inefficient too, just not so maliciously so as Williamstown.'

In his view, GAF was the worst industrial site in the whole of Australia. A managerial arrangement was in place which was little short of 'bizarre', with a departmental official and the head of the union group rotating in the manager's chair. Its performance, warranting such adjectives as 'appalling' and 'disgusting', was – according to Hickman – a tribute to the social theories which Howe had formerly indulged; as a result, the whole place needed to be 'rectified'.[57]

Apart from its management structure, GAF was facing another serious problem. Although it was one of the nation's two main locations for designing,

After part of the Clothing Factory was moved to new premises at Brunswick in 1952, the space available was used to commence production of embroidered items such as badges of rank, insignia, flags and regimental colours.

Australia's decision in 1954 to adopt the Belgian L1A1 rifle of 7.62mm calibre was taken in conjunction with Britain and Canada. The multi-national steering committee which guided this project is pictured during a three-day meeting at Ammunition Factory Footscray in November 1957.

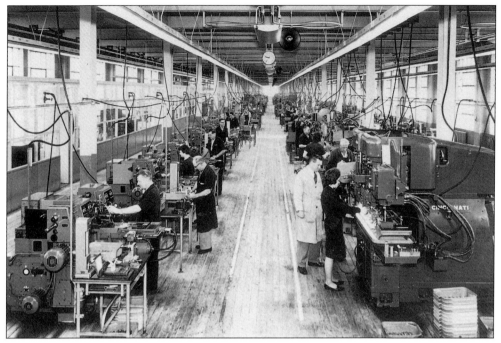

The L1A1 program led to reorganisation of the Small Arms Factory at Lithgow from 1956, which left it looking like a relatively modern facility.

View of the Munitions Filling Factory at St Mary's during the late 1970s. The main administration was in the multi-storey building on the left.

The main administrative building at Ordnance Factory Maribyrnong. The recurring problem of fluctuating work loads saw this facility depend heavily on commercial work to retain its viability from the early 1960s.

The main aircraft assembly plant at Fishermen's Bend in the 1960s, showing the production lines for the Mirage III–O fighter (foreground) and the Jindivik target drone (at rear). From the 1970s GAF faced an increasingly uneven flow of orders, which made it difficult to keep a regular workforce fully employed.

From 1968 the Anzac Park West Building, located at the base of Canberra's Anzac Parade, housed the central office of the Department of Supply and its successor organisations. During 1982–84 the headquarters staff of the Department of Defence Support numbered some 1200 people.

The Minister for Manufacturing Industry, Senator Jim McClelland (centre), is shown a machined hollow forging during a visit to Ordnance Factory Maribyrnong in March 1975. With him are the factory manager, Les Amos (left), and Neil Currie, Secretary of McClelland's department. In the nine years between 1974 and 1982, the defence factories underwent no fewer than five changes according to the government portfolio under which they fell.

Computer technology, such as this cloth cutter at the Coburg clothing factory, began playing an increasingly important part in the defence factories' efforts to make themselves more efficient and competitive.

A 1970s view of the nitrocellulose area at Mulwala Explosives Factory, looking west. The brick building in the background is the Nitration House, with the manufacturing process moving east to the Boiling House, Pulping House, Poaching House, and finally to the closest building for blending and wringing. The nitrocellulose was then loaded into rail cars and moved to the powder area.

This giant Sulzer marine diesel engine was one of 29 ships' engines manufactured between 1949 and 1974 at the Australian Government Engine Works, Port Melbourne. After attempts in 1975 to turn the factory into a viable commercial industry failed, AGEW was closed down in 1979.

In 1981 the Fraser government announced its intention to sell or lease the Clothing Factory at Coburg, but after two years nothing came of this plan and the incoming Labor government decided the keep the facility publicly-owned.

Although advertised for sale in 1982, the Bendigo Ordnance Factory drew only one response — and this was not regarded as a serious offer. In July the Fraser government decided that the factory would not be disposed of, after all.

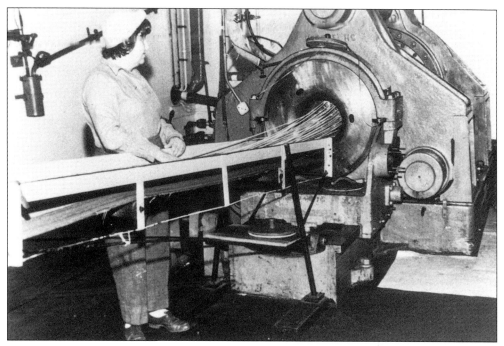

A horizontal press at the Albion Explosives Factory extrudes propellant for use in 4.5-inch naval guns. The future of the Albion facility had been in doubt for more than a decade before the decision to begin closing it down from 1986 was announced.

Williamstown Naval Dockyard in Victoria was the principal site for warship construction in Australia. Until it was bought by a private operator in 1988, the yard was notorious for its inefficiency and union strife.

The scene in the plastics workshop at Explosives Factory Maribyrnong. In 1989 the Defence Minister announced that this facility would not be transferred to ADI but closed down instead.

A celebratory drink follows the signing of the deeds of transfer in the Parliament House office of Minister for Defence Kim Beazley, 3 May 1989. Seated (from left): Ken Harris, Beazley, Alan Woods; standing (from left): Brian Conway, Bill Mitchell, John Barclay, John McCorquodale, Patrick Walters, and Tony Ayers. (Defence PR, neg.#CANA 89.90.10)

producing and overhauling manned and unmanned aircraft, and guided weapons, there was a diminishing need for its services. With the end of its principal project involving the assembly and testing of F/A-18 fighter aircraft for the RAAF already approaching, no new defence workload of any significance was in sight. More commercial work needed to be obtained for the factory to remain viable. It was in this context that the decision was taken that GAF's future must depend on its ability to compete with local and international aerospace companies. Allowing market forces to impact upon GAF's activities would compel it to become cost-effective and innovative or else go out of existence.[58]

At the same time as announcing the extent of workforce reductions to apply at Williamstown, Garden Island and GAF, Defence Minister Beazley's statement on 18 July 1986 also included the announcement that a government-owned company was to be created to take over the operations of GAF's jointly-managed facilities at Fishermens Bend and Avalon and to continue them on a commercial basis.[59] A company structure was considered to be the best way of allowing competitive forces to influence GAF. In turn, this was expected to influence the degree of competition within the Australian aerospace industry and thus maximise the government's return on its investment. In an effort to minimise the impending loss of military work and give GAF the best chance of off-setting the effects of this occurrence, it was proposed to set up the new company as quickly as possible.[60]

Harris claims the credit for having suggested this novel solution to the malaise at GAF, although at this distance in time Woodward, for one, is not so sure about where the idea originated. He recalls it as having many authors, himself among them:

> While I signed the documents which went to Beazley, the architectural strategy they contained were the product of contributions from a whole series of people working on the problem.[61]

In accordance with Beazley's announcement, a new and separate legal entity called Aerospace Technologies of Australia Pty. Ltd. (or ASTA) was created. This was incorporated on 28 November 1986, with three shareholders in the company: Defence Minister Beazley held ten shares, while Alan Woods (who had become Secretary of Defence following the retirement of Cole the previous month) and Harris had one each; each individual held their shares on behalf of the Commonwealth, by virtue of their official positions.[62]

ASTA became operational in March 1987 with the appointment of a board of directors. This was led by Sir Brian Inglis, the head of Ford Asia-Pacific and chairman of the Defence Industry Committee, and included such high-calibre businessmen as Jim Leslie (chairman of Qantas) and Leigh Masel (former chairman of the National Companies and Security Commission). Also on the board was Harris, although he personally felt very uncomfortable with combining his responsibilities here with his role as a government official.[63] After carrying out a thorough review of GAF's assets and capabilities to determine which of these had a commercial future, the new company progressively assumed responsibility for GAF. The transfer of assets and liabilities was completed in early October, prior to which the company finalised its management and workforce structure.

George Stuart, a former BHP executive who became the new company's managing director, was determined not to take over the whole of GAF's former workforce of 2000. In the event, positions were offered to only some 1400 of them and another major redundancy process was initiated. This provoked industrial action during August not just at Fishermens Bend but also Williamstown, where dock workers went on strike in support.[64] While those GAF workers not transferred were offered a retrenchment package, many of those who still had the promise of a job also eyed these benefits. The decision by the Public Service Board not to transfer people against their will inevitably led to a 'run on the package', and it became necessary for Defence to decree that those refusing to join ASTA would be given employment elsewhere. As a consequence, some 40 workers spent several months in limbo at a building in Queens Road, Melbourne, while jobs were found for them.[65]

The position at Williamstown could scarcely be regarded as much better than that at GAF. Promotional material produced for the dockyard during its time under the administrative control of Defence Support contained the soothing bromide that:

> Quality control and assurance operations are being updated and reorganised to allow further attention to quality related problems, the prevention of defects, and closer co-operation with procurement and production divisions.[66]

Such blandishments, however, merely helped to disguise the plain fact that Williamstown was a huge loss-making operation. Beset by an industrial relations scene which was a nightmare, through demarcation practices caused by union rivalries, and weighted down with middle-managers, the yard was so inefficient that its whole future had long been hanging in the balance.

As previously narrated (see chapter 3), the government's response to the 1981 Hawke committee's review was to retain the yard, introduce new management arrangements, and pursue a program of reform. Despite the great promises apparent at this stage, matters had not materially improved over succeeding years. In a decisive move – for which Woodward accepts full responsibility for proposing – Williamstown was put up for sale to the private sector in April 1987. While requiring the new owner to maintain the yard, the Commonwealth's interest would be protected by the government retaining a degree of control over dockyard assets through a 'special share' arrangement. In addition, it was announced that the lease on the government's Cockatoo Island dockyard would not be renewed after refit work then being undertaken on Oberon Class submarines was completed in 1992.[67]

Bought in 1988 by Australian Marine Engineering Consolidated (AMECON) – which firm later became Transfield Amecon, and later still Transfield Shipbuilding Pty Ltd – the yard was promptly shut down by the new owners in a highly controversial move following a confrontation with the unions. With ACTU help, the industrial relations aspect was finally sorted out. A largely-new workforce was recruited and the number of unions represented at the yard reduced from 23 to only three.[68]

Under Australia's first enterprise agreement, crippling work practices and demarcation rules were removed in favour of such innovations as multiskilling. New management was also brought in, while a large part of the former middle-management structure was dispensed with.[69]

Thus reformed, Williamstown survived to carry out the building of two American-designed FFG-7 guided missile frigates for the RAN, which were delivered in 1992–93. In 1989 Transfield also won the contract for ten modified Meko 200 (Anzac Class) frigates – eight for the RAN and two for the New Zealand navy; the first of these ships was launched at Williamstown in 1994.

That Garden Island was not treated in a similar way is probably due to two factors. Firstly, it occupied a somewhat different position to Williamstown in that it also housed the RAN's fleet base. In this capacity it had another function to fill, whereas Williamstown had no real purpose if it was not building warships. Secondly, Garden Island was under a management which was committed to a process of reform and steadily producing results. After achieving a productivity increase from the first round of workforce reductions of roughly 10 per cent in 1986/87, the shipyard had launched itself on a second efficiency drive in April 1987. Given the title 'Full Speed Ahead in 1987/88', this program aimed to yield measurable gains in productivity of 14–22 per cent, chiefly by breaking down demarcations and rigid work practices which created inefficiency.[70]

In effect, this meant taking on the powerful Painters and Dockers Union, which was the leading cause of time lost through industrial disruption at Garden Island – then running at quadruple the national average.[71] Berlyn maintains that, on first taking up the general manager's post during the days of Defence Support, he had attempted long and hard to use the consultative approach favoured by Howe. Becoming disenchanted with the idea that this would ever lead anywhere, he began moving to actively counter the antics of the painters and dockers and to minimise their influence.

As at Williamstown, it was discovered that this was an effort which other elements of the union movement were quite prepared to support, having realised that things simply could not continue as they had before. Beazley recalls approaches made to officers of his department from unions demanding to know if the latest attempts to reform Garden island were serious or not:

They were saying things to us like, 'Look, people have said before that there has to be reform here and then they haven't done anything about it, and the Ship Painters & Dockers do us over. Are you going to stick at this? Because if you are, you've got to be aware that it means something physical as well as moral to a lot of our members. Unless you stick with it, we're done'.[72]

Such representations left little doubt that reform was not a process to be lightly undertaken and, once embarked upon, had to be seen through to conclusion.

In addition to the measures mentioned, Berlyn was also eager to see his facility using commercial costing and pricing procedures. Accordingly, Garden Island began following the principle of full cost recovery from July 1986. This meant that all indirect wages and other overheads previously funded under departmental budget allocations were charged to customers and recovered from receipts from orders. While the change provided a more accurate and realistic picture of the operations of the facility, its immediate effect was to raise the prices of ODP products and services dramatically. With hidden subsidies now highlighted and the true cost of operations of the facility fully revealed, it was no longer possible to secure work by offering unrealistically low quotes which made the dockyard appear competitive.

The real point of bearing the pain associated with such a change was to directly confront a facility's management with the full scale of the adjustments which had to be made if its establishment was ever to achieve economic health. Berlyn's goal behind accepting such a challenge was to promote a climate in which the proportion of Garden Island's load which was made up of commercial work might increase to 30 per cent. He even harboured hopes that the yard might have a future as a government business enterprise in its own right, perhaps with a separate arm operating on the west coast of Australia once the RAN had carried out plans to base a portion of its fleet there.[73]

The principle of full cost recovery was introduced into all the munitions factories from 1 July 1988.[74] Other economic measures were also made, including 'sensible involvement' in modern equipment and products which increased efficiency and productivity, such as automated systems and processes, and more vigorous marketing of the capabilities of ODP establishments. The need for such changes was increasingly being forced on the facilities by virtue of a steady peeling away of the sheltering under which they had formerly operated. As the 1987 Defence White Paper made clear, the new approach being taken by government required that:

… unless there are compelling reasons to the contrary, defence work will be allocated on a competitive basis using fixed price (as opposed to cost–plus) contracts, with payments against milestones (rather than elapsed time) and with other incentives for improved performance where appropriate. Wherever possible, opportunities are to be provided for Australian organisations to bid as prime contractors ... Progressively, the Government expects that the [ODP] establishments will enter collaborative arrangements with local and overseas industry and will compete against local commercial enterprises for defence and other work.[75]

In accordance with these expectations, the ODP establishments more and more found themselves treated by the 'customer' elements of Defence as simply another source of goods and services. Since parts of the same department could not enter commercial contracts with each other, work given to ODP became the subject of Production Management Agreements (PMAs). These operated the same way as legal agreements with civilian firms, even including penalties for failure to 'perform to contract' in the form of authority to withdraw work rather than monetary damages.[76] Unmistakably, the defence facilities were facing not only demands for greater internal discipline but a requirement to function in a climate as competitive as that which had existed in the 1930s.

By mid-1987, a considerable distance had been travelled towards achieving ODP's corporate objectives of becoming more efficient and improving the productivity of the various factories and facilities. The specific goal attached to the latter objective had been to attain a 30–50 per cent boost in the five-year period from July 1985. Over the next three years up to 30 June 1988 the actual improvement reached was 28 per cent, nearly half of this figure being attained in the last of these financial years.[77] Most notably, the number of people employed within the organisation was cut by 43 per cent to 8500, with reductions not just at establishments but also ODP's head office. The net effect of all this reform was to reduce expenditure on defence production by some $150 million a year.[78]

Decision to corporatise ODP

Completion of the process described saw ODP standing on the threshhold of a new era. The number of actual defence facilities had been reduced and other cuts were in train elsewhere in the organisation. As an information booklet from 1988 noted:

> ... the new head office structure signals the end of the period in which reductions were the target. The new businesslike structure signals the beginning of a commercial assertiveness in ODP, building on the advantages of a lean organisation.[79]

The implied expectation that the rump of the old ODP which remained would continue largely as before, but with renewed vigour, was not a vision of the future shared in all quarters however. The experience gained through hiving off of

Williamstown and GAF had inevitably raised the question of whether ODP might not also prosper better in some different form.

An internal briefing paper dated as early as February 1987 took heart from the gains made up to that point and the fact that ODP was then in the process of 'throwing off the effects of the pillar-to-post existence of … recent years'. But this document still stressed the pressures for even greater efficiency from the organisation, 'especially in terms of its management performance and its workforce productivity':

> Despite becoming progressively more efficient and cost-effective, the cyclical nature of defence procurement (which we are seeking to even out) is such that most ODP establishments will continue to look for commercial and export work to subsidise uneconomic strategic capabilities.

> All these factors are pushing ODP in the direction of a more commercial approach … .ODP's future depends on improving its performance.[80]

Following the completion of his work on the restructuring of GAF, Harris had moved on to a different job running the Facilities Division of the Department of Social Security. Although still a director of ASTA, he had no continuing connection with ODP. He nonetheless found himself involved once more with the fate of the facilities, after Woodward moved to become Head of the Defence Logistics Organisation and his successor as CDP, Dr Malcolm McIntosh, was also promoted to a deputy secretary's job in Defence after only six months. Phoned by Woods about the vacant appointment, Harris was initially reluctant to apply. Not having enjoyed his experience of Defence committees, he recalled his response:

> Having done ASTA and seen the way the defence bureaucracy handled these things, I was pleased to have left and can't say that I leapt into this. Hence I was somewhat reluctant. I said, 'Look, I'm not insane, you know, I've had enough. I don't know how people can live with that committee system.'

Woods persisted, and prevailed on Harris to submit an application which was to prove successful.[81]

Even before taking up the CDP job on 18 February 1988, Harris' mind again turned to the central dilemma facing his organisation.[82] He began his analysis of what to do with the obvious question of whether ODP needed to be preserved in any form at all:

> It was a serious consideration whether it was really worthwhile giving the place a chance. Why bother? Would we be better off, for example, shutting it down? I wasn't a long-term defence official. I had no loyalty to the organisa-

tion. I guess that's one of the advantages of bringing in outsiders who don't need the job – they can be more objective than people who have spent all their lives there.[83]

The solution which he finally settled upon was disclosed to only a few close associates, one of whom was Brian Conway as director of the secretariat section. A member of Harris' staff during the process of corporatising ASTA, he had acted as company secretary and was thus familiar with the events of that time.

Conway recalled the first inkling he received of what was in store came when:

Ken called me into his office one day and showed me these large display panels which had logos on them. These were very similar to what became the ADI logo but were in different colours and different names across the top – green for Weapons and Engineering, blue for Naval Engineering, or something like that. He asked, 'What do you think of this?' I thought, oh no, here we go again, but said 'That looks quite interesting, Ken. What's this all about?'

Harris explained the designs away as merely part of an exercise which he had called for from ODP's marketing branch under Les Targ. But it was shortly after this that Conway was instructed to visit the companies office and reserve the name Australian Defence Industries Pty. Ltd.[84]

This was effectively the beginning of what would become the new company identity of ODP Harris at this stage had yet to seek formal approval for such a step, and was merely ensuring, as quietly as possible, that the company name which he had selected was available when and if required. Although careful to avoid alarming or alerting people to what might be in the offing, the very need to not broadcast his plans brought complications. A problem emerged when Conway received a phonecall from the companies office advising that someone else had applied to reserve Australian Defence Industries as a business name, as distinct from an incorporated company body.

In the event it was discovered that the other applicant was Targ, also acting on instructions from Harris to reserve the name for marketing purposes. In Conway's words:

Ken didn't realise that our paths were eventually going to cross. I had to get Les to write a letter foregoing his reservation in favour of our other application.

By this stage, clearly, the idea which Harris was pursuing was beginning to take firmer shape.

The principle at the heart of Harris' plan was simply that production for defence purposes alone was not an economical option, particularly in peacetime.

The various facilities had to be able to obtain business in competition with commercial firms on the open market to become and remain viable, yet this was not possible while they were hampered by the 'constraints that come from attempting to operate in a business-like way within a government department'. While ever the factories stayed under their present form of administration they would, he argued, be disadvantaged in their financial management by the elaborate control systems relating to expenditure to which they were subject.[85]

The restructuring which Harris proposed was not a unique or totally untried experiment. Indeed, the rationale for what he wanted to implement was similar to that which he had seen behind government enterprises elsewhere:

> I was interested in what was happening overseas, what other countries were doing. There was an awful lot being written about it … books, articles, and the like, which I read. And I'd been to Sweden several times earlier on, and was very impressed with the relationship between Swedish companies and the government. Thatcherism was a big issue at the time as well, with governments being inspired to look at ways of managing commercial operations in which they were involved. I admired what Thatcher was doing in Britain and the way her ideas were sweeping the world, although I can't say that we purposely adopted that model. The problem wasn't so very difficult that we needed to import a complicated theory. When you went through the range of possibilities, there weren't too many of those. It boiled down to a question of which organisation is most distant from the bureaucracy? Answer: a company. It really wasn't any more sophisticated than that.[86]

On 7 June 1988 Harris prepared a minute addressed to the Minister for Defence which set forth the options for further commercialising ODP's operations. Leaving the organisation as 'a standard public service unit within the Department of Defence' was rejected, as was the alternative of converting it into a statutory corporation. While he considered that the latter course held some promise of eliminating many of the controls which hindered performance, in his experience such bodies 'often become half-breed organisations unless they are large', like the Commonwealth Bank. The conclusion he offered was that the creation of a government-owned company provided 'the best chance of turning ODP into a competitive, businesslike organisation'. Although he acknowledged that there was a risk such an entity would have diminished links with the Defence Department, he outlined a number of measures which could be implemented to safeguard against this happening.[87]

Taking his proposal to the Defence Secretary the next day (a Wednesday), Harris succeeded in gaining Woods' endorsement. In a covering minute prepared for the minister's consideration also, the latter agreed that:

ODP will never be able to compete while it is part of a government department. Nor can it compete better with the private sector for its survival and growth if it is denied the means to become more competitive.

Woods argued that Harris, by virtue of his experience in the creation of ASTA and his government and private sector background, was the man who could pull off such a major task, adding that 'I would like to see him given three years and a fairly free hand to turn the organisation around, liaising as necessary with key elements of the Department'.[88] Armed with this support, that weekend Harris flew to Perth, having made an arrangement to see Beazley at home in his Swan electorate.

In the minister's kitchen on Saturday morning, 11 June, Harris elaborated his arguments for the course he was proposing to take. He recalled that it was not an easy interview, though not for reasons which he might have anticipated:

> We were trying to make some coffee and there was a builder doing some renovations out the back who kept interrupting all the time looking for instructions, in between the Beazley children coming in and out for money for videos. It was very difficult going through this ODP thing, and eventually he asked, 'What do you want to do, Ken?' I said, 'Well, I think we should give it a go as a company'.[89]

Beazley does not specifically remember the details of this meeting. He was, he says, impressed though by 'the runs' which Harris — and before him Lionel Woodward — had put on the scoreboard in this area. He was therefore 'basically happy to go along with' what Harris, as his chief adviser here, determined would be an appropriate corporate structure. There were, he acknowledges, other important considerations. The level of defence spending on capital equipment had shrunk significantly during the early 1980s, at a time when the department had in its program several large and expensive acquisitions. In addition to the $5 billion Anzac frigate project, it was planned to purchase six Type 471 (Collins Class) submarines at a cost of another $4 billion.[90]

The minister well understood that Defence was unlikely to enjoy growth in its share of government allocations to fully meet expenditure of such magnitude; increased savings from within its own budget, such as Harris was proposing, were crucial:

> We gained from that process something like $200–300 million a year as a relaxation for the Defence budget. That was equivalent to about three per cent real growth. Knowing that we were not going to get a sustained growth of that size, which was almost necessary for the White Paper's goals to be realised, the only place we could get this money was here. The outcome achieved by this gave my whole life as Defence Minister credibility. I would not have survived as Defence Minister if it hadn't happened, no chance at all. When defence items

surfaced in Cabinet and it was asked whether we could really afford the ambitious equipment program called for by the White Paper, I was always able to answer yes, because of the changes taking place in the factories.

It was hardly surprising therefore that, after asking a few questions to satisfy himself on key points, Beazley gave his agreement. Across the bottom of Woods' minute, he wrote: 'I have asked Mr Harris to proceed with the Company option for ODP.' With this endorsement in his pocket, Harris returned to Canberra to set the wheels in motion for the upheaval which was to follow.

After prolonged vacillation and ineffectual tinkering with the problem of making Defence's production facilities into viable economic undertakings, at last the decision had been taken to take a gamble with a bold new approach. Within little more than three years, the crumbling edifice which ODP had inherited from a succession of failed government departments was swept away in spectacular fashion, replaced by two government-owned companies while other facilities were placed into the hands of private enterprise.

Whether factories established to meet the specialised needs of a particular government activity like Defence could survive in a commercial environment was problematical, notwithstanding the increasing number of examples of business undertakings being created from former public instrumentalities. While the wisdom of this highly experimental course would be established in the passage of time, there remained a vast amount of work to be accomplished just to take the facilities out of their former departmental setting.

5

TRANSITION

In Australia in the mid-1980s there were many government business enterprises (GBEs); indeed, about half of all Commonwealth civilian workers – representing about 3 per cent of the Australian workforce – were employed in such organisations. Yet, as Harris contemplated the task in front of him, he quickly realised there were very few local precedents for the sort of exercise in which he was about to engage. Despite the number of GBEs, or the fact that some of these even operated as companies, none could readily serve as a model for the process which ODP was about to undergo. He knew that:

> Certainly the government owned Qantas, for example, but it did so simply by buying shares in a company that already existed. It had established statutory corporations before, but as far as I could find out there were no large-scale corporatisations where someone actually took part of a department outside of government and made it something else, and tried to keep it operating during that complex process. So there was no handbook to draw on, no form to follow.[1]

There was, of course, the experience which had been gained in creating ASTA. While this had been a much simpler undertaking, being both smaller in size and not involving facilities of differing type spread across several States, it did serve as a 'dry run' in terms of the mechanics of setting up a company.

In this period the government had also been defining what it expected from its own enterprises, as part of a process of reforming Commonwealth public sector administration. GBEs were now recognised as constituting an important business sector in their own right, and providing a significant proportion of infrastructure for the rest of the national economy. The loan and equity capital of the sixteen largest GBEs alone totalled an estimated $12.3 billion in 1986. Understandably, the Hawke government had begun focusing on 'achieving the highest levels of operational and financial efficiency' in these enterprises.

An information paper issued in October 1987 by the Minister for Finance, Senator Peter Walsh, had set out policy guidelines for such organisations. This document was followed in May 1988 by a further package of reforms aimed at reshaping the eight major transport and communications GBEs: Qantas, Australian Airlines, Australian National Line (ANL), Australian National Railways (AN), Telecom, Overseas Telecommunications Commission (OTC), AUSSAT and Australia Post. Outlined in a major statement to Parliament, the new provisions aimed to replace a range of controls on how these entities operated with streamlined management practices which emphasised performance, implementing a philosophy of 'letting the managers manage' with appropriate accountability for results. In view of the currency of these two documents, inevitably they formed an important basis for approaching the task of creating a new GBE.[2]

Harris admits that, in initially thinking about what should be done with ODP and developing the plan to put to the defence minister, his preference was to follow the example provided by Williamstown:

> I said to Kim Beazley, 'I'd like a Transfield thanks'. I wanted to shut the place for six months, retrench everybody, and give ourselves the breathing space to restructure. Then we could bring back the people – or some of them – as company employees, having shed all of their connections with the Public Service, and we'd have a clean start. But I knew it wasn't possible, because unlike Williamstown … where the dockyard was expendable to some extent … we had to keep going. We had to keep producing clothing and ammunition, keep repairing warships and making rifles, and so on. Somehow or other, we had to keep the organisation manufacturing at the same time as it went through very traumatic and fundamental change. That's what made this whole thing a complex exercise.[3]

The only logical course to adopt, he decided, was to effect the fairly standard commercial practice of a takeover. This would entail first creating the legal entity he had in mind as Australian Defence Industries and then transferring to it the assets of ODP.

Three weeks after Harris returned from Perth, he summoned a group of key people to a meeting in Sydney. This was held on the morning of 3 July 1988 – a Sunday – in a small conference room at the Airport Hilton Hotel. The choice of a venue away from Canberra, and the somewhat clandestine air to the arrangements, was deliberate. Harris was determined to prevent premature speculation about what was about to happen, either publicly or within ODP itself.

Those attending this gathering, apart from Harris, were: John McMahon, first assistant secretary heading the Budget & Support Division within ODP's head office; Dr John Barclay, who since May had been heading a newly-created division of ODP called Corporate Development as first assistant secretary; Ron Evans, general manager of the Footscray ammunition factory; Nigel Berlyn from Garden Island; Neville Rogers, general manager of the Bendigo ordnance factory; and David Holmes, from the accounting firm Ernst & Whinney (which was filling the role of corporate adviser).

To this group Harris now told of the plan agreed to by Beazley. He advised them that they were the group he had chosen as a steering committee for the conversion of ODP into a government-owned company. At the same time small cells would be set up in each establishment to handle specific issues, and a team would be created at ODP's head office under Barclay. Discussion then ranged across the many aspects involved in such an undertaking and the many actions which would be necessary to achieve the desired transformation.[4]

First among the steps taken was to legally incorporate the new entity as a proprietary company limited by shares. After articles of association signed on 19 July 1988 were lodged, this was achieved two days later. The share capital – just $12 – was drawn from ODP petty cash. As with the creation of ASTA, the nominal shareholders for the new organisation were Beazley, Woods and Harris.[5]

By this stage Woods was on the verge of retiring from his position as Secretary of Defence and the Public Service, although he had accepted the part-time appointment as chairman of the Civil Aviation Authority newly created under an act of parliament. His successor had already been named as Tony Ayers, then Secretary of the Department of Community Services and Health.[6] Knowing of his former mentor's impending availability, Harris moved to obtain Woods' services for the company. He recalls:

> I said to Alan, 'Well, you're the guy who brought me back into this and now that you're about to leave there's something I want in return. I'd like you to be the first chairman of ADI'. He said that would be fine, if I could talk Kim Beazley into it. So that was the deal between us.[7]

A board comprised of Woods as chairman and Harris as managing director was appointed by Beazley for initial six-month terms commencing on 19 July 1988.

A team established

In line with the course agreed upon by the steering committee, a 'merger implementation' group – later more commonly referred to as the 'transition team' – was set up in Canberra to handle the changeover to independent company status. Harris had hand-picked Barclay for the task of heading this team, after marking him out as a man of special talent and ability soon after becoming Chief of Defence Production. Deciding that his first act as CDP would be to make a self-drive familiarisation tour of facilities, Harris' first destination during February 1988 was the Lithgow factory. Barclay, aged 40 and with an engineering degree from Melbourne University and a doctorate gained in 1976 from the University of Aston (at Birmingham, UK), had then been manager at Lithgow for almost two years.

Thinking back on that visit, Harris well remembers their meeting:

We talked a lot that night. I guess in the back of my mind I knew already something had to happen to ODP. I couldn't just go there and continue to run it while ignoring the numbers, that was just impossible. I said to John, 'If the government decides to support me in reforming the place, do you want to live at Lithgow for the rest of your life?'. He said no, he'd be interested. So I targeted him in the early days as someone who I'd want to bring into it.[8]

When Harris approached him after returning from Perth about leading the transition team, Barclay now replied that he would not know where to start. 'Oh, its really quite easy', Harris assured him. 'You just do it.'[9]

With his 'trusted lieutenant' Barclay as team general manager, Harris recruited three other officers from within ODP to create the small group he wanted. To handle financial matters he selected Bill Mitchell, Director of Budgets and acting Assistant Secretary in the Accounting and Budgets Branch, whom he already knew to be 'a smart operator and a guy who could weave his way through the bureaucracy'. Kevin Callinan, the Personnel Manager at Garden Island, was chosen for his expertise gained from more than 20 years spent in that industrial relations crucible. Keith Farquhar, Director of Executive Co-ordination, had worked with Harris on the restructuring of GAF, Garden Island and Williamstown, and was brought on board to handle administration.[10]

Each of these men, to Harris' mind, exhibited the sort of qualities which he considered necessary for the task at hand. While they were all people who could work very well as public servants, a different sort of spirit also had to be present:

I had to pick people who were quick on their feet, intelligent, articulate, but they had to be committed too, to have drive, and like to achieve things. They needed to be able to say, 'Well, I don't know what this is all about, but I'm prepared to take it on trust and learn as we go'.[11]

While these individuals became the core members of the transition team, others were added from time to time as particular areas or problems came to be dealt with. For example, Conway frequently became involved in his capacity as company secretary, and Jim Kelaher (ODP's Assistant Secretary, Finance) helped where assets aspects of the transfer framework were concerned. In addition, a number of outsiders became involved when required, such as Russell Miller and Neal Parkinson from the commercial law firm Sly & Weigall, and Denis Page of the Arthur Young firm of chartered accountants. Specialised financial advice was also obtained from Rothschild Australia.[12]

The issues which needed to be addressed and worked through were numerous, varied and complex. Reflecting back, Mitchell says:

> What stunned people more than anything was the sheer scope and size of the task, and that came from both within factories and other elements of the bureaucracy.[13]

One part of the process involved setting up an independent company, with its own corporate structure and premises, starting balance, stock and bank accounts. Once this was established as a legal entity, the fixed assets of ODP could then be transferred to it from the Commonwealth: land, buildings, machinery, work-in-progress, contracts and people. Other matters – ownership of intellectual property, an amount of operational funding, and an appropriate capital structure – would have to be resolved along the way. Ultimately, all these many activities would be embodied in a transfer agreement which formalised the arrangement.[14]

The first step in the process was to get ADI functioning in a normal way. To this point nothing more had been done than to gain the minister's concurrence and fulfil the formal but very basic requirement of registering a company name. To go any further required broader government endorsement for the plan. On advice obtained by Harris, this did not, however, entail a need for legislation or even the formal approval of Cabinet. Under the Defence Act, Beazley already had the necessary authority as minister to create an enterprise for the defence of Australia. This issue was not explicitly addressed in a letter dated 16 June sent by Beazley to the Prime Minister, but in his reply Hawke also did not directly raise it either, merely stipulating that the new entity should be 'consistent with changes currently being introduced for a range of established Government business enterprises'. Hawke required only that Beazley consult with his colleagues, the ministers for Finance (Walsh) and Industrial Relations (Ralph Willis), and 'initiate discussions with the ACTU and relevant unions at an early stage'.[15]

Although the possibility of a misfire in Cabinet was thus averted, the process of consultation proved only marginally less messy. Plans for the defence minister to make a public announcement regarding ADI on 12 August (a Friday) produced a requirement for haste which meant that Beazley got around to consulting with his ministerial colleagues only in the corridors of Parliament House. In the scramble leading up to the announcement, moreover, the briefing of the secretary of the ACTU, Bill Kelty, was somehow overlooked. As Barclay recalls:

> From memory there was a bit of a fuss about that afterwards and I don't remember how it was resolved. On the whole, though, the thing went off moderately quietly. The bureaucrats were basically caught off-guard.[16]

Coincident with the public announcement, a nameplate was erected outside the main entrance to Anzac Park West signifying the location of the registered office of Australian Defence Industries Pty. Ltd. (which happened to be Harris' room). This had been done previously for ASTA, which had its registered office in the same building. The screw holes remained in the wall to show where that sign had once been fixed. Conway remembers often walking up the steps and thinking to himself that soon there would be another plate to replace the old ASTA one:

> Seeing a nice brass nameplate with paint-filled black lettering up there was another tick in the right box. Of course, we were legally bound to display the company name out the front, but we probably didn't have to do it as pretentiously as that. I guess we were sort of making a statement at the same time … [17]

The minister's announcement that ADI was expected to become fully operational in March 1989 created a tight timetable for the transition phase.[18] Although this allowed six months for transfer arrangements to be completed, this period was hardly generous in view of the complexity of the issues to be resolved. The imperative for speed was, of course, largely self-imposed by Harris, who offered no apologies for pressing the pace:

> This wasn't a theoretical exercise on paper. There were thousands of people with families, millions and millions of dollars worth of plant and equipment. There were orders to satisfy and the defence of the country to consider, because the joint was servicing warships and making weapons, and that had to be kept going. You couldn't sit there all day writing learned memos on the subject. The thing was always going to be messy and difficult, so why prolong it – better hack in and finish it. We just had to cut through any red tape and anybody who got in the way of that, watch out![19]

A consequence of this approach was that keeping copious and detailed records of every action taken, apart from essential legal and commercial documentation, was not high on the transition team's list of priorities. One member later justified this situation on the grounds that the sheer pressure to keep abreast of developments dictated such a course,[20] but another offers a somewhat different explanation:

> About that time there had been problems with Freedom of Information. Here we were in a bit of no-man's land, in that we were still public servants while trying to set up ADI. So we deliberately decided on a strategy of working so fast that we were unable to keep any personal records and diary notes. No-one was going to be able to trip us up, bloody oath they weren't.[21]

Complicating matters was, Harris maintains, also a need for secrecy regarding much of the early work which had to be done, since sensitive industrial relations and other issues were involved. A consideration of no less importance was that of staff morale, a factor which McMahon is quick to acknowledge:

> I've always found the greatest demotivator for people is uncertainty over one's own future. This was a period with a hell of a lot of change going on, rumours were rife and so a lot of people became quite despondent.[22]

The need was therefore recognised early on to think through carefully what had to be done and only announce the decisions once action had been approved, but to keep quiet in the meantime.

While the transition team carried the burden of day-to-day detailed work, they did so under Harris' personal direction. From the very first day, there was never a doubt in anyone's mind that he was the prime 'change maker' behind the process. By Barclay's account:

> It was being run by Harris, with us feeling a bit schizophrenic doing what we were doing as Defence employees. He set the agenda, and we would then basically do it to achieve the outcome he wanted. We did an awful lot of writing of correspondence, but he wrote much of it too. The tactic was to put the words into people's mouths so then he could wave a piece of paper saying that they said it. Invariably he signed or saw the policy stuff that went to the Minister. In a group effort like that it is very difficult to work out how much was his and how much was other's work, but Harris was clearly the driving force and the philosophical pin.[23]

Harris' guiding hand remained in firm evidence throughout the process, even after he stepped out of the CDP's chair to become the company's first (and for a while sole) employee. The position of managing director of ADI was advertised as would be the case normally, and Harris was among about thirty candidates who applied. After attending an interview on 16 December which was presided over by Alan Woods as company chairman, he was formally appointed on a five-year contract from 2 January 1989. Resigning from the Public Service and moving out of the CDP's office to another room on the first floor of Anzac Park West, Harris was succeeded a week later by John McMahon.[24] The latter acted only in an acting capacity, however, since the job would go out of existence when ADI actually took over; until then, it was needed to keep things going and to exercise delegations which were the CDP's prerogative. This change made little difference to the arrangement which operated, though, since Barclay states that while he 'nominally answered' to McMahon he continued to take all his directions from Harris.

Given the level of Harris' involvement, inevitably the team's methods and manner of proceeding came to directly reflect his personal style. Again recounting Barclay's recollections:

> He doesn't take any prisoners, and he's got some fundamental points of view which we all know and love. He was convinced that as soon as we let ourselves get engaged in debate, we'd lost – the bureaucrats would win because they'd talk us to death. If we became involved in consultation, and set up committees or whatever, then nothing would ever happen because everybody's view would be taken into consideration. We were actively discouraged from talking to the people who did ASTA because Ken would say 'I know all that', and we were discouraged from talking to other GBEs. It wasn't to say that we couldn't … but we sort of didn't do it. I think he just didn't want everyone getting involved. He really wanted to present everybody with a *fait accompli*, or he feared it wouldn't happen.[25]

From Harris' perspective there was more at stake than simply minimising interference. As he later put matters:

> We were the people who were going to be responsible for making it work, and I didn't want to have to live with a compromise. We had to put in place the best possible set of commercial arrangements to give the company a chance. Tackling this as a genuine take-over meant that we were going out on a limb. As the group running it, we had to take the whole thing very seriously, to make certain that we didn't negotiate ourselves into bankruptcy. We had to be bloody interested in the outcome, rather than have some committee do it and present a *fait accompli* to some poor wretch who then tries to run it but finds he can't because of all the compromises built into the structure.[26]

Concerns on this score were not entirely without justification, as was rapidly discovered. Callinan recounts how, within days of the ministerial announcement of the intention to set up ADI, the transition team was summoned to a meeting at the Public Service Commission. At the appointed time Barclay and himself duly went to the nominated venue at offices in Barton:

As we walked in the door on the ground floor there was a notice saying that the ADI meeting was in conference room so-and-so on the second floor. So we went to the lift and there was another big sign saying the meeting was upstairs, and as we came out on the second floor there was another one. We walked down the corridor to where there was this large conference room with a table which would have seated probably thirty or forty people. When John and I went in there must have been eight or nine spare seats, and after we sat down someone decided to open the meeting. The chairman wanted to know where was the rest of our team? 'We're it', we answered. Then he said, 'Well, the purpose of this meeting is to tell you how you're going to go about doing your job. We've got representatives here from Public Service Commission, Department of Finance, Industrial Relations … ', etc. We said, 'Sorry, we're doing this job, not you people. These are the broad principles of how we intend to do it – bang, bang, bang. Do you have anything further you want to discuss. No? Well, thank you very much'. And we got up and walked out. Those people weren't there to help us in any way. They were a bunch of assistant secretaries who'd simply been instructed by their superiors to make sure that things were done their way.[27]

Apparently confirming the view of team members, that there was a generally negative reaction to their mission within parts of the bureaucracy, was a letter received in November from Stewart West, the Minister for Administrative Services. West's letter, which was copied to other departments, stated that his officials had been asked to arrange the transfer of ODP properties to ADI, an action which he considered to be inconsistent with a recent Cabinet decision regarding assets sales. On the basis of such claims, the Minister for Finance, Senator Walsh, also wrote to assert the need for extensive consultation on a range of property and other issues.[28] Although West's information was wrong, as Beazley wrote back to tell him – DAS's assistance had only been sought in identifying the title to properties – this exchange was taken as indicative of a determination to place obstacles in the team's way and frustrate the transition process. While understandable, perhaps, such a perception meant that a hostile construction would often be placed on the actions of officials who also were only doing their job.

To break the deadlock which developed between departments would eventually entail the creation of a 'Committee of Deputies' – deputy secretary level officers from Defence (Ron McLeod) and Finance (Eric Thorn) meeting with Harris – and several face-to-face meetings between Walsh and Beazley. Even now, more than six years later, Patrick Walters, who in October 1988 took over as Beazley's principal private secretary (or senior adviser, as this position subsequently became known), says that:

The overwhelming recollection that remains is of the very difficult time we had in convincing the Department of Finance that ADI should be allowed to function as a fully-fledged public company ... Officials there were constantly chipping away at this; they just didn't want it to be more than a glorified statutory authority. I well recall Kim going across to Walsh's office over several months, trying to persuade him to give a bit more.[29]

For the most part Harris dodged attempts to lock him and his team into protracted negotiations by ignoring them. He was inclined to attribute instances of obstructive attitudes and behaviour to a natural tendency of bureaucrats to resist surrendering any power:

People would say things like, 'Well you guys are just cowboys. You're trying to get away to do things in your own way without following the established process'. That expression 'cowboys' was used about us quite a lot. I've also noticed that there is a deep suspicion of business inside the Canberra bureaucracy, the notion that profits are somehow evil. The idea of making a profit out of defence contracting was seen by some as being a particular problem, yet it is profit that generates investment and investment generates defence infrastructure; without one you don't have the other.[30]

There were, though, other factors influencing the reaction of many areas of the bureaucracy, particularly within the Defence organisation. Harris himself accepts that there was a strong legacy of resentment left over, not without some justification, from the days of the Department of Defence Support. Beazley also holds to this view:

There was good reason for the defence bureaucracy being reluctant to relinquish control during the transition phase to ADI. They'd had such trauma with Defence Support that they were trying to know everything that was going on, and to second-guess every management decision down to the factory level. It was the only mechanism they had in place for dealing with the lunacy that had prevailed up to that point, and naturally they were going to resist any invitation for ADI to remove themselves from detailed scrutiny.[31]

Others point to uncertainty as a factor which also caused 'very mixed feelings' within both civilian and military elements of the Defence department. McMahon recounts that soon after the ministerial announcement, the Chief of the Naval Staff, Vice-Admiral Mike Hudson, wrote to the Secretary of Defence (Ayers) expressing 'grave concern' for the operational readiness of the Navy once control of Garden Island passed into the hands of a separate entity. As he says: 'It was a legitimate concern – I mean, we didn't know the answers either. All we could do was try to convince Navy that their interests wouldn't be jeopardised.'

McMahon and the Director-General of Fleet Maintenance in Navy Office, Commodore Ian Holmes, were put to work to draft a memorandum of understanding between the service and the company. In the event this was never signed, due to legal impediments, but eventually letters were exchanged between CNS and Acting CDP which confirmed the substance of the draft agreement anyway. As McMahon later remarked:

'This whole episode was only because of people's uncertainty – it was all so new. The evolution of thinking that occurred was really terrific.'[32]

Assets and valuations

A major step which had to be undertaken in preparation for the formal transfer of properties owned by ODP involved finding the necessary land titles. With some of these documents dating back a century, as in the case of Footscray, this was no easy task, especially after it was discovered what state the records were in. Barclay remarks that they were 'a shambles':

The titles had been mucked around with, abused and neglected since these places had been formed, so we had to deal with the Australian Government Survey Office to define a title to begin with.[33]

Further problems emerged when it came to placing a value on these properties, for the purpose of calculating the amount of debt to be entered on the company's books. Initially the team engaged a firm of commercial valuers, Mason, Gray and Strange (MGS), but later the Australian Valuation Office (AVO), the Department of Finance, and the Property Group of the Department of Administrative Services all became involved. This was because the land was to be transferred under the Land Acquisition Act, and there were established procedures which required the government to make its own valuation.

Major arguments ensued over what were reasonable values based on the 'best and highest use' to which the various land parcels could be put. On nine sites the difference between MGS and AVO assessments was less than $5 million (or about 7 per cent of the highest total), although on several of these places the discrepancy was as high as 20-30 per cent. In the separate case of St. Marys, though, the AVO arrived at a valuation nearly double the MGS figure. Again, in Barclay's words:

The AVO would go to a place like St. Marys, see it all as real estate for housing sites, and put a high value on it. We didn't want ADI to come into existence with a balance sheet loaded with all these expensive assets which weren't performing, so we talked the AVO down on the basis of potential demolition and decontamination costs.[34]

Not so easy to move on this issue of land valuations was the Department of Finance, which insisted that the highest possible figure be placed on all properties. Try as the ADI team might to argue that such values were in excess of market levels, Finance would not budge – to the point that the company's takeover of ODP was being put in jeopardy. The ADI Board finally gave way on this issue, enabling land acquisition submissions to be forwarded to the Minister for Administrative Services. But, as Harris later recalled, the Board also advised the Government that it would only be a matter of time before the value of the properties had to be written down and would show up as a loss in the company accounts:

> In fact, the properties had to be written down by $105 million in 1992 and this had to be carried forward ever since as a loss on the balance sheet. It is another example of the bureaucracy knowing better than the market.[35]

One problem which was identified while sorting out the land titles was the realisation that some $16 million would be payable to State and Territory governments in stamp duty on the conveyancing of these properties. In addition, once the protective shield of the Crown was removed from the facilities, ADI would be immediately subject to the different (though not necessarily higher) standards required under state and local regulations governing land zoning, the manufacture of dangerous goods, pollution control, and so forth, which previously did not apply because of their departmental status. The company might therefore find itself meeting not just these expenses in the future, but also liable for rectification in areas where currently there was non-compliance. These costs were estimated to be at least $60 million. The only way around this situation was determined to be special legislation to amend the Defence Act, exempting ADI from all state transfer charges and giving the company a period of six years in which to meet the requirements of local regulatory laws.

Another unexpected hitch was found to have arisen as a result of action recently taken to establish the Defence Housing Authority (DHA). Defence-owned houses on land adjacent to some of the factories had been transferred to DHA, at no cost, in December 1987. It was now discovered, however, that the loss of control of title created potential encroachment, safety and security problems at what would become ADI sites. Worse, the haste with which the DHA exercise was accomplished had caused 'fundamental errors of fact and law' to be made, resulting in the whole of the Lithgow and St. Marys sites being transferred, and for factory land at Mulwala also to be affected. The ADI Board decided to request that the relevant properties be transferred back to the Commonwealth for subsequent transfer to the company, again at no cost.

When attempts to negotiate a way through this difficulty at official level failed – DHA was only prepared to sell the houses to ADI at their market value of $4.9 million – an informal approach was made by Beazley to the Minister for Defence Science and Personnel, Ros Kelly, but without success. While directing that action was taken to correct the mistakes over the Lithgow and St. Marys facilities, Mrs Kelly rejected the request to transfer the houses themselves. On 25 March 1989 she wrote to Beazley complaining of the presumptive tone and confrontational approach adopted by ODP representatives with DHA officers, claims which were rejected by others present on the relevant occasion as simply not true. In the event the ADI Board dropped its claim to title of the houses, opting instead to create subdivisions at the effected sites which enabled the houses to be excised from titles, and to settle for assurances regarding their rental or disposal.[36]

Handling this messy and complicated business was mainly the task of Dr John McCorquodale, head of one of the contracts branches in the Commercial and Drafting Division of the Attorney-General's Department. As with members of the transition team who often found themselves 'wearing two hats', he also comments that:

> My role was a bit incestuous really because, although always acting in the Commonwealth's interest, at times this meant advising the Department of Defence – that is, ODP – and at other times Department of Finance, or even Administrative Services when issues of the national estate were involved.[37]

He was assisted by officers of the Crown Solicitor's office in Sydney and Melbourne who identified the services and easements, and associated requirements. However, much of the work also fell to Bill Mitchell within the ADI team, and to Barclay who dealt with Finance on the issues which were periodically thrown up.

The explosives factory at Maribyrnong was not to be included among the properties transferred to the company. An analysis of the commercial viability of the Maribyrnong facility, conducted by Ron Taylor (Special Advisor, Production) in September 1988 had recommended that it be closed down in preference to being incorporated in the ADI structure.[38] A public announcement to this effect was made by Beazley on 27 February 1989, stating that the factory would stay with Defence until its closure was progressively effected over the ensuing 18–24 months.[39]

Although ADI was not taking over the operations of the factory at Albion, or the explosives works at Maribyrnong now either, the company found it impossible to remain aloof from developments at both these places. Albion was already in the process of winding-down, its capabilities being progressively transferred to Mulwala, and the Maribyrnong plant was earmarked for closure by December

1990; both were to remain Commonwealth establishments within Defence until their final disposal. On the recommendation of Harris, the ADI board had decided in October 1988 to 'express no interest' in taking part in the commercial redevelopment of the Maribyrnong site,[40] but this proved not to be the end of company involvement.

Since capabilities from the Maribyrnong explosives works were being transferred to other factories which would be joining ADI, and a reorganisation at the plant was expected to produce surplus staff by March 1989 'much the same as at other establishments', ADI retained a vital interest in what was happening there. In February 1989 it was proposed that the closure of both Albion and Maribyrnong explosives factories be managed by an administrator acting under the Supply and Development Act, and that this person be an ADI employee agreed to by the Department of Defence. ADI would therefore manage the closure on behalf of Defence.[41]

Also not to be transferred to the company were Garden Island, and the Production Development Facility at Salisbury. At the former, the intertwining of the dockyard and the Navy's fleet base meant that transfer was out of the question – quite apart from the $245–296 million price tag attached to the site. Similarly, the PDF was an integral part of the defence complex at Salisbury. In both cases, therefore, these were to be leased to the company but remain under Commonwealth ownership. Initially considered for lease, too, was an ODP-run explosives magazine at Longlea, Victoria, until it was decided that this area was not required.

Not actually wanted but forced onto ADI was the factory at Mulwala, then currently being upgraded under Project REFA. Because of the new facilities being constructed there costing $137 million, the value of which the company was expected to assume on completion, there was strong resistance to taking this on. As Barclay put it:

> REFA was a contentious one. Defence put it in the transfer arrangement and we couldn't get it taken out so we finally accepted it.[42]

The policy of taking over the facilities as working entities meant that values had to be put on the work they were currently performing. Each facility was asked to identity all contracts which they held, and to predict which were expected to be 'loss-makers'. Admittedly, not all those likely to bring in losses were commercial disasters, as some merely reflected changes in accounting policy, escalation factors, exchange rate variations, and so forth. For each of these liabilities there were then negotiations to strike a commercial rate at which the company was prepared to take them over, with the government paying an 'adjustment' which eventually turned out to total over $30 million. Similar arrangements had also to be reached over special production capabilities which Defence particularly wished to see retained for strategic reasons, rather than commercial viability – what were termed defence required support capabilities (DRSC).

Before the assignment, or novation, of existing contracts to ADI, agreement to do so had first to be obtained where customers other than government agencies were involved. Intellectual property held by ODP, and such things as patents, trademarks and technical drawings, had also to be identified and transferred, sometimes with other interested or originating bodies – such as the Defence Science and Technology Organisation (DSTO) – placing qualifications or restrictions on their use.

Arrangements had also to be made over the transfer of ODP's human assets, its workers. While personnel issues are discussed further in the next section of this chapter, here it should be noted that agreement had to be reached to share costs such as workers compensation, superannuation, leave entitlements, etc., according to the length of time an employee had served with the Commonwealth and went on to spend with the company.

All these sorts of issues needed to be settled, to enable a funding package to be assembled to allow the company to actually operate at takeover. An amount of one million dollars had already been made available to ADI during the months after the August public announcement to allow the company to meet its running costs, such as managing director's salary, stationery, bank fees and various other accounts. Among these anticipated expenses was the finding of suitable office space to house the company's corporate headquarters. During April 1989 arrangements were made to lease a floor of the National Capital Planning Authority's building at 10–12 Brisbane Avenue, in the inner Canberra suburb of Barton close by the parliamentary triangle. These offices were occupied by ADI on 1 May.[43]

Personnel issues

A key element in the plan evolved for helping the new company to break free from the straight-jacket which had bound ODP and its predecessors was a strategy to attain greater efficiency and productivity from the workforce in the facilities. To do this, a new industrial award was needed which simplified job classifications and did away with the basis for the innumerable demarcation disputes between various trade unions.

The need for such a change had been recognised well before ADI appeared on the horizon, having been raised at an ODP industrial manager's conference in May 1988. As a result of this gathering a group had been established, with factory representation, to undertake the rewriting of the award covering defence munitions establishments. Work towards this end had been well advanced when the decision to form ADI was announced, and was used as a start point for a new award to cover the bulk of the company's workers.[44]

Kevin Callinan was notified two days before the August ministerial announcement of the intention to form ADI that he was the man selected to carry through the process of negotiating the new award. He was asked to develop a broad strategy for what needed to be achieved and produce a paper for the consideration of the steering committee by early October. Describing the philosophy adopted, Callinan states that:

> The fundamental principle was to create a situation where managers had the freedom to manage and also the responsibility to manage as well. We had to get away from having everything prescribed, and to that end we took around twenty-seven awards, three Acts of Parliament, two other major awards and a myriad of unregistered and unsigned agreements, and dispensed with the lot.[45]

While Callinan recalls that there was uproar when the company's plans for a single, demarcation free award became known, this was not the cause for the industrial unrest which initially greeted the announcement of ADI's formation. Causing much greater concern was news of a staffing reduction program to be undertaken, to realign manning levels to current workloads and ensure that creation of the new company was not burdened with excess overheads. Under this plan only about 6700 of ODP's existing workforce of just over 8000 would be invited to transfer to ADI – a reduction of 1300, or 15 per cent.[46]

Not unnaturally, there was widespread anxiety over the extent and terms of such a program. Announcements of retrenchments at various factories inevitably triggered fears among remaining workers at where the process would end, and whether cutbacks were, in fact, a surreptitious prelude to closure. When 67 workers at the Bendigo ordnance factory were informed in February 1989 that they would not have jobs after the facility became part of ADI, this was met with a protest stoppage by some 200 fellow employees who objected to thirteen non-voluntary retrenchments being included.[47]

Countering such concern, however, was the position of the ACTU, which had recognised that restructuring before the ADI takeover was largely inevitable. The advice given to Bendigo workers by an ACTU industrial officer, Bob Richardson, was that they should 'flow with' such changes, since the process was 'irrevocable'. The view publicly expressed by Richardson was that the defence factories would have to be competitive and get work in order to keep jobs, and that a positive attitude by unionists would strengthen Bendigo's chances of maintaining its strong role in defence manufacturing.[48] Despite these rational pleas from such a significant union source, some unrest remained.

Anxiety was not confined to the outlying facilities, but extended to ODP's head office in Canberra as well. Concern here was well justified, because while this had been trimmed down from about 1000 in its heyday in 1984 to only about

250,[49] Harris was determined to take the barest minimum of personnel across with him to ADI's corporate headquarters. He admits to having been influenced in this aim by his experience of working in Sydney with Boral Ltd.:

> I would go to meetings with Sir Eric Neal, Boral's chief executive, and see the complete focus on the profitability of the organisation. I also saw the importance of systems which lacked complexity, that allowed decisions to be made quickly. You could take a risk at Boral, without having the endless committees which are there in the Public Service to eliminate risk but usually ensure that by the time a decision is taken the business opportunity has passed by.

> I prefer to deal with small groups anyway – makes communications easier – but it seems to me that effective organisations don't run with big staffs. A small headquarters was a feature of Boral, they made almost a fetish of it. When I was leaving, Sir Eric Neal showed me around the reorganised office in Norwich House, in O'Connell Street. He said to me, 'You probably wonder why I'm squashing everybody onto the one floor. The answer is that organisations always want to grow, so when they come to me about more space I tell them I haven't got any money for it but more importantly we're hemmed in by the concrete walls of the building. If you've got no room to expand its another way of keeping the numbers down.' I thought that was a very practical solution and that's how I approached ADI.[50]

In the event Harris resolved to have no more than about 40 people at his new head office. In January 1989 assistance was obtained from a private consulting firm which specialised in providing advice on organisational structures, job descriptions, salary levels and issues of that kind. Based on their suggestions on what a suitable structure might look like, selections were made of the existing staff of ODP who should be asked to transfer to ADI. Conway recalls that, as company secretary:

> I had the dubious distinction of quietly walking around the Office of Defence Production giving people letters signed by Ken and saying, 'This is from ADI. Keep it quiet, don't tell'. The ones who didn't get a letter had a choice of being redeployed within the department or taking a redundancy package.[51]

Another important administrative issue which had to be addressed concerned the composition of a company board and remuneration of its members. The two-man board appointed by Beazley in July had commenced holding meetings just four days after the public announcement of the company's creation was made on 12 August. By the next monthly meeting, the board's attention had turned to the appointment of an additional director and filling the full-time chief executive's position (that is, the job then filled by Harris) on a permanent basis.[52]

To find a third director, an approach was made to Russell Fynmore, at that time executive general manager for Business Development at BHP. This was a step taken at the suggestion of Woods, who had known Fynmore for more than 20 years. The latter recalls:

> I had a lot to do with Alan when he was Secretary of the Department of Resources and Energy. This was not the first job that he had suggested me for, although I didn't get to know about it directly from him. I happened to be in Sweden at the time, on a government science mission led by Senator John Button. I was in my hotel room and received a phone call from Patrick Walters, Kim Beazley's private secretary. He said the minister had asked him to determine whether I would be prepared to be the deputy chairman of ADI, a company that Defence was developing, but he needed to know then because a list of names would be going to Cabinet the next day. My response was, 'Well I work for BHP and I can't take on any role without their permission. I can't get back to BHP but my feeling is that if the government wants me to do that job BHP would go along with it. That's their history.' So it was on that basis that my name was put forward. When I came back to Australia I went and saw Brian Loton [BHP's chief executive] and he agreed.

Appointed by the Minister also for an initial six-month term from 19 October, Fynmore attended his first meeting at the end of that month when he was named as deputy chairman of the board.[53]

To facilitate the selection of a chief executive, the Board resolved in September to consult the Remuneration Tribunal and seek a determination on a pay level appropriate to such a position, and also for annual fees to directors. This would ensure that the company conformed with other GBEs. When the tribunal's ruling was received, it was found that ADI had been placed among the middle tier of public office holders. This was not, of itself, unreasonable, since it now ranked alongside OTC, the Federal Airports Corporation, Australian Nuclear Science and Technology Organisation and CSIRO.[54] What rankled, Conway explains, was that:

> We were also pegged to ASTA, which was a bit off and not necessarily a good move because ADI was a larger organisation with a larger capital structure. We ended up in an argument with the Tribunal, but rather than move us up they kept us at the bottom of the pile.[55]

Meanwhile, work on developing an ADI award was proceeding. One problem experienced stemmed from the fact that ODP staff were employed under any one of three Acts: Public Service, Supply and Development, or Naval Defence. While the defence minister had existing powers under the first two to transfer people to the company, this was not the case with the Naval Defence Act which covered Garden Island workers. A new piece of legislation had to be put through Parliament before this could happen. An amending Bill was accordingly introduced into the House of Representatives by Beazley on 3 November 1988 and gained assent the following month.[56]

Distillation of all the awards and regulations under the various Acts ultimately led to the development of only two draft awards covering middle management and paid rates employees (the executive group was covered by individual contracts with separately negotiated salary packages), and these were tabled for discussion with unions on 11 November.[57] The work done along the way, embracing the rationalisation of job classifications and the introduction of multi-skilling, had put ADI in the vanguard of the process of industrial reform which was then underway across Australia.

Acceptance of such a radical outcome was obviously dependent on the co-operation of the ACTU and unions, and required a concerted effort to keep these on-side. A key part of the strategy towards this end was to ensure that all parties concerned were kept informed of what was happening as events unfolded, a sensible precaution to prevent the spread of rumour. A communications plan was devised which entailed the distribution of monthly newsletters and stop-press bulletins when appropriate. Callinan also had a hand in this process:

> In addition to that, each time I met with the unions we put out a one or two-page brief on the outcome, on what points were discussed, etc. These were jointly signed by myself and the ACTU and were in the hands of each facility for distribution to the workforce before lunchtime the next day. This was to ensure that the correct message got to people.[58]

The company's laudable aims in this matter were not universally appreciated. It was here that Harris was given a glimpse of the irritation felt towards his team within areas of Defence:

> In the run-up to ADI's takeover we had an enormous communications problem trying to keep all the plants and twenty-odd unions up-to-date with information. We had people constantly standing beside fax machines feeding paper into them, and I thought that this was a waste of time. I wanted to get one of those fancy broadcast faxes, and asked if I had the necessary authority. I was assured that as a deputy secretary I did, but first I needed to clear it with some first assistant secretary in Defence. When I told this guy what I was going to do, he said, 'No, you will not buy any faxes. I'm in charge of that'. What's more, he decided to conduct a major review of fax requirements throughout the department and, once he'd done that, then he would tell me what I could have. He even wrote me a letter confirming it, which ended with something like,

'You think you can get away and do everything you want without following the department's process'. So obviously we didn't buy the faxes – we leased them instead, which was the same thing.[59]

Explaining what the company wanted to do and what the new awards would mean was never going to be easy. Callinan was given to understand this from a very early stage, when he went to provide a background briefing to the ACTU soon after the ministerial announcement:

That first meeting was very dynamic. The unions turned up for it with anywhere between three to eight representatives from each of our facilities, so there was a hundred-odd people in the room all going for the jugular of myself and John Barclay. It was pretty fiery.[60]

Again it was ACTU officials who played a crucial moderating role in the process that followed. Once the impossibility was acknowledged of having substantive talks between the company and 26 unions, a negotiating committee was formed with about nine instead. Again, to quote Callinan:

Even amongst that group there was a diverse range of views, so it was very important to have someone like Bob Richardson, the ACTU rep, to co-ordinate those views. He is a bit of a reformer and very positive about the need to improve industry and bring about change in respect of performance and conditions. We worked together fairly closely, so ADI had the support of both him and Kelty to do what we wanted. Provided we delivered certain things and gave reasonable assurances, then they came along with us.

Despite such valuable support, the way forward was frequently rocky. Individual unions were alarmed at the prospect of losing particular awards and conditions, to which the company responded with assurances that, in Callinan's words, 'the baby was not going to be thrown out with the bath water':

We told them we were going to create a new situation which would improve their lot rather than damage it, and we gave undertakings about people not losing their fundamental entitlements and conditions of service. That was certainly true in the aggregate sense, but we did muck around with the margins quite substantially.

By no means happy with such changes, the unions took the step of notifying the Conciliation and Arbitration Commission (renamed the Industrial Relations Commission from March 1989) that they were in dispute with ADI. At a formal conference held before the Commission in Melbourne on 25 January 1989,

Commissioner Peter Nolan endorsed the concept of the parties negotiating a package of conditions, and encouraged everyone concerned to reach agreed positions in preference to formal arbitration.[61] Further conferences in the Commission followed, but the outcome on the demarcation-free award still hung in the balance as the date for ADI's takeover in early May neared. As Callinan recalls:

> The unions kept trying to walk away from some of the things that were in the award package. Commissioner Nolan likened the package to a string basket that you took to the shops – full of holes and things kept falling out. That was a pretty apt description. We tried to achieve acceptance by consent, without having arbitration as such imposed, and it was really up to the unions. That was the whole point.

Complicating the issue was a last-minute intervention from the Chamber of Manufacturers, which objected to provisions for the company to buy out 'ratbag conditions' for an additional payment to workers of $10 a week. This was against wage fixing principles, the Chamber argued, and the company did not have the right to reach such an accommodation with the unions. Callinan had earlier found the Department of Industrial Relations similarly opposed to ADI's position, but had steadfastly refused to accept that department's advice despite eight or nine meetings on the matter. To counter this latest attack Callinan brought in the MTIA, Australia's manufacturing, engineering and construction industry association, to lend support for what ADI was doing.

On the eve of the ADI transfer, with a number of issues still outstanding, the award was listed for a final hearing on 3 May. Such was the importance attached to resolving the matter that a national wage case already being heard before a full bench of the Commission was rescheduled. Callinan recounts a chance encounter with one of the commissioners on the night before:

> I was staying at the Travel Inn Motel in Carlton, which a lot of union people used and was very good for gathering intelligence over a beer at the bar. After dinner this night, a few of us were sitting having a drink about 9.30 when this commissioner from Western Australia walked in and plopped himself down at the table with us. He and a commissioner already in the group were both also members of the bench hearing the wage case. He turned to this commissioner and said, 'What's this bloody Aida mob? We're told to adjourn the national wage case for them so we can get this Aida award up and in place. I want to get home to the West.' The other commissioner turned, nudged him in the ribs while pointing to me, and said, 'He's Aida'.

Next day, in the hearing itself, things began to go horribly wrong and it appeared that the whole process might actually collapse. When union representatives started detailing different parts of the award which they still opposed, it became clear that they were aiming to pick and choose over the package's provisions. Callinan, sitting around the packed table before the bench with his back to the commissioners, made clear the unacceptability of this with much shaking of his head.

The president asked to see the union representatives in his chambers, and suddenly found space at a premium as 50–60 people packed in. Recalls Callinan:

> Apparently the talking was pretty rugged even before I was invited in, to be told that the unions wouldn't cop this and wouldn't cop that. So I said, 'OK, its quite simple. If you want to go down that path, we'll let you off. We'll withdraw the whole package and all bets are off'. You see, what we were doing was creating an award for a new industry called the defence support industry, but if that wasn't ratified by the Commission then all the old awards would still stand. I pointed out that the new benefits which had been negotiated wouldn't apply. They hadn't appreciated that was an option available to me, and they were suddenly in a diabolical position. There was deathly silence in the room for probably 30–40 seconds, just stunned amazement. I repeated my position, and then the judge said, 'Gentlemen, he's quite right in what he's saying. He can do that if he likes and you've got no other recourse'. So then we shaved down all the issues to just three that were the real sticking points, and the unions agreed to accept arbitration on those. It was close.

Deeds of transfer

The culmination of the transition process was the preparation of legal deeds which set forth the detail of the assets being transferred to ADI. In addition to listing the individual facilities being sold or leased to the company, the main deeds of transfer provided comprehensive schedules of the buildings, plant, stock on hand, contracts, intellectual property and other items included at each site. Among the sites covered in this way was the company's head office in the Australian Capital Territory. Since arrangements to actually transfer the land had not been completed by the expected takeover date, an additional deed was needed to enable the company to occupy the various facilities on short-term lease.

A key part of the transfer documentation was a letter addressed to Woods as ADI's chairman from the Minister for Defence, as representative of the share-holder/owner (the government), which set out how the company was expected to operate.[62] As well as containing guidelines to directors, which were a modified version of those issued to the boards of ASTA and Qantas, this laid down the basic framework for the transfer. Here was detailed what had been agreed on a whole raft of issues, and the government's expectation of 'a sound commercial customer/supplier relationship' being established between ADI and the Defence department. Fundamental to this was an understanding that it would be 'business as usual' between the two organisations, most tangibly through the negotiation of five-year contracts 'to cover a range of consumables and spares as well as relevant goods and services traditionally supplied by ODP'.

Among the matters addressed in the minister's letter was the transitional funding package provided to ADI, amounting to $275.4 million. Almost half this amount comprised a government commitment to provide the company with a capital contribution of $26.3 million in its first year of operations, with another $103.7 million to follow, phased evenly over the next two financial years.

Another question covered concerned indemnities, since the company could not adequately insure its business against such events as an explosion on board a visiting warship berthed at Garden Island, or at its works at St. Marys or Footscray. The company's liability was accordingly restricted to payment of a million dollars, with the Commonwealth self-insuring against the remaining risk.

A significant matter which was purposely left for future resolution was the issue of the capital structure of the company – essentially the level of debt which ADI should assume in respect of the assets transferred to it. Understandably, the company's position was that to load a new and fragile business with debt was adding unnecessary risk; it therefore argued that the fixed assets it received should be reflected in shareholder equity rather than treated as the company having received a loan to purchase its assets. Finance, though, would not hear of that. Barclay maintains that:

> We kept saying, 'Look, you can't load up the company with fake debt – and that's what it is. You've really got to look at the business and its future ability to borrow'. Finance wanted fake debt because they saw it as guaranteed interest income, and because they didn't trust the Board to give them a dividend otherwise. The business had been losing $300 million a year as an organisation some years earlier, and now suddenly they wanted it to have dividends!. It was unbelievable![63]

As deputy chairman of ADI, Fynmore was also heavily involved in arguments over this issue:

> Various people in the Department of Finance were saying that we needed this much debt, this much capital. But we didn't know whether ADI would be able to repay debt – we didn't even know whether we would ever make a profit – so I argued that we couldn't determine what the capital structure should be. In a meeting with Alan Woods and myself with Dr Michael Keating, the Secretary of Finance at the time, we all agreed – I really don't recall who made the suggestion, or even whether it came from any one person – that the sensible thing

to do was to run the company for twelve months and get a feel for what its capability was as far as payment of debt.[64]

It was on this basis that the capital structure issue was left to be revisited in a year's time. Significantly for the future resolution of this question, it was Fynmore who suggested a possible one-third/two-thirds ratio between debt and equity. This figure was written into the draft letter for the minister's signature, in Barclay's words, as 'a sort of objective agreed for the sake of the transfer'.[65]

Negotiating the fine detail contained in the Deeds of Transfer had been a protracted business, carried out in the main by Barclay and Russell Miller (of Sly & Weigall, solicitors), or occasionally McMahon, for the company. As Barclay recalls, 'Defence would invariably turn up with a football team, to their great cost because they were all representing sectional interests'. [66]

The ministerial letter was itself jointly agreed beforehand and passed through numerous drafts before finalisation. It was drafted in the first instance by Harris, Barclay and Mitchell, with departmental officials taking a hand at the final stages to reduce what they regarded as 'hype' in the document. Some elements in the arrangements were still not completely resolved, even at the eleventh hour. A major problem was caused by a last-minute letter from Finance questioning the means by which the Commonwealth would receive a return from ADI for the use of Garden Island and Salisbury.

With the letter and deeds due to go to the Minister for Defence for signature the next day, the ADI Board was obliged to hold a hurriedly-convened meeting in the company's new offices at Barton to review the situation. That same afternoon the Board flew to Sydney for a summit conference with Beazley and Walsh, which enabled matters to at least proceed. Barclay maintains that, by questioning many of the actions which had been taken up till then and seeking 'to slow the whole thing down and introduce a lot more consultation', Finance had come close to derailing the ADI engine.[67]

With all the delays and complex negotiations involved, progress towards completing the transition process inevitably fell behind the target date. The announcement by Defence Minister Beazley that the company would commence operations 'in March' 1989 had been interpreted by the transition team to mean 1 March. This slipped to 1 April, then 3 April, and finally fell behind another month until 1 May. When 3 May (a Wednesday) was finally set as the new start-up date, wags in the ADI team dubbed this 'March the 63rd'.[68] Even then, it seemed, it might be touch-and-go whether *this* target was met.

On the morning of the great day, there was a last-minute flurry in RFP (Resources, Finance and Plans) Division of the department to correct a typing mistake discovered in one of the documents, before copies of the deeds were rushed across to Parliament House. The signing ceremony took place in a small conference room in the executive area which featured a table made from Monkey

Pod timber, and on its completion glasses of champagne were passed around the room to toast the occasion. With the formalities out of the way, Harris, McMahon, Barclay and Mitchell went for a chinese lunch at the Tang Dynasty restaurant in the nearby Kingston shopping centre. Barclay recounts that the mood of the party was subdued rather than jubilant: 'We all felt a bit flat. It was like sitting your last exam really.'[69]

That afternoon, Beazley introduced into Parliament the Bill to amend the Defence Act to temporarily protect the company from State transfer charges and regulatory laws. Despite enjoying bipartisan support which ensured easy passage through both Houses, it was another month before the Bill gained Royal assent and became law.[70] While celebrations were under way in Canberra on 3 May, in Melbourne Callinan spent the day before the Industrial Relations Commission. Not for another five days could he, too, savour success.[71] The IRC approved the ADI awards with effect from 8 May but ordered that they remain in force for the relatively short period of only six months, in the expectation 'that further changes are to occur'.[72]

6

A NEW BEGINNING

From 4 May 1989, ADI was at last master in its own house. A week later, on 10 May, Beazley announced to parliament that ADI had commenced full operations and publicly hailed the company's take-over of the old ODP as 'one of the most ambitious corporatisation exercises ever undertaken in Australia'.[1] Precisely what was the condition of the ADI structure, and how solid its foundations, was then unknown – indeed, would be essentially unknowable until a decent interval had elapsed.

Development of the company's first financial plan covering 1989/90 had commenced in November 1988. Such were the uncertainties associated with the transition exercise, however, that the financial forecast presented to the Board the following March could only predict a result by June 1990 which lay somewhere between the range of a $10 million profit and a $16 million loss.[2] The company might be – as the defence minister informed his parliamentary colleagues – starting out as the largest single supplier of defence equipment and services in the country, with an annual turnover of $400 million,[3] yet there could be no doubting, as Harris had pointed out to Beazley, that ADI was 'off to a shakey start'.[4] It would be, as the Board appreciated, 'a fragile organisation for some time to come'.[5] Even a year later the company's precarious financial position remained a key preoccupation for Harris, as one manager concerned with this side of the house recalls:

> Ken would come along to my office and ask, 'Have you managed to pinpoint the date that we're going to fall off the cliff yet? When does the till run dry?'.

And I'd say, 'Not yet, we're right for a while' That was the sort of banter that went on.[6]

Nonetheless, at least now the company's future was in the hands of its own management, acting under the direction of its own chief executive. When Sir Brian Inglis, the chairman of ASTA, wrote a fraternal letter to Harris on 28 February 1989 in which he referred to ADI's senior executives as 'generals', he was quickly assured that 'There will be only one general in the Company'.[7] Like any good commander, though, Harris recognised how much he owed to his subordinates and troops. Addressing the managers and headquarters staff by letter on transfer day, he confessed that:

I haven't had much time over the past couple of months to do anything other than concentrate exclusively on the transition to ADI. I have had to let a lot of things slip and the thing I most regret is the lack of communication that was a direct result of the task … I would like to thank all of you for being so patient with us while the transition activity has been underway … Quite frankly, there have been a number of occasions over the past 4 or 5 months when I had serious doubts that the system was capable of producing this result.[8]

In a separate message sent to senior officers on the same day, the managing director also stressed that:

Firstly, until the full Board is appointed, the transition process is complete and key executives are in place I want a 'steady as she goes' mode of operation. No major new initiatives should take place.[9]

Elsewhere Harris stated his intention as being to put the company 'into hibernation for the first three months to give an opportunity for the new senior managers to work out their roles'.[10]

Initial business structure

In planning for ADI, it had been assumed initially that the new organisation would take over all the establishments belonging to ODP – excluding the explosives factories at Albion and Maribyrnong, and a subsidiary storage site at Point Wilson (on the shores of Port Phillip Bay between Melbourne and Geelong), which were to be retained by the Commonwealth or progressively closed down. The number of facilities which remained was large, although some of these were not, strictly speaking, concerned with production.

Elsewhere in Victoria were the ordnance factories at Maribyrnong and Bendigo, the ammunition facility at Footscray and the clothing factory at Coburg (with a small annexe located on the site occupied by the Bendigo ordnance works). There was also an explosives storage area situated at Longlea, 9 kilometres east of Bendigo, and a testing site for small rocket motors at Ravenhall (on Robinsons Road, Deer Park) on Melbourne's western outskirts.[11]

In New South Wales was the small arms factory at Lithgow, the explosives factory at Mulwala on the Murray River west of Albury-Wodonga, and at St. Marys the munitions filling factory. At St. Marys, too, was the Guided Weapons & Electronics Support Facility (GWESF). Also within that State was the naval dockyard at Garden Island, along with six annexes spread around Sydney which operated in conjunction with it. These comprised workshops at Marrickville and North Sydney, a warehouse at Alexandria, a small craft repair and refit facility at Ryde, a technical school for training apprentices at Roseberry, and offices located in the Remington Centre.

At Salisbury, South Australia, was the Production Development Support Facility, representing the result of several years' involvement by ODP in development work on Project Nulka, a ship-launched electronic decoy system. Established in 1987–88, in conjunction with the Defence Science and Technology Organisation also located at Salisbury, this facility undertook the filling and assembly of cast composite rocket motors used as the propulsion unit for Nulka. As the successor to ODP, ADI was, naturally, interested in gaining the business generated by the Nulka project and hence agreed to take over this facility and its staff of more than 30, mostly engineers and technical officers.[12]

As a result of negotiations during the transition phase, the number of sites which would actually be transferred to ADI ownership was reduced considerably. As previously mentioned (see chapter 5), it was decided that Garden Island and Salisbury would only be leased, while Longlea was left in Commonwealth hands. Mulwala was among the properties originally transferred, but as soon as the cost of taking its assets and land onto the company books was realised arrangements were put in place to sell these back to the Defence Department and a lease substituted instead. Of the dockyard annexes only those at Roseberry and Ryde were actually owned by the Defence Department while the rest operated under leasehold arrangements; the leases on the latter properties were therefore either assigned or sub-let to the company.

Regardless of the means by which various sites were passed to ADI, the new management faced a considerable challenge in bringing unified control to such a disparate conglomeration. This was a problem which, understandably, had been addressed prior to the actual transfer, as Harris explains:

I wasn't going to try and run a joint that had all these facilities or factories, each doing their own thing. Do we have any businesses here? That was the question. When we looked at it, we decided there were four. So we specifically dropped the term 'factory' and spoke about 'businesses' instead.[13]

The distinct business units – or 'divisions' as they became known – which had been identified were: Naval Engineering, made up of Garden Island and annexes, along with the GWESF at St. Marys; Ammunition & Missiles, combining the facilities at St. Marys, Footscray, Mulwala and Salisbury; Weapons & Engineering, grouping the ordnance and small arms facilities at Maribyrnong, Bendigo and Lithgow; and Military Clothing, comprising the Coburg facility and its Bendigo annexe. Each division would have a headquarters based in either Sydney or Melbourne. Of these divisions, Naval Engineering and Ammunition & Missiles would be the largest, generating approximately 37 and 35 per cent of the company's business respectively; Weapons & Engineering would manage about 20 per cent, while Military Clothing was expected to account for 8 per cent.[14]

In an effort to get away from the perception of the former factories as separate and independent enterprises, Harris also instructed the adoption of a standard company logo in place of the separate crests and other corporate badges previously used. The new symbol was triangular in shape to represent the letter A in Australian, enclosing two concentric circles (representing a target to suggest the military-defence nature of the company's products) split by vertical and horizontal cross-hairs (suggesting precision and quality).[15]

To ensure that the significance of the change which had come about was fully understood, there was great insistence on every part of the company using the new logo without variation. The only exception allowed to this rule was in the matter of colour-coding; while the corporate headquarters used red, each division was allocated a separate colour.[16] Even this concession was quickly rethought. By late 1989 Harris conceded he had made a mistake in allowing it, declaring that:

> It has become apparent to me at trade shows that the use of different colours merely confuses customers and is acting to continue some of the barriers that still stand in the way of a genuine cross-divisional corporate approach.[17]

Having decided on the new company structure, the next hurdle to be faced was the recruitment of suitable executives to run each operating division. In addition to these officers, to be titled Chief General Managers, were others required to manage the key functions which would be handled within the corporate headquarters. Here it was planned to have Group General Managers controlling finance, marketing, development and defence liaison.[18]

In finding candidates for these senior appointments Harris looked to both former ODP executives and outside applicants, selecting roughly half-and-half between these sources. Rear-Admiral Berlyn, who had by now left the Navy, was appointed to take on Naval Engineering, and was the only CGM announced at the time of the transfer. By August, however, the remaining CGMs had been chosen also. Control of Weapons & Engineering was vested in Graeme Phipps, who had wide experience in British engineering firms and previously worked in Australia with the Comeng company before becoming general manager of Boral Windows Ltd. Bryan Padman, formerly the managing director of roof tile operations for Monier Ltd., was appointed to head Ammunition & Missiles, while Brian Lanigan, already the general manager of the Coburg factory, was picked to run Military Clothing.[19]

When it came to filling headquarters positions, the choice understandably settled on some who already had an intimate association with the company's fortunes, with Barclay appointed as GGM Development and McMahon as GGM Defence Liaison.[20] Les Massey, formerly General Manager Treasury with Bell Resources, was chosen as GGM Finance,[21] but no appointment was immediately made for the marketing position.

One of those involved at this level offers an observation about the process at work here, remarking that:

> The policy adopted from the very beginning was to get the executive team right, and to get the culture of that team right. It was a simple and effective approach to say, 'Well, we'll have half the people from the old organisation so we've got the corporate memory, and half brand-new whiz-bang killer-types with Masters of Business Administration degrees. Put them together, and we'll have got a very good team'.

> Interestingly enough, because there were constraints on salary packages, we couldn't go out and buy killer MBAs like the merchant banks. The sort we were able to attract, though, were older people who weren't concerned about having the killer instinct but were very experienced and qualified. They were a certain type, just as good as anybody else, but it was the fact that we were able to offer them an interesting challenge which attracted these people more than the salaries.[22]

Also joining corporate headquarters from outside the old ODP was the person filling the important post of Company Secretary. In July 1989 the first holder of this office, Brian Conway, resigned to take up another position within the company. In his place was appointed Dr John McCorquodale, who had been involved in providing advice during the transition period in his capacity with the Attorney-General's Department. He recalled that his recruitment to ADI was Harris' idea:

> We were walking away from a meeting with Beazley sometime about the previous February, where I had been explaining the necessity for the series of documents which the Minister would have to sign. Ken began musing on the sort

of position needed for a legal officer within the company, and an appropriate title I suggested 'Corporate Secretary/Legal Counsel', and said that, based on my knowledge of Britain and elsewhere, this was a common practice.

He jokingly proposed that I should consider taking up such a position with ADI, at which I said, 'Well, make me an offer I can't refuse'. Some time later such an offer was made and I decided to accept it. Since the transfer of assets had still to take place at that stage, I immediately transferred the handling of all matters concerning the company to another officer in a different branch of my division, to avoid any conflict of interest arising.[23]

Although Conway had resigned as company secretary, he was still required to assist in that capacity until he submitted a second resignation with effect from 15 October 1990. Mrs Patricia Russell was appointed in his place as additional company secretary to McCorquodale. An ex-ODP member, she had worked in that office's executive co-ordination unit and since joining ADI had been working on building the company's corporate identity.[24]

The ADI board

A key element in the scheme for effectively reforming the former defence facilities had been the hope of bringing their operations under the influence of sound commercial knowledge and skills. An ADI spokesman later declared that it was 'deliberate policy to establish a strong Board and [an] equally strong management team significantly different' to that of ODP.[25] From the beginning Harris had accepted the importance of having the company controlled by 'a group of independent people who were willing to spit the dummy' if their advice was ignored: Ultimately they might have to say to the government, 'Look, this isn't going to work, and we don't want to be involved in it'. Because that then puts pressure on the government to listen to these people, to accept that they're commercially experienced and know what they're doing.[26]

During the period before May 1989, action had been taken to place the interim ADI board onto a permanent basis. In February, Woods' initial six-month term as chairman was extended, while Harris was reappointed for the duration of his employment contract; the latter also announced his resignation as a director of ASTA.[27] In April, with the transfer less than a month away, Defence Minister Beazley wrote to Woods asking him to stay on, saying:

A major part of the reason for my confidence [in the long-term future of ADI] is the fact that you have been prepared to act as Chairman of the Board during the lead-up to the formal takeover … I know that you accepted the job on an interim basis only but I would regard it as a significant advantage to the

Company if you would consider extending your appointment as chairman into the next stage of development.

At the same time, the minister similarly invited Fynmore to accept reappointment as deputy chairman for up to five years.[28]

Consideration was now also given to expanding the board to a more workable size through the appointment of additional directors. In his letters to Woods and Fynmore, Beazley had emphasised the importance he attached to ADI having a 'commercially experienced' board 'with the right blend of skills'. As Fynmore recalls:

> Assembling the board was really a case of – without putting too fine a point on it – Alan and me sitting down and coming up with names. He already had Major-General Derek Deighton in mind, and also Elizabeth Bryan. We wanted an engineer so I suggested Malcolm Kinnaird.[29]

The first two of these new directors were appointed for five-year terms commencing on 6 June and took their seats at the board's monthly meeting on 27 July. General Deighton, aged 58, had retired in November 1987 as chief of the Army's Logistics Command. His 39 years' experience as a military logistician had brought him to Woods' attention during the latter's time as Defence secretary, and as well he carried the personal recommendation of the Chief of the Defence Force, General Peter Gration, a fellow graduate of the 1952 class from the Royal Military College, Duntroon.[30] Kinnaird, aged 55, was the chairman and chief executive of Kinhill Engineers Pty. Ltd.

Elizabeth Bryan was appointed for a similar period from 15 June but did not attend her first meeting until 1 September. She had become known to Woods through the Australian Industry Development Corporation (AIDC), where she was the 43-year-old general manager of the Development Investment Division and Woods held a seat on the Board. She recalls:

> When he asked me to take on ADI I was a little bit hesitant about the industry, thinking that arms manufacturing probably wasn't my strong suit really, but he was quite persistent. There was considerable fuss inside AIDC over me, as a woman, being appointed to this directorship. It created a bit of jealousy maybe, and I think other names were put forward. So it was a long haul for me to be given permission to take it up and I doubt that if Alan hadn't been on our Board it would have got through.[31]

The possibility of still further appointments to the board arose from a request by the Minister for Defence that a union representative be considered. The board adopted this advice, deciding to approach Garry Weaven, the assistant secretary of the ACTU, to seek the nomination of 'some suitable candidates for consideration' and inviting Weaven himself 'to consider the position'.[32] While the intention to investigate this possibility of appointing a union representative was carried through, and discussions with Weaven subsequently held, the board was later moved to make a mild assertion of independence over this issue, resolving that:

> If the ACTU could nominate only one person the Board would not oppose the appointment. However, the Board requested the Managing Director to suggest to the Minister that the primary basis for Board appointments should be ability to contribute. Eventually joining the board for a five-year term from 25 January was Iain Ross, the ACTU's 30-year-old Scottish-born legal officer, who attended his first meeting in February.[33]

Tragically, at this point the company also suffered the untimely loss of its founding chairman, Alan Woods, who died on 13 January 1990, aged 59, after a brief battle with cancer.[34] First diagnosed with his illness in May, just as ADI had finally come into being, he had begun receiving treatment in Canberra over succeeding months. He was already a very sick man by the time the ceremony was held on the morning of 27 July at which Beazley formally opened the company's offices at Barton. His wife, Anne, recounts that:

> That same afternoon I drove him to Sydney for an appointment at the oncology department of Royal North Shore Hospital. The weather was terrible, pitch black and pouring with rain by the time we arrived. Alan underwent radical surgery there, from which he was able to recover for some time. Having gone into remission, he was able to continue in the ADI job until about November, when he picked up an infection and had to give it away.[35]

According to Harris, the plan had always been that Woods would give the company guidance for five years, by which time Fynmore would be ready to retire from BHP and thus available to move into the chairman's job.[36] Sadly, this succession came about sooner than anyone wished. During the board meeting in February, it was announced that Fynmore had been appointed by the minister as the new chairman.[37] While continuing to fulfil his primary obligations to BHP until 1992, Fynmore proved a strong figure and formidable advocate at the company's helm.

Strangely, the new chairman's authority derived from the very fact that he had important commitments outside of ADI. As he expressed the situation:

> The fact was I didn't need the job as ADI's chairman; I was doing it as a public service. At first I thought, 'Well, if I can't do it my way, I can always resign'. I could drop the director's fees I get from ADI and it wouldn't make one iota of difference to my lifestyle or anything else.

The more you get involved, though, you realise that whilst you have the luxury of being able to walk away, very few of the company's staff have that option. You need to curb your enthusiasm for using the resignation threat for those issues where it is really right to do that.

So I have never as yet threatened to resign on an issue – that is, to the Minister. Ken Harris would have heard me say it on occasion, and I suspect that sometimes he has used that to advantage in negotiating with other people. Obviously it is one of those things you can't use too often, but clearly it is the ultimate decision for the chairman of a government corporation to make clear that he won't support a course being forced on him.[38]

Also at the board's February session the question was considered of a number of possible additional directors, according to 'their capacity to contribute particularly to strategic planning and marketing'. This issue continued to feature at board discussions, most notably during the next meeting. In this regard members felt that 'a valuable addition would be someone with current practicing accountancy qualifications who could also act as Chairman of an Audit Committee'. It was agreed that, until the board was fully constituted, all present directors should act as the audit committee. Once the board's composition was finally settled, though, 'it [the audit committee] should comprise three members (one with accountancy qualifications, one with a legal background, and one other)'.[39]

The view still prevailed that any additional director should also be someone with senior-level planning experience 'who could provide inputs to the strategic direction of the Company in making informed judgements'. Both requirements were duly met with the appointment of 57-year-old Kevin Fellew for five years from 20 April 1990. A senior partner and National Industry Director for Government Services in the commercial advisory and accounting firm Deloitte Ross Tohmatsu, he brought to ADI extensive experience gained in manufacturing and engineering companies. ADI now proudly claimed to have 'one of the most commercially experienced Boards of any company in manufacturing industry in Australia'.[40] At the board's subsequent meeting in May, Fellew was made chairman of the audit committee, with Bryan and Ross as its other members.[41]

The question of board appointments arose again following the death in Melbourne of General Deighton on 16 April 1991.[42] Discovered to have an inoperable cerebral tumour four months earlier, he had continued his involvement with ADI until the month before he died.[43] At its meeting three days later, the Board paid tribute to the general's contribution to maintaining and enhancing the company's harmonious relations with the ADF. When it came to considering a replacement, however, the meeting drew a link between this and other outstanding issues requiring resolution. Arguing that it was inappropriate to make any recommendations at that time, any appointment of new directors was deferred.[44]

The board's stance was maintained at the following meeting in May, with members deciding to make no approaches to prospective appointees until the question of the company's capital structure had been cleared up (see later in this chapter). It was not until July that the board accepted a proposal from Beazley's successor as defence minister, Senator Robert Ray, to appoint Steven Harker (a 36-year-old executive director of the investment bank Barclays de Zoete Wedd Australia) for a five-year term, enabling him to attend his first meeting the next month.[45] Even so, debate over the company's capital structure dragged on for some months yet.

Another addition to the board was made on 25 February 1992 with the appointment of Anthony Bowra, the former Executive Director of Manufacturing and Development with IBM Australia. He had held senior management positions with IBM in the United States and Japan, and was a director of IBM Australia from 1979 until his retirement from that company in 1992 at age 55.[46]

Further changes occurred early in 1993, with the resignation of Ross on 7 January, and the appointment next month of Arthur Apted as his successor from the ACTU. With a background as an industrial officer working in superannuation and financial service matters, the 37-year-old Apted admits that he had little idea of what he had let himself in for, or the slow and subtle process of education on which he was embarking:

I discovered that there wasn't a great liking of unions among members of the ADI board, and it was quite a shock initially. I actually rang up the Minister's office after attending my first board meeting and said 'Who are these people?'. The thing that surprised me most was the attitude that although the government owned the company, government was stupid and had to be kept out of it.

Over time I came to understand where they were coming from with some of these attitudes, because – there is no doubt about it – government is very slow and operates in a very complex environment. People with a private sector background found, I am sure, the processes of government and dealing with government all very mystifying and difficult.

So far as the board's attitude to unions was concerned I found that my ACTU background and experience was a useful thing for ADI, because on a number of industrial matters I was able to inject some notes of realism and encourage a different route to that which the company might otherwise have taken. I also discovered that when push came to shove there was always accommodation; in reality the company's bark was definitely worse than its bite.[47]

Later that same year, in July, Bowra was appointed Deputy Chairman of the ADI

Board. This position which had not been formally filled since Fynmore moved up to become chairman more than two years earlier.[48]

Judged against the company's publicly-stated object of building a high calibre board, it could fairly be said that ADI had achieved this aim. Blending long experience and business competence with youthful vigour, ADI's board could even be regarded as forward-thinking in shedding old gender stereotypes – something still relatively rare in Australia, despite corporate protestations to the contrary. The proof of the Board's determination to face the challenge with which it was presented would be shown by the results produced.

Issues to be resolved

In his parliamentary statement announcing ADI's takeover of ODP, Defence Minister Beazley had declared that the company's advent represented 'a further significant step away from the bureaucracy and politics that have bedevilled these defence establishments for so many years'.[49] While undoubtedly a belief sincerely held, and an outcome most definitely sought, at this stage it was little more than a pious wish. Important matters were outstanding, even after the formal transfer date, which inevitably made it impossible for the company to become divorced from difficult dealings with a range of government departments and agencies.

During the months which followed the minister's initial announcement of August 1988, the transition team had found itself caught up in a series of battles regarding employees' conditions – especially superannuation and workers' compensation – and whether or not the new company should be free to make commercial arrangements for such services as auditing. The problem concerning superannuation arose from the board's desire to establish its own fund for employees, rather than maintain their coverage under the Commonwealth Superannuation Scheme (CSS) for public servants. This was a concern not just to existing employees, but for prospective new personnel which the company was, even then, attempting to attract to advertised positions.

The principal issue here was, from the company's perspective, a simple one of the cost difference between private sector schemes and the CSS, since the former operated on a capital accumulation basis whereas the government scheme was basically an unfunded pension related to the salary level of a retiring employee. The problem ADI had was the surcharge of 19–24 per cent on its salaries bill that the CSS entailed, which – compared with the cost of 8–10 per cent borne by other firms – affected the company's competitive performance. While all ODP 'white collar' workers were currently in the government scheme, only about 10 per cent of 'blue collar' workers had this cover. As a result of the negotiations then taking place over the new industrial award, ADI was in no doubt that union pressure would be applied for the benefit to be extended to everyone, resulting in a large

Influx of new contributors to the CSS which would greatly increase the cost burden facing the company.[50] The position taken, therefore, was that no new employees should be eligible to join the CSS and that personnel who transferred to the company should cease contributing to that scheme. The principle behind the latter requirement was simply, as Harris later explained, that if 'people wanted private sector salaries they couldn't expect government superannuation'.[51]

In explaining the objective behind ADI's proposal to Finance Minister Walsh in February 1989, the company chairman (Woods) emphasised that it was imperative for the new organisation to mirror efficient manufacturing firms in its cost structure and mode of operation. Superannuation, he said, 'affects our competitive ability in two ways':

> First, the Commonwealth Superannuation Scheme is quite expensive to the employer and represents an additional element in our costs that our competitors do not have to bear. Secondly, our ability to attract good staff is strongly influenced by the superannuation arrangements that we can offer them. It is for these reasons that the Board believes that it is appropriate for the Government to allow ADI to establish a company superannuation scheme in line with that available in the manufacturing sector.[52]

Responding to this approach at the end of the same month, Senator Walsh said that he had no objections to personalised superannuation for senior executives on fixed-term contracts of less than five years, but he was 'much more concerned' about proposals to take other employees outside the CSS. While some GBEs – Australia Post, Telecom and OTC – had been authorised in May 1988 to have their own schemes, this approval was still subject to guidelines which were to be drawn up in the course of a review of the CSS then under way:

> In effect, the test for the establishment of a separate scheme is now that the authority must be in at least as competitive position as Australia Post and Telecom and would face similar penalties because of the costs of the CSS.

> … I am extremely reluctant even to consider ADI making its own superannuation arrangements in advance of Government decisions on the Review … In any event, in order to make a decision on any ADI proposal, I shall need to be informed in some detail of ADI's operating environment … [53]

In a letter to Beazley early the next month, Woods appealed for support in pressing the case with Finance. Stressing that the company faced stiff competition as a result of the government's policy of turning ODP into an arms-length, unsubsidised contractor, he noted that 'ADI's competitive position is not good':

Ken Harris and I met the chairman and executives of Transfield two weeks ago. This company is emerging as ADI's major competitor in the ship maintenance business. It was clear from our discussions that Transfield's costs are significantly below ours. ADI will never meet the competition while burdened with non-commercial arrangements such as Commonwealth Superannuation. Not only will the continuation of the present arrangements remove another opportunity for us to cut costs but, perversely, will add significantly to our costs.[54]

Discussions between Beazley and Walsh in April led to an agreement that, to avoid damaging the company's recruitment efforts, it could be stated that Finance had agreed 'in principle' to ADI establishing its own superannuation arrangements. When confirming this in writing, however, Walsh was at pains to point out that:

My approval is still required to any specific scheme that is negotiated between ADI and employee representatives. The parties should be advised that I will not be in a position to consider any specific proposal until the Government has completed its current review of the Commonwealth Superannuation Scheme. The Minister concluded with a reminder that in May he would be bringing to Cabinet guidelines for GBEs which were already authorised to have their own schemes, and 'I would not wish to prejudge before then whether ADI should be subject to these guidelines or to more formal control arrangements'.[55]

When, in June, the company formally outlined to Walsh its proposed superannuation arrangements, Finance responded the following month by forwarding a copy of the recently-finalised guidelines to apply to GBEs which were authorised to establish separate schemes. The Minister for Defence was invited to put his views on the matter in due course:

In the meantime, consistent with the spirit of the guidelines approach, you may wish to institute a process of rigorous self-assessment of your proposals against the guidelines ... I note in passing that you are proposing enhanced benefits for senior staff which would not comply with the consistency guideline and which I would not normally be prepared to approve.[56]

Eventually, the company got its way in this matter, and was enabled to set up its own scheme, the ADI Superannuation Fund, from 1 June 1990. The outcome was not everything that it might have wished, however, as it actually found itself contributing to two other funds as well – including the CSS – on behalf of its employees.[57] However, as the residual members of the government scheme were few in number and located in the lower paid category, the issue was not a major one for the company.

Much the same issue of costs lay at the core of the board's handling of the legal obligation to provide its workers with insurance cover for work-related accidents and injuries. As Harris saw it, workers' compensation had come to be viewed by many ODP employees 'as a form of income supplementation' and he was highly critical of the arrangements the new company would be inheriting in this regard. As part of the drive to reduce ADI's operating costs, in December 1988 the Board decided to seek competitive quotations from a number of private insurers as well as the Commonwealth's own agency, Comcare, in an effort 'to better understand the options available'.[58]

In discussions with the ACTU negotiating team over the new industrial awards the company was seeking, it became clear that nothing less than retention of the present level of compensation benefits would be acceptable to trade unions. The company accordingly acceded on the point, even though there was 'little doubt that this agreement places us at a disadvantage to our competitors'.[59] The only option to obtaining a suitably attractive bid from those insurers invited to tender for ADI's business was for the company to become a self-insurer under the terms of the Commonwealth Employees Rehabilitation and Compensation Act, as two other GBEs (Australia Post and Telecom) had been allowed to do on a two-year trial basis.

When word got back to Comcare in April that ADI was contemplating the latter course, the chief executive officer of that organisation, Sandra Halley, wrote to Harris in an attempt to dissuade him. The record of ODP establishments with regard to accident prevention and management practices was extremely poor, she noted, and in these circumstances Comcare 'would be advising our Minister that any move by your organisation to seek self-administrator status be deferred until the end of the pilot self-determination exercise with Telecom and Australia Post'. After additionally pointing out the financial and administrative implications for ADI, the letter ended with the assurance that:

> Comcare's price is competitive and Comcare's service is professional and comprehensive … I believe that it would be in the best interests of ADI and its employees for the self-administration proposal to be at least deferred and that Comcare be allowed to continue to manage ADI's workers' compensation claims.[60]

With just a few days to go before formal transfer, Harris wrote to advise Halley that ADI would insure with Comcare at least until late the following year – by which time it was expected that the experiment being conducted with Australia Post and Telecom would have been completed and evaluated. Then ADI would be seeking to establish itself as a self-insurer. As Harris' letter made clear, there was no suggestion of a company back-down over this issue:

> This result has occurred not because of our choosing but because, in the end,

we really had no choice. You need to understand that, even adjusting the quotes from private insurers to meet the Commonwealth's level of benefits, your premium is about $2.55m higher than it should be …

It also needs to be said that Comcare was rated at the very bottom of the scale as far as performance was concerned … From our perception, and after reviewing the proposals from the private insurers and yourself, Comcare has yet to establish its credibility as a good performer. The fact that my Company also has a long way to go in this area heightens my concern.[61]

To emphasise ADI's dissatisfaction with the course it had felt obliged to pursue, Harris also wrote to the Minister for Industrial Relations, Peter Morris, the same day. Again he did not mince words in expressing the concerns he had, declaring that the government's determination to open up more of ADI's area of business to competition meant that the company was finding its contract bids were too high and likely to cost jobs. He therefore gave notice to the minister that, following the pilot program involving Australia Post and Telecom, ADI would be making a further submission to argue the case for being allowed to run its own workers' compensation program.[62]

After an unexplained delay of nearly four months, Morris eventually responded by lamely professing faith that Comcare was 'well on the way to providing … a competitive compensation system based on efficient claims administration and the dissemination of effective rehabilitation and prevention strategies':

I hope that by working closely with Comcare over the next 18 months or so, Comcare will establish itself as your preferred long term option by providing a level of service to ADI which will lead to major reductions in injuries and workers' compensation costs.[63]

Ultimately, the company had the satisfaction of achieving its objective of becoming a self-insurer.

By comparison with both the above issues, the dispute which developed over the board's insistence on the right to retain auditors of its own choosing became a far more protracted and bruising affair. As already recounted, at the outset of the process of establishing a company structure, the Arthur Young firm of chartered accountants was appointed in August 1988 to provide audit services for ADI, as well as tax and financial advice. This was for an initial six-month period, until long-term arrangements were settled, reflecting a requirement of the Companies Act for an auditor to be appointed within four weeks of incorporation. Although the Commonwealth Auditor-General got in touch at this time to explain what was entailed to appoint his office to fill this role, the fact was, as Harris later told the Secretary of Defence, that:

The procedure is so cumbersome that it would not have been possible [to] appoint the Auditor General within the statutory period. The appointment of Arthur Young and Company was done within a day.[64]

Having spurned the bid from the Australian Audit Office (AAO), Harris and his team found themselves the targets of considerable pressure to reverse this stance. Representations to the Defence department during October 1988 made clear the view of the Auditor-General, John Taylor, that his office had an automatic right to the business of GBEs. Harris did not agree, and approached six firms to submit proposals that would meet ADI's requirements for internal and external audit services, as well as advice on taxation and general financial management. The AAO was also invited to make a proposal but declined.

In February 1989 the board resolved to formally recommend to its shareholder, the government, that Arthur Young be confirmed as ADI's auditors.[65] Writing to explain the basis for this choice to Defence Minister Beazley the same day, the company chairman described the valuable role which 'the right audit firm' could play in guiding the development of a new enterprise:

This appointment will give the Company access to one of the top commercial firms in Australia … The awarding of the contract for external audit will mean that the firm will be able to provide invaluable support to assist … our Company. It is impossible to over-emphasise the significant lack of commercial experience within ADI and the great reliance that we will have to place on the appointed firm.[66]

Of course, Woods said, the board was well aware of the Auditor-General's views, and despite the absence of a proposal from that party it was still possible to compare the performance of the AAO with Arthur Young:

Frankly, the Auditor General is not in the same league as far as commercial expertise is concerned. This is not meant to be a criticism of a fine organisation but is simply a fact of life that the Auditor General does not have the experience that would enable him to be a serious contender for auditing the accounts of this Company. Needless to say the Auditor General has little, if any, expertise that would enable him to use any knowledge he gains of our affairs to guide and assist the Company in establishing a commercially acceptable structure. An additional major factor was the matter of fees. While the AAO had declined to name a price for its services, based on past charges for services to ODP this was expected to be in the order of $1.5 million – three times the amount negotiated by the preferred firm.

Harris also later recounted that one of the issues discussed privately and somewhat tentatively at the time concerned the future possibility of privatisation. In his words:

> [If] we could get the Company in sufficiently good shape to be privatised, the purchaser of the Company would probably place little store in the accounts unless they were signed off by one of the big private audit firms. At the time, of course, there were varying degrees of confidence, or perhaps lack of confidence, around the board table about possible privatisation but, nevertheless, we saw this as an issue in our insistence on a private sector auditor.
>
> The practice followed by other GBEs was for the audit office to be the auditor and sub-contract the work to a private sector auditor, hence the signature on the accounts was that of the Australian National Audit Office. Why was our argument for having the private sector carry out the audit and report to the board and hence sign the accounts along with the audit office such a big issue for the government machine? Rice bowls?[67]

Beazley was willing to lend his support to the Board's stand, declaring that he found 'the arguments advanced for … a commercial audit firm compelling'. Addressing this issue in a letter to Senator Walsh, he said that the main goal behind the government's reform of GBEs was 'the quest for efficiency and cost minimisation through the pressure of competition':

> In this situation I believe it is appropriate for ADI to look for the most cost-effective service providers. The real question in this debate is why the providers of services to government business enterprises should be given monopoly positions and made immune from competition themselves.[68]

The Minister for Finance was not persuaded, and countered that, to protect the Commonwealth's financial interests, it was more appropriate for ADI to take the Auditor-General's services. A very close relationship between the Commonwealth and ADI would remain for a long time, with Defence continuing to be the company's main customer and making further large payments for things such as DRSC (defence required support capability). The AAO would, moreover, be involved also in the closure of ODP trust accounts.[69]

Even within Defence there were those who disagreed with the handling of this issue by ADI's management. Among the critics was Woodward, who was watching events with a discerning eye from his position as Head of Defence Logistics. Dismissing the notion that competition was the key element in such matters, the personal view he expressed to the Secretary of Defence was that, of course, the Auditor-General ought to audit a government-owned company:

> The more fundamental issue is whether the Parliament should expect, through

the Auditor-General, reports on a company established with considerable Commonwealth funds and continuing to draw heavily (at least for a period) on Commonwealth funds. At a more pragmatic level I question why such an issue would have been allowed to develop such a 'head of steam' with the very agency (Finance) which will be critical to ADI's survival – surely there are more important battles to fight. If ADI were to have private equity I would, of course, be more sympathetic to the ADI position.[70]

There was, in any event, little prospect of the Auditor-General taking ADI's course lying down. During January Taylor had written to the Prime Minister on the subject of several GBEs (ADI among them) who were threatening to slip the AAO's net.[71] Hawke duly wrote to Beazley on the question, warning that for such a bold step as the transformation of ADI entailed it would be counterproductive for the company to alienate 'groups which can affect its future'. He urged the need for further consultation on 'establishment matters':

> Without commenting on the merits or otherwise of such a proposal, I am unaware of any Cabinet agreement for ADI to appoint an auditor of its choice. Because of the Parliamentary responsibilities of the auditor, and in the interests of ensuring continuing public sector accountability … I believe any proposal for the ADI to appoint a private auditor should be handled in a manner consistent with the GBE reform process.[72]

At a meeting with officials on 6 April 1989 the ministers for Defence and Finance decided that the Auditor-General would carry out the annual external audit requirement for ADI on a shared basis with Arthur Young, though without ADI being required to bear the AAO's costs for this service (which would be met by Defence). As Beazley recounted to the Prime Minister, he was aware of the feeling of board members that, 'as they would be personally liable under the Companies Act for their actions as directors, their views on an external auditor should be given weight':

> On the other hand, the Minister for Finance and myself could see the case for a role for the Auditor General, particularly in the early stages of the life of the Company.[73]

The two ministers therefore agreed that, once ADI had established itself more fully as a commercially-viable operation, it might then be decided to dispense with joint audit provisions.[74]

This agreement went a long way towards defusing the difficult situation which had developed between ADI and the Australian Audit Office, and allowed for the two organisations to get on with the essential task at hand. There was, however, no pretence that the fundamental differences between them had been resolved. Giving evidence to the Senate Standing Committee on Finance and Public Administration, Harris could not resist taking a swipe at the AAO by expounding on a theme of whether that organisation was 'necessarily the best organisation to provide the most cost effective commercial auditing services':

> If I might say so, there appears to be a dangerous philosophy developing in this country that the Australian Audit Office is to be placed above criticism and protected from the normal commercial pressures applying to other commercial enterprises.[75]

In August, after the AAO delivered a damning report on the financial records and accounting practices at Garden Island, Harris took the trouble to write to Beazley pointing out that these findings related to 1987/88, which was a period before the dockyard became part of ADI. It would be, he said, quite wrong 'to infer that ADI could be responsible':

> The combination of many years of Government management and Government auditing almost brought that organisation to its knees and the Auditor General must share the responsibility for that state of affairs. A private audit firm would have rolled up its sleeves and helped solve the problems but the Australian Audit Office either through inexperience or a peculiar sense of independence, has always been more interested in finding problems than in solving them. Describing the important changes which ADI had put in train since it had been in charge, he added that: 'It must be said that the Australian Audit Office's role … is negligible. The office's main concern appears to be with classical [sic] empire building activities.'[76]

The board was certainly not happy with the joint audit arrangement either, a point made at its meeting in October. After hearing presentations from the Audit Office and the firm it preferred (now under the name Ernst & Young), it approved the internal audit plan which concerned solely the latter but 'noted, rather than approved' the external audit plan. Whether there should be a joint audit conducted of all the company facilities was left for later consideration.[77]

The dispute over the freedom of the company to make its own choice of auditors pointed to a more thorny issue as to whether directors on the ADI board had any genuine independence or would always be expected to accept the dictates of the company's owner in such matters. Clearly the latter's point of view could not be disregarded, especially since the question of accountability was closely intertwined in such instances. The board had acted in the only way open to it, in continuing to press the owner to modify its position to satisfy the board's concerns.

If nothing else, the conflict on the audit question had served to heighten sensitivity within ADI to the matter of accountability. This focused specifically on the strong legal requirements imposed under the Corporations Law, rather than the more general notion of accountability for a company which had the government as its owner on behalf of the Australian public and taxpayer (since this was perceived as being really a political issue). Concern on this score had been expressed in the Senate at the time of the transfer, during debate over the Defence Legislation Amendment Bill, when the Opposition spokeswoman on defence matters referred to the 'problem of scrutiny of the company … [as] a government instrumentality'.[78]

At a meeting on 3 October 1989 the board resolved to change ADI's status from an exempt proprietary company to a fully fledged limited liability company.[79] The point of making this recommendation was because, as a limited liability company, the reporting obligations required by the Companies Act were significantly higher. The board already accepted the heavier obligations, having told the defence minister in February that it would be reporting to him as though ADI was a listed public company:

> This will place on us the highest commercial reporting standards which the Parliament has deemed to be necessary for the protection of shareholders in those companies. The Board believes that the acceptance of this high reporting obligation by us will provide you as the shareholder with sufficient information to understand how the business is being conducted.[80]

Even before receiving a suggestion by the Senate Standing Committee on Finance and Public Administration, however, the board had considered that 'there is some sense in making the reporting obligation a legal requirement rather than a voluntary obligation'.[81]

After obtaining the minister's approval, the directors called a special general meeting to immediately follow the annual general meeting on 7 December. This was to consider the board's recommendation on the question of the company's status. The proposal was duly adopted with effect from 1 July 1990, which meant that the company's name would then formally become 'Australian Defence Industries Limited'.[82] Delaying the change until the next financial year would simply provide time for stocks of stationery and business cards to be run down. In promulgating the new name around the company, Harris also took the opportunity to urge greater use of the shorter form 'ADI':

> I have been very surprised at the speed with which the acronym ADI has been picked up both in Australia and overseas. Just as many other companies have moved away from their full name to an acronym it was always my intention to make this move two or three years down the track. Perhaps the defence business is more used to acronyms than other businesses and as from July next year

we will start to emphasise in our letterheads, business cards, brochures etc the acronym ADI instead of the full name.[83]

Six months after the company's takeover of ODP assets, the issue which nearly scuttled the transition process at the last moment abruptly resurfaced. The question of the lease fees to be paid by ADI on Garden Island and Salisbury had not been settled at the time of transfer, and the level of these rents had still to be finalised. During negotiations with the Australian Property Group (APG), the company tried to push the view that consideration of this matter should be deferred until the end of the company's first year of operations, arguing that it must be considered in the context of the rate of return to the shareholder which was set as the company's target.

In November the head of the Defence & Government Division in the Department of Finance, Eric Thorn, expressed disagreement with ADI's interpretation of how the matter should be handled. Finance's understanding of what had been agreed in May was that the company 'was to be given opportunity to initiate the process of setting the fees by putting forward its own proposals to the Department of Defence':

However, as ADI has declined to proceed on this basis I believe that APG should now provide advice to Defence and Finance on what it considers to be appropriate lease fees reflecting the nature of the current business conducted at the sites. I understand that preparatory work … is still proceeding but I do not believe that this is an impediment to … proposing lease fees now.[84]

Responding to this letter, McMahon (as CGM Defence Liaison) confirmed that ADI was adhering to its view that the rent question was bound up with the larger question regarding the company's capital structure:

It makes no sense to consider this issue in isolation from other aspects of the rate of return. In any case, the basis of lease premiums, whether they are resolved in the context of the overall rate of return or separately, can only sensibly be based on the revenue earning capacity contributed by the assets concerned … Garden Island particularly has a number of major complications still unresolved concerning the assets to be leased.[85]

This exchange was an early indicator that resolving the capital structure issue was not going to be a simple affair. At its meeting in March 1990 the board made clear that it wished to be involved in the initial discussions with the government on this matter, with the result that at the next meeting Harris outlined the substance of a letter which needed to go to Defence under the terms of the Beazley-Wood letter the previous May.[86]

The question which had to be settled was the level of debt/equity ratio which the company would have to accept, or whether it should begin paying interest on the Commonwealth's investment from May of that year. At the board's meeting in June 1990, Harris tabled a paper dealing with the company's debt level which detailed a compromise position put forward by the new defence minister, Senator Robert Ray. The board chose to accept this, considering that the position needed to be resolved before ADI could present its corporate plan. Also recognised was the fact that the board had clear responsibilities concerning its annual accounts, and the sooner outstanding issues were resolved 'the less that needs to be said by the Directors in their Report'.[87]

Deciding in August on the response which the board should make to Senator Ray's letter, it was resolved that the chairman and managing director should privately brief the minister on the corporate plan which the company had developed and 'the essentiality of having a no-debt capital structure'. In any event, no detailed discussions of this issue could proceed with the departments of Defence and Finance until ADI's accounts had been audited and passed at the company's annual general meeting.[88]

Consultation with the Department of Defence on the issue of the level of debt which the company might have to accept continued, with Harris reporting to the October board meeting on his discussions with the secretary, service chiefs and the minister's office. The board, however, could do little at this stage. Since the question seemed unlikely to be resolved before the company's annual report was due, the directors proposed seeking further assurances from Ray through an exchange of correspondence.[89]

In a later meeting between the managing director and Ray over the capital structure issue during 1991, the minister informed Harris that he felt he needed advice from a non-ADI source if he was to carry any debate in Cabinet. After initially proposing a broad-ranging inquiry into the company's market prospects and structures, he now wished to obtain a report from a merchant bank on the available options. When this development was related to the board on 12 March, it considered that the minister's draft terms of reference were 'too intrusive', even though their scope had been significantly reduced from the original proposal. Further, members considered that:

> … the idea of a Government appointed enquiry followed by Cabinet consideration of a public service prepared submission on ADI's future was incompatible with the basis on which they were appointed as directors.[90]

Deciding to have alternative terms of reference drafted for Ray's consideration, the board resolved that the chairman should follow up with a letter to the minister outlining other forms of equity that could be applied to ADI. In accordance with the minister's wishes, an inquiry into the capital structure issue was undertaken by the Macquarie Bank over the next few months. The company duly co-operated with the bank officials conducting this exercise, who also held discussions with the departments of Finance and Defence. The report which resulted from the inquiry was finalised in June and matters arising from it considered by the ADI board the following month.[91]

The company might have hoped that this would see an end to a prolonged debate, but this proved not to be the case. Instead, in October the board received terms of reference for a further study of ADI's business plan which the minister wanted the Macquarie Bank to carry out. While members understood that the minister felt this might help him obtain support in Cabinet, they could only express their concern at 'yet another review'.[92] Clearly, their patience was beginning to wear thin. In the event, the outcome of the second Macquarie Bank inquiry proved more benign than company executives obviously feared it would be. When the board considered the bank's report at its meeting in November, in preparation for a subsequent discussion on the capital structure issue, members agreed that these findings were fundamentally supportive of ADI's own position.[93]

By the year's end a draft submission had been prepared for consideration by Cabinet, where it was hoped the matter would finally be resolved. Instead, the matter dragged on for another year, providing a basis for continuing ill-informed and speculative press comment. When Fynmore appeared before the Cabinet's Structural Adjustment Committee on 14 October 1992 to speak in support of a recommendation (from the Macquarie Bank as well as the company) that ADI's $442 million asset debt be converted into equity, this was reported in one newspaper as the company seeking a 'capital injection' of that amount which – when added to existing debt – supposedly meant the government would have invested $900 million in the company.[94] This was, of course, a complete nonsense which misrepresented that the government was being asked to reclassify its existing investment in the company as share capital, not provide any further cash.

Harris did what he could to answer such claims, even sending a letter to the editor which was duly published.[95] He also took the action of writing to senior executives, asking them to assure employees that the reports which had appeared did not really reflect what was happening in the company, and to point out the mistake of inferring from such sources that ADI's hoped-for commercial success was not going to happen. But he had to admit that:

> Regrettably, there is nothing ADI can do in the short term to publicly counter these stories. We need to keep our heads down and to hope that, next week, Cabinet makes the correct decisions.[96]

When the outcome of the Cabinet's consideration of the issue eventually became known on 20 November, for most company employees this news was again received first via the press.[97] Harris could only confirm the elements of the story that the government had decided to convert 86 per cent of the company's debt burden to share capital, giving the company an issued share capital of $366 million. The balance of the debt amounting to $60 million was to attract a commercial rate of interest and would be repayable in 1999. Harris commented:

> I believe it would have been more practical to have resolved the capital structure issue with a clean balance sheet, but the important thing is that the result does not affect the Company's cash flow. It may affect our ability to pay dividends in future but that issue is further down the track.[98]

As it happened, the level of debt had actually been reduced from $442 million to $426 million, mainly due to an agreement at the time to return the Mulwala facility to Commonwealth ownership. Even so, the figure was substantially inflated by the very high valuation placed on land the company acquired on its establishment, notably the St. Marys property. A statutory revaluation of all of ADI's properties in 1992 resulted in a write-down of $105 million – an outcome which had been predicted by the board when it warned the government that transfer values which were insisted upon were far in excess of market values.

Unkept promises

Complicating the entire task of moving ADI onto a sound and viable footing was uncertainty surrounding some matters which were crucial to the company's future and survival. The letter handed to the chairman by the defence minister when the deeds of transfer were signed on 3 May 1989 had been intended to provide a clear and dependable basis on which to establish the relationship between the Commonwealth and the company. Yet the worth and dependability of the 'further and better assurances' contained in that document very quickly came into question.

The most serious problem developed over issues of funding. The letter contained a specific promise by Defence of a funding package worth $275.4 million to meet the costs of creating ADI – to cover such things as employee entitlements, adjustments for pre-existing loss-making contracts, outstanding capital works and maintenance obligations, and expenditure to remedy deficiencies in financial systems. Among the commitments given was an initial $47.7 million in the 1988/89 financial year. Initially the board had been expecting money for this purpose to be made available in a single payment on transition, but in March 1989 – little more than a month before the big day – it was learnt that the department was proposing to stretch out payment into the 1989/90 year. Writing to the Defence Secretary (Ayers) on this matter, Woods said that:

On its own, such an approach may be tolerable (provided, of course, that any changes in costs caused by the delayed payments are borne by the department). What the Board finds difficult to accept however, is that there appears to be a reluctance to give a commitment that the staged payments will actually be made.[99]

What disturbed the ADI directors even more was 'an implicit unwillingness to accept the validity of some of the funding proposals', particularly a promise that Defence would provide a capital contribution of $130 million over three years to provide the company with an asset replacement reserve. The board had been dismayed to discover that Defence was budgeting for only $30 million, less than a quarter of the figure which the company had planned on. As Woods explained, the creation of such a reserve was 'fundamental to the viability of ADI':

> Any prudently managed business creates resources not only to replace assets as they wear out, but also to provide a buffer for the bad times. The next couple of years are going to be very difficult for ADI and it cannot survive unless it is given a reasonable start.[100]

The level proposed by ADI was, Woods also argued, 'quite a modest request', given that it represented less than two years' worth of investment expenditure and the company would be funding its own investment in future. Moreover, as Harris pointed out to officials in Finance and Defence at this time, the total funding required to cover the costs of the transition to ADI was well inside the budgetary provision for ODP within the Five Year Defence Program ($606.4 million); the company was not seeking additional money, simply that allocated funds be brought forward within the program.[101] Defence still stood to reap a massive saving through the changeover to ADI, even if the company was given everything that it sought.

The $130 million figure was subsequently included in the funding package specified in the attachment to the letter given to the chairman on 3 May, with $26.3 million of this money due to be paid on the passage of the 1989/90 Supply Bill. Included in the body of the letter was an assurance from the minister that: 'I and my Department will do everything possible to ensure that funds are paid to the Company in accordance with the understandings reached.'[102]

On 7 August Ayers wrote to ADI's managing director, explaining extraordinary pressures which had built up on the Defence department's finances as the result of an 'eleventh hour' additional budgetary cut of $105 million. It had been necessary to make some quick and unpalatable decisions in areas of expenditure which were discretionary or could be deferred – including the $130 million capital contribution to ADI. While it might be possible, he said, to make some funding provision late in 1989/90, or the next year, the bulk of the money would have to be deferred until later.[103]

When this news was presented to the board, directors refused to accept deferral of payment as proposed by Defence, and resolved that Harris should tell Ayers as much.[104] Following the board meeting in October, Woods also wrote to Ayers to point out the serious consequences which ADI faced without the funding which had been originally envisaged:

> Unless the Company uses … earmarked cash for investment (a risky course of action) we have no spare cash for maintenance of our capabilities or for pursuing business opportunities. The Commonwealth has refused to allow the Company to borrow on its own behalf without the prior approval of its officials. In any case, for the moment our expenses are greater than our revenue.

(Indeed, while Woods did not say so, the fact was that about the only real source of cash the company had was the funds negotiated for loss-making contracts which it had taken over from Defence.) Stressing that fulfilment of the commitment given by Beazley was essential to the success of ADI, the chairman sought at least 'to put the issue of principle beyond doubt even if specific amounts and timing of their payments need to remain flexible'.[105]

Although an approach made by Harris to Beazley on 4 December received a sympathetic response, there was ultimately no satisfaction to be had over the missing capital contribution. When Ayers responded to Woods' representation, he stated that he had instructed his officers to 'examine the prospect' of identifying some amount for ADI's purpose in future estimate bids but declined to give any firm commitments or undertakings that the $130 million would be forthcoming.[106]

All a sadly-wiser Harris could do was to denounce, on the company's behalf, the Commonwealth's failure to honour its promises whenever invited to give public addresses to business groups regarding the formation of ADI. In such forums he warned listeners engaged in any similar exercise to corporatise government instrumentalities to beware:

> Again, for those looking for practical lessons, apply a very heavy discount factor to any funding offered in letters or in a form that has no legal enforceability … [These] are more likely to be broken the further one moves away from the moment when the commitment was given. I stress that this is more likely to be an issue with businesses owned by a government – any government – because I do not believe that, deep down, they take their own businesses as seriously as they do other peoples' businesses.[107]

Unfortunately, capital contribution would not be the only area where the company was given to feel that it had been abandoned by Defence. In devising an appropriate financial arrangement on which to set up ADI, care had been taken to ensure that liabilities incurred by ODP were not saddled unfairly onto the new organisation. In relation to employees brought across to the new organisation, it was specifically agreed that the government would meet the costs of sick, recreation and long service leave to which personnel were already entitled, at such time as these eventually fell due.

In 1991 the company was shocked by suggestions that the Commonwealth might not honour its promises to pay its share of employee-related liabilities under certain circumstances. This was despite the fact that the government's commitments were incorporated into the deeds of transfer, and were thus legally-binding, and that these documents contained no qualifications on this obligation. As Harris later observed of this situation:

> Under normal commercial arrangements one party breaching this contract would be quickly sued by the other. It is much more difficult in practice for a government-owned company to sue its owner for breach of contract.[108]

As 1989 drew to a close, ADI had survived the initial test of transition and begun to find its feet as a new organisation with its own identity and culture. Yet, while it enjoyed new-found freedom to conduct its affairs in ways previously unknown to the old ODP as a government instrumentality, some painful lessons about the nature of the relationship between the company and its shareholder/ main customer were also becoming evident. The company had stepped out from under the cloak of Defence, but now stood in the department's shadow.

In the lead-up to ADI's takeover of ODP, Harris had sometimes complained about 'a general unwillingness [in Defence] to let go the controls'.[109] After nearly eight months of the company actually in operation, the same battle was still being fought. When a Defence official wrote to request information from ADI as a GBE falling within the Defence portfolio, the managing director shot back a reply which challenged the characterisation of the company in this fashion. ADI operated under guidelines emanating from Finance as much as Defence, and observed requirements prescribed by the Corporations Law:

> Accordingly, the Company objects to the proposition that it will continue to be subject to a range of ad-hoc guidelines, draft or otherwise, which arrive unannounced and upon which the company is expected to comment at short notice.[110]

Much as such assumptions about where the company fitted in relation to Defence might be resented, a measure of confusion in many minds was at least understandable. The links remained close, deliberately so, with an instruction circulating Defence jointly signed by the Secretary and the Chief of the Defence Force calling for 'business as usual' with ADI.[111] No sooner was the company in control than it was looking to negotiate five-year contracts to continue supplying

Defence with a range of items traditionally provided by the old ODP, drawing on British experience when Royal Ordnance had been sold to private interests three years earlier.[112] Even though it was expected that ADI would be 'progressively competing in the market place for defence business',[113] it was clear that – in the words of Beazley's letter of 3 May 1989 – ADI would 'remain within the Commonwealth' for some time to come.

7

BROADENING HORIZONS

The first six months of ADI's existence as an independent entity was a harrowing period, particularly for Harris as he worked to get a clear understanding of the company's state of health and a firm grip over its operations. He recalls that:

> It was a very worrying time for me, because we had no real idea whether we were bankrupt or not – the systems simply weren't there to support the financial information that was coming in. With no confidence whatsoever in that, we were really flying by the seat of our pants. By about December we were feeling a bit more confident, but until then it was very difficult.[1]

Other events had helped at that time to provide a firmer basis for believing that the colossal gamble that had been taken with ADI might actually prove to be workable. The company's interim industrial award was finalised shortly before Christmas 1989, although only after ADI's Clothing division found itself at the centre of a national test case over paid maternity leave. The issue here was not that the company objected to this form of leave but that it considered the existing public service arrangement operated as little more than a pay bonus, rather than encouraging women to return to the work force after having their child. Notwithstanding that there was political interference which ultimately forced the company to back down, ADI was able to achieve an outcome which satisfied its broad objective of significant industrial reform.[2]

In particular, the arrangement was confirmed which saw 24 awards with 1200 pay points consolidated into just two awards, providing a single company-wide structure having 35 pay points. The new scheme involved an agreement linking improvements in productivity and efficiency, and the adoption of a multi-skilling process, to job classification in ADI's plants. As the second phase of the company's wage deal, a review would now be implemented of individual employee skills in tandem with a pioneering program of job redesign aimed at maximising each employee's contribution to efficiency. In essence, individuals were now expected to perform whatever work was safe, practical and legal for them to perform, rather than only those jobs which related to whichever union they had joined.

In February 1990 the company could also announce that 'the major phase of its executive recruitment' had recently been completed, following further middle-management appointments.[3] While a number of those closely associated with the transition from ODP already filled General Manager positions in the new organisation – Callinan (Employee Development), Kelaher (Management Accounting), Mitchell (Defence Liaison), Targ (Capital Investment) and Taylor (Strategic Development) among them[4] – others subsequently came in from the private sector, and some from the military.

Among the new arrivals was Michael Beary, a former general manager of Dowd Corporation and Victorian regional manager of Venture Stores, who became Business Development Manager for Military Clothing Division; and Harry Hickson, recruited from the Maritime Services Board in Sydney as General Manager Operations in the Naval Engineering Division. Among the ex-military recruits was Brigadier Peter Badman (formerly Director-General of Operations and Plans in Army Office, Canberra), who became General Manager for Defence Requirements at headquarters, while Commodore Peter Mitchell (formerly Director of the RAN's Anzac Ship Project) became Head of Weapons and Electrical in Naval Engineering.

The company was also greatly pleased to obtain the services of Dr Ross Babbage, a prominent academic and former public servant who was then deputy head of the Strategic and Defence Studies Centre at the Australian National University, Canberra. His appointment as General Manager for Strategic Analysis should, Harris said, be seen as part of a strategy 'to become an even more significant participant in the international defence business':

> Any company wishing to survive, let alone grow, in our business needs to have a deep understanding of world events and strategic issues. Dr Babbage will strengthen our understanding of the future world and thus make a major contribution to our corporate planning processes.[5]

For many of the company's employees, especially those coming from the public service, adapting to the environment of private enterprise was no easy transition. Callinan recounts that some were not used to, or ready for, having true management flexibility:

> I had people who hadn't absorbed what was in the ADI awards ringing me up

and asking 'Can I do this, can I do that?'. They were still looking for the pre-scriptive guidance that was in General Orders, or the Public Service Acts and Regulations. My response was always, 'You asked for freedom, you've been given it – and a pay rise. Now manage'. I wasn't going to become their crutch all the time.[6]

In the same vein, Conway recalls that:

There were a few people who initially came across to the company but ulti-mately left for one reason or another. They didn't like the way it was set up, or didn't believe they could make the change from the public sector to the com-mercial world, etc.[7]

Notwithstanding that there was a constant process of change underway throughout and at almost every level of the company, the stage had been reached for determining some longer term goals for the organisation. Management was able to focus on finalising business development and corporate strategy plans. The purpose of these were, in Harris' words, to work out 'what we'd need to do to make … [the company's] businesses profitable and to stop the bleeding'.[8]

This process entailed arriving at a no-nonsense assessment of the current con-tracts held by individual facilities, the capabilities they possessed, and the prospects of securing other work. Out of this exercise was derived the goal of halving the company's dependence on ADF orders (then accounting for 80 per cent of its busi-ness) over the next eight to ten years. Achieving this target would require building up a strong base of commercial, non-military business – even while retaining, and perhaps increasing, the amount of work done for Defence.[9]

Such a result would mean, though, that at a minimum ADI would have to dou-ble its present annual turnover of $505 million within five years, with almost all growth coming from new non-ADF contracts, just to maintain its existing level of turnover in real terms. Commenting publicly on this ambitious goal, Harris acknowledged that 'to reduce our dependency this way will require significant effort in both commercial and defence exports, and the development of new prod-ucts'.[10] Privately, he elaborates on the thinking behind such statements:

When we asked ourselves whether there was really a long-term future for the company with just the four businesses we had, the answer was no. We looked then at what we needed to do to round-out the company, to make it a broad-ly-based defence contractor. In other words, what capabilities don't we have that we should have. There was another question as to whether we were mak-ing best use of what we had, whether there were already some capabilities that had commercial application which we weren't pushing enough.[11]

Adding new businesses

The process of striking out in new directions had never been put on hold entirely. Within four months of the company's formal take-over, Harris reported to the board that ADI had obtained the assistance of the government of Western Australia to establish a commercial reference standards laboratory in that State. Opened in November and incorporated into ADI's Naval Engineering Division, this facility, located in the southern Perth suburb of Bentley, offered a service which enabled the RAN and local industry to calibrate and test vital electronic measuring devices.[12]

As part of Harris' determination to seek out and pursue new business opportunities, however, came a decision in late 1989 to extend the company's marketing efforts overseas. An International Marketing Group was established at headquarters with Les Targ as general manager, who had done work in this area for the old ODP organisation. Targ recalls that he had been performing this function for ADI – in addition to his other formal role – all along:

> Ken decided right at the start that he didn't want to do anything on the international front until he had time to assess things, so really there was a moratorium. I was firstly appointed General Manager, Capital Investment, but he said to me 'I want you to keep international enquiries just bubbling along, without being proactive for the moment'. So effectively I had two jobs. Within about six months Ken realised that he couldn't sit on things any longer, because there was too much happening and I think by then he had begun to gear up his own plans anyway.[13]

In February 1990 an ADI office was established in the Malaysian capital, Kuala Lumpur, run by William Grassick (a retired colonel who was the former defence attaché at the Australian high commission there) as general manager. The office was officially opened by Malaysia's defence minister on 19 March. As ADI's representative throughout the member countries of the Association of South East Asian Nations (ASEAN) and the Pacific, Grassick's charter was to seek opportunities for 'collaboration' with local companies in the design, development, manufacture and marketing of defence and commercial products.[14]

In March 1990, too, Harris reported to the board on the possible acquisition of the New South Wales government's clothing facility in the inner western Sydney suburb of Leichhardt. After examining the proposal in detail,[15] the directors decided to back this venture. The result was that in June an announcement was made that the company had bought the equipment, stock and intellectual property of the factory, and signed a lease for an initial three-year period.

Explaining the rationale behind ADI's take-over of this business, Harris pointed to the modern plant and equipment contained in the factory, and 'an impressive client list' which included the New South Wales fire brigade and police department. The company was counting on being able to apply different management techniques to transform it into a viable enterprise, by offering more competitive prices, faster delivery and better sales service. More importantly, this acquisition would enable the company to expand its activities into the potentially lucrative commercial uniform market, while establishing a manufacturing and sales presence in Sydney.[16]

In May 1990 a chief general manager was appointed for a new Electronics Division to be based in Sydney. Announcing the commencement of this new business unit in June, Harris stressed the importance being placed on 'ideas rather than manufacturing' and said that it would focus on services and systems as much as products. By August, the head of this new enterprise, Graham Shepherd (who previously worked for Plessy and Telecom Australia), had commenced formulating a business plan and provided a briefing to the ADI board on prospects in the area. By year's end the business plan was complete, and the division had been established in premises in the western Sydney suburb of Silverwater with three additional executives appointed.

At the board meeting of August 1990 the directors also received a briefing from Babbage. He addressed the opportunities for ADI to establish an analytical and studies service to the Defence department and other agencies in the defence field, specifically in strategic, force development, and system and tactical analysis. The directors supported moving into this business too, by creating a small Consulting Division in Canberra under Babbage's direction. It was particularly noted that:

> ... the main advantage to ADI would not be in the revenue generated directly ... but in the retention of key contacts in the defence and government networks and the use of first hand product, service and systems development information by other elements of ADI.[17]

After initially-abortive negotiations, by July 1990 ADI had also acquired an interest in the ailing Dart Defence Industries Pty. Ltd. located at Albury, New South Wales. This company made an advanced target system which had already been sold to more than 25 countries around the world, for use on firing ranges in training defence, police and paramilitary forces. Acquiring the exclusive rights to manufacture and market Dart products provided the basis for a new Training Systems Division based in Melbourne under the direction of Neville Rogers as CGM, previously the general manager of the company's ordnance facility at Bendigo.[18]

Other parts of the company's existing structure were also separated out into new business divisions under chief general managers at this time. Industrial Decontamination, under Ron Taylor, was established primarily to meet the company's requirement to deal with several of its properties found to be polluted with chemicals after it was decided to restructure the ammunition business (see chapter 8). When it was recognised that the company was acquiring considerable expertise in this area of activity, the decision was made to seek further commercial opportunities for the new division in treating old Defence and disused industrial sites.

Logistic Support, headed by Peter Badman, was established in the hope of seizing opportunities thrown up by the Defence department's commercial support program, which aimed to place the provision of more work and services with private contractors. Targ's group in headquarters was set up as an International Marketing Division to develop both defence and non-defence business overseas for the company. These three divisions were all based in Canberra, but – to emphasise that they (with Consulting) were not part of corporate headquarters – were to be located away from Barton, in a separate building in the suburb of Deakin.[19]

A decision taken within a few months of ADI's take-over from ODP to begin work on some major restructuring issues, described later in this chapter, led to other big changes at Corporate Headquarters during early 1991. In January, Harris announced the establishment of a Major Projects Group with John Barclay as GGM. Although nominally head of Development, he had been fully occupied in project work for almost a year while his other functions were shared between Harris, McMahon and Massey.[20]

The decision was now taken to formalise that arrangement, by bringing in Nigel Berlyn from Garden Island to take over on development issues. Berlyn's place at Naval Engineering was filled in February with the appointment of Bryan Gibson, formerly the managing director of Joy Manufacturing Pty. Ltd. of Moss Vale, New South Wales, a heavy engineering company specialising in making and marketing equipment for the underground coal mining industry. Gibson's prior experience included a long period with Australian Wire Industries, a subsidiary of BHP.[21]

During April 1991 ADI announced the purchase of the East Bendigo factory formerly run by the Perfectfit company, which had moved its clothing manufacturing operation to Thailand in 1990. To ease congestion at the Coburg facility, the shirt production section of Clothing division's business would be moved to Bendigo and eventually employ 150–200 workers there. The 50 people at the small annex already engaged in making shirts at ADI's ordnance plant in the town would be transferred to the new factory.[22]

In May 1991 the company's base in Western Australia was augmented through the purchase of the assets of Universal Defence Systems (UDS), a leading computer software engineering company.[23] The attraction of UDS to ADI was the fact that it was one of only a few businesses in Australia with an Ada software capability, which was the mandatory language requirement for all new computer programs for the United States Department of Defence and more and more the preferred software language for Australian and European defence force systems. With increased commercial application being found for Ada, ADI's ability to compete for business in the electronic systems field would be considerably enhanced. More than this, however, the acquisition also reflected the company's determination – even at this early stage – to break free from 'old manufacturing' and recreate itself as a player in the field of systems engineering.

No less important to ADI was the projects in which UDS had been involved, which ADI would now be completing. These included the RAN's maritime intelligence support terminal and the Australian Army's electronic warfare command and processing sub-system (EWCAPSS), and brought with them a ready-made relationship with two other firms which were important in the field, Perth-based Clough Engineering and E-Systems in the United States. In conjunction with these companies, ADI now planned to use its newly-acquired intellectual property to tender for the Australian Army tactical command and support system (AUS-TACSS) contract, worth $20–40 million.[24] The calibration and standards centre already operating in the west was merged with the UDS business, both becoming part of Electronics Division. Together they were known as ADI's Perth facility, and sent to run it was Kevin Manie, who had earlier succeeded Rogers as general manager at Bendigo.[25]

Later in 1991 Harris rethought his approach to the company's activities overseas and had international marketing reabsorbed as a group at headquarters. In the board there was also discussion of whether Canberra was an appropriate base for the company's activities, with a decision being taken 'in principle' as early as May 1991 to transfer the Corporate Headquarters to Sydney.[26] An announcement was not finally made to staff until February 1992, with the move expected to take place at the end of the year. Although explained formally in terms of the company's 'growing maturity as a commercial entity',[27] the reason for the transfer was described less guardedly by the general manager for Corporate Relations, Leigh Funston, as stemming from a desire to escape from 'the centre of bureaucracy … to be in one of the major commercial centres of Australia'.[28]

A small element of the headquarters staff would remain in the national capital to keep in day-to-day contact with the Defence department and Canberra-based elements of the ADF. Among other company units which would stay behind was a new Property Division headed by Bill Mitchell, which was set up in September 1992 to manage the commercial redevelopment opportunities created by ADI's decision to vacate a number of its sites in Victoria and New South Wales (see chapter 8).

The new headquarters offices, located in Sydney's eastern suburbs at Bondi Junction, were formally opened by Defence Minister Ray and the New South Wales Minister for State Development, Peter Collins, on 14 December 1992. Left behind in the old Canberra headquarters was the conference room named in honour of the great English cricketer, Dr W.G. Grace, famous for remarking when bowled first ball during a country match, 'Put the bails back. They paid to see me bat, not you bowl'. According to one press account, this encapsulated the ADI philosophy too. replace the bails and continue batting.[29] Also left behind in the main Canberra offices was another conference room known – somewhat provocatively – as 'The Thatcher Room'. At the board's first meeting in the new headquarters, held on the same day as its official opening, the directors decided to name their new meeting place the 'Alan Woods Room', in honour of the company's inaugural chairman.[30]

Following the transfer to Sydney, there was a rationalisation of company-occupied office space in Canberra. The Major Projects Group had remained behind in the move and was mow merged with the Ammunition Division, under Barclay as CGM. This division had shed its missiles component on the closure of the Salisbury facility in May 1993, with production of the Nulka rocket motor being retained but moved to Mulwala (where overhead costs were much lower).[31] A Minehunter Project Division was also created during 1993 (see later in this chapter), so that the number of divisions which made up the company actually rose to eleven.

Ship repair

In the company's bid to boost its turnover, particularly in the non-defence area, much hope was pinned on the significant heavy engineering capability and expertise possessed by ADI, particularly within Naval Engineering Division (NED) centred on Garden Island. The dockyard, along with Weapons & Engineering Division, was – Harris said – expected to lead the 'charge for new business'.[32]

Of course, the company was largely guaranteed the lion's share of work which the Navy required to be done on its ships, under a five-year contract promised at the time that ADI took over from ODP. The umbrella agreement covering ship repair was not, however, signed until February 1991.[33] And, contrary to the claims of some critics,[34] it was never intended to give ADI a 'free ride' or a monopoly on government business. Its purpose was merely to avoid confronting the company with full competition for all its work from the day of inception – something which would have killed it off before it had a chance to establish itself. NED was still expected to perform efficiently and be competitive.

The take-over of the Garden Island facility by ADI came mid-way through a program of large and costly projects to upgrade the RAN's main combat vessels. The refit of the three Adams Class guided missile destroyers (known as DDGs) was in its final stages, with work on the last of these, *Hobart*, having commenced in March 1989, barely two months before ADI took over the Garden Island facility. She entered the dockyard in June for work to commence below the waterline and returned to duty with the RAN in August 1991, her two-and-a-half year refit having been completed a week ahead of schedule.[35]

Running concurrently with the DDG modernisation program was another for work on the newer FFG-7 Perry Class guided missile frigates. HMAS *Adelaide* was just completing an upgrade lasting 19 months to enable it to operate the RAN's new Seahawk anti-submarine helicopters. This involved major modification to the ship's flight deck, including extending the stern transom with a new three-metre replacement section to allow for a flight retrieval system to be installed for helicopter operations in heavy seas.[36] When this work was finished in December 1989, it was announced that *Canberra* was to receive the same treatment. The award of the new $40 million contract to ADI was, Defence Minister Beazley declared, a recognition of the 'job very well done' with *Adelaide*.[37] Entering the dry-dock in August 1990, she emerged transformed in December the following year.

What was particularly different about the refits of *Hobart* and *Canberra* was that both contracts were on a fixed price basis, with excess costs (or savings) shared between the Commonwealth and ADI. Also included was a performance incentive, which was a bonus payable on the strength of Navy's assessment of ADI's performance on the contract. Equally remarkable was NED's practice in the case of *Canberra* of carrying out a great proportion of outfitting work ashore, both to save time and reduce the difficulty of working in confined spaces.[38]

While the *Canberra* modification represented the end of the Navy's program of large capital projects, there was other work which came NED's way. A contract to refit the destroyer escort *Torrens* was completed in May 1991. Conversion of a former civilian vessel commissioned as the trials ship *Protector* was also carried out in that year, and a refit of the fleet replenishment ship *Success* begun in August.[39]

The division also scored work unexpectedly as a result of the Australian government's decision to become involved in the Gulf War. On 10 August 1990 (a Friday) the Prime Minister, Bob Hawke, announced that ships of the RAN would join a Multi-National Naval Force enforcing United Nations trade sanctions against Iraq following that country's invasion of Kuwait eight days earlier. A weekend of intense activity followed at NED as *Adelaide* and another FFG, *Darwin*, were readied for active service, before sailing from Sydney on Monday, 13 August.[40]

Following the despatch of the initial Australian task group, preparations were begun for the frigate *Sydney* and the destroyer *Brisbane* to relieve them after three months. When it became apparent that the Australian task group might become engaged in active hostilities with Iraqi forces, involving a high threat of air attack, a key part of the replacement ships' preparation entailed fitting *Brisbane* with two Phalanx close-in weapons systems (CIWS) – components of which were partly 'borrowed' from one of the FFGs then under construction in Melbourne and partly delivered urgently from the United States.

The Phalanx rapid-fire guns, designed to defeat incoming anti-ship missiles, are highly complex weapons. While Garden Island staff had gained experience through retrofitting Phalanx to FFGs, space had already been provided in these ships when they were built. The task with *Brisbane* presented a much greater challenge, because

CIWS had never before been fitted to a ship of this class and a DDG was the smallest ship in the world fitted with two such systems. Equipment already in the positions required by the CIWS had to be relocated elsewhere in the ship, so that installing the weapons entailed 11 000 man hours of design work and 40 000 man hours of labour. To have them successfully installed during the seven weeks available before the RAN vessels departed for the Persian Gulf on 12 November meant that many ADI personnel worked 12-hour shifts seven days a week.[41] The destroyer *Perth* was later fitted 'for, but not with', CIWS, in case she, too, was wanted for duty in the Gulf.[42]

Subsequent refits carried out at Garden Island included that of *Darwin* in 1993,[43] and a 10-month $30 million overhaul of *Brisbane* completed in May 1994. The latter was finished within budget and returned to the fleet by the specified completion date, despite the fact that the work required by the Navy had risen by 120 per cent during the course of the refit.[44] Similarly, *Perth* also underwent a nine-month refit which saw her returned to the RAN in March 1995. Again the task was completed on time, and within budget.[45]

While much of the work described was only what was due to come to ADI under its long-term agreement with the Navy, the company was also successful in winning work which was put out to open tender. In July 1990, for example, the company was selected as the preferred tenderer for the last two of the RAN's Oberon Class submarines which had yet to undergo major refit. This contract, worth more than $100 million, was regarded as a major win for the company, as previously such work was performed at the Cockatoo Island dockyard. The government had, however, decided against extending the life of that facility (already earmarked for sale and redevelopment) for this purpose – even though there was some risk, not to mention cost and difficulty, involved in setting up new refit facilities at short notice.[46]

Award of the Oberon contract to ADI predictably drew criticism from the other two contenders in the bidding – Australian Shipbuilding Industries (ASI), which was the Western Australian subsidiary of Transfield, and Clough Engineering – both of whom had proposed performing the work at Cockburn Sound in the west. The absence of other orders for Western Australian shipyards added an edge of anger to their protests, especially as the project encountered delays in finding space at Garden Island which prevented the first boat, HMAS *Onslow*, entering a purpose-built slave dock until November 1990 – by which stage, it was alleged, ASI could have had the job substantially under way.[47]

Matters did not get any easier for NED as further problems emerged. A major part of this situation was due to 'emergent work' – that is, repairs found to be needed only after the vessel was stripped down and examined. Regrettably, delays continued to mount, until the *Onslow* ended up not rejoining the fleet until October 1993 – having been in dock for 120 weeks instead of the 97–101 originally anticipated. The most serious of the problems encountered was that of authenticating the spare parts planned to be fitted into the submarine, a crucial aspect because of the Navy's emphasis on quality and the requirement for a 'safe to dive' certificate to be issued after the refit. This demanded the developing of new procedures and work methods to ensure that all stages of the project could be tightly monitored and controlled. ADI had also based its bid on an assumption that the RAN could supply the necessary supporting documentation required, which proved to be ill-founded.

Inevitably, the difficulties experienced over the submarine contract were regarded in many quarters as a failure by ADI.[48] Defence Minister Ray found himself under intense pressure from Western Australian interests to have at least the refit of the second submarine, *Otama*, transferred to ASI's yard.[49] The whole experience was, as ADI's GGM Defence Liaison (McMahon) candidly admits, highly damaging to the company in such an early stage of its history:

> With the benefit of hindsight, we're all saying [in ADI] that we should have let Transfield win that refit, because they'd look bad now too – probably worse than we do. To an extent it was a disaster going to happen anyway.[50]

Understandably, great effort was put into ensuring that the same problems did not recur with HMAS *Otama* when it commenced its refit late in 1991.[51] This contract went very smoothly and won high praise for the company's performance.

Despite the steady volume of work for the RAN which initially flowed through the dockyard, there were several worrying portents for the future which the company had to address. Bryan Gibson, Berlyn's successor at Garden Island, recalls that when he arrived the company's forecast for his division predicted that revenue for 1991/92 would equal the current year. This expectation was, however, soon proved highly inaccurate, since within months the yard had experienced a 40 per cent decline in the volume of its workload.[52] Even though the guarantee which ADI enjoyed under the umbrella agreement with Defence would remain in place until mid-1995, funding problems within the Navy meant that the number of scheduled naval refits declined sharply from mid-1992 anyway. Added to this reduction was a Navy decision not to refit its major surface vessels in future, just retire them earlier. Moreover, the government's declared policy of basing half the fleet in Western Australia by the year 2000 seemed likely to ensure that such work as did become available would be divided between new shipyards on the west coast as well as the established ones in the east. If demand was fragmented in this way, there was a real fear whether highly-technical fit-out work would continue to be an economic proposition at Garden Island, which – under the lease terms finally reached early in 1993 – was costing ADI $3 million a year in rent.[53]

Further fuelling doubts over Garden Island's future was the question mark which arose over continued use of the site for naval purposes. In July 1993 the Prime Minister, Paul Keating, requested Defence Minister Ray to 'look into the possible relocation of the Navy 'as a matter of priority', suggesting that the fleet base be moved west of the Sydney Harbour bridge, possibly to White Bay near Balmain. When news of this proposal became public the following year, a vigorous debate ensued which only raised fresh uncertainties.[54]

In response to the severe decline in naval work levels and the continuation of this downward trend, in September 1991 NED announced its intention to cut up to 500 jobs from its current work force of 2300.[55] After some 60 employees opted for voluntary redundancy packages just before Christmas, in January 1992 the company took the step of retrenching immediately another 365 workers with pay in lieu of notice.[56] Gibson explains that this was done because:

> There was a lot of concern among managers that if we gave people notice and then let them work their time out, there would be all sorts of sabotage, absenteeism and sickness – all the things that people could trump up. With hindsight, that was the worst thing we could have done, because while there were a large number of larrikins among those involuntarily retrenched – poor performers, troublemakers, etc – everyone got treated the same way. The blokes who knew they were getting their just desserts didn't lose too much sleep, but it was bloody terrible for the good guys.[57]

The mistake was not repeated when, in November 1992, the division found it necessary to trim down by a further 500 workers. Advice was given that retrenchments would occur in March–April of the following year, the names to be announced in February. As Gibson recalls, the five weeks of notice passed productively and there was no surge in absenteeism: 'There were only three minor acts of sabotage, and a fourth involved filling up a foreman's boots with grease, which was a fair cop.'

Because of the declining amount of naval work passing through the yard, commercial ship repair became increasingly important to Garden's Island's turnover. The problem was, though, that not only was work of this nature low-margin and comparatively easy, but – as Harris asserted – it did little to 'exercise key military technical capabilities essential for maintaining the operational readiness of the Fleet'.[58]

While commercial work was perhaps a poor substitute, here at least the Garden Island's vastly improved record of performance now attracted customers. In September 1992, for example, the 22,000 tonne P&O cruise liner *Fairstar* entered the dockyard for a week to undergo major maintenance and repairs to its power generation systems.[59] So satisfied were the owners with the work done on this occasion that, when further work on the ship was required the following year, ADI was again asked to carry it out. Unfortunately space was unavailable at Garden Island and the vessel had to be turned away to the Singapore Dockyard. In a unusual compliment to NED, however, the company was asked to send personnel to Singapore to supervise the critical tasks involved.[60] ADI continued to win work from the *Fairstar*, as in November 1993[61] and February 1995[62] – further proof that the ADI facility was operating to world standards.

Early in 1993 NED drew international attention when it was able to dock the Egyptian-registered 36,000 deadweight-tonnage bulk carrier *Qena*, while it was fully loaded with a cargo of bauxite worth around $100 million. Although docking of fully-laden ships was virtually unknown for a decade, because of the risk of structural damage, ADI achieved this complex feat without mishap. The extent of the repairs needed was far greater than first thought, entailing a rebuild of the main engine and three diesel alternators, yet the job was completed in under 40 days.[63]

So well recognised was NED for its efficiency that a total of 37 commercial ships, mostly Australian and New Zealand, passed through Garden Island during 1993–94.[64] Even then, however, because of the requirement for the ADI facility to be primarily responsive to the needs arising from the RAN fleet base next door, some non-defence work had to be declined. During 1993, the division was obliged to refuse four or five requests from civilian customers. Not everyone, it must be said, applauded the heavy volume of traffic through the yard anyway, as periodically there were complaints from Woolloomooloo residents about excessive noise levels and other inconvenience.[65]

Contracts lost and won

Other divisions of the company were equally successful in finding new business opportunities in what was becoming an increasingly competitive marketplace. Through the specialised engineering capabilities which it possessed, Weapons & Engineering Division (WED) won a variety of contracts associated with the six new Type 471 Collins Class submarines being constructed by the Australian Submarine Corporation (ASC) in South Australia. The value of these contracts progressively grew in value to more than $40 million. Included among the parts supplied by ADI were high technology hoistable masts to carry the radar, electronic support measures and snorkel/induction equipment for each boat,[66] propulsion shafts, forgings and weapons discharge systems for torpedoes, frames for the main electric motors and generators, and hatches and cover plates. In 1990 the division's Bendigo facility commenced the manufacture of components for the Hedemora diesel engines which powered the submarines (three each, weighing about 27 tonnes piece, per boat). The first three of these engines were imported from Sweden, but in accordance with local content rules the remaining fifteen were manufactured in Australia, then assembled and performance tested at NED (Garden Island).[67]

Bendigo also won a $3 million contract from ASC for the manufacture and supply of centrifugal bilge and circulatory pumps for fitting in the new submarines. The pumps were of an innovative design – the brainchild of a Melbourne firm, Pump Technology Pty.Ltd. – and were chosen over four international competitors.[68] Not only were the pumps smaller and lighter than any other on the market, but they had a number of features which were then unique. These included high efficiency (meaning less battery power was needed than for conventional pumps), easy maintenance, ability to withstand corrosive tropical waters and – most vitally for avoiding detection when on operations – low vibration and noise levels.

To the Bendigo plant also went the distinction in 1992 of making the huge controllable pitch propeller blades required to drive HMAS *Newcastle*, the last of the FFGs being built for the RAN at Williamstown. Previously made in the United States, the technologically-advanced blades had the ability to form an envelope of air around the revolving propeller, thus deadening the sound of the transmission system and disguising the ship's noise signature. Manufacturing the blades entailed using a computer controlled machining tool to produce fine three dimensional contours on aluminium–nickel–bronze surfaces.[69]

During 1991–92 Bendigo's role in manufacturing Dyad influence sweeps led to important commercial opportunities for the company. These were innovative new devices designed to counter mines laid against naval and merchant shipping, employing special towed magnets which could be arranged to simulate the magnetic field of specific ships. Developed by DSTO over ten years and recently taken into operational service by the RAN, the use of the sweeps enabled fishing vessels and merchant tugs to be quickly converted as minesweepers at a fraction of the cost of dedicated mine countermeasures vessels. On the advice of Commodore Hector Donohue, a mine warfare specialist who had retired to join Consulting Division, ADI recognised the sales potential of the group of mine countermeasures equipments being developed for the RAN. In December 1992 an exclusive licence agreement was negotiated with the Commonwealth to market and supply these worldwide as an integrated product which ADI dubbed AMASS (Australian Minesweeping and Surveillance System).[70]

Winning fresh contracts was, of course, crucial to the continuing viability of the Bendigo factory, especially as existing long-term contracts were completed. For instance, the manufacture of a total of 129 105 mm Hamel light field guns for the Australian and New Zealand armies – produced under licence from the UK – had begun back in 1985 but came to an end in November 1992.[71] In such circumstances, other commercial business became increasingly important to the future of the facility.

As part of its program of diversification WED targeted a number of new areas, among them power generation in the renewable energy sector. ADI's breakthrough here came in March 1991 when it was awarded a $7 million contract to refurbish two of the Snowy Mountains Hydro-electric Authority's underground power stations, located near Cabramurra in south-east New South Wales, over several years.

This required eight of the giant water turbines and 80-tonne main inlet valves to be dismantled, parts refurbished at the Maribyrnong facility or replaced, and then reinstalled and the equipment tested.[72] During 1992 WED also won a $4.2 million contract to design, supply, install and commission a wind farm west of Esperance, 720 kilometres south-east of Perth, Western Australia.[73] Based on the success of this bid, WED decided to set its sights on the $20 million contract for a 10 megawatt wind farm proposed to be established at Toora, on Wilson's Promontory in Victoria's south Gippsland region. In June 1993 ADI was named as the preferred tenderer for the project, but less than a year later the Victorian government decided it was not prepared to give the necessary commitment and withdrew its support.[74]

On other occasions, too, WED's hopes of finding new business were frustrated. There was bitter disappointment at Bendigo in 1990 when ADI missed out on three major contracts worth more than $100 million to supply parts for the Anzac frigates, these all going to cheaper overseas bidders.[75] Even though the division subsequently scored work worth $17 million to manufacture below-deck equipment for these ships' 127 mm guns,[76] an announcement followed in January 1991 that nearly 180 Bendigo workers would be retrenched in a further attempt to make the facility more competitive.[77] Similarly, in December 1992 it was learnt that ADI had failed to win a $120 million contract to supply 97 light armoured vehicles for the Army.[78]

Since 1982 the Bendigo factory had also enjoyed an association with the General Electric Aircraft Engines company of Cincinnati, USA, through which ADI received ongoing export orders. The value of this work was not great initially, being worth less than $1 million in 1988/89, but four years later had risen to nearly $10 million. By this time ADI had become the sole supplier of precision-fabricated base structures for GE's LM2500 marine gas turbines, each of which weighed seven tonnes and provided power for standby electricity generators and the main propulsion system for ships such as the RAN's FFGs. In 1993 Bendigo received a hotly-contested $43 million contract to manufacture a range of other components for these engines, including the rotating aft shafts (a highly complex task requiring machining to produce a mirror-like surface), exhaust ducts and acoustic enclosures. By December 1994 the value of export work carried out for GE in the previous three years exceeded $50 million.[79]

Important though this work was, the factory could not maintain its current level of activity without new contracts. Although a contract was announced in 1994 to build the power plants for new RAN minehunting ships, the value of this – initially expected to be $70 million but later reduced to $40 million – would not fill the gap created by the completion of Bendigo's current orders associated with the submarine project. When the latter ran out in mid-1996, the facility would be faced with the loss of roughly a quarter of its workload. In anticipation of this drop, in May 1995 the company implemented a restructure plan which entailed the loss of 81 jobs.[80]

Although Lithgow began its existence in WED with firm commitments promising work for several years, its prospects of future business also began to fade. Under a small arms replacement program (SARP) begun under ODP in 1983, ADI held the contract to supply the ADF with 67,000 assault rifles and 3420 light support weapons. Selected to meet Army's requirements were the 5.56 mm Steyr AUG (Armee Universal Gewehr) A1 automatic rifle designed by Steyr-Mannlicher GmBH of Austria, and the 5.56 mm F89 Minimi machine gun designed by Fabrique Nationale Nouvelle Herstal of Belgium, both of which were manufactured at Lithgow under licence. The lightweight Steyr, made in part of polycarbonate plastic, also included components manufactured in New Zealand.

A pre-production batch of 500 of the Australian F88 version of the Steyr (dubbed the AUSteyr) was delivered for testing by the Army in November 1988. A problem was encountered during trials early the next year, however, when – after firing extremely prolonged bursts – some weapons failed to fire every time the trigger was pulled. A modification program was instituted by ADI which overcame the fault and full production commenced at Lithgow some six months late. Although the company's performance inevitably had its critics on account of this occurrence, the Army's Assistant Chief of the General Staff-Materiel, Major-General Duncan Francis, put the matter into proper perspective by pointing to the difficulties which arose in transferring technology from one country to another: 'Manufacturing, particularly of small arms, is an art and it cannot be rushed.'[81]

The first production weapon was formally handed over in October 1990, and the full contract was expected to be completed by 1995. In the 1993/94 Defence Budget, however, a further order for 8600 rifles was approved, which promised to carry production at Lithgow up to May 1996.[82] The first troop trials batch of 50 Minimis was supplied during 1990 and the contract for these weapons was due to be finished in October 1995. The majority of components were initially imported, but by early 1995 the proportion of each weapon made up of local parts increased from 13–50 per cent. A subsequent order for another 4207 of these guns, approved in the 1994/95 budget, was also expected to see production last until September 1997.[83]

Adding to the SARP production run at Lithgow were orders for the New Zealand Defence Force, which bought 18,000 Steyrs. The first 5000 of these weapons were made in Austria and delivered directly from there in March 1988; the second batch of 5000, delivered in September 1989, contained some Lithgow components; the final shipment of Australian-made weapons was received in 1991.[84]

Unfortunately, problems were experienced with each of the lots coming from Lithgow. In the case of the second batch, some weapons were found to jam or have faulty safety catches. Ironically, these safety catches were unique to the New

Zealand order and adopted at this customer's insistence; modifications were carried out under a shared-cost arrangement. In the last batch a different problem was discovered with the gas plug, which necessitated the company undertaking a rectification program. A ten-man ADI team was despatched to inspect and, if necessary, rework each weapon prior to acceptance by the New Zealand Ministry of Defence.[85]

With the finish of these contracts in prospect, Lithgow also found itself on the lookout for new work. In a move reminiscent of the 1930s, engineers at the plant began development of a new type of rotary shears for sheep, derived from a local inventor who might otherwise have sold the patents overseas.[86]

Avenues for overseas sales of Steyrs to other than New Zealand were also explored, although Malaysian production of the same weapon presented ADI with strong competition in the region. One small sale of 2600 Steyrs to the Sultanate of Oman was achieved in 1991,[87] but a potentially more valuable order to a Pakistani anti-drug police unit was vetoed by the Australian government on the grounds that supplying that country could add to instability on the Indian sub-continent.[88] Also missed in 1992 was an offer to Papua New Guinea of 600 Steyrs under Australia's defence co-operation program with that country, aimed at standardising weapons used by the PNG and Australian forces. This was refused and instead the PNG Defence Force bought weapons from the United States Colt manufacturer at a higher price, a transaction which became the subject of a controversy in April 1992 when an internal ADI memo was leaked to a Melbourne newspaper.[89] In the document cited, the GGM International Marketing (Targ) reported to Harris that the limited opportunities arising for ADI to make further sales must ultimately mean that 'once the current orders for the Australian Defence Force are totally satisfied, there is very little possibility of us keeping the production line open'.

For a time, hopes were held of a major export deal with Thailand, but this prospect, too, foundered in late 1994 amid a public controversy over Australian government and media assertions that Thai army officers were trading with Khmer Rouge guerillas in neighbouring Cambodia, and there was a high risk that Australian-made weapons could fall into communist hands. The Thai army commander was reportedly offended by such statements and vetoed the purchase of rifles from ADI. Although the government in Bangkok subsequently gave assurances to Canberra that the Australian proposal would be dealt with on its commercial merits, nothing further was heard of this opportunity.[90]

A repeat of this episode accompanied press reports early in 1995 that the Australian government had given 'in principle' approval to a company proposal to export $100 million worth of Steyr rifles to Indonesia. In the furore by human rights groups and East Timorese activists which followed, it scarcely mattered that ADI had not applied for an export licence, that Indonesia's Minister of Defence and Security denied that the country's armed forces were in the market for Australian-made weapons, or that Defence Minister Ray had declared in the

The ADI board of directors in 1994: (standing, from left) Malcolm Kinnaird, Kevin Fellew, Elizabeth Bryan, Steven Harker, Anthony Bowra, Arthur Apted; (seated, from left) Russell Fynmore and Ken Harris.

The Deputy Premier of Western Australia and the Minister for State Development, Ian Taylor, inspects metrology equipment during a visit to ADI's Perth facility in 1992. With the Minister is the company's Managing Director, Ken Harris, and facility staff member, Gareth Edwards.

The company opens its first overseas office, in Kuala Lumpur, in March 1990. Ken Harris introduces Air Vice-Marshal Barry Gration of the RAAF to the Malaysian Minister for Defence, Tengku Ahmad Rithauddeen, who performed the opening. Visible over the Minister's shoulder is the manager of the office, Bill Grassick.

ADI's chairman, Russell Fynmore, addresses the gathering at the opening of the new Corporate Headquarters in Sydney, 14 December 1992. Seated behind him are (from left): Dr John Saunders, Director-General of the NSW Department of State Development; Ken Harris, the Managing Director of ADI, and the Minister for Defence, Senator Robert Ray.

A pre-fabricated stern transom is fitted to a RAN frigate at the Garden Island facility run by ADI's Naval Engineering Division.

In 1994 it became publicly known that the prime minister, Paul Keating, had suggested relocating the Navy from its Garden Island site. Debate over such proposals compounded uncertainty over the economic vialibity of ADI's continued operating lease of the dockyard facilities from the Commonwealth.

The port-side Phalanx weapon system is installed by ADI onto the guided missile destroyer HMAS Hobart. The rapid-fire 20mm guns provide close-in defence against missile attack.

The ten-month refit of HMAS Brisbane at Garden Island, completed in May 1994 on time and within budget, was a turning point in ADI's sometimes difficult relationship with the RAN.

HMAS Onslow rejoins the fleet in 1993 after completing a major refit at Garden Island – the first carried out on a submarine at ADI's dockyard.

Completion of the refit of HMAS Canberra, shown here proceeding to sea after her return to the RAN in 1992, marked the end of the most complex program ever undertaken to modernise the Navy's warships. From 1984 three destroyers and three frigates underwent the major refit process at Garden Island.

In need of urgent repairs, the Egyptian bulk carrier Qena docks fully laden at ADI's Garden island facility in 1993. Although risky, the operation was successfully completed without mishap.

Hedemora diesel engines leaving Garden Island for the ASC's yard at Osborne, South Australia where they were installed in the new Collins Class submarines.

The hand-over in 1993 of the first two hoistable masts built at ADI Maribyrnong for the Collins Class submarines.

On 11 July 1991 the company's Managing Director, Ken Harris, and Snowy Mountains Hydro-electric Authority Commissioner, Charles Halton, signed a $7 million contract for ADI to refurbish power-station components.

In 1992 ADI won the contract to install a wind-driven power station near Esperance, Western Australia. Here the 27-metre blades of one of nine generator units are about to be hoisted up to the turbine atop its 30-metre tower.

The 105mm light gun (shown here during live firing at the High Range Training Area west of Townsville, Queensland) was the first complete artillery weapon made in Australia since the 1940s. Manufactured at Bendigo between 1985 and 1992, 105 of these howitzers were for the Australian Army and another 24 were sold to the New Zealand Army.

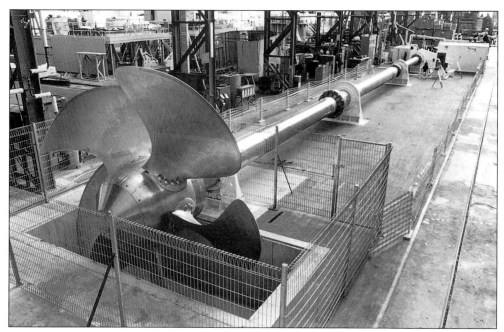

The propulsion system for the first Australian-made FFG–7 frigate (HMAS Melbourne*) sits ready for spin testing at ADI's Bendigo facility in 1990. Much of the system was manufactured under licence from American and Swedish companies, but the five blades of the controllable-pitch propeller – requiring advanced machining technology – were fabricated in the US and imported. When the second locally-built FFG (HMAS* Newcastle*) was launched in 1992, she carried blades produced at Bendigo.*

The RAN auxiliary minesweeper HMAS Wallaroo, *shown towing a maxi-influence sweep during Exercise Dugong off Townsville in November 1992.*

A member of the ADF firing the ADI-manufactured Steyr F88 assault rifle. The soldier is also wearing an ADI-made disruptive pattern uniform.

The Minimi light support machine gun is manufactured at ADI's Lithgow facility for the Australian Army.

In the shadow of Mt Fuji, the Japanese Ground Self Defence Force trains its soldiers on an ADI range system in 1993.

With a roar which startled spectators, this Caterpillar D8L burst from hiding behind haybales to 'turn the first sod' on ADI's new factory at Benalla. The start of excavations was the finale to the contract-signing ceremony on 2 July 1993.

Having scaled difficult heights in transforming ADI into a thriving business, the five remaining members of the company's board of directors – (from left) Arthur Apted, Kevin Fellew, Russell Fynmore, Ken Harris and Anthony Bowra – savour the view from the top of Sydney Harbour Bridge in June 1999.

Combat system integration activities are under way in the shore integration facility at ADI's minehunter ship site at Newcastle, New South Wales. The shore integration facility is used to integrate and test the full array of complex and sensitive electronic systems which make the Huon Class minehunter the most advanced of its type in the world.

ADI's Command Support System in use at headquarters Australian Theatre. The Joint Command Support Environment has been extended from the headquarters of the Australian Defence Force to all major headquarters in Australia.

The Strategic Munitions Agreement, replacing the (not-so-long) Long Term Ammunition Supply Agreement, was signed on 10 July 1998. Pictured at the signing are, seated, Ken Harris (left) and Rear-Admiral Simon Harrington, the Support Commander, Navy; standing (from left): Rob Tannahill, GGM Finance, ADI; John McMahon, GGM Government Relations, ADI; Darryl Page, GM Ordnance Marketing & Product Development, ADI; Brigadier Greg Thomas, Director-General Support Concepts & Capability; Paul Barratt, Secretary of the Defence Department; and Admiral Chris Barrie, Chief of the Defence Force.

The members of ADI's executive team gather in the board room at Corporate Headquarters Sydney, in July 1999: (from left) John McMahon, Ross Babbage, John Barclay, Ken Harris, Merv Church, Steve Milner, Rob Tannahill and Les Targ.

Senate on 2 February that ' there are no plans by Australia nor Indonesia for a large scale purchase of Steyr rifles to the value of $109 million or even $1 million'.[91]

Considering the attitudes surrounding the question of arms exports, ADI's Lithgow facility was condemned to a process of accelerating decline. There had been considerable dismay when, in January 1991, the company had made a relatively small-scale rationalisation at the factory entailing 97 retrenchments, followed by more staff reductions in May 1992. There was anger in April 1994 when another 70 jobs were cut, with the entire production work force immediately going on strike. By the time of the announcement in March 1995 of a further loss of 90 employees, the mood among the local community was more one of resignation than surprise, it being realised that there was very little the company could do without new contracts in the offing.[92]

The prospect of increased orders was also somewhat restricted for the Ammunition division, given the nature of the products which it had to sell, although opportunities in this area were pursued. Here, too, ADI quickly came up against the strength of public objections to any perception of Australian companies playing the role of 'merchants of death' on the international arms scene. Approaches received from Sri Lanka, for 76 mm tank ammunition in 1990 and fragmentation grenades three years later, each became the focus of a public furore when enquiries made by the company to the Department of Foreign Affairs and Trade regarding export licences for such munitions were leaked to the press.[93]

Production demand for propellant had actually increased between 1991 and 1993 due to stockpiling to meet ADF needs while ADI was rationalising its ammunition operation; the number of employees at the Mulwala plant rose during this period from 220–330. At the end of 1993, however, the factory was faced with virtually no further defence work until 1996, and securing commercial orders became critical to its survival.

Remarkably, Mulwala was able to establish itself as the exclusive supplier of the United States firm Hodgson Powder, providing propellant for sporting rifle and shotgun ammunition.[94] As a result of this success, the division achieved exports in 1993/94 which were expected to reach a record total of $5 million.[95] Notwithstanding that such a substantial avenue had been found to replace defence sales, in January 1994 it was still necessary to retrench 62 members of the work force of 273.[96]

The commercial limits to this business, and the cost of the investment made by the Commonwealth in the buildings and plant at Mulwala, prompted the company to change its mind in 1993 about becoming the plant's owner. Instead, it was agreed with Defence that the factory should be regarded as a 'strategic facility' and retained in government ownership, but operated by ADI under a lease arrangement.[97]

The division also undertook the marketing of a 'family' of hand grenades developed by the company's Ammunition Product Development Centre at

Footscray and which gave greatly-improved performance at lower unit cost than other types of grenades available. Designed around a high explosive fragmentation grenade, the many variants in the family could be thrown more than 35 metres by hand, projected from both the Steyr and M16A2 rifles without modification to a range of 200 metres, or rigged in a booby trap role using a firing demolition device. First shown in November 1991 at the International Aerospace and Defence Exhibition in Dubai, United Arab Emirates,[98] the grenades were among a range of marketable products which prompted the company to open an office in Abu Dhabi.

In addition to obtaining a contract in 1992 to cleanup the site of the former explosives factory at Albion, the Industrial Decontamination Division (IDD) began securing other business. Late that year, for example, ADI was engaged to clear asbestos and chemicals from an abandoned site in the Sydney suburb of Ashfield.[99] After receiving contracts to clear unexploded ordnance from military ranges in South Australia, the company also looked to develop an international business in bomb disposal, initially in Kuwait which was littered with munitions debris after the Gulf War.[100]

Among overseas contracts which came ADI's way during 1992 was work to undertake environmental remediation at sites in the former East Germany once occupied by the Soviet Army. By the next year no fewer than eight such contracts had been won, and the company had sufficient work in this region to warrant the establishment of an office in Berlin.[101] By late 1994 the company created a subsidiary there – ADI Deutschland – which was expected to have eleven employees by January 1995.[102] In North America, too, IDD proved successful in winning contracts to carry out ground surveys for buried ordnance at ex-military sites, using an advanced digital-imaging magnetic detection system developed by the Geophysical Research Institute of the University of New England in New South Wales.[103]

In March 1995 ADI, in conjunction with Bains Harding Ltd., won a $25 million contract from the Victorian government to demolish the disused power station at Yallourn, a complex of five coal-fired installations near Morwell in the Latrobe Valley. The task, to begin immediately and expected to take two years, was considered to be the biggest of its type ever undertaken in Australia and involved the removal of large amounts of asbestos and other hazardous materials.[104] Ultimately, this project proved an unhappy experience for the company after the customer, the Victorian Government Electricity Commission, cancelled the contract. ADI claimed this was unwarranted and subsequently won the case in an arbitration procedure, but nonetheless failed to make any money out of it.

Throughout this period ADI's Electronics division was equally engaged in an aggressive hunt for business. In July 1992 it was announced that a contract had been won in partnership with two British firms, GEC-Marconi and Logica, to supply a computer-based military command support system for the Royal Navy.

The software, which ADI was to develop, would provide naval and marine commanders with communications, intelligence, geographical displays, tactical databases and various aids for planning and controlling military missions.[105]

By October of that year the Perth facility had also completed (on time and within budget) the $18 million EWCAPSS contract which it had inherited when it took over UDS. This system, based on ADI's proprietary Ada software technology and claimed to be among the most advanced of its type in the world, enabled a user to quickly sort, verify and display information derived from an enemy's radio communications and for commanders to decide their own counter moves and control resources to best effect.[106]

In July 1993 the division publicly revealed that it had developed a computer software system at its Perth facility which it also regarded as a world leader when applied to mine warfare. The new system enabled a naval force to hunt, detect and counter enemy mines and minefields, and also provided intelligence information of enemy and allied military capabilities. With expressions of interest already received from several US corporations, and an invitation to display the software at a British defence exhibition later in the year, the company hoped to reap millions of dollars from defence and commercial exports.[107]

Electronics division had also just signed at this time a $36 million contract for Project Vigilare, the upgrading of the RAAF's air defence system. Within months of this success came the news that the division had also won a $2 million five-year contract to repair and test radio and radar communications equipment in the nose cones, or radomes, of all RAAF aircraft.[108] Hard on the heels of this win came two others in December 1993: a contract to supply the Civil Aviation Authority with an instrument landing system for the new third runway at Sydney's main airport, and another worth $7.5 million for installing Norwegian-made instrument landing systems at six ADF airfields around Australia.[109]

In tendering for Vigilare, the company had teamed with Westinghouse Electric Corporation and AWA Defence Industries. Unfortunately, the key to the ADI bid was imported components from Westinghouse, which were subsequently discovered not to meet the technical requirements of the project. The company found itself in the position of being unable to offer a fully compliant system, and was obliged to terminate its agreement with the big American firm and attempt to retrieve the situation through an arrangement with Unisys. Ultimately ADI's contract was cancelled in January 1995, and the project put up for re-tender later that year.[110]

Notwithstanding that such a project went sour, in October 1994 ADI's Electronics division was still awarded a $5 million contract to supply command support systems for several major ADF headquarters. This would offer formatted military messaging, situation display, and briefing and office automation tools. The company was again prime contractor, with responsibility for project management and most of the technical work, but this time ADI teamed with Compucat

(Australia) for communications facilities and an American firm, Booz Allen Hamilton, for advice on security aspects.[111]

In 1994, too, the division was successful in winning a contract to provide the RAAF with calibration services. The contract, worth about $36 million over six years, was expected to cut the annual cost of calibrating 10,000 items of technical equipment by 20 per cent, and was won in competition with five other commercial firms. While moving this work into ADI's own laboratories at Sydney, Melbourne and Perth – allowing the closure of six RAAF centres – the company would operate existing centres at air force bases at Darwin, Edinburgh (South Australia), Richmond (New South Wales) and Amberley (Queensland).[112]

Continuing its push into this field, in 1993 Electronics division also joined a team bidding for a $500 million contract to refurbish the RAAF's P-3C Orion maritime patrol aircraft. The company was not seeking to have prime carriage of the project, merely to become the sub-contractor with responsibility for developing software for the airborne data management system and interfaces among new and existing systems. Accordingly, the company signed a memorandum of understanding in February with GE Aerospace to pursue this project, but when this preferred partner was bought in April by the United States Martin Marietta Corporation, however, ADI found itself unable to reach a suitable teaming arrangement with the new organisation and withdrew.[113]

Subsequently the company joined a group led by Rockwell Systems Australia Pty. Ltd., which included Ferranti Computer Systems Australia Pty. Ltd. and the North American Aircraft Modification Division of Rockwell International Corporation. When, in January the next year, three of the five contenders were shortlisted for further evaluation, it was an interesting reflection on the changed environment of Australia's defence industry that the Rockwell team was named in competition with the Martin Marietta group and another led by E-Systems which included ASTA. Ultimately the last-named consortium won the contract.[114]

ADI's Training Systems division also hunted new sales opportunities. Its ability to provide a comprehensive service of design, construction and installation of high technology small calibre, armoured fighting vehicle, air-to-ground and special forces ranges was claimed to be rivalled by very few companies in the world.[115] Central to the company's marketing effort was its state-of-the-art projectile locating system, which allowed a supersonic projectile – rifle, cannon or tank – to be electronically detected, regardless of whether a target was struck or missed, and the fall of shot scored and displayed instantaneously to the shooter on a video terminal.

Some valuable contracts were secured in 1991 and early 1992, such as target equipment worth $450,000 for New Zealand, in addition to military ranges at Singleton and Kapooka in New South Wales and Greenbank in Queensland. The company was also involved in range projects with Middle Eastern countries such as Bahrain, Oman and the United Arab Emirates. In April 1992 the division won an order from the Japanese Ground Self Defence Force for electronic targets valued at just under $1 million.[116] Hopes that this might be followed by further big orders from that country went unfulfilled, however, and in July that year the 88-strong work force at Albury was reduced by one-third.[117] To keep the plant operating, small-scale light engineering work had to be transferred from WED's facilities at Bendigo and Maribyrnong.[118]

Subsequently the division's fortunes improved, as interest in live-fire training systems rebounded from a worldwide slump experienced after the Gulf War. A order for eight ranges, worth $18 million, was received from Singapore in 1993, and in May 1995 the division won – in competition with a Swiss bidder – a $4.2 million contract for two training ranges to be installed at Army bases at Townsville in Queensland and Holsworthy in New South Wales.[119]

While the nature of Consulting's business did not make a large contribution to the company's revenues, this division also secured some important consultancy tasks – mainly commissioned by senior officers in the Department of Defence. One example was the devising of certain parts of the course program to be taught at the new Australian College of Defence and Strategic Studies in Canberra from 1995. Other work came from within the company itself, providing advice on policy issues and organisational aspects such as restructuring.[120]

Another important activity in which the division had earlier become involved was the organisation of a major international conference dealing with changes in the maritime environment of the Asia-Pacific region. This event, held in Sydney on 21–22 November 1991 under the co-sponsorship of the RAN and ADI, brought together strategic and political analysts from the Asian region as well as from Europe and the United States and proved a remarkable success. Attending it were 200 participants from a range of countries, including Indonesia, Malaysia, Singapore, the Philippines, Japan, India, Pakistan and New Zealand.[121]

On other fronts, the Logistics Support division was actively pursuing opportunities under the Defence Department's Commercial Support Program (CSP) aimed at having non-core support tasks and services carried out by private enterprise. To take advantage of the steady redeployment of ADF elements to Australia's north, as foreshadowed in the 1987 Defence White Paper and the later Defence Force Structure Review, in February 1992 ADI opened an office in the Northern Territory.[122]

In July of that same year ADI teamed with two other firms to win the base support contract for the Harold E. Holt Naval Communications Station at North West Cape, Western Australia.[123] The facility was important for its role in providing radio communications to RAN and US Navy submarines, and the ADI team was expected to provide all operational support and maintenance services, including management and administration, communication systems, utilities and emergency services from December 1992.[124]

In August 1993 the company won a three-year contract worth $21 million to provide operational support to the satellite control station jointly manned by the United States Air Force and ADF at Nurrungar, located 500 kilometres north-west of Adelaide, and the Woomera village 20 kilometres away. The deal, won in conjunction with two partner companies, covered the operation and maintenance of the satellite communications and computer equipment (under military command); the provision of supply and transport functions, emergency services, catering and cleaning; the operation of community and recreational facilities; and administrative support.[125]

In October of that year, too, the company took over the management of the Army clothing store at the Royal Military College, Duntroon, under a $1 million three-year contract to provide tailoring services to some 2500 Army personnel based in the Canberra area. Subsequently ADI also took over the operation of the shop supplying a wide range of military-related memorabilia to staff and cadets at the college.[126]

Clothing division initially had a quite healthy order book, by virtue of contracts for 275,000 sets of disruptive pattern combat uniforms, and female uniforms for the Army and Navy, which would last for several years.[127] This situation was further enhanced by the signing in the first half of 1991 of a five-year contract with Defence worth nearly $66 million,[128] which here again would buffer the company from commercial competition while it sorted itself out. As was recognised even in 1990, though, the company needed to look to improve its future prospects in this field, as 'the volume of military work available is directly related to the level of defence spending'.[129]

ADI's acquisition of the Leichhardt factory in June 1990 was followed almost immediately by an announcement that the company had won an open tender to supply the New South Wales Fire Brigade with 2000 firefighting jackets worth more than $1 million.[130] In March 1991 the division also won a $723,000 contract for uniforms for Victoria's Public Transport Corporation (PTC).[131]

The official opening on 2 August 1991 of ADI's new clothing factory in Bendigo was accompanied by expectations that this might lead to generation of sales worth $10 million annually.[132] Within little more than a year, however, the company found itself retrenching nearly 280 staff in the Clothing division – 12 at Bendigo, 68 at Leichhardt and 196 at Coburg – as a result of a slowdown in Defence department orders which had cut workload by 30 per cent.[133] Somewhat ironically, shortly afterwards the company had to deal with a rush job in December 1992 to provide 1200 wide-brimmed camouflaged hats within a week, these being needed for the ADF battalion group being sent to Somalia for service with the United Nations.[134]

Subsequent efforts to diversify the range of ADI's customers enjoyed some success. By late-1993, in addition to producing its traditional products, Clothing had become an important supplier to major outlets in the fashion industry. Among these were the Coles-Myer and Country Road Clothing chains, the latter exporting to the United States.[135] Whereas the division had been shedding staff a year earlier, in November 1993 the company was announcing a $1 million dollar expansion of its Bendigo plant and the expected hiring of an additional 30–50 workers.[136]

Clothing had begun to realise its goal of expanding into the specialist niche corporate wardrobe market, winning contracts from such big-name companies as Kodak and Thomas Cook. Efforts to continue growth in this area led ADI to Queensland, where it sought to gain a foothold by entering into a teaming agreement in November 1993 with a Brisbane clothing supplier, Designer Workwear Pty. Ltd.[137] Despite some success which such measures brought, Clothing continued to be an area of uneven development.

The minehunter project

The Defence Force Structure Review paper, released in May 1991, accorded priority to the acquisition by the RAN of larger coastal minehunters in place of a prototype inshore minehunting program which had not produced the results expected. It was quickly recognised within ADI that the company ought to be involved in any program which resulted from this recommendation, since this would represent one of the major defence acquisition contracts of recent years. An early assessment of the existing types of vessels available overseas also evaluated that the two designs with the greatest prospect of success in gaining selection by the RAN were those from the British firm Vosper Thornycroft and the Intermarine company in Italy.[138]

Vospers was able to offer the Sandown Class of ship, which utilised the latest glassfibre reinforced plastic (GRP) technology in its hull stiffened internally by lateral and longitudinal ribs. The Royal Navy already had the lead ship of this class in service and another four on order, and orders were in hand or expected from two foreign navies. The Rome-based shipbuilding company Intermarine SpA, part of the Italian agro-industrial and chemical group Ferruzzi SpA, was the maker of several types of vessels featuring GRP monocoque hulls and an ingenious suspension system which separated major machinery items from the hull to protect them from damage during a mine explosion.

The Lerici Class, introduced into service with the Italian navy in 1985, had performed successfully in the Persian Gulf in 1991, and earlier in these waters during the Iran-Iraq conflict of 1987–88. Ships of this type had been acquired by Malaysia and Nigeria, and the US Navy had recently awarded Intermarine a contract for eight of a larger variant dubbed the Osprey Class. Among the variants of the Lerici ships was the Gaeta Class, 52 metres (171.6 feet) long and displacing 700 tonnes. Not only was this about the right size to satisfy the RAN's requirement but ships of the class had a conventional propeller (so essential for traversing a long coastline like Australia's) in addition to the thrusters used as 'egg-beaters' during mine hunting operations.

Based on information gleaned through initial contacts in Britain and Italy, the company considered the options for pursuing the minehunter opportunity early in 1992. Visits were made to both Vospers and Intermarine, to follow up on what was beginning to look promising as an opportunity to win the RAN contract.[139] As Harris recalled, the main obstacle to be overcome among the directors was that they did not want ADI to become a shipbuilder, and 'we had to work hard to convince them that it was, in fact, a systems project'.[140]

That same month Defence conducted industry briefings, prior to issuing a formal RFP (request for proposal) on 1 May for the acquisition of between four and six ships. After it was decided that any bid by the company could not be won by managing it out of Garden Island, a project team was set up within Berlyn's group at Corporate Headquarters. This was headed by Barrie West, a retired rear-admiral who – before joining the company in March – had been the RAN's Chief of Materiel. At the board's meeting during April, West and Hector Donohue (then engaged in developing the AMASS system to be marketed by ADI) told the directors that – while the company had kept its options open with all overseas companies with designs likely to be contenders for the RAN ships – the relationship with Intermarine was the strongest, and accordingly an arrangement was being developed with them. A decision to team with the Italian company was publicly announced late in June.[141]

The company's courtship of Intermarine was not without its difficulties. For a start Intermarine was caught up in a crisis of the first magnitude, with its parent – the Feruzzi Group – on the verge of bankruptcy due to a scandal involving its chief executive who had committed suicide. As Harris recalls:

> We were getting daily stockmarket prices for the Feruzzi Group to warn us of any further deterioration of their financial position. During these events, there were some very interesting exchanges with people from Feruzzi and from Intermarine to try to make certain that this crisis did not impact on our bid. Guiseppe Sirignani, the chief executive of Intermarine at the time, played a wonderful game of poker with his parent to keep the relationship with ADI alive. There is also the story of Intermarine being courted by the Transfield Group, with one of the co-founders of Transfield – Franco Belgiorno – owning a house just up the coast from La Spezia where Intermarine was based. We wondered how we could possibly win this courtship with the Italian company when Transfield appeared to have a stronger relationship with them.[142]

The task undertaken by West and members of his team was also complicated by the decision to offer both the Gaeta (Italian) and Osprey (United States) variants, together with a range of sonars and combat systems. Design and technical aspects were prepared by Intermarine, while preliminary assessment of the effects of building in Australia, integrated logistic support, and Australian industry involvement was done by ADI. After hectic months of work, the response was completed and submitted by the required deadline in September. Ultimately there were to be seven organisations which responded to the RAN's request for proposals, including bids from ADI's rival Transfield (in a joint venture agreement with Vosper Thornycroft to promote the Sandown design) and ASC (offering a lengthened version of the Swedish Landsort ship).[143]

On 23 December 1992 the Navy shortlisted three of the contenders – ADI, ASC and Transfield – to undertake Defence-funded project definition studies. Each of these groups was also selected to receive the request for tender when it was finally issued on 5 July 1993, with a requirement to respond by mid-December.[144] Having made the short list of contenders, the company now lost the services of West and was obliged to find a replacement as head of the Minehunter team which handled all aspects of the company's bid from offices in Bondi Junction close by, but separate to, Corporate Headquarters. Mervyn Church, the General Manager Commercial at NED, was selected and appointed in November 1992, under the direction of Nigel Berlyn as GGM Development.

On 12 November the deputy chairman of the ADI board (Bowra) announced that the company, in developing its bid, had chosen Newcastle, New South Wales, as the place to build the minehunters – should it be successful in winning the contract. In what was described as a 'slick ceremony' at the Newcastle Workers Club, Bowra – accompanied by Church – promised that an ADI win would see some 2000 jobs and $300 million income created for the Hunter Valley region. The construction site selected was at Throsby Basin, Carrington, then used as a maintenance depot by the Hunter Port Authority. This already offered modern buildings, as well as deep water adjacent to a wharf which provided safe manoeuvring space for ships.[145]

Hard on the heels of this announcement came further news on 22 December – one week after tenders for the project officially closed – that an enterprise bargain agreement, which had been negotiated specifically for the company's minehunter bid, was registered with the Industrial Relations Commission. The agreement, reached with the Automotive Metals and Engineering Union and the Association of Professional Engineers & Scientists, contained a special emphasis on 'dispute avoidance and resolution' and was intended to ensure harmonious employee relations at the proposed ADI facility. It also provided, as Harris explained:

> ... a sound basis for wage fixation, a co-operative approach towards applying skills-based career structures, employee development and continuous improvement strategies for the benefit of a project of national importance.[146]

Further emphasising the attractiveness of the ADI bid was the company's ability to show that its proposals were proceeding trouble-free. In March 1994 the Newcastle City Council approved ADI's application to develop the Carrington site. The scheme presented included a construction hall 120 metres long, 40 metres wide and 21 metres high, a concrete marine railway extending approximately 100 metres into the water, wharfage facilities, ancillary offices, workshops and storage areas – all of which were passed without any amendment being required.[147]

The company also sought to stress that its commitment to the Newcastle region went beyond simply securing the lucrative minehunter contract; there would be lasting benefit in the form of a state-of-the-art facility as the core of an ongoing local industry. In May – with the final selection now looming – ADI announced that it was funding a $2 million research project in conjunction with CSIRO and the Co-operative Research Centre for Aerospace Structures. The object of this effort was to find new applications for lightweight, super-strength composite materials – such as components of building structures, railway carriages and wagons, ship superstructures, vehicles, bridges and offshore platforms.[148]

To meet the RAN's schedule for introducing the minehunters into service, and also to ensure the smooth transfer of GRP technology, the company made known that it planned to build the hull of the first minehunter in Italy. This would be done using existing moulds at Intermarine's plant at Sarzana, on Italy's north-west coast (a second facility at La Spezia specialised in completing and trialing the vessels), and transported to Newcastle for final fit-out – by which stage the construction facility at Carrington would be finished and ready to begin work. It was still expected that the level of Australian industry involvement in the program would stand at a minimum of 78 per cent, well above the RAN's requirement of 60 per cent.[149]

The benefits of these various strategies were plainly demonstrated when the Lord Mayor of Newcastle, John McNaughton, publicly endorsed the ADI bid while speaking on local radio. Although the other two contenders were – if successful – proposing to construct their ships at Tomago, on the north channel of the Hunter River on the city's northern edge, he declared that:

> ... the thing that impresses me about the ADI plan, it is clearly the one that is best for the City of Newcastle. We'll get more out of that one than we'll get out of anything else.[150]

On 2 June 1994 Defence Minister Ray announced that the outcome of what he described as an 'extremely close' contest. While all three bids 'were of excellent quality, offered high levels of Australian industry involvement and met the Navy's stringent requirements', ADI was the preferred tenderer for the Minehunter contract.[151] After detailed negotiation of an agreement, a contract was formally signed on 12 August at ADI's Carrington site for delivery of six vessels (of what would become known as Huon Class minehunters), beginning in 1998 and with the last one due in 2002.

Literally within minutes of the contract signing, work began at Throsby Basin with the demolition of a building to make way for the new construction hall costing $16 million. Harris also announced that the 30 members of ADI's minehunter group, including senior management, would be moving soon to Newcastle.[152] This transfer took place at the end of August, when the ADI team moved into temporary quarters at the old state Dockyard site at Dyke Point, on Newcastle Harbour, expected to be its home for some months until offices at Throsby Basin were ready to receive them.[153]

On 16 September the first of 300 eight-metre long timber pylons was driven into the ground, in preparation for the pouring of the construction hall's concrete floor. By the end of November the work of erecting the steel columns of the huge building was ready to start,[154] it being expected that the shell of the hall would be ready by March 1995 but not completely fitted out until September. A local firm, Anderson Rea of Argenton, was given the $3 million contract to build the 200-tonne mould used to cast the hulls of the five boats built on the site, beginning in August 1995 – about the time that the first hull arrived from Italy.[155]

Other orders for equipment and items required by the new Huon ships were generated both within Australia and overseas. Eighteen Isotta-Fraschini 1300 generating sets were to come from Italy. So, too, would the first of the GMT (Grandi Motori Trieste) 230 non-magnetic and silenced diesel engines for main propulsion, but the remaining five would be manufactured under licence by ADI itself at Bendigo. Twelve remote-controlled mine disposal vessels were ordered from Bofors Underwater Systems AB in Sweden, although a large part of the work on these would be done in Australia.[156]

Winning the minehunter project – at $1.2 billion one of the largest naval contracts ever awarded in Australia (after submarines and frigates) – was clearly having an immense impact both on the Newcastle region and on ADI's development. As Harris acknowledged in the company's 1994 annual report, it not only added 'significantly to ADI's growing order book' but also to 'its reputation as a strong industrial and project management company'. In many respects, this one contract was the big break which the company needed to establish itself as a major player on the international defence scene.

The intensive effort put into marketing ADI's products and services had unquestionably started to pay off – even before the minehunter contract was won. Up until 1993, about $600 million in new business had been secured since the company's inception, some $130 million of this in export orders; the extent to which annual turnover was dependent on the nation's defence budget had been reduced from 80 per cent to about 65 per cent.[157] Notwithstanding ADI's special relationship with the Defence department, such ADF contracts as the company was awarded were won in the face of intense competition from many other local and international commercial firms. This, in itself, was a tribute to the extent to which the company had improved its standards and performance.

Inevitably, ADI had not always been able to demonstrate that it was the best contender for contracts on which it bid. Equally, some of the ventures which it pursued did not always prove to be good business or as profitable as expected, and there is little doubt that mistakes were made in the course of exploring and taking up the business opportunities which they were thought to hold at the time. The haste and poor judgement involved had been directly behind the departure of the Company Secretary/Legal Counsel, in August 1991.

McCorquodale had become increasingly irritated at being excluded from the executive decision-making process within ADI headquarters, regarding this a shortsighted view of the role which he could play to the company's benefit:

> I was particularly frustrated that arms of the company were entering into deals which made little commercial sense but only involving me afterwards, or at second hand. Some of these transactions were hopeless, but here I was arguing that an 'ounce of prevention is worth a ton of cure' and getting nowhere.[158]

Reflecting on this situation Harris offers a slightly different view of the situation, suggesting that:

> [At] the time ADI was experiencing some difficulty in injecting stronger commercial legal considerations in its business activities and avoiding the sorts of legal issues that would normally concern government organisations. I suspect that this problem led to some of the business units trying to find alternative legal advice.[159]

When approached about a position as Deputy Government Solicitor (Commercial) in Attorney-General's, his former department, McCorquodale decided to accept the offer. On his departure the functions he had been performing were split. Trish Russell took over as Company Secretary and Andrew McKibbin was subsequently appointed Legal Counsel (and additional company secretary,[160] to provide for occasions when Russell might be absent).

With the number of operating divisions having grown, and a range of important developmental aspects receiving attention within headquarters, the company was fast becoming a complex business. The task of running it was made more demanding by Harris' resistance to any notion of expanding the size of management. As he said in a minute to his senior executives in March 1991:

> In setting up the new business units I deliberately chose not to add another level of management between me and the Chief General Managers. I know there are some people who argue that the span of control is becoming too

great but it should be possible to run a multi business operation such as ours with no more layers of management …

Clearly, some additional staff work is required on operational issues. I need to spend more time on strategic issues and make more time available to the Chief General Managers. It is becoming increasingly difficult, now that we have 10 very active business units for me to keep abreast of all operational issues.[161]

Such rapid expansion of the company's structure was open to criticism on other grounds as well. As a former manager of the Bendigo facility in pre-company days was moved to complain, ADI had spread itself so widely that it ought to change its name to 'Australian Diversified Industries'.[162] Fynmore later candidly acknowledged the question mark which hung over the company's move into so many areas of non-defence business:

I guess I have a concern as to whether we have a future in some of the new fields in which we're dabbling our toe. I've been strongly supportive of pushing into those areas, but we've had criticism that these are pretty well looked after by the private sector – why are we entering them? My argument is that, if we're to be a well-rounded company, we need to be there. We shouldn't be condemned to being in the pre-Second World War industries and not into the future industries.

Our track record on some of the things we've taken over hasn't been all that good. Some have become the nucleus of our new technology areas, but … to be fair, some of my fellow directors probably would have preferred that we opted out of one or two of the others by now. I've been supporting management in sticking with it a little longer, but we need to get some runs on the board soon or I'll have to acknowledge too that perhaps we shouldn't.[163]

In a more philosophical mood, Harris had no doubts about the wisdom of the strategy which was followed:

Not all of the array of businesses that we have will survive. There may be some that don't make it, and that's OK. You can never get a 100 per cent hit rate anyway. Its all about risk management … We worked on the assumption that if we got about 70 per cent of our decisions right then we were ahead of the game. That's all you could expect, as long as they were the right 70 per cent.[164]

8

MODERNISING AMMUNITION PRODUCTION

Although appointed GGM Development on ADI's headquarters staff, as already mentioned Barclay was soon diverted onto special project work. The task which Harris asked him to undertake, beginning in about September or October 1989, was nothing less than the rationalisation and restructuring of the various elements of the ammunition and heavy engineering businesses which the company had inherited. It had been recognised from the start that there were serious problems with this part of the new organisation's structure.

The main deficiency was that there was too much duplication and fragmentation of production across the factories as a whole. Under existing arrangements, no fewer than seven factories were engaged in parts of the ammunition making process, and these largely employed mass production techniques which were relics of the Second World War. Even with the closure of the Albion and Maribyrnong explosives works coincident with ADI's formation, there was still an excess of capacity over future demand – especially for ammunition, where the Army in particular seemed intent on cutting purchases.[1]

In the case of many of the facilities, the most valuable or attractive thing about them was the land they occupied – a fact which Harris acknowledges was not at all lost sight of when setting up the company: 'One of the reasons why we negotiated so hard on the real estate, why we wanted to own and not just lease it, was because of its value. That was our capital.'[2] Barclay says the same thing:

I think it went right back to when we were chasing the title for the land. We played it very low key, saying that we could not possibly operate these factories if we didn't own the land – we wouldn't be masters of our own destiny, and so on. But we always knew that what we would do was then sell them.[3]

Further impetus for re-evaluating what these assets were actually worth to ADI stemmed from the wish of Ammunition and Missiles Division (as it was then known) to get control of the ordnance facility at Maribyrnong. This played an important part in the division's activities – forging shell projectiles, for instance – yet it was actually part of WED. Although Harris told the head of Ammunition (Padman) not to pursue this initiative, it was clearly becoming imperative to resolve questions about the future of some of these plants.[4]

Project Alaric

While the broad thrust of what needed to be done was undoubtedly in Harris' mind from a very early stage, he was not certain initially of the scale and precise nature of the problem. Accordingly, Padman's division was told to undertake analysis into why the company was losing so heavily on this part of its operations. Harris was particularly troubled by the fact that ADI's ammunition prices were well above other suppliers on the world market. It disturbed him even more that the division's performance to its customer – the ADF – was frankly 'pathetic', with only 64 per cent of orders received being delivered in the year required, which meant that a huge backlog of unfulfilled orders had been built up.[5]

After getting Barclay to look into matters in more detail, the issues became clearer. The problem was seen by Harris as simply one of rational economics:

Looking at it from the perspective of the balance sheets, we could see that we had an awful lot of assets there. How could we make a return on assets of that value? Could we increase the volume of the business? Well no, short of World War III occurring – thanks to the ending of the Cold War, which was a dreadful thing when you happen to be an arms manufacturer. If we couldn't rely upon exports, we had to accept that our business was of a certain size and likely to get smaller. It followed that our assets base here was too big, that a lot of the company's capital was being wasted through being tied up in ammunition production. We could do better things with those properties than have ammunition plants on them. By now it seemed obvious to him that drastic action was called for; he resolved – in his words – to 'king-hit the joint'.[6]

Following what was now a tried-and-proven approach, Harris formulated his tactics: keep plans secret until finalised, obtain endorsement for action at the highest level, then move rapidly and ruthlessly before any opposition had time to block, delay or force modification of the plan. It was a philosophy which perhaps owed something to Harris' reading of Sun Tzu, the fourth century Chinese theorist, whom he was fond of quoting.[7] Then again, as a solution it was very much just an extension of the process which had begun back with ASTA and Williamstown dockyard, of which ADI's creation was itself just a part.

Drawing further on proven methods, Harris next set up a very small implementation group under Barclay's direction. With Barclay was Bill Mitchell – another with demonstrated ability on such tasks – and Ron Taylor, who had been heavily involved with Project REFA. To keep the team's members insulated from day-to-day distractions, in May 1990 Harris had them moved out of Corporate Headquarters (then still located in Canberra) into rented office space in the National Press Club building, located a few streets away on National Circuit, Barton. Here, in what Harris jokingly referred to as 'the little hot-house in the Press Club', they set down to work. Within three months Taylor moved on to head up the Industrial Decontamination Division, leaving the other two to continue on their own for a time. Later Brian Conway moved across to join them, bringing together another of the major players from ADI's transition period.[8]

The first phase of the team's efforts was focused on identifying the alternative courses of action which were available. In Barclay's words:

> We looked at about nine or ten options, costed them, and it boiled down to two or three. The main one was to stay at St. Marys, on the eastern edge of the site. Basically, put up a fence along there and keep just that bit. But then, it was worth more shut than it was open, and we were concerned about devaluing the whole lot. So in the end we went for the greenfields option.[9]

In essence, this meant closing down a number of the older plants and shifting production to a completely fresh site altogether.

On 1 September 1990 the chairman and managing director of ADI met with Senator Ray. In Harris' words, the purpose of the meeting was to give the minister, 'as the new owner, a realistic appreciation of the state the Company is in, and what we should do to create a strong business'. This session was not undertaken without a certain amount of misgiving, since the company had previously refused to reveal details of its affairs to the Defence Department until key points underpinning the corporate plan – meaning mainly, but not exclusively, the capital structure – were resolved. But, Harris noted in a minute to his senior executives, 'we are running out of time, patience and money and cannot wait any longer'.[10]

The document which Fynmore and Harris delivered was a frank assessment of how far ADI had come and the extent to which it could be expected to achieve its objective of providing 'a cost-effective industrial underpinning to the Australian defence effort'. The broad thrust of the argument presented was that three of the company's existing four main businesses could be 'made to perform reasonably well in commercial terms'. The fourth, the Ammunition and Missiles Division, was judged to have no commercial future 'as presently structured'.[11]

According to the projections included in the company's paper, the ADF's requirement for ammunition was expected to fall from approximately $150 million in 1990/91 to an annual average only one-third of that figure for the next five years.[12] During this period the division would accumulate losses of $60 million, even though ADF orders were later anticipated to rise – but only to about 60–70 per cent of their 1990/91 level. Export opportunities for this product were limited, both because of a world oversupply and the Australian government's nervousness at acquiring an image as a promoter of lethal products. There was little prospect either of setting the existing factories on a more economic path: 'Costs are excessive, response times are long, plant is outmoded and industrial working conditions are sometimes Dickensian.'

The conclusion to be drawn from this assessment was that the sensible commercial option was to close the business down and import the nation's ammunition needs from overseas. Such a course was, however, unacceptable to the ADF, which considered local manufacture of ammunition to be essential to Australia's self-reliant defence capability. On this basis, therefore, the business had to be completely restructured to provide a smaller number of automated plants geared to production in small batches. This approach, Ray was told, had been discussed with the Chief of the Defence Force, General Gration, who strongly supported the plans which the company had formulated.

Restructuring the company's activities was, the document argued, the key to setting ADI on a sound future footing. Without such action, the company was 'slowly going broke'. Depending on how much of the debt covered by the interim capital structure was ultimately converted to equity, the company must run out of cash between 1992–94 and in any case would start having negative cash flows from 1991. Neither the board nor presumably the government wanted 'to be associated with yet another high profile, government-backed corporate failure', so the alternatives were really very few.

Under the scheme proposed, the costs of WED would be reduced by closing Maribyrnong and expanding the heavy engineering capability at Bendigo. Doing this would also save the Defence vote $8 million annually in funding DRSC (defence required support capability). Closing Footscray and St. Marys, and setting up a new integrated manufacturing factory at a new site to be determined, offered further major advantages. Not only would this see the nation left with 'a modern, flexible ammunition facility, sized to the needs of the Australian Defence Force and geared to the next century' – something which the report wincingly referred to as 'ADI's gift to Australia' – but the whole project would be self-funding. The costs of establishing this new factory would be met through the sale of company assets at the closed sites. Revenue from this same source would also be applied to furthering the company's development, with any left over being returned 'to the shareholder in the normal way that companies deal with surplus capital'.

Achieving this outcome would mean that the company had to bear heavy costs initially, through preparing the land for sale and progressively releasing lots onto the market to maximise the return on its value. In short, ADI would have to make substantial borrowings and endure negative cash flows for probably the first five years – something which was extremely risky while ever the question of the company's debt levels associated with the capital structure issue remained in doubt. All the minister was asked to do was commit himself to 'the broad direction proposed' and to 'charge the Board with the responsibility to implement this plan'.

Senator Ray accepted the advice contained in this special report, without attempting to pressure the board into changing its mind. His only intervention was a later request that the public announcement regarding factory closures be delayed until 30 November.[13] On that date Harris duly made public the company's intention to shut down the three targeted plants. The closures would be phased, with Maribyrnong the first to go in December 1992, followed by Footscray and St. Marys no later than mid-1994.[14]

With the initial thinking now done and the resultant plan announced, Harris moved to set the restructuring team onto a formal basis in January 1991 by creating it as the Major Projects Group, with Barclay as Group General Manager. Mitchell was named as General Manager Operations, while Jim Ruming became Accountant & Manager Administration. Small cells were also established in Melbourne and Sydney, occupying offices at the Maribyrnong facility and the National Mutual Building in Market Street respectively.[15]

Showing a macabre sense of history, the process of restructuring was dubbed 'Project Alaric'. The name was not an acronym, but that of the Visigoth king who sacked Rome in the 5th century. Perhaps concerned that this choice might be taken by critics to indicate that the creation of ADI had been a 'slash and burn' exercise after all – despite public denials at the time[16] – Harris moved to end speculation as to the name's significance. In May 1991 he humorously invited company personnel to suggest 'the most inventive use of these initials' and promised a bottle of wine for the winner.[17]

The holding of the Alaric competition received wide attention, and from circles well beyond the company itself. As Harris recalls:

There was a lot of interest in it. One of the entries was sent in from Robert Ray's office. Ian MacDougall [Chief of the Naval Staff] sent an actual plaque from the submarine HMS *Alaric*, on which he'd served, as his entry – on loan only. Staff at the Canadian High Commission got involved as well.[18]

When the large number of entries received were assessed, the managing director took a judicious course and declared himself the winner with 'Authoritarian Leaders Are Really Intensely Conceited'; he then awarded prizes to six runners-up and all the remaining entrants.[19]

End of an era

News of the planned closures came as a severe jolt to a lot of people. Anticipating that this would be the case, Harris had taken the precaution of summoning his plant managers to a briefing at Melbourne's Tullamarine Airport a few days before the official announcement. Here it was explained to them what was about to happen and why, in an effort to obtain their support beforehand. According to one account, 'Those who were expected to "have difficulty" with the news were dealt with separately first'.[20] Among the latter were the chiefs of the three plants concerned: Ron Evans (Footscray), John Pettifer (St. Marys) and Russell Thomson (Maribyrnong).

Harris admits that this was a very difficult meeting in itself:

> Their reaction was absolute shock. Ron Evans in particular had spent his whole working life in only two places, Maribyrnong and Footscray, and here I'd come down to tell him I was shutting both. He was quite upset, but being a total professional he got on with it.

> What shocked people most was that the decision had been taken so quickly, and it was all happening. We weren't there to get their advice, just telling them that Friday the announcement was being made. Now I think everybody recognises that it was the right thing to do – it wasn't all that complicated really because there was no other choice.[21]

Pettifer confirms that what he and the others heard was indeed unpleasant news. In his case it was almost doubly so, since to him had fallen the task of closing down the Albion explosives factory prior to his arrival at St. Marys in May 1987. He had put more than three years of effort into tackling the problems at his new location, and had good grounds for believing that this process was reaching a stage of paying off to ADI's benefit:

> By 1990 we'd actually got the place back to just about breaking even. We'd cut our overheads and restructured, all long before the other factories. We hadn't got it all right by any stretch of the imagination – we were still having problems with deliveries, for example. Our deliveries had got up to about 75 per cent, instead of closer to 50 per cent when I started here, so we were definitely getting better. Certainly we knew where we were, which was more than we did before. We had a handle on what the factory was doing, and that was a big thing at that stage.

> And then we were told, 'Right, we're going to close you down'. Whack! I had no idea until very shortly before the announcement. We knew something was

up, but never thought that St. Marys would be one of those to close. I was kept out of all discussion in the planning stage, which I felt a bit bitter about at the time. If I'd known I might have argued vociferously against closure, but once the decision is made then one turns around and implements the decision. Today, I don't think it matters. I just think, 'That's that'.[22]

The shock felt by the managers was, predictably, fully mirrored by the large number of employees at the three factories: 552 at Maribyrnong, 570 at Footscray and 406 at St. Marys – a total of 1528, although some were expected to be relocated to other plants or join the new factory's work force of several hundred when this was built.[23] The loss of so many jobs during the depths of a national recession naturally caused a great deal of anxiety among those workers affected. Finding new positions in areas of western Melbourne and western Sydney already hard-hit by high unemployment was clearly going to be a daunting prospect for many.[24]

Added to such concerns was a feeling of disappointment that institutions with long histories, particularly Footscray and Maribyrnong, were suddenly being swept away. For some, the connexion had become familial, with sons and daughters following their parents into the work force of these places. As Evans later commented about Footscray to one television news service: 'Third generation members of families have worked on the site so, you know, that's sad.'[25] Even the then premier of Victoria, Joan Kirner, counted her father among those who had spent part of their working lives at Maribyrnong.[26]

A degree of anger was felt by unions, too, who considered they had been ambushed and to an extent betrayed after lending their support to earlier company initiatives to make the plants profitable. Objections promptly expressed to the government from this quarter derived a measure of comfort from statements by the Minister for Finance, Ralph Willis, that the proposed ADI restructure had not been discussed – let alone approved – at Cabinet level, and that agreement by the government to fund such a large number of redundancies would not necessarily be forthcoming when the matter did come before Cabinet.[27]

Union representatives were reported as accusing Harris as having 'acted outrageously' in pre-empting Loan Council approval for redundancy funding by his announcement, and challenged him to state 'where the money was coming from'. Rather ominously, warnings were sounded of union determination to fight the company on the issue of closures, if need be with industrial action.[28]

Despite the conciliatory tone initially adopted by the finance minister, attempts to force government intervention on this matter did not get very far. Now the advantages of forming these factories into an independent company came to the fore, in allowing ministers to distance themselves from commercially necessary but politically unpalatable decisions. When questioned about the closures in the Senate on 4 December 1990, Defence Minister Ray was able to respond:

I think I should point out, firstly, that the facilities…are not Defence Department establishments but are, in fact, owned by Australian Defence Industries … . ADI is run by a board of experienced business people charged with the responsibility of operating modern, efficient and competitive defence industries in this country. While in the final analysis ADI is answerable to its owner, the Government, we do not seek to intervene in the day-to-day commercial decisions of the company. In this context, it is important to understand that the announced closure … is an ADI proposal based on its commercial assessment of its future. It is not a Government decision. Having said that, I should point out that ADI consulted the Government and the Defence Force prior to last Friday's announcement.[29]

The terms of this reply made clear that Ray had no doubts that, had he failed to support the ADI board's judgement on this issue, probably all the directors would have resigned.

In the months that followed, passions aroused by the company's plans occasionally found expression in acts of sabotage by workers at the affected plants. There were, though, clear limits to giving vent to feelings by such means, given the work performed at these factories. As Pettifer recalls at St. Marys:

We had broom handles stuck in machinery, accusations made that could never be substantiated, and things of that nature. The key thing that happened was when a piece of copper pipe was found inside the incorporator and jammed it up. But in this business you don't dare to sabotage too much because it turns dangerous. This went on for a period of probably eighteen months and then the 'troops' settled down and accepted the situation.[30]

With the slump in morale which inevitably followed the announcement, keeping up production levels was going to be difficult. In fact, however, the problem was not nearly so bad as might have been expected. To quote Pettifer again:

The productivity kept on coming because we were able to convince people that May 1994 was a long way away. We also said, 'Right, we don't agree with the decision but we're not going to try to change it. We accept that its irrevocable, but we will make it our mission over the next three years to prove that the company has made a mistake. You're all going to lose your jobs, but if you go out on a high note you stand a very good chance of getting another good job because you can show you've come from a successful business rather than a down–and–out one'.

We also instituted an incentive system which gave people a monthly $150 bonus, payable at the time of their retrenchment, which was linked to meeting production goals. That worked, because they could see how well they were doing and they were getting money for it.[31]

With encouragement coming in this form, worker output actually hit new highs. Notwithstanding the closure edict which had been passed on St. Marys, throughout 1992–93 production targets were routinely being met almost in full and often exceeded, as were delivery schedules.[32] In May 1992 the facility was also granted Class 'A' accreditation for manufacturing resource planning by the Oliver Wight organisation of the United States, and as well won the prestigious 'Company of the Year' trophy for 1992 awarded by the Australian Production and Inventory Control Society (APICS).[33]

The same picture emerged at Footscray, where in 1993 the first batch of a major order for half a million 20 mm cannon cartridges required for the RAAF was delivered well within schedule. To complete the order, it had been necessary to recommission an entire manufacturing system but this had been achieved a month early. Evans pointed out that:

We had to substantially revamp some materials handling equipment to improve occupational health and safety, but that did not prevent us quickly getting on with the task. The alternative to re-establishing the line would have been to bring in the cartridges from overseas.[34]

This record of increased achievement at Footscray was slightly tarnished in May 1994 when it was revealed that four large batches of 5.56 mm ammunition delivered to the Army, totalling approximately a million rounds, included a very small number of cartridges which did not contain enough propellant to discharge the bullet from the Steyr rifle firing them. This meant the batches had to be returned to ADI so that all rounds could be weighed to check that each was not faulty.[35]

At Maribyrnong, too, a similar upwards trend was observed. Zoltan Janka, who managed this facility from July 1991 until its closure, recalled in 1993 with pride that:

We built into our budget a ten per cent allowance for loss of morale due to the retrenchments program. But we managed to avert that, and instead it actually went up. In fact, we've bettered our budget in the last two years quite significantly. I think that shows that if there is work to be done, and the work is seen as worthwhile, then people respond pretty well.

Part of the answer to this lay in the fact that, because of the close-down of factories and the phased start-up of the new plant, there was a program to buy for stockpiling purposes. That meant Defence orders increased in volume, and you can achieve a lot with larger throughput. Having a firm order book for, say, two years in advance helps planning, so you can utilise both plant and equipment in the most efficient manner. We certainly implemented lots of improvements to our manufacturing methods that led to productivity gains.[36]

Despite the efforts of a small group who formed themselves into a 'Save Maribyrnong Committee', the majority of people at the facility reconciled themselves to facing the reality of their situation. The factory's management tried to facilitate that process by frankly telling each worker how long their employment was expected to last, to provide them with a sound basis for deciding their own future. To make it easier for those considering early retirement or wishing to re-establish themselves in new employment, the company engaged a firm of consultants, DBM Australia, to provide 'out-placement' services and other on-site assistance. Apart from providing advice and counselling, the consultants set up what amounted to a job centre to help workers prepare resumes and tap into the large number of positions available which are never advertised. According to Harris, the proportion of former Maribyrnong workers seeking new jobs who found them was 80 or 90 per cent.[37]

Notwithstanding that the continued operation of the three factories was not in the company's long-term best interests, there was little doubt that their departure from the scene would be missed on several scores. Janka recounted in the period leading to Maribyrnong's closure that:

Each week I'm getting phonecalls from businesses who are rather concerned that we are closing our place. What are they going to do about orders that we used to do for them, they ask? Its a bit of a problem they've got. In many cases we can solve it by suggesting someone else that might be able to do what they need, but in others they may find that there is a gap they can't fill. While commercial work has only been 5–25 per cent of our normal production here, that proportion has been fairly significant in terms of the top end of technology. Our organisation is and has been in the forefront of things like electron beam welding and forging.[38]

There was also no mistaking that the armed services also stood to lose in certain respects as a result of the closures. With the consolidation of heavy engineering work at Bendigo, the ADF – and Australia generally – would be foregoing some capabilities previously possessed at Maribyrnong. For example, the Defence department had decided that the forging of barrels for medium-calibre artillery and tank guns within Australia was no longer a strategic requirement and on this basis was being purposely and knowingly dispensed with.[39] While some capacity for producing these items might remain at Bendigo, it was doubtful that the steel making capability to manufacture suitable forgings existed elsewhere in the country. As Janka observed:

While its certainly feasible to buy gun barrels from overseas in peacetime, as soon as there is a conflict most countries – particularly USA – closes the doors to any exports and so there isn't any more. So I can foresee a situation where, if we get ourselves into a general conflict, we will have to go about re-establishing some of the capabilities we have given away.[40]

There was also some criticism of apparent wastefulness arising from the move which received publicity, such as the fact that a new $10 million shell filling building at St. Marys might possibly be demolished without ever being used. Despite the furore which erupted, the fact was that construction had been commenced by the Department of Defence in November 1988 – while ADI was still in the course of being set up. By the time the company had realised that the structure would probably never be commissioned for its intended purpose, it was nearing completion. The decision therefore had been made to carry on to lockup stage, but not proceed to install the plant ordered (which would go to the new greenfield site), in the hope that a developer still might find a suitable use for the building.[41]

Closing Footscray (which covered 94.7 hectares) and Maribyrnong (36.65 hectares) would release valuable real estate in an area of Melbourne's inner western suburbs. Plans were developed for public comment envisaging a mix of residential, commercial and light industrial uses on each of the sites, with varying areas of public and private open space preserved. Also retained would be historic buildings, some of which might be refurbished.[42] When, in November 1993, the sites at Maribyrnong and Footscray were rezoned to enable a redevelopment scheme worth $350 million to go ahead,[43] this news was positively reported by the press. Construction of 1650 dwellings for about 4200 people was expected to create more than 3000 jobs in the building industry over the next five to seven years.[44]

In New South Wales the state government was also initially keen on the idea of throwing open for redevelopment the huge tract of 1535 hectares at St. Marys, which was near Parramatta – one of the fastest growing parts of Australia. Approaches begun by ADI shortly after the closure announcement resulted in the site being included on the State's Urban Development Program during 1991.[45] In October 1991 premier Nick Greiner also announced that he had asked the federal government to contribute $73 million over five years under the Commonwealth Building Better Cities program towards building a new model city of about 40 000 residents.[46]

In the wake of the decision announced by ADI in February 1992 that the new ammunition facility would be located in Victoria, the support of the government in Sydney for the St. Marys redevelopment scheme evaporated overnight. The Minister for State Development and Tourism, Michael Yabsley, angrily labelled the decision 'one of the most blatant examples yet of the Federal Government using raw political muscle to influence what should have been a straight forward commercial decision'.[47] It was, in fact, quite untrue that there had been any government influence in the matter, but attempts to inform New South Wales ministers and officials to this effect were strongly rebuffed.

Adding to the expressions of outrage, the next month Premier Greiner notified Canberra that his government was withdrawing its submission for Better Cities funding for St. Marys.[48] A week after this the state Minister for Planning and Energy, Robert Webster, made clear the extent to which the company would be punished for its decision. Speaking in Albury on 23 March, he declared that government pledges to give priority to ADI's application to have the site rezoned had been conditional on New South Wales winning the new plant. Now the company would have to decontaminate the site and apply 'through the usual channels'.[49]

After considering the position in which it was now placed, in August ADI announced that it intended to press on with its plans for St. Marys. To assist in financing the undertaking – estimated as likely to worth more than $1 billion – the company would seek to enter into a joint arrangement with a commercial developer, the choice of whom would be decided after negotiations yet to begin.[50] In March 1994 the company announced that its partner in the venture would be Lend Lease Corporation.[51]

The main impediment to these plans was the need to engage in major cleanup programs at all three sites. This entailed undertaking careful assessment of the heritage significance of the numerous buildings which covered each property, followed by not just the demolition and removal of unwanted structures, but also the decontamination of soil which over long years of industrial occupation had become impregnated with a range of chemical pollutants. Even allowing for some recovery of costs through recycling items such as pressed red clay bricks, the job involved was long and expensive.[52] Remediation costs would ultimately total approximately $90 million, most of which had to be outlaid before a cent would be recovered from sale of these assets.[53]

The worst feature of this task was the element of uncertainty regarding precisely what activities had gone on at the various sites over time, even where problems were suspected or known about. As Bill Mitchell (CGM Property Division) remarked:

> At St. Marys it turned out that from time to time over 50 years they'd been disposing of obsolete ammunition, only some of the components had not been completely destroyed. We found parts like small fuses which hadn't combusted, or residues of RDX and TNT, or residues of propellant. And we have found a bit of a cocktail in a couple of places, with stuff like asbestos impregnated by paint or chemicals. A few years ago we were very surprised when these things came out, though now I'm over being surprised by anything.

> I think in the 1990s we tend to forget that when these places were operating at their peak during times of crisis, the nation was very grateful to have them.

Practices went on which are not acceptable now, but they were acceptable back then and no-one really cared. Our approach has been essentially to get on with the task of cleaning the mess up, without getting all emotive. People are slowly accepting that.[54]

The extent of the contamination discovered was neither unduly serious nor unmanageable. A $1 million soil-testing study begun by the company in April 1991, and carried out under the supervision of the State Pollution Control Commission, had established that less than 1 per cent of the entire area was in any way affected. As the head of ADI's Industrial Decontamination Division (Taylor) told one journalist: 'By far the biggest problem we have on this site is general rubbish.' Contamination from chemicals, organics and heavy metals was limited to less than 1 per cent of the property, and none of these areas were beyond the scope of existing technology to remedy.[55]

Notwithstanding the company's best endeavours to deal with the decontamination issue, a considerable obstacle was encountered in the form of the Blacktown and Penrith city councils – the two local government authorities within whose boundaries the St. Marys site lay. The concern of these bodies was understandable, since the granting of rezoning approval while doubt existed as to whether all areas affected by pollutants had been discovered, and properly dealt with, left them liable for potentially huge legal damages in the future. Added to the difficult situation were pressures placed on the two councils by a diverse range of community groups. Among these were groups arguing for surveys to be conducted of former workers at the factory whose health had allegedly been damaged; neighbouring residents concerned about the fate of the natural bushland and 2500 kangaroos and 50 emus roaming within the high wire-fence surrounding the grounds; objectors to proposals to road transport a quantity of low-level radioactive waste which the federal government had placed in temporary storage on the site; and still others promoting such unrelated causes as support for rebels on the island of Bougainville.

Attempts to find a solution to the impasse which developed were not helped by the attitude of the federal government, which initially declined to comprehensively indemnify the two councils against future problems which might be experienced with contamination. This was despite the fact that any such occurrences which were discovered would have been occasioned by activities carried on during the Commonwealth's period of occupancy. A more limited form of indemnity offered by Senator Ray in June 1993 was rejected,[56] although eventually an acceptable indemnity was negotiated which left all parties satisfied.

Not only did the initial approach harden the councils' stand as to the assurances they demanded, but the Commonwealth's attitude was scarcely helpful to ADI either. Up until February 1992 a mere $8 million of the $30 million promised to ADI under the agreement with Defence as compliance funding had been received.[57] Now that the company was proposing to sell off these properties,

Defence and Finance began arguing that the process of cleaning-up for redevelopment should be financed from proceeds of real estate sales. This was despite the fact that there would be no such proceeds for quite some time, and that the government had already reneged on the pledge of a capital contribution which might have allowed the company to finance such a venture in the first place.

Plainly underpinning the view frequently adopted towards ADI in Canberra was a belief that the company was somehow taking advantage of the taxpayer with its redevelopment plans. As Mitchell more accurately summed up matters:

> There is a perception that ADI has got away with these terrific landholdings which are worth lots and lots of money, and we shouldn't have. Well, frankly, what we got away with were properties inappropriately zoned, contaminated and making ammunition that nobody wanted. They might be in desirable locations but no-one was going to touch them without the value-adding process being undertaken. That's the reality as well.[58]

Eventually more funds for the purpose of cleaning-up the ADI sites were forthcoming, to the tune of $38 million by 1995/96 – but it came in the form of a loan.[59]

By early 1994 – with production at St. Marys in its last days before closing on 17 March – some movement over the site finally became evident, when the Penrith council agreed to hand over responsibility for planning control to the State's planning minister. Whereas previously the council feared being associated with the ADI property in any way, now it was willing to assist in drafting a regional environmental study (RES) – provided it was indemnified by the state government. This shifted stance prompted Blacktown to follow suit in April by also agreeing to take part in the RES process, although the council continued to maintain that no development would be allowed to proceed without an indemnity.[60]

On this basis Kinhill Engineers, a private consultancy, was commissioned in October by a joint planning team (comprising the Department of Planning and the two councils) to conduct twelve studies over a period of four months which would form the core of the RES.[61] Even while this work was proceeding, the battle over indemnities spilled over into 1995.[62] It fell to the general manager of Lend Lease Development, Steve McMillan, to point out to the 24th national congress in Adelaide of the Urban Development Institute of Australia what the outcome of this bureaucratic nightmare would be:

> The consequential costs to ADI are likely to exceed five years and $1 million by the time the zoning of the land [at St. Marys] has been determined by the Minister for Planning. ... While recognising the undoubted importance of environmental issues ... ways have to be found to handle zoning procedures with greater cost-effectiveness, because otherwise equally important social

objectives such as affordable housing become less feasible as a consequence of overall cost increases.[63]

The last word of the dismal episode perhaps belongs to Barclay, who – when reflecting on the negotiations which took place back in 1988–89 on the transfer of title to ODP's properties – was moved to comment that:

> If we knew then what we know now about how difficult it would be to get St. Marys rezoned, I think we would have talked down its value a lot further than the $36 million that we did ...[64]

The Benalla site

Concurrent with the process happening at the closing plants, a hunt was under way to find a suitable spot for the new replacement factory which was planned. This was intended to be one of the world's most efficient, modern and safe facilities, utilising technology and manufacturing techniques such as robotics and automated materials handling devices. Here would be manufactured the full range of Defence's ammunition needs, from 5.56 mm small arms rounds to 127 mm naval shells, as well as grenades, pyrotechnics, aircraft bombs and other explosive stores.[65]

Although the area required for production was only about 250 hectares in size, the site acquired would have to be about 1500 hectares in extent to provide wide surrounding safety zones. Much of this buffer area would still be available for uses such as farming. No chemical processing would be carried on at the site and – the assurance was given – all statutory environmental requirements would be met. Whichever community ended up hosting the facility could expect to see around $9 million a year injected into the local economy in the form of the plant's annual wages bill.

The announcement of the company's requirements not unexpectedly produced a large number of offers to host the plant when applications closed in May 1991. In all, 47 submissions were received from state governments and local authorities in all states except Western Australia, proposing no fewer than 93 specific sites.[66] As with the broad restructuring plan, the issue of the new factory site was one which Defence Minister Ray deliberately stayed clear of, asking only that the board discuss with him those which were shortlisted for consideration.[67]

In September 1991 the company announced that it had decided on 'the preferred region' in which it wanted to establish the new ammunition facility. The search for a specific property would now be confined to a 'land corridor' extending from Wagga Wagga in southern New South Wales, through Albury-Wodonga astride the Murray River and on to Benalla, about 200 kilometres north-east of Melbourne. As Harris explained, this zone had been chosen:

… not only because of its ability to provide the level of manufacturing and technical support required by ADI but also because it enables ADI to achieve significant operational economies [in relation to Mulwala]. The climate, social infrastructure, transport network, land availability and industrial back-up also significantly favour this area as providing the region of greatest opportunity to ADI.[68]

By November the choice of sites appeared publicly to have narrowed to four: Wagga, Ettamogah (on the north-eastern outskirts of Albury), Barnawartha (south-west of Wodonga, on the Victorian side of the border) and Benalla.[69] In reality, though, the field had secretly shrunk even further in July, when the board approved negotiations on a confidential basis with the owners of only two sites to secure lease or purchase options. No firm commitments were to be given, however, prior to the range of studies and approvals required being obtained, nor – in particular – until a firm commitment had been obtained from Defence regarding purchases from the new plant.[70]

On 11 February 1992 the board received a presentation from Barclay regarding the siting question. The directors also heard the chairman report that Defence Minister Ray had told him 'that he had no suggestions to make about the choice of site: the Board was expected to make a commercial decision'.[71] They then proceeded to give their unanimous preference to a tract of sheep-grazing land near Lake Mokoan, about seven kilometres north of Benalla, a verdict which was finally announced publicly three days later. This choice was based on the judgement that the anticipated costs of constructing and operating the plant were lowest here, and that it would be 'well supported by the surrounding region including the cities of Benalla, Wangaratta, Shepparton and, for some less crucial products and services, Albury, Wodonga and Melbourne'.[72]

According to Barclay, though, the key factor behind the decision was the planning issue:

> The Victorian government had pre-empted the process by providing a temporary zoning for the Benalla site even before we chose it, to allow defence manufacturing. Furthermore, the Victorian government had overruled the need for a full blown Environmental Effects Statement (akin to the New South Wales EIS process) but rather required ADI to prepare a comprehensive report which addressed all environmental issues but removed the right of third parties to appeal against the intended use, i.e., defence manufacturing. It was this certainty of process for appropriate zoning and ultimate environmental clearance that most strongly influenced the planning team and led to an unequivocal recommendation in favour of the Benalla site.[73]

But the Board was also adamant that the new facility would not go ahead until negotiations with Defence for a long-term agreement covering ADF ammunition requirements from the plant were concluded. Given this constraint, ADI did not propose to commence construction until early in 1993, which meant that the factory would become progressively operational from 1995.

Next stage in the process was the compilation by independent consultants of a comprehensive environmental report (CER) on the site for presentation to the Shire of Benalla. This document, completed in September, involved no fewer than six consulting firms which examined a range of aspects such as archaeology, flora and fauna, safety, air quality, noise, waste management, traffic and visual/landscape setting. The report found that the proposed site was 'a desirable and acceptable location for the new facility', a conclusion accepted by the Benalla shire council in November when it formally approved a permit for the company's plan.[74]

While the matter of selecting a suitable site had thus been satisfactorily resolved, the project now became entangled in a different dispute over ADI's insistence that it did not wish to find itself building a factory from which the ADF would not buy. The Defence Department was understandably reluctant to give the company what amounted to a monopoly over its requirements for such munitions products. For its part, however, the ADI board was determined that it would neither buy the Benalla site nor commit itself to future expenditure until a long-term contract had been agreed.[75]

A stalemate developed over this issue which for a long time seemed insoluble. At the meeting of the board at the end of March 1993, the company's directors 'noted with considerable irritation' that the department had still been unable to agree to a long-term contract and reaffirmed its policy of refusing to spend further on the project until the matter was settled.[76] Knowledge that this question was preventing the work on the factory from proceeding naturally engendered increasing nervousness in Benalla that the whole project 'may stumble at the last hurdle'.[77]

The problem centred around ADI's insistence on an agreement which provided a guaranteed rate of return on its investment. Knowing from history how readily the Defence Department changed its mind on the quantities of ammunition required from year to year, it favoured a 'take or pay' contract of the kind common in the resource development business where, for example, a company will invest in gas distribution infrastructure if a gas utility guarantees a return irrespective of the volume taken. From ADI's viewpoint, such an arrangement seemed an innovative way of sharing risk with its customer, allowing it to drop prices if the Defence department accepted the risk associated with fluctuating volumes or, if the department wanted the company to bear the risk, set prices at a higher level.

The reluctance of Defence to accede to company demands for a long-term agreement stemmed from a belief in senior echelons of the department that a monopoly contract was inconsistent with the concept of ADI being in an arms-length relationship to its customer and in competition with other suppliers. It needed to be convinced that the prices quoted by the company were indeed the best that could be managed, and that the return on investment upon which ADI insisted was fair and reasonable in the circumstances – particularly for the reduced element of risk which the company carried under a take or pay arrangement.[78]

For its part, the company countered with arguments that there was no way it could match spot prices offered on global markets during the current supply glut, but equally there could be no certainty that quantities would be available at marginal prices when required in the future. This provided the case in favour of producing within Australia, which Defence already accepted and insisted upon, so that obviously some premium was unavoidable to retain the capacity for local supply. The prices set as targets for the new facility were approximately 10 per cent lower than those under existing contracts. This was, admittedly, still 12–20 per cent more expensive than purchasing the equivalent ammunition from the United States under the foreign military sales system, although this was not really the same as buying in the marketplace. It was also not unreasonable considering the small volumes involved. If Defence were to double the quantities of 5.56 mm rounds that it planned to order, for instance, the price for this product would drop by 23 per cent. Even so, the prices ADI was forced to charge still represented an annual saving to Defence of $30 million a year.[79]

These differing points of view generated robust debates and some frustrating moments during negotiations by Harris, McMahon (in his defence liaison capacity) and Barclay (who became chief general manager of Ammunition Division early in 1993) with senior officials in Defence. One of the latter, the Deputy Secretary Acquisitions & Logistics, Andrew Podger, recalls that, despite this:

> We did some good work between us trying to see if we could test whether ADI's costs were consistent with international competitiveness, that if Defence were to go on and order more ammunition the marginal price would be in the same ball park as overseas. Although you couldn't actually prove the point, we were satisfied. I know the services still thought they were being done in the eye. The Army in particular didn't accept that they were reducing their order so dramatically that it was having the acute effect on the economy of scale issue as claimed. But I think ADI was right, and Army was being a bit precious on that.

> The major debate was over the issue of profits and the company's accounts. At one point we raised the question of whether, bearing in mind the monopoly, ADI's dividend payouts ought to be directed to the Defence budget rather than consolidated revenue, as with other GBEs. There was a strong feeling that we probably had the strongest case of any department in such a situation, but we didn't win. For Defence to complain too bitterly about that is a bit hard because we made some big savings out of the setting up of ADI.

To get an assessment of what constituted a reasonable profit level, though, required an understanding of the company. Now, with a contract which involves full competition you don't need to get into the intricacies of the company's arrangements, but a long- term monopoly contract always requires more transparency in the accounts and this Chinese wall had to be breached. There were a series of issues that had to be resolved. Interestingly, we had difficulty in getting competent advisers from other departments – like Treasury and Finance – who were meant to be experts in the field. They gave us various views but they did not know some of the technical side of businesses. We ended up calling in three different consultants on aspects, because it was such a genuinely complex issue.[80]

Not until April 1993 was the question of rate of return finally agreed, and it was a further month before the board could be briefed that other details for a 20-year contract had been stitched together at last.[81] The agreement itself was formally signed at the site of the new Benalla factory on 2 July 1993. This provided for the supply of ammunition to the value of up to $75 million a year (worth a total of $1.4 billion) and offered a number of benefits to the nation. One was that the department had been forced – for the first time – to seriously consider what its medium- term needs for ammunition might actually be. Another was that it gave the ADF a 20 per cent reduction in the price paid for ammunition in the past.

With the agreement finally reached the company proceeded to acquire the Benalla site of 1550 hectares from two landowners; subsequently 300 hectares would be sold as surplus to ADI's requirements. After the construction company Baulderstone Hornibrook was appointed in early September 1993 to manage the building of the new $150 million plant,[82] work on the site was due to commence late the next month. This program – involving erection of six kilometres of security fencing two metres high, construction of site offices, roads, stormwater drains, water storage dams and wastewater ponds – was slightly upset when the Benalla region suffered a disastrous rare flood at the start of October, but stayed broadly on schedule by proceeding the following month.[83]

On 2 November 1994 Senator Ray officially opened the first building of the complex, and started up the production line for small arms ammunition cartridge cases which it contained, in advance of the production of pilot lots of small arms rounds the following March. Two years later, on 9 August 1996, the main plant was officially opened by Ray's successor as Minister for Defence, Ian McLachlan. By then 37 buildings had been completed (eventually 42 would be built), occupying only 155 hectares of the total site, and full production of 5.56 mm and 20 mm ammunition was under way with the manufacture of large calibre munitions soon to commence. Although the new facility would be producing only 70 per cent of the quantity of ammunition which the factories it was replacing had made in recent years, it would have the capacity to increase output substantially should there be a war or if demand increased to meet heightened readiness levels.

The dramatic changes associated with the restructuring of the ammunition facilities was a long-awaited step which was fundamental to placing Australian defence production onto a viable and efficient basis. Though recognised as necessary for at least a decade before – in 1981 the Eltringham report had pressed for some form of rationalisation to be carried out – it had taken the advent of ADI to make this course a practical possibility. A confluence of factors, in the form of managers willing to take hard but sound commercial decisions and a government now sufficiently distanced from the political consequences to be prepared to support it, allowed this far-reaching reform to be implemented not just rapidly and confidently but in a period of great economic hardship. While the closure of facilities which were so strongly a part of the nation's early manufacturing history undoubtedly represented the ending of an era, with the opening of the modern facility at Benalla there was also no doubting that a new era had begun at the same time.

9

FORGING AHEAD

On 21 July 1993, Harris took to lunch the senior members of his Ammunition Division in acknowledgement of their work in finalising the long-term ammunition contract. It had slipped his memory that this date happened to be the anniversary of the company's incorporation five years earlier, but it did not escape the attention of two of those present. Having been present at the birth of ADI, and of Project Alaric, Barclay and Conway handed their chief a boxed bottle of wine appropriately labelled 'Alarmagnac'.

The dubious winemakers' notes accompanying this gift referred to the success of 'renown vigneron Ken Harris' in producing a 'startling new variety' from vines first grown at Footscray in 1889. Early cuttings from these plantings had resulted in proliferation of the grape species 'Financius Extravagentius', which became known for 'its lack of body, poor character and high cost of production'. But Harris' 'selective grafting', it was claimed, had produced a 'viticultural revolution':

> Whilst further maturation will develop the wine further, the concentrated spirit which has emerged displays all the robust, vigorous characteristics that has quickly become its trademark and should be consumed with great satisfaction. It is testimony to the positive effects that good commercial management can have on the public vineyards despite severe headwinds, outbreaks of financius phyloxera, slanted growing fields and some minor erosion of the left macquarie bank.

The self-congratulatory spirit behind the gesture was unmistakable, and it was in the same spirit that later the same day Harris copied the bottle-label to all his fellow directors, group and chief general managers to let them in on the joke.[1] But it was not as though a sense of satisfaction at what had been achieved was in any way unjustified. The transformation of the moribund defence factories into a vibrant – and profitable – enterprise in such a short period was little short of amazing.

Financial turnaround

The first report presented by the company on its financial affairs covered a four-teen month period from May 1989 until 30 June 1990. Considering the immense effort required to transfer the company's financial operations to accrual account-ing and to standardise accounting and reporting procedures across ADI's disparate businesses so that these could be consolidated, the outcome contained a welcome surprise in the form of a $23 million operating profit and an unqualified audit report from the joint auditors, Ernst & Young and the AAO. The size of the profit – reduced to $15.7 million after tax – was, admittedly, a fairly meagre return of only 3.6 per cent on the shareholder's investment. Moreover, it was an outcome which had been achieved with the help of interest totalling $37.3 million ($22.8 million after tax) earned on short-term deposits, which offset 'abnormal' items such as termination payments and superannuation; if this contribution had been excluded from the accounts, an $11.9 million loss would have been the result shown.[2]

At the conclusion of its second year of trading, ADI was again able to report a positive result. After-tax profit on 1990/91 operating revenue of $466.3 million was $16.2 million (compared with $14.1 million for the equivalent twelve-month period). While a 15 per cent increase on the previous year's effort, it still repre-sented a return on investment which – as Fynmore observed – no one 'could pre-tend … is yet satisfactory'. Again, without the income derived from investment capital, abnormal expenses would have left the company looking at a $4.1 million loss.[3]

In 1991/92 after-tax profit on revenue of $479.2 million had risen to $20.4 million, though if interest income was not included the profit stood at only $9.1 million. The chairman also reported that:

> As has been the case in many other corporations, the directors, acting on advice from independent valuers, were required to revalue most of the Company's properties … this revaluation created an abnormal loss of $105.1m … [4]

As noted previously, this situation was one about which the board had warned during its dispute with the government over the property values forced upon ADI at the time that assets were transferred to it. The bottom-line now, however, was that the company had an underlying loss of $84.7 million, although this should not obscure the fact that trading performance was quite clearly 'in the black'. In particular, ADI was showing – for the first time – a profit on its operations without having to rely on investment earnings.

Despite a drop of $15 million in revenue to $463.7 million, pre-tax operating profit for the 1992/93 year managed to reach $40.26 million. After both tax and abnormals, the profit level still stood at $23.9 million, which Harris noted in his managing director's review was especially noteworthy for having been 'achieved during a period of tight Defence spending and a continuing severe recession'.[5]

By 1993/94 the company was able to record its fifth consecutive year of profitable business operations. Sales revenue had risen to $562.5 million, exceeding the previous year's figure by almost $100 million – largely due to increased production and disposal of ammunition stocks prior to the closure of factories for restructuring. Profit grew by $4.6 million, or 13.4 per cent, to a record of $39 million. After paying $5.22 million in tax and providing for a loss on abnormals of $5.8 million (caused by bringing to account about $12 million in restructuring costs) profit for the year stood at $27.9 million. Although the company still had accumulated losses of $39.7 million, this was down by $13.9 million on the level of twelve months' earlier.[6]

Most remarkable of all was the fact that half the 1993/94 annual profit, some $14 million, was returned to the government (as owner) in a first-ever fully franked dividend payout of 3.82¢ a share.[7] The achievement of this milestone was of special significance to Harris:

> During the arguments to settle our capital structure, some people in the bureaucracy were so keen to load us up with debt because they were effectively saying, 'This is just ODP in another guise, its never going to pay a dividend, so let's get a return in the form of interest'. We responded by saying that, as business people, we would take it as a great achievement to get the company into a position to pay a dividend. In fact, we pointed out, we were actually budgeting to pay half of our profits in dividend when we finished restructuring. Those statements were greeted with horselaughs in the bureaucracy, but, I mean, in a capitalist society we must judge our company against the standards of that society, and a dividend is the mark of achievement.[8]

Confirming that the 1993/94 result was no aberration were the figures for the following year, which showed that despite a $60 million drop in operating revenue – a trend which had been fully predicted in connection with the restructuring – profit after tax and abnormals actually rose to $33.4 million. On this basis another fully franked dividend of 4.6¢ a share was declared, amounting to $16.8 million.[9]

All this was a far cry from the situation immediately preceding the company's creation. In just the five years between 1984 and 1989, the facilities which were eventually to become ADI had drained $1.3 billion out of the Defence vote (see Appendix I) in what amounted to a direct taxpayer subsidy. Now, in the subsequent five years, that trend had been totally reversed. Not only was ADI returning dividends to the government as shareholder, but the profits it was making were in addition to paying the full range of taxes and charges which both federal and state governments levied on businesses.

Of course, the facilities which ADI took over from ODP were not the defence establishment's only loss-makers prior to 1989; also contributing then were Williamstown dockyard and GAF. If the subsequent performance of these are added to ADI's results, then an even more amazing picture emerges. Neither organisation to which Williamstown and GAF now belonged – Transfield and ASTA respectively – retained a linkage to the Defence vote in the same way as ADI (through compliance, workers' benefits and redundancy funding), but both contributed to government revenues through taxes in the same way as the company did, particularly the Transfield group which boasted an annual turnover of $1.2 billion. On this basis it can be fairly said that the swing of the pendulum observable from 198–89 was even more dramatic than first apparent.

Other yardsticks give a clear measure of the extent to which operations had improved in profitability. For instance, the value of annual production/sales achieved per employee had risen from about $20,000 in 1984/85, in the days of the Department of Defence Support, to just over $40,000 in 1988/89 when ADI took over from ODP, and to $148,000 just five years later; by 1996/97 the figure stood at $180,000, and was expected to reach $220,000 by 1998/99. This result was brought about as much by a reduction in the size of the company's workforce as through increase in turnover, which emphasises that the change – though both highly desirable and necessary – had come at a heavy cost in jobs. Instead of the 6780 employees who were on the books when ADI took control in 1989, the company had just under 3800 five years later[10] and in 1998 just over 3100.[11]

The process of downsizing which had taken place, however justified, had also dented the company's standing in certain quarters – as Callinan, ADI's GM Employee Development, fully accepts:

> There is a fair bit of credibility gone out of our relationship with the ACTU and the unions as a result of what they see as just continual slash and burn. They feel that the reward for their co-operation in achieving a number of good outcomes was taken away by the fact that we kept on reducing, reducing, reducing.[12]

It was only understandable that for ADI employees made redundant – especially those living in rural centres like Lithgow and Bendigo, where the range of work opportunities was limited – there was no consolation in knowing that their former job had not been 'real', or that ADI's facilities could not be allowed to operate as 'sheltered workshops'. These were abstract considerations far removed from the concerns of ordinary people.

Impressive though the scale of the turnaround achieved through the advent of ADI undoubtedly was, it was apparent to those in charge of managing the company that they faced an even greater challenge in maintaining that success. As Harris put matters:

> The formation of the company might have been initially undertaken to achieve savings in the Defence budget that could be redeployed elsewhere, but ADI had to be a company with a future if those savings were to continue.[13]

Despite the ambitious goals talked about in 1989 of doubling turnover within five years, the plain fact remained that scope for such growth in Australia was limited for a company such as ADI. Quite simply, the volumes generated by ADF requirements were low and likely to stay that way (short of a major conflict erupting), and the nature of the businesses which were traditionally conducted by ADI were, in many instances, narrow in their civil applications. The company was thus operating in a field of inherently marginal profitability.

In these circumstances it was only natural that ADI would initially look to exports as the key to large-scale future expansion. Harris admits that this idea was in the minds of ADI's founders back in 1988,[14] and indeed the speech to Parliament made by Defence Minister Beazley at the time of ADI's takeover of ODP in May 1989 had specifically referred to the aspect of defence exports, remarking that this 'fairly specialised' area had 'the capacity to foster and maintain specialist skills and reduce the cost of such goods on the Australian market'.[15] Subsequent events, however, consigned such notions to the 'forlorn hope' category. The Australian government's guidelines covering exports were actually tightened in 1989, so that sales of defence goods abroad slumped from $157 million in 1989/90,[16] and $130 million in 1990/91,[17] to around $37 million in 1992/93.[18]

While ADI, as one of the nation's leading defence manufacturers, was as well placed as anybody to develop a sizeable export component to its business, its performance in this area remained disappointing. In its 1994 report, for example, the company could only point to export sales of $30 million, and admitted that this result was almost double the previous year's level.[19] Though this represented a miserable 5 per cent of ADI's 1993/94 operating revenue, it was still a vast improvement over the performance of the old ODP, which had managed less than $1 million worth of exports in 1988.[20]

Not discouraged by these figures, in April 1994 the company continued to believe that it was about to achieve a major breakthrough on the world arms market. As the GGM International Business (Targ) expressed matters:

The major thing when you're talking about big contracts is critical mass. Nobody wants to deal with a little company; they want to deal with companies of the right size to handle contracts of that sort. So a very important part of why we're on the verge of international success is because we have a company of substance with tremendous capability, a strong balance sheet, a growing track record. And we can match that with managerial commitment.[21]

Six months later the reality of matters was brought home by a report tabled in Parliament by the Joint Standing Committee on Foreign Affairs, Defence and Trade titled 'Implications of Australia's Defence Exports'. While two-thirds of the committee was 'relatively supportive' of the existing guidelines and policy regarding defence exports, a group of six members signed a minority report arguing that Australia should abandon plans to sell defence equipment to the region, describing the Asian market as fiercely competitive, sometimes corrupt, and subject to arbitrary political whims.[22]

Just a month before this, Harris had let it be known through the company's annual report that ADI was pursuing about $2.5 billion in export opportunities and that he was 'hopeful of closing a healthy proportion of this amount over the next 12 to 18 months'.[23] After the findings of the committee became public, Harris was moved to comment that he was no longer 'so sure' about Australia's prospects of doing better in promoting international sales of defence related goods:

Our problem is not in the excellence of our goods and services. They are frequently judged the best in the world. Nor is our pricing a serious obstacle. We are often very competitive commercially. The heart of the problem is the difficulty that the government system has in dealing with actual sales as opposed to framing the policy. Despite Australia's remarkable success in foreign relations we have a reputation for clumsy handling of the sensitivities of our Asian neighbours. This behaviour could lose us very large contracts.[24]

What Harris was plainly alluding to here was the fact that, while other countries of varying shades of respectability might engage in the international arms trade, for a small but vocal section of the Australian community it would never be an acceptable form of activity for their country. As proof of this, from time to time the company and its premises were periodically targeted by special interest groups operating on the fringes of political opinion.

In January 1992, for example, the Sydney Peace Squadron staged a 'mock killing' outside the company's Market Street offices in Sydney to protest the Indonesian occupation of East Timor.[25] In July 1993 it was about 50 demonstrators attempting to invade the Footscray plant to protest against Australia's alleged role in providing military aid to Papua New Guinea for use against rebels on Bougainville – it did not matter that ADI did not sell ammunition to the PNG

Defence Force.[26] Easter 1995 saw protests in both Sydney and Benalla, with the Sydney Peace Squadron trying to invade Corporate Headquarters to voice objections to reports (which were false) of planned rifle sales to Indonesia,[27] while a National Women's Peace Camp at the latter site ended with seventeen trespassers being arrested.[28]

Faced with the sobering conclusion that exports would not preserve the gains won, nor provide the means to continue transforming the company's fortunes, ADI's management began seeking new and better directions along which to set the company's path. In Harris' words:

> We tried to mirror what we were seeing happen to defence budgets all around the world. When we looked at Australia it was no different to elsewhere, in that there was not a lot of growth in the total money allocation. But its composition was changing very significantly, with a much higher proportion going to high technology areas such as electronics, communications, and command and control.[29]

Others in the company, like Ross Babbage, also recognised the impact of other global factors at work, such as the shift in strategic thinking which has been dubbed the 'revolution in military affairs' (RMA). According to him:

> RMA is already starting to have an influence on acquisition plans in Australia. There are things that have been in the Defence Department's pink book, the plan for capital acquisition, for a few years but which are being pulled out and cancelled. And there are other things which haven't been there at all that are being put into the pink book, because of the concepts that are being developed. This is stemming from more than just the idea of doing more with less. It comes from a recognition that there are some opportunities that are largely provided by new technologies, and smarter use of some existing technologies – more a case of technology plus innovative strategy plus organisational change.[30]

Realising this reality of the future, the company formulated a strategy to shift the emphasis of its business away from traditional engineering activities and into these new growth fields.

Revamped business structure

In May 1994 the organisational structure of the company underwent another revision, which was to take effect before 1 July. As initially announced, there was no basic change to the set-up at Corporate Headquarters, but it was intended that there would be just five business groups instead of the existing eleven units.

Under the new arrangement the Naval Engineering and Electronics divisions were to continue largely as before under the management of Bryan Gibson and Graham Shepherd, but would be known henceforth as ADI Marine and ADI Electronics. Instead of Weapons & Engineering Division, there would now be ADI Engineering (comprising essentially the Bendigo plant) under Graeme Phipps. The former Ammunition Division would be replaced by ADI Ordnance under John Barclay, taking in Mulwala and Benalla as well as the former Training Systems Division at Albury and the Lithgow facility. The Consulting, Logistic Support and Industrial Decontamination divisions were to be brought together as ADI Services, under James Kelaher as Group General Manager.[31]

Under this plan, the Clothing division would not be considered part of the company's 'core' business, but Kelaher (its former CGM) would continue to look after it 'for the time being'. Likewise, the Property division (under Bill Mitchell) and Minehunter Project Team (headed by Merv Church) were to remain as separate operations reporting directly to Harris as managing director at headquarters. By the time this new establishment came into being, however, it had been decided to create Church's team as a separate group dubbed ADI Minehunter, so that the number of business groups now totalled six.

The point of this adjustment was explained in terms of a need to streamline the organisation to take greater account of changing patterns of business growth,[32] and to 'make the company's internal structure more focused and manageable'.[33] Despite this claim, there was strong speculation – both within and outside of ADI – that the real purpose lay in preparing for eventual privatisation, through constructing compact and functional entities more suitable for disposal as separate businesses.

While regrouping may have had the incidental benefit of making ADI more attractive to potential commercial buyers, there had been considerable pressures on the company to make changes for some time – deriving mainly from problems being experienced by Clothing division with diminishing profitability and uncertain long-term prospects. In mid-1992 Harris had attempted to turnaround the fortunes of this business by appointing a new CGM in the person of Kelaher.[34] Serious thought also began to be given to selling off this division, but soundings made with potential buyers found that there was no real interest in acquiring the site at Coburg (which ADI owned rather than leased) as a going concern.[35] Continued low-key efforts to achieve a sale resulted in only one informal offer, of about $1 million purely for the real estate.[36]

In the meantime, Clothing division's Sydney operations were relocated from Leichhardt to more spacious leased premises at Marrickville. Here manufacturing and warehousing activities were able to be consolidated at one site, along with offices and a modern display area, in hopes that efficiency could be improved. Attention was given to developing a 'total apparel management service', described by Clothing's sales manager David Rountree as being 'where we carry a complete range of corporate clothing on behalf of corporate clients, then pick, pack and dispatch nationally to meet individual requirements'.[37] Moving to Marrickville, which was near Sydney airport, held advantages for such a service through providing faster distribution.

In the last months of 1993, the board approved proposals to rationalise Clothing's operations in Victoria. This entailed proceeding to sell Coburg and concentrating production at East Bendigo. The directors also called for the development of an 'exit strategy' to enable ADI to quit the clothing business altogether – either by sale as a going concern or through closure when current contracts were completed in 1995.[38]

Under the plan implemented during the first quarter of 1994, Bendigo focused on military clothing orders while the Marrickville plant carried out the manufacture of all protective clothing and corporate wardrobe distribution.[39] The Coburg site was closed and sold at auction on 21 April.[40] The question of the clothing business' future continued to be kept under examination with a view to bringing sale options to the shareholder's attention at an appropriate time.[41] In July 1995 the board actually decided to sell the business and authorised Harris to enter negotiations with potential buyers, with the result that by October the business was sold to a consortium calling itself Australian Defence Apparel Pty. Ltd. and ADI had exited the clothing field entirely.[42]

As the second major restructuring of business activities in the space of five years demonstrated, ADI's management felt the need to constantly keep reacting to changes in the trading environment. There was a clear perception that any degree of ossification in outlook, particularly at such a young stage in corporate age, could well prove fatal. In the circumstances it was probably no less fortunate for the company's future direction that it could look to enjoying stability at the top. At the end of 1993 Fynmore was reappointed as a director and chairman for a further two years, followed by Harris' reappointment for another three years early the next year.[43]

Barely a year after the second reorganisation of the business structure, the company underwent a third major wave of change – this time bringing it down to just three major business groups shaped around functional roles rather than purely activities. Now there was an Operations Group, a Technology Group and a Systems Group, each headed by a chief executive officer. While Operations under Bryan Gibson focused on depot level warship maintenance, heavy engineering and ordnance manufacturing, the Technology Group headed by John Barclay managed warship repair, minehunter construction, mine countermeasures technology, logistic support and environmental technologies, and Systems handled command support systems, software engineering, and combat systems from ADI Marine. The latter group was under David Robinson, a newcomer to the company who had taken over from Graham Shepherd in June 1995.[44] Later, Major Projects would be separated out from Corporate Headquarters and replace Technology as the company's third business group under the direction of Berlyn as CEO.

One effect of this change was that it made for a much smaller management team in the company, which made it easier for Harris to stay in regular touch. Apart from regular Monday morning meetings in his office with the three Group CEOs and the three GGMs at Corporate Headquarters (McMahon, Targ and Tannahill), Harris made a point of holding monthly dinners with the eight members of the senior executive team at the Union Club in the city.[45] The core of this group was still those who had made the original switch from the public service at the time of the company's creation – the so-called 'Long Marchers' (an allusion to the epic trek from Kiangsi to Shensi undertaken in 1934–35 by the army of Chinese communists led by Mao Tse-tung) – but there were some new faces. Apart from Robinson, another new addition to the company now headed Operations Group in the person of Steve Milner, who arrived from Metal Manufacturers Limited followed the resignation of Gibson early in 1996.[46]

Reflecting the updated vision which the company now held of itself, in July 1995 the board adopted the managing director's suggestion to change the company's name.[47] Having been surprised by the speed with which the ADI acronym had found acceptance within the defence and broader business communities, Harris states that he merely decided to formalise the situation by replacing 'Australian Defence Industries Ltd' with 'ADI Limited'. The change became effective on 1 January 1996,[48] and was accompanied by a change in the corporate logo which Harris decided had become a bit old-fashioned. As he says: 'I think every company should look at updating its image every few years, and I felt the logo should reflect what the company had become.' [49]

Shifting emphasis

These changes were not solely cosmetic, since they were backed by some fundamental shifts as to where and how the company was doing business by 1996. In recognition that some ventures had not been as successful as hoped, decisions were made to withdraw or reduce the scale of involvement in certain areas. For example, in late 1996 the industrial decontamination division began to pull back from its exposure in Europe in the face of increasing evidence that governments were reassessing their budget priorities in the light of deteriorating economic circumstances, thereby reducing the opportunities which had initially prompted ADI's move into the region.[50] Back in Australia, however, remediation activities continued at a steady pace, with contracts won to clean up localities such as Coode Island in Melbourne, Pyrmont and Homebush Bay (site of the 2000 Olympics) in Sydney, and Armidale in northern New South Wales.

Operations at Lithgow, too, underwent substantial reduction once the end of the Steyr production had been reached and the last of 75,674 weapons handed over to the Army,[51] with the facility being reduced to core personnel only.[52] In the event something of a reprieve was gained early in June 1995 when a new order for 4207 Minimi light machine guns was obtained from Army which would carry the facility into late 1997.[53]

Property development was another area that began encountering significant problems. The planned redevelopments of Maribyrnong and Footscray were able to proceed without much difficulty, due largely to the sympathetic approvals procedure that operated in Victoria.[54] After the Lend Lease Corporation was signed on as development partner in June 1995, detailed planning commenced for the subdivision, construction, infrastructure and marketing of the two sites. By the time the estate at Maribyrnong (given the name Waterford Green) was officially opened on 20 February 1998, nearly 300 of the 540 residential blocks available there had been sold, some homes were completed and the area's first residents had already moved in.[55] Elsewhere, at St. Marys, the idea of returning unused real estate to public uses had run into obstruction and delay, held hostage to a cumbersome process, minority pressure groups and political manoeuvring.

Other of the company's traditional sites were also in trouble, with the marine engineering and heavy engineering facilities at Garden Island and Bendigo respectively both faced with serious downturns in business. The former had won a contract to refit HMAS *Manoora*, one of two ex-US Navy tank landing ships acquired for the RAN, but ADI missed out on the more lucrative job of converting both these vessels to training and helicopter support ships. A bout of retrenchments at Garden Island followed, although the board acknowledged that cutbacks in the workforce there would have been necessary in any event in view of the reduction in the volume of work entering the dockyard.[56] Competition between the large number of dockyards around Australia, and Navy practices which allowed 'tin shed' contractors to operate at the fleet base at Garden Island because of their ability to tender low for work, meant that ADI's workforce there had fallen to about 430 by the early in 1998.[57]

The Bendigo facility also found itself in the doldrums, reflecting the fact that heavy engineering – by nature an industry of high peaks and low troughs anyway – was in general decline across Australia.[58] Here, however, the gloomy picture was relieved by the company's success in building a new business in military and specialist vehicles. What had begun as an initial response to a requirement stated by the Army in 1994 for a light engineer tractor capable of moving long distances at convoy speed had grown a couple of years later into a small group of products which held good prospects of success both in Australia and overseas. The first of the ADI vehicles, known as the High Speed Engineering Vehicle, combined a 100 kph road speed with outstanding cross country performance, four wheel drive and the earth moving capability of a tractor; as well as back hoe and front end loader functions, it had fork lift, light crane and drilling capabilities.[59] Interest in the vehicle expanded from the local requirement, resulting in an order during 1997 for a test vehicle for the Canadian Defence Force even before the Australian Army placed its order for 27 HSEVs early in 1998.[60]

Another Army project, Mulgara, gave rise to ADI's second specialist vehicle, the Flyer. After the Army stated its requirement as being for a fast, highly mobile vehicle for use in surveillance and reconnaissance operations in the remote and rugged conditions of northern Australia, ADI teamed up with a Californian company with experience in producing off-road racing vehicles. With an appearance resembling a dune buggy, the Flyer's 100 kw diesel engine gave it a top speed of more than 130 kph and an ability to carry more than a tonne of gear across the most difficult terrain.[61] By the end of 1996 the first overseas contract for 29 of these vehicles had been received and was being met for a south-east Asian country. Although another regional customer also placed an order for these vehicles, the Australian Army cancelled the $250 million Project Mulgara in October 1997 without making a selection of type.[62]

Finally, the company entered into the competition to tender for a large number (expected then to be 455, later reduced to a minimum of 340) of armoured infantry mobility vehicles for the Army under Project Bushranger. The initial ADI solution was rejected for selection to the Army's shortlist in June 1995,[63] but this disastrous situation was retrieved when the company bought the rights to the Bushmaster vehicle produced by Perry Engineering, a subsidiary of Boral Limited, and proceeded to heavily redesign it. Using a Catepillar six-cylinder turbo diesel engine and an Allison seven-speed automatic transmission, the Bushmaster could meet the Army requirement for eight different variants. These ranged from the standard version able to carry nine soldiers (including the driver) in air conditioned comfort over long distances, to others adapted for use as ambulances, command posts, recovery vehicles, mortar carriers and so on. With this design ADI became one of the two contenders for the Army contract in early 1998.

Success in building up this field of activity was largely attributable to Koos de Wet, a South African designer of military vehicles who joined the company in November 1996. The specialist skills and knowledge in landmine protection which he possessed enabled him to develop the Bushmaster design in less than eight months, commencing the task on 29 January and completing it on 17 September 1997. In addition to his vision of creating a 'family' of specialist military vehicles, he also began looking at non-military opportunities and by 1998 had also devised a vehicle uniquely adapted to fighting bushfires.[64]

Other new openings were pursued in the electronics field, reflecting the belief that ADI's future increasingly lay in systems development and application. In pursuing this goal, the former UDS facility in Perth became a crucial centre of activity and produced some notable achievements. In 1995, for example, a command support system required for use in the ADF's major exercise in the Kangaroo series later that same year was supplied at short notice. The system was also put into service in Malaysia during 1997, as part of a new air defence system supplied to the Five Power Defence Arrangement. Early in 1998 a $3 million contract was received to develop, supply and support the RAN's Maritime Intelligence Dissemination and Analysis System. Greg Tunny, who managed this facility since the start of 1994, maintains that it was his deliberate policy to shift the focus of his team from being a defence software business to an information technology software house which derives only part of its business from defence.[65]

During July 1996, however, ADI also acquired the businesses and assets of Stanilite Pacific Ltd., an Australian-based electronics company which had got itself into financial difficulties through loss-making contracts in Russia and Argentina. This company produced and marketed a range of high technology products relevant to defence as well as civilian applications; among the former were tactical radio communications equipment and switch systems, while the latter included a range of digital trunk radio and cellular telephone systems. The acquisition, entailing assets valued at $33.8 million, provided an opportunity to obtain both capabilities and intellectual property of considerable value to Systems Group, although not all the Stanilite businesses were crucial to ADI's plan and an offer from a Canadian firm for its emergency lighting division was quickly accepted.[66] Within days of the purchase being completed, Systems Group began moving from their existing accommodation at Silverwater in Sydney into the former Stanilite offices at North Ryde, to make this their new base.[67]

Economic downturn would effect the success of attempts to enter the commercial phone markets in China, South East Asia and Eastern Europe, and significant problems were encountered in the course of absorbing Stanilite into the ADI structure and culture. Nonetheless this one acquisition played an important part in repositioning the company and building its standing in the market place where it wished to operate. As Harris observed in the company newsletter, ADI 'now has a significant systems business – number 2 or 3 in Australia – and we are well placed to compete strongly in the growing systems market.'[68]

Of course, many of ADI's existing capabilities continued to flourish and contribute to the company's revenues. Examples of this fact could be found in contracts won for the supply of rocket motors, launcher and canister for the Nulka missile decoy; the development of launching equipment and components for the Evolved Seasparrow missile, to be fitted in the RAN's new Anzac frigates; the commencement of filling and assembly of the Penguin anti-ship missile warhead used in the armament of the Super Seasprite helicopters for the Anzac frigates; and the AMASS minesweeping system, which began attracting orders from Europe beginning with the Royal Danish Navy. The minehunter project ran so smoothly that it came to be regarded in many circles as something of a model defence project, with the first ship officially launched at Newcastle on 25 July 1997 and commissioned as HMAS *Huon* on 15 May 1999.

Arising from the efforts of the Major Projects Group, further opportunities for the company on the same large scale as the Minehunter project were targeted and bids prepared. Nigel Berlyn, who headed this group until his retirement early in 1998, recalls that:

> The company liked getting a billion dollars worth of business in one hit … My job was to set up an organisation that could identify these project opportunities and evaluate them in a rational way, help the company to decide which ones to invest in. Digging for major projects was really like trying to win the Melbourne Cup, but to enter every race and place your bet – with any chance of winning – meant you were going to expend at least one per cent of the contract value on preparing a bid. What we did was ensure the company had the best odds for the projects it went after.[69]

Included in this category were the programs to upgrade the Navy's six guided missile frigates (FFGs) worth almost a billion dollars, and a similar program to improve the war fighting capabilities of the RAN's Anzac Class frigates (known as the Anzac WIP), also worth over a billion dollars. ADI also teamed with Eurocopter, and several Australian partners, to bid for a $1.2 billion project to provide 25–30 armed reconnaissance and fire support helicopters for the Australian Army.

A matter of safety

Not everything that ADI touched turned out to be a shining success, and sometimes the company suffered intense public scrutiny and criticism as a result of its actions. One controversial moment came with revelations that the company had received a large payment, eventually totalling more than $700,000, for old surplus weapons and spare parts surrendered under the government's guns buy-back scheme. The scheme had been devised as a means of removing dangerous firearms from the community after a series of tragic crimes, and it hardly mattered when the company responded that it had no choice under the terms of the relevant legislation.[70] The howls of public outrage made clear that many in the community considered the company's action to be an abuse of the good intentions behind the policy, although it remained a moot point whether the same reaction would have ensued if ADI's owners had not been the Commonwealth government itself.

Many instances of adverse publicity arose from high profile mishaps involving explosives. On 14 November 1995, for example, a blast occurred in a building at St. Marys where grenades were being assembled and checked by seven female workers, causing serious injuries to four of the women. Although production here had closed in March 1994, some parts of the facility had been reopened to finish off last minute orders. After the explosion incident made headline news around the nation, the entire factory was shut down several weeks early.[71] On 12 November 1996 there was a similar occurrence at Mulwala, which drew even greater adverse publicity. A 35-year-old male worker was killed when an explosion demolished the structure in which he was conducting a routine procedure to melt down a pentaline explosive. Witnesses described the blast as 'like an atomic bomb' that shook the surrounding district and was heard up to 50 kilometres away.

Finally, there came another tragedy on 5 May 1998 when a fire broke out in the engine room of HMAS *Westralia*, the RAN's fleet supply ship, off Perth and resulted in the deaths of four sailors. Investigations revealed that the blaze had begun when flexible fuel hoses recently fitted to the ship's engines developed leaks and sprayed diesel fuel onto hot surfaces before igniting into a fireball. The fuel hoses had been fitted by ADI's sub-contractor in Western Australia, and the media was quick to point the finger at the company as being to blame for the tragedy. In fact, as the company tried to point out to the naval inquiry held in relation to the accident, ADI had merely been responding to requirements spelt out to it by the RAN, which in this case had itself been taking technical shortcuts in breach of its own rules and safeguards.[72] Further, as the company went on to point out in other forums, the conduct of this inquiry only gave rise to an unfortunate impression of the inherent unfairness of allowing the RAN to sit in judgement upon itself in such instances rather than allowing an investigation by independent authorities[73] – a view endorsed the next year by a parliamentary committee examining military justice.[74]

Ultimately the issue at the heart of all the episodes in which the company's good name suffered so badly was the question of worker safety. In fact this had been a constant cause of concern to ADI's management, from the board level down. Minutes of board meetings periodically reflected directors' dissatisfaction at the standards being observed at various facilities – nowhere more so than at Garden Island, where the frequency of accidents prompted an expression of 'continued concern' in October 1995.[75] This aspect was also strongly reflected in issues of the magazine for company employees, *Pursuit*, which constantly carried exhortations for individuals to make safety a particular focus of attention.[76] In the final analysis, however, it must be said that the scale and frequency of accidents were a direct reflection of the dangerous nature of much of the manufacturing activity which lay at the core of the company's existence.

The years 1995–97 represented a second period of transition for ADI and the people responsible for managing it. Having fought and won the initial battle to create a viable company from the dismal inheritance of ODP, the challenge had become one of finding a future for the company and redirecting its path. Inevitably this meant that ADI itself must change, letting go some of the areas of activity with which it had become traditionally identified and taking up new ones. Once again this challenge was met and by the end of 1996, the company had essentially taken on a new identity and found a new position within the business community and, in particular, the defence industry. Having read the future trend into systems engineering ADI had become not just a new player in the pack but in many respects a leader on the local scene. In reaching this point, however, a final and more decisive crossroad had been reached that would determine the company's ultimate destiny.

10

THE QUESTION OF OWNERSHIP

Once ADI was firmly established as a well-run, economically-viable commercial entity returning respectable if not spectacular profits, inevitably the issue was raised of whether it should remain in government ownership. From the late-1980s the same question was being asked about a range of other GBEs. Subsequently, governments representing both sides of the political divide in Australia began a steady process of divestment of public assets, culminating in a partial float of the telecommunications corporation Telstra in November 1997 worth $14.3 billion alone. By the start of 1998 it was claimed that, nationally, matters had reached the stage where most 'big ticket' items had been sold. Leaving aside the possibility of a further sell-off of Telstra, either in full or another tranche, only a number of smaller and harder-to-sell assets were left for disposal. Even so, by the time of the budget statement in May 1999, the government was still expecting an aggregate return from asset sales of nearly $16 billion during the 1999/2000 financial year.[1]

Of all the government enterprises previously considered for the privatisation treatment, the one of most obvious relevance to ADI – if only by virtue of its common origins – was ASTA. As early as May 1989, even as ADI was taking over from the former ODP, government ministers confirmed that negotiations were then under way for the sale of the planned ASTA subsidiaries.[2] An announcement in the August 1993 Budget indicated that privatisation of ASTA would indeed be considered during 1993/94, after a consultant's report and a strategy from the company board had been obtained.[3] The following December the federal government announced its decision to offer for sale all Commonwealth equity in the company.[4]

Towards the end of 1994 calls were made for expressions of Interest 'from parties wishing to consider the purchase of ASTA', preferably as a whole although 'purchase options involving individual business units or subsidiaries may be considered'.[5] In the first months of 1995, after jolts caused by the sudden resignation of the company's managing director and release of annual trading figures which showed a loss of nearly $61 million in 1993/94,[6] the government announced that the Australian subsidiary of the United States corporation Rockwell International had been selected as 'preferred purchaser' – subject to successful conclusion of sales negotiations.[7] Subsequently ownership passed into other American hands, after Rockwell was taken over by Boeing.[8]

Debate over privatising ADI

Predictably, suggestions were heard that ADI should be sent down the same path as ASTA. Indeed, according to the former finance minister and senator Peter Walsh, privatisation had been the expected endpoint of the transformation process occurring with ODP from the very beginning:

> Corporatisation of the defence factories was, perhaps naively, seen as a prerequisite for getting rid of some of their inefficiency and/or an intermediate step to privatisation … To the best of my recollection, privatisation was not identified as the eventual goal of corporatisation in any of the official Cabinet papers. But it was certainly seen [that way] by me, almost certainly by Hawke, and a few other people. I'm not sure about Beazley, but Dawkins was sort of that way.[9]

When indications were received that the privatisation of ADI was being seriously thought about in government circles, the directors did not directly oppose such a course being pursued but instead urged the government not to be too hasty in throwing away what undoubtedly had been a major success. Countering the views expressed in a review carried out in 1993 by the Macquarie Bank, the advice the board offered to Defence Minister Ray was only that, while selling off the company might well be 'a realistic option' at some point in the future, it recommended 'waiting until the initial restructuring program has been completed in 1996/97 before contemplating a sale'.[10]

This was a message which Harris went out of his way to reinforce when asked publicly about the issue at this time. To one interviewer in late 1993 he said:

> Of course they [the government] should look at that issue … [of whether] is privatisation an option – if it's not now, when is it? My view is that it's not yet there. We've still got to get the Benalla investment under our belt, there is still

the new businesses to get on to their feet, and there is still the naval engineering business to understand a bit better. There are two years ahead of us before we could say that the original restructuring program has been completed ... Whether they will privatise when we get the company finally restructured, I don't know – only the government knows. But I think that it's right and very healthy that they should look at the question from time to time.[11]

One of the ironies of the situation was that the more ADI diversified its activities into non-defence work, and the more it improved profits and dividends, the greater was the temptation of the government to realise the investment in the company by selling it. The Macquarie Bank report had found that there was no continuing rationale for the Commonwealth to retain control of the company, not least because there were no more significant gains to be had from restructuring. The course it proposed was a sale by 'flexible tender' – meaning (as with ASTA) as a whole, or each division or subsidiary separately, rather than through a public floating of the company.[12]

Harris did not hesitate to reject suggestions which appeared in one professional journal that, in response to the Macquarie Bank findings, ADI was 'honing their lobbying skills to keep the enterprise out of private hands'. Such claims, he said, were 'ludicrous':

ADI has consistently taken a pragmatic position and has not sought to tell its owner (the Commonwealth Government) whether the interest in the company should be disposed of or retained. Our job is to put the company in the best possible commercial position so that the owner can make a sensible choice, based on business criteria, about whether to sell or hold, and when to make that decision.[13]

Noting that 'some people see privatisation as an ideological issue', Harris asserted that actually it was not 'an end in itself' but simply a 'rearrangement of ownership'. In his view the real issue behind the debate was 'which ownership arrangements will give the company the best chance to continue its growth and development'. He could see a number of outcomes which were possible, some of which might be preferable to existing arrangements:

One outcome could be a government owner that supports the company as institutional investors do. Another outcome could be a group of private owners who could bring in some form of commercial advantage ... The issue should be decided on the basis of practical business judgement, not on ideological views that were going out of date 10 years ago.

The company's management was genuinely as sanguine as it sounded about this whole issue. In private, senior executives were convinced that ADI could even win handsomely out of privatisation, through getting rid of the dead hand of government interference.[14] Fynmore, equally, saw little to get too excited about. For him, a far bigger aspect of the public debate had passed relatively unnoticed:

> You know, everyone thinks of privatisation as selling the company to a bunch of shareholders and getting money for the shares. It is, though, just as much an act of privatisation to have developed the new site at Benalla and released that very valuable land in Sydney and Melbourne for conversion to better uses. The money from that will be channelled back to the nation through the Treasury, so I claim it as a privatisation, too, and I think that has been our single best achievement so far.[15]

In contrast to the relatively relaxed view adopted within ADI's senior levels, there was considerably more heat generated among the company's workforce and elsewhere outside. The extent of resistance to the idea of ADI's imminent privatisation which was apparent within both the union movement and the left wing of the Australian Labor Party (usually strident in its anti-defence attitude) was really another irony of the situation. In Bendigo during April 1994 a rally by 400 angry ADI workers demanded an end to all proposals for selling off the company, believing that any short-term gain realised by the government would only come at the expense of their jobs.[16]

The next month a conference of left-wing Labor members heard a paper by Senator Kim Carr, developed in preparation for the ALP's national conference at Hobart during September, which opposed selling or allowing foreign ownership of defence industries and related assets on the grounds that this held 'serious implications for Australia's defence preparedness'.[17] That Senator Ray was prepared to lend his support to the same position, giving as his personal view that ADI should not be privatised, was sufficient to secure withdrawal at the Hobart conference of the Left faction motion opposing the company's sale.[18]

In May 1995 Finance Minister Kim Beazley confirmed that the issue was not high on the government's list of priorities.[19] A short time earlier Beazley had expressed the view that:

> I think this [question of privatisation] is something that we need to think through a bit carefully. There's a distinct difference between ADI and ASTA, as the latter simply has to survive entirely separate to the Defence Force. It has such a low, and now lessening, component of defence activity as its principal function, and whether or not its going to realise a suitable or good price, it just has to go.
>
> With ADI I think the issue is complex. I don't think there's anything more

to be gained in privatising ADI. The factories are about as efficient as they are ever going to be. They're not going to be any more efficient in private owner-ship. I don't know exactly how we are going since I'm not as closely involved as I once was, but I was a pretty strong believer in the great importance in clothing, feeding and keeping those government industries alive simply because they are absolutely central to the self-reliance strategy and serve a pos-itive good in keeping Australian industry up to speed generally. That was con-stantly at the forefront of my mind [as Defence Minister].[20]

Finally, in late June 1995, Defence Minister Ray announced that Cabinet had put off 'for the foreseeable future' any plans of privatising ADI, deciding instead to retain the company in Commonwealth ownership.[21] This remained the govern-ment position until the Labor Party lost office at the 1996 election and was suc-ceeded by a Liberal-National Party coalition headed by John Howard as Prime Minister.

The decision taken to sell

By late 1996 the feeling within ADI was that the company's fortunes had progressed to the stage where privatisation should be examined as a viable and desirable option. The restructuring which had caused the company's earnings to fall heavily during 1995/96 – down to a pre-tax profit of just $4.7 million (actually a net loss of $19.4 million after tax and abnormal costs) compared with $24.3 million the year before[22] – was now largely complete, and figures for 1996/97 were expected to be much stronger with the first returns from the Minehunter project and reopened munitions production coming onto the accounts. Having weathered this period entailed in cleaning up the mess left over from the old ODP days, the need was now seen for the company to focus on its future direction.

As already recounted in the previous chapter, considerable effort had been devoted to repositioning ADI within its primary defence market, shifting away from the traditional engineering activities which were its original base and increas-ingly into the systems area. This process of reinventing itself, according to one senior manager, presented important challenges which could best be met only through privatisation:

We were seeing the nature of the market, and the players in that market, chang-ing quite rapidly. Overseas mergers between major defence manufacturers were having an effect, but coincidentally many of those large companies were look-ing to Australia as one of the priority places for them to expand into. Whereas in the early 1990s there were only two or three main players on the local scene

– including ADI – who were regarded as prime contractors for defence work, and these Australian companies received special consideration in tender evaluations because of their Australian-ness and had the opportunity to go overseas to find technology partners, now more and more of these partners were creating their own links into Australia and that access was being closed off. Privatisation was therefore an important part in getting access to technology, and that made it critical for business development.[23]

Not everyone was completely persuaded that a change of ownership was essential. Among members of the ADI board, for example, Apted admits that his public sector background left him unconvinced that the existing arrangement was necessarily a bad thing:

The ideological view I held, though not a strong one, was that I couldn't see why the government should sell its defence manufacturing and supply capacity. I felt it was a public good to have ADI in government hands, with all the spin-offs that the situation provided, like using it as an interventionist policy for industry development. And I felt that in a small economy like Australia's that might have added substance.

In the end, though, I realised that it just doesn't matter, really. There are plenty of overseas examples of equivalent functions being in the private sector for quite long periods, and they seem to work pretty well. The government is always able to influence the public policy outcomes of defence procurement, simply through the process that it is ultimately the buyer. After that realisation dawned on me I was quite comfortable with the idea, though, frankly, everyone else on the board had reached this conclusion way ahead of me and this was just me coming to terms with my own thinking on the issue.[24]

Accordingly, in December 1996 Harris visited the Office of Asset Sales to 'volunteer' the company for privatisation and seek advice on what was entailed. He recalls being warned that, as managing director, he would not like the process. For a start he was about to partly lose control of the organisation. Whereas he had been used to running the company largely as he saw fit, he was about to be disempowered and forced to place his trust in other people.[25]

In mid-February 1997 the chairman of the ADI board, Russell Fynmore, wrote to the Minister for Defence, Ian McLachlan, to offer the views of himself and his fellow directors on the options for privatising the company.[26] He began by addressing the consequences for the company of not proceeding along this course. The first factor noted was 'the subtle but nevertheless real influence that governments have on companies they own', principally through the dilution of commercial resolve to meet the demands of a competitive market and the needs of a shareholder 'whose objectives are often more than simply profit related'. The second consequence concerned access to capital – a factor of major importance to a high technology company like ADI which in future would need funds for further acquisitions and other investments. Given the board's assessment that the government could not be relied upon to provide capital as the shareholder, or to allow the company to borrow (since this added to public sector debt), here was an additional reason why privatisation should be seriously considered.

The board's own examination of whether it was commercially possible to privatise the company now left it 'confident that potential investors would value ADI at a price in excess of the Government's equity stake', but it warned that the price obtained would depend on several factors – probably the most important of which was the method of sale employed. While it was not possible to be precise in the amount likely to be realised, the board offered its own best estimate as 'upwards of $400m'.

Noting that privatisation could be achieved, essentially, in two ways – either by trade sale or public float – Fynmore asserted that the company had been established with the eventual possibility of the former in mind. Both ADI's creation as a normal limited liability company and its determination to have accounts signed off by an internationally recognised audit firm was expected to eliminate complications from the sale process, since potential purchasers could have confidence when they came to examine the accounts. A trade sale was certainly feasible, considering the valuable position occupied by the company within the market, and there was little doubt 'that ADI could be sold quickly and for a good price if the Government placed no restrictions on foreign ownership':

> The Company could operate effectively as a subsidiary of a foreign defence contractor, and I am sure that the Government could extract from any purchaser commitments about how the Company would be integrated into the purchaser's international business.

On the other hand, to achieve a float would depend on how the market viewed the company and the business sector in which it operated. For it to succeed, potential investors 'would need to feel comfortable with the fact that ADI has a dominant, sophisticated customer that is sometimes influenced by politics', but this was an arrangement which could well be made to work with the right sort of 'anchor investor' – indeed, 'this method of privatisation would probably be the most satisfactory of all the options'. It would depend on how the issue of foreign ownership was resolved by the government, and on ensuring that the shareholding of the anchor investor did not frighten off other companies with which ADI would want to do business. While the company had so far avoided becoming committed to technology companies except in regards to specific projects, this was a situation that was unlikely to continue once its current batch of projects began to decline and a link with a major international high technology company became more important for ADI's future.

Fynmore emphasised that the board was not making any recommendation as to the best form of privatisation to adopt, recognising that the decision ultimately rested with the government; instead, it saw its role 'as assisting the shareholder to achieve its objective while, at the same time, ensuring the Company is not damaged by an extended process'. Once the government announced its intention to privatise ADI, the company 'will find it difficult to attract teaming partners and to sign long term contracts':

> This will be the case as long as there is uncertainty over the future ownership arrangements. This will adversely affect not only the order book, but also the morale of management and other employees. The value of the Company will be eroded over time if the privatisation process is prolonged.

The board's strong preference was that the government resolve as many of the policy issues of concern prior to making any announcement 'then proceed with its chosen form of privatisation as quickly as possible thereafter'.

Fynmore then further canvassed a range of factors which currently determined where the company stood within the market, including its origins, size, range of businesses, the effectiveness of its management, and understanding of how to deal with the Department of Defence as its main customer. These elements gave rise to considerations which would need to be addressed along the path to privatisation, such as ADI's position as a major competitive force in the defence industry and the fact that it was the repository of a number of assets or skills which Defence might regard as important. Whatever course the government chose, it had to take account of the extent to which business corporations were becoming global in their focus, the need to retain strong competition within the local defence industry even while achieving a restructure of that industry, and 'whether the complete exclusion of foreign ownership to satisfy domestic political considerations will enhance or undermine the ability of the Company to grow in the local market and become more heavily involved in the international market'. In working through all these issues, however, the government could be assured that the Board and management 'view privatisation as a positive step and are prepared to assist and cooperate … in any way to ensure the process is undertaken smoothly and swiftly'.

ADI's views were very well received within the office of Defence Minister McLachlan, who later recalled that from the outset he was immensely impressed (as a former businessman himself) by the quality of advice coming to him from that quarter:

> I had no problems. I was well reported to by the managing director, whether things were going well and badly. It was a good set up, and the company had a

very good board – people with a great variety of business experience who weren't frightened to speak up. There was never a problem about whether the Liberal and National parties were going to privatise the thing, and everyone was aware that that's where it was going.[27]

Speaking in parliament on 27 February 1997, McLachlan stated that the company was fit for sale to the private sector and that he imagined that such a transaction would occur 'in the next year or so'.[28]

As anticipated, the question of privatising ADI duly received a mention in the budget papers in May 1997, when the Minister for Finance stated that the government would decide on the timing and strategies for privatisation and other relevant issues during the 1997/98 financial year – thereby confirming that mid-1998 was the most likely time for achieving a sale.[29] This announcement was followed by several public expressions of interest in becoming the new owner of ADI by companies such as the Visy Industries group, although there were also other approaches being made quietly behind the scenes. Harris was quoted as saying that he knew of eight to ten proposals from potential investors or buyers, and expected more now that the government's intention to privatise had been officially confirmed.[30] On 1 July the finance minister announced that the government had chosen the firms of Baring Brothers Burrows and Blake Dawson Waldron, as business and legal advisers respectively, to assist it in deciding how to proceed in the matter.[31]

With the decision announced and the first steps under way, there were some painful adjustments now made within ADI. When the board met on 11 July the chairman advised that Malcolm Kinnaird, who was absent, had formally notified the Minister for Defence of his 'inability to continue as a Director', as a result of a potential conflict of interest arising from the merging of Kinhill Holdings with a company that intended to explore the possibility of making an offer for ADI. Elizabeth Bryan, who was present, also announced that because of the possible involvement in the privatisation process of her employer she, too, felt obliged to withdraw.[32] The board had previously lost the services of Steven Harker, whose resignation to take up a position in London had been announced in May 1996, so these two new departures meant that the board's membership had been cut from eight to five in little more than a year. None of these vacancies would be filled, despite the fact that the company was plainly entering a difficult and demanding period.

According to one director present on 11 July, there was another factor behind Bryan's resignation which served as a sober warning to her fellow directors. Apted recalls that:

The most pertinent comment I heard about privatisation came from Elizabeth. She said, 'You all think it will be twelve months and it will be a pretty straight-forward exercise. I reckon you could all be still sitting here in another two to three years. You have no idea what you are going to go through, but I've been through it before. Despite all the assurances you get, it is going to take a hell of a long time, you are going to get tied up in it, and there's a real risk that the place will lose its focus.' Basically she just felt that she didn't want to be part of all that again, so she said 'I'm out of here'! Unfortunately she has been proved right.[33]

Harris, too, acknowledges that Bryan's forecast proved accurate, recalling that upon meeting up with her on a later occasion he was prompted to remark, 'Elizabeth, you were quite right that I was going to hate the privatisation process. But you should have told me how much I was going to hate it!'.[34]

No-one in ADI had been prepared for the scale of the disruption caused to daily activities by the requirements of the privatisation process. From mid-1997 the company found its affairs under detailed scrutiny firstly by the government sales team (impishly known as the GST after an equally unpopular tax measure), which was trying to establish a complete picture of ADI's shape and health to determine the government's options, and later by potential buyers keen to discover the same information under what was called 'due diligence'. Although personnel from the Office of Asset Sales proved to be experienced and professional, in dealing with them ADI members often found themselves returned to the mires of the bureaucracy. Les Targ, who took on the day-to-day management within ADI Headquarters of issues and matters related to privatisation, relates that:

Whenever the GST visited us at Bondi Junction we always found ourselves short of chairs and coffee cups. There would always be me and three or four other ADI members flanked by about twenty GST advisers, and the atmosphere was quite stifling. At one stage we were told that the GST wanted the company management to rehearse their presentations to bidders in front of it. I queried this, saying 'None of us are actors, but we know our business and we'll do it properly at the time.' 'Ah no', said one man from the Office of Asset Sales, 'we want to see how you perform when placed under some pressure'. I told them we were happy to receive their advice on do's and don'ts, but we weren't prepared to waste time on dummy presentations …

It was difficult enough for managers to meet their budget targets and contractual commitments anyway, but it was worse to have a process that requires a full and ongoing disclosure of all material issues affecting the company for a period that ultimately stretched out to more than two years.[35]

The practical and physical demands of the situation were immense. Not only did the company have some 500 commercial agreements in place that would have to be considered in determining its value, but the requirement for ADI to hand over information for examination – even if considered only marginally relevant – by mid-1998 had caused 12,000 documents to be placed in a Commonwealth 'library'.[36] The sheer volume of material meant that there were huge difficulties in being categorical about the accuracy or completeness of documentation. And once bidders actually started their inquiries there was a steady stream of formal written questions, usually involving highly technical detail, to which the company was obliged to respond with letters which had to be legally signed off by the board.[37]

It was in the context of impending privatisation that keen public interest was focused on the figures for ADI's trading performance for 1996/97 which were reported at the start of September 1997. These showed that for the first time revenue had exceeded $600 million (actually reaching $624.7 million), which made ADI far and away Australia's largest defence manufacturer. On the strength of this turnover, the company's pre-tax profit had bounced back to $42.3 million – a ninefold increase on the previous year – which enabled payment of a total dividend for the year of seven cents per share.[38] This return to profitability was, in the words of Defence Minister McLachlan, 'an excellent result ... [which] provided a welcome backdrop to the Government's consideration of the optimum timing and method for privatising ADI Limited'.[39]

By late 1997 the report commissioned from the government's financial advisers, Baring Brothers Burrows, had been received and the issues associated with privatising the company were back on the government's agenda. The ADI board was not provided with a copy of this document, but on 19 November was invited to offer any views held regarding privatisation which it felt might be helpful to the government's consideration. In response to this request, a week later the chairman sent a letter to Finance Minister Fahey and Defence Minister McLachlan which addressed further issues that the Board believed were crucial to understanding the options regarding any move to sell the company. Among the questions raised were the likely consequences of allowing it to be sold as a whole or broken up, whether the development properties at Footscray, Maribyrnong and St. Marys should be included in the sale, and a number of presale measures that could be taken to enhance the company's value.[40]

Throughout these last months of 1997 there was also much jockeying for position among potential buyers of the company. By far the most visible of the contenders was a consortium being assembled by Visy Industries, which made known its interest in merging ADI and the Australian Submarine Corporation (ASC) to create a publicly-listed giant engineering company for both civil and defence projects. Visy's chief executive was none other than Dr John White, the man credited with revitalising the former government dockyard at Williamstown on behalf of Transfield, whose stated aim was to turn ADI into Australia's premier technology company with annual revenues of more than $3 billion within a decade.[41] By mid-November the National Australia Bank (NAB), the nation's most profitable listed group, had joined the Visy-led consortium as a partner.[42]

Also announcing at this time an intention to make offers for ADI were the Swedish company Celsius AB,[43] and the recently-separated arms of the Transfield Holdings group – construction and infrastructure company (Transfield) and its shipbuilding and defence offshoot (Transfield Defence Systems, or TDS) – which would make rival bids.[44] Within days Transfield had formed a consortium with Raytheon International, the third largest defence contractor in the United States,[45] while TDS (renaming itself Tenix from 20 November) was already linked to Lockheed Martin through an established strategic partnership. The French conglomerate Thomson-CSF, Europe's largest electronics manufacturer, also added its name to the list of contenders, and British Aerospace expressed an interest in acquiring some parts of ADI's business.[46]

On 9 December a joint media release was issued by Finance Minister Fahey and Defence Minister McLachlan announcing the government's decision to dispose of its shareholding in ADI through an open tender sale to be conducted by the Office of Asset Sales and Information Technology Outsourcing, in consultation with the Department of Defence. Preference was for the company to be transferred to new ownership as a whole, but the sale of individual or groups of business units would also be considered. Expressions of interest in acquiring the company would be sought in the first quarter of 1998, with the sale expected to be completed later in the year.[47]

While the government had been considering the simultaneous sale of its shareholding in the ASC, it had now also been decided to defer any move to dispose of its stake in the Collins Class submarines until the second half of 1998. Though this had the effect of giving priority to the privatisation of ADI, such an outcome was not actually the prime factor behind it. The real reason lay in problems being experienced with the new Collins boats, and the determination of McLachlan (himself a South Australian) to keep the two separate until the submarines had been 'fixed up':

> A linkage with the ADI sale would have hindered the submarine program. I wanted to get the submarines in the water and working properly. I didn't want a takeover or a merger interfering with or distracting from that.[48]

A week later the two ministers further announced a timetable of events regarding the sale process. Under this, expressions of interest would be called by the end of February 1998, with shortlisted contenders having from May until late July to conduct due diligence and submit final bids. The remaining steps – evaluation of offers, purchaser's final review of classified information, and government approval of the sale – were expected to completed by August or September.

The government's guidelines for potential bidders had still not been released in early March 1998 when ADI issued figures for its trading performance in the half-year to December 1997, showing a net loss of $9.3 million as a result of writing off nearly $40 million in abnormal expenditures (including almost a million dollars in preparing documentation needed for due diligence) aimed at putting the company into shape ahead of its sale.[49] At the same time the likelihood of meeting the stated deadline for completing the sale seemed remote when ADI became one of two prime contenders – Tenix was the other – for the Navy's $1 billion FFG upgrade program; final proposals for this project were lodged only in March and a decision was not expected before near the end of the year. Winning this contract was expected to add substantially to the company's prospective price, so it became increasingly likely that the sale would be deferred until the outcome of the contest for the FFG contract was known. (This action proved justified when, in November 1998, it was announced that ADI had won the FFG upgrade tender.[50])

The bidding war

In anticipation of the government's call for expressions of interest, the field of contenders began to line up. Again taking the lead was the Visy-NAB partnership, which on 15 April announced that a memorandum of understanding had been signed with Celsius to form the Systems Engineering Consortium of Australia (SECA); this new group would continue to seek further members or allies from engineering and investment companies both locally and overseas.[51]

Unfortunately, a fresh cause of delay arose a week later, when Finance Minister Fahey announced that the need to allow ADI time to complete negotiations on a new ammunition supply agreement with the Defence Department meant that the planned call for expressions of interest had been deferred until early June.[52] This was an announcement which overshadowed ADI's success right at this juncture in winning a $250 million contract as sole worldwide supplier of enclosures and modules for General Electric's LM2500 marine gas turbines,[53] an achievement which emphasised the company's potential value to any new owner.

The announced deferment added greatly to a growing sense of frustration within ADI. Contrary to the impression being created publicly that the company was itself in some way to blame for delays in the privatisation process – an impression the board decided in March to take steps to dispel[54] – the impetus for revisiting the terms of the long term agreement covering the supply of munitions (signed only in 1993 and meant to last 20 years) came directly from the Department of Defence. In December 1997 the company had been notified that the GST wanted the department and ADI to 'tidy up' the details of the contract, to make sure that it was an appropriate commercial document to put to bidders for ownership of ADI. Company officials were therefore upset to find that this review involved

Defence winding back consideration to such fundamental questions as whether ammunition should be manufactured in Australia at all or simply imported – an issue supposedly resolved before the company had invested heavily in the new factory at Benalla. Says Harris:

> Neither ADI nor the GST expected that what was a fine tuning exercise was going to develop into a root-and-branch renegotiation of such a major contract, but that's what happened. And it took some eight months to do it.[55]

The revised ammunition agreement reinforced the commercial principle of 'take or pay' and provided ADI with a more even cashflow over the period of the contract than had been the case with the original contract. Anticipated cashflows over the first seven years of the revised agreement were now considerably better than under the old agreement. At the same time a greater degree of certainty was introduced into the revised agreement, to the advantage of both parties, through clearly defining matters such as termination provisions which had been left hanging in the air in the original agreement. The new agreement is an 'evergreen' arrangement, requiring negotiations to take place between the parties from time to time to extend the period beyond the initial seventeen years. From Defence's viewpoint, ammunition pricing was now less volatile than envisaged with fluctuating order levels under the old agreement.

It was not until mid-year that this obstacle was substantially settled and out of the way (though even then the new contract was not formally signed until 9 July). The government's call to potential purchasers was finally made public on 12 June with a closing date of 9 July.[56] Now a second consortium comprising Transfield and Thomson-CSF – not Raytheon as expected – announced it would also enter the competition, followed by Tenix which confirmed on 24 June that it, too, would be submitting a proposal of its own in conjunction with Lockheed Martin. Two British contenders, GEC-Marconi and British Aerospace, also emerged publicly at the last minute as contenders.

On 31 July another joint announcement was made by Ministers Fahey and McLachlan that from 'a strong field of candidates' the government had shortlisted five consortia (without naming them) to proceed to the next stage of the sale process, involving the undertaking of due diligence and preparation of final bids for assessment against the government's objectives.[57] This statement referred to the impact of the FFG upgrade project, which implicitly meant that finalisation was unlikely before early in 1999 and, as one newspaper pointed out, more likely meant later in the year if all consortia were to be allowed time to consider the contract negotiated for the FFGs.[58] The ministers also made clear the government's strong preference for selling the company as one entity, although not now included in the assets being offered, however, were the development properties at St. Marys, Footscray and Maribyrnong. In recognition that none of the bidders, all of whom were defence contractors, were keen to become engaged in the real estate business (especially overseas companies which had little background to help them value these assets), the decision had been made that the properties would be 'dealt with separately'.

Despite hopes that matters would now push ahead with more speed, in fact there continued to be substantial delays caused in part by the sheer scale and complexity of the process involved. Another complication proved to be the calling of a federal election for 3 October, even though this resulted in the return of the Liberal–National coalition but with a new Minister for Defence, John Moore, to replace the retiring McLachlan. The most interesting aspect of the election was the anti-privatisation platform adopted by the Labor Party under the leadership of Kim Beazley, which included a proposal to consolidate ADI and the ASC into one venture called Defence Manufacturing Australia based in Adelaide[59] – a plan which promised to kill privatisation of the company stone dead if Labor had won office. Such a prospect was felt as a deep disappointment among ADI's senior managers, especially for Harris. His appointment as managing director had recently been extended to September 1999, specifically to cover a period of transition to new ownership, but the idea of no sale going ahead prompted him to resolve to leave in December 1998 under the terms of his existing contract if Labor won the election.[60]

In the midst of the election campaign the company was also obliged to release its annual report for 1997/98 which showed that an operating profit of $37.5 million had been converted into a loss through the posting of $51 million worth of abnormal costs, much of which were associated with privatisation. Noting that the process was not expected to be concluded until the second half of 1999, the directors took the opportunity to complain at the 'excessively slow' pace of the sale and point out the intense demands placed on the company's management team and other damaging effects on the company's health and outlook.[61]

Within a month of the election the bidding contest for ADI took a dramatic turn when Tenix withdrew without giving any reason publicly (because of nondisclosure agreements with the Office of Asset Sales and IT Outsourcing binding all bidders).[62] Less than a week later the SECA group took on board two new partners: Western Australia-based firm Clough Engineering, and the giant United States defence software company Science Applications International Corporation (SAIC).[63] By December it was public knowledge that British Aerospace had withdrawn too.

This was not the extent of the changing character of the field which was active in the contest. By the end of March 1999 the United States aerospace firm Raytheon – which had been excluded at the initial shortlist stage the previous August – re-entered as an additional member of the SECA group; it was also reported that Tenix had re-entered as a partner to GEC-Marconi. Since the latter's defence electronic interests were on the verge of being taken over in the UK by

British Aerospace, this represented a highly significant consolidation and enhancement of one of the three remaining bidders for ADI.[64] Its immediate effect, however, was to cause the privatisation process to be extended by a month to allow the revised team to catch up with other contenders in carrying out due diligence studies.[65]

Finally, in mid–May, came the bombshell that the SECA group was withdrawing. After having been the most prominent among ADI's potential buyers from the beginning, and in many circles regarded as the frontrunner, it had decided to drop out citing unspecified 'commercial reasons' – although any further explanation was prohibited by confidentiality provisions.[66] As one newspaper observed, amid the mass consolidation of the world defence industry, bidding for ADI had now come down to a battle between consortiums led by the warring families who just three years previously jointly controlled Transfield.[67]

Throughout this wave of turbulence, ADI, too, continued to be buffeted by the effects of the protracted privatisation process. When the company's financial results for the half year to the end of December 1998 were made public in February 1999, these revealed an outcome that was significantly below budget. A small drop in operating profit (down from $12.1 million to $11.4 million) had been completely eclipsed by one-off losses of $35 million associated with restructuring costs and write-downs in further preparation for the company's long-awaited sale.[68]

Acknowledging the strain and uncertainty the whole situation had placed on ADI's employees, and the demands it had made on their performance, the managing director, Ken Harris, took the opportunity presented by the launch of the third minehunter *Norman* at Newcastle on 3 May – coincidentally the tenth anniversary of the company's creation – to publicly praise the commitment of the workforce 'right across ADI'.[69] As the keynote speaker at the ceremony, Finance Minister Fahey also used the occasion to express to reporters present his understanding of the frustration felt within the company over delays, but added that the tender process would be 'well and truly under way' by the end of the financial year. All bids had to be lodged by 30 June and an announcement regarding the successful tenderer was expected by 'late spring'.[70]

Considering the toll which, by this stage, had been exacted among the field of bidders and within ADI itself, it was understandable that Harris, when speaking on 1 June at the signing of two contracts collectively worth over $1 billion (for the FFG upgrade and the supply of 370 Bushmaster vehicles for the Army), welcomed what he saw as the kick-starting of the final phase in the sell-off. Lamenting the disruptive effects of the process which had forced his executive team to split their time between running the company and showing around potential bidders, he said: 'There's no more reasons for delays in the sale. The prospective buyers can go away now and do their due diligence on these two contracts. These are the last pieces to fall into place, and the bidders will be able to see the company in full.' The people at ADI, he emphasised, were keen to move into the hands of private sector owners who would bring capital, technology and increased international market access to the company. Warning against any further delays, he declared that 'the only certainty in our business is that if we continue to be owned by the government, the place will die'. [71]

And the winner is ...

When the deadline for firm offers to the Office of Asset Sales closed on 30 June 1999 there were just two bids lodged. Although the government announcement the next day neither confirmed this number nor named the parties, [72] they were immediately identified in the media as coming from the Transfield–Thomson joint venture and from Tenix. Claims swiftly surfaced that the latter had lost GEC–Marconi as its partner at the last minute, but had gone ahead with a bid on its own account. [73] Later it was reported that although GEC–Marconi had indeed withdrawn, it had provided a letter supporting the Tenix offer and indicated its continuing interest in the sale. [74] Even with the deadline past, the bidders still had until 21 July to carry out further due diligence on the value of the FFG Upgrade and Bushmaster contracts, before making final revised offers. [75] During this interval, and in the weeks immediately following, the media rumour mill slipped into overdrive. Among the stories that gained currency were claims that members of the now defunct SECA consortium had complained to the Australian Competition and Consumer Commission about the sale process which had been followed, and monopoly aspects which would arise should Tenix emerge as the successful bidder; [76] and that Celsius – one of the former partners in SECA – had approached the Office of Asset Sales about re-entering the bidding separately, but seeking a six-week extension to proceedings which the OAS was unwilling to countenance.[77] More disturbing were claims which began appearing from early August. These were to the effect that the whole sale process was in disarray or 'floundering' with the real prospect that it would be either postponed or called off entirely, possibly with the company being retained in government ownership by being 'folded' into the Australian Submarine Corporation.[78] The reasons behind such assertions were various, but often seemed sufficiently well-grounded to be possibly true.

The most common rumour put forward was that the prices offered by the contenders were only about half the figure of $400 million which the government had hoped to raise – $225 million from Transfield–Thomson and $220 million from Tenix. This immediately gave rise to speculation that the government might prefer to risk further damage to the company by delaying matters for several months while it held a second round of bidding, in the hope of eliciting better offers – otherwise, some commentators charged, it would be merely engaging in a 'fire sale'. So persistent was the belief that the prices offered were too low that it scarcely mattered when ASI tried to point out that such figures, even if correctly reported, did not take into account the development properties (valued at $157 million) which the government had decided to sell separately.[79]

Another factor in the evolving equation was the uncertain impact of serious convulsions with the Defence Department right at this juncture, after a highly critical external report into the controversial submarine project had been made public on 1 July. This produced a personnel shake-up in the Defence Acquisitions Organisation and moves by the Minister for Defence to remove the public service head of the department. Within ADI's management there were now serious concerns that the individuals most likely to be considered as replacements would refuse to accept the criteria established at the outset by the government for the sale and seek belatedly to intervene by moving the goalposts.

Other concerns arose in claims that an intense debate regarding the sale had been triggered within government circles on political, diplomatic and security grounds, because of French connections of Transfield's partner, Thomson–CSF.[80] Even ADI's latest success in winning a $56 million contract to build twelve new fast ferries for use on Sydney Harbour (the first three in time for the 2000 Olympics) was portrayed as 'the most recent complication' in the 'involved saga' of the government's attempt to sell the company.[81]

Eventually, on 17 August, and despite all the doomsayers, the announcement was made. The ministers for Finance and Defence had decided that the Transfield–Thomson joint venture would be ADI's new owners. The ministers' statement made clear the basis on which the choice had been made:

> The Transfield–Thomson Joint Venture is expected to build on ADI's strengths and standing within the Australian defence industry. The Joint Venture has indicated its commitment to the continued operations of ADI's existing businesses at their current locations. In particular, it is expected that ADI's operations at Bendigo, Lithgow, Newcastle and Albury will continue and, where commercially possible, be strengthened by the development of new business activities, presenting opportunities for regional employment.[82]

From the company's perspective, the decision was greeted with scarcely concealed delight. A statement released that same day was headed 'ADI Welcomes Announcement', and made it clear that management considered that the three objectives it had wanted to see achieved from any sale – and which the government had effectively endorsed – were now within reach. As Harris commented, 'ADI would be greatly advantaged by having Transfield and Thomson as its new owners', and he pledged that the company's management team would work closely to achieve a smooth transition.[83]

11

REFLECTIONS

In terms of simple chronology, the decision taken in 1988 to corporatise Australia's defence production facilities undoubtedly falls within a recognised broad historical trend. As Harris later paused to reflect ten years after the company's creation:

> The timing was right, in that it was the era in which Margaret Thatcher's view of capitalism was sweeping the world. Five years earlier – or even now – and the corporatisation of ADI might not have happened. We were caught up in the change of attitude to the role of governments everywhere that she initiated, and we were very conscious of her legacy.[1]

Yet in a sense, this global movement formed no more than a backdrop to the process which took place in this country in respect of the creation of ADI. This is because the individuals who both inspired and carried through this enterprise were not driven by ideology so much as a simple awareness of the need to find a practical solution to the serious and ongoing problem besetting the industrial sphere of defence activity.

In the view of the then Defence Minister, Kim Beazley, Australia was fortunate to have the individuals that it did occupying the positions at this crucial juncture:

> Whatever drive there was coming from the top in this exercise, the whole thing was put together by Lionel Woodward and Ken Harris. They are unusual public servants, and not like most public servants I've come across in the

Commonwealth. I doubt very much that without them the job would have been done … and it was a unique set of circumstances which enabled it to be done. They were the catalysts, but I think the person who started it all was probably Bill Cole.[2]

Obviously the key figure among the group named was Harris, to whom the bulk of a difficult and daunting task was entrusted. Speaking in jocular vein at the opening of ADI's first corporate headquarters in July 1989, the company's inaugural chairman Alan Woods left no doubt of his admiration for the managing director's mettle when he said:

While this is clearly ADI's day, it would be wrong of me to single out any individual except 'Genghis Ken', whose energy and enthusiasm has enabled him to climb Mt. Everest, leap skyscrapers, overcome Finance and become a friend of the Auditor-General.[3]

For his part, Harris was not so sure that the effort had been worthwhile, candidly admitting that:

From a personal point of view, had I realised how difficult it was going to be I doubt very much that I would have taken it on. But, you know, you start on a path and once you do it's difficult to get off.[4]

Those credited by Beazley with achieving the ADI exercise are equally conscious of the part which he played in helping the process along. Observes Harris:

As a basically decent person, I think Beazley was a bit appalled at what went on at some of the defence factories. He saw the need to clean up the organisation as well, and to knock it into shape, but unlike a lot of ministers he was prepared to say, 'Well the bunch of people I've got there seem OK. If its going to succeed, there's a good chance that they'll be able to make it work, so I'll go along with them'. That was a most uncharacteristic attitude for a minister to adopt.

Other ministers wouldn't have done it that way. They'd have had endless consultants coming in, and interdepartmental committees. They would probably still be talking about it and meanwhile the organisation would be dead! Being a strong personality he knew how to deal with other ministers and get his way. But the other thing that I think he knew, better than most, was the potential of defence industry to be not only a great contributor to the defence of the country but also a contributor to economic growth and jobs and exports. So I think he was motivated not only by money but the need to make the place efficient in any case, and also maybe the idea that this was something that eventually we could be proud of.[5]

Beazley acknowledges that he was in a fortunate position during his tenure of the Defence portfolio:

It was a great personal advantage that there were no political pressure points on me over the defence factories. No-one could come whining to me about what might happen to my preselection, so I was in a very strong and different position to many of my colleagues. I do think that it required a defence minister from Western Australia to deal with it, or perhaps one from Queensland. You couldn't have had one from New South Wales or Victoria and had him sane enough for another Cabinet post afterwards. It would have been his last great act of politics.[6]

Of course, after the company had been launched it was not just Beazley who, as political chief of the situation, played a critical role in giving it direction, but his successors too. As Harris later freely acknowledges: 'ADI was extremely lucky in the succession of ministers – Beazley, Ray, McLachlan and Moore – it had to deal with while the major decisions were being taken that shaped its future.'[7]

If the nation was fortunate to have had at the top the confluence of able and motivated people necessary for ADI to become a reality, the same was true of managers working at levels further down. The contribution of these people received particular acknowledgement from Fynmore, who remarked:

I think it was a big achievement to convert what was basically a public service management team into a private enterprise-oriented business group. I've been most impressed with the John Barclays, the John McMahons and, at the next level down, the chap now running our land development area, Bill Mitchell. As a new board member I met them when they were coming up with the plans and valuations for converting ODP into ADI. They were all public servants at that stage, but the way they have been able to convert into their new role has been very significant. It means they were very good quality people, whether or not they had chosen to become public servants. With a board that has encouraged them, they've become … well, most of them could find their way into any private sector organisation in the country.[8]

The ability of former members of ODP to adapt to the challenge of the new commercial organisation so rapidly and successfully was an interesting surprise to a great many people, belying one of the cherished traditional beliefs held by detractors of the public service. ADI's former company secretary, Trish Russell, commented on this phenomenon in the following terms:

When the company was first formed those of us who transferred from ODP saw a lot of people coming in from outside, people of great ability with commercial backgrounds. We felt like the 'country cousins' and were a little bit in awe of them. As the years have gone on and I've looked back at how people have performed, I realise that those who were selected to come to the company from the public service were enormously high achievers, with incredible ability and capacity. I say to people now, 'Don't ever feel like the country cousins any more', because the John Barclays, the Bill Mitchells and so on, have simply made huge progress.[9]

The transformation from the public service approach to a commercial outlook was, of course, the fundamental objective of the whole exercise. Harris is insistent that setting up as a company is the only sensible course to be followed in trying to make former areas of government activity into viable business entities. As he puts it:

Whenever anybody tells me that they are thinking about corporatising something and asks for my advice, the first thing I do is say 'Don't do it' and second is to then tell them that if they must do it, do it as a take-over.[10]

Not only was this an approach which involved a clear-cut set of commercial arrangements, but it provided all the necessary incentives for everyone concerned to appreciate the different environment within which they were required and expected to function. Some commentators felt a twinge of concern at claims that ADI was urging its employees 'to think of themselves as belonging to the private sector, notwithstanding its public ownership', emphasising the potential for loss of control and accountability.[11] It makes little sense, however, to go to the bother of corporatising without reaping the full benefits in terms of efficiency entailed by the resulting 'change of culture'.

Having such a change fully understood and accepted had been one of the hardest aspects to address, and an area in which the company's experience was least satisfactory – hence Harris' injunction against lightly embarking on the corporatisation path in the first place. From time to time the ADI board voiced frustration at attempts to limit or restrict its independence to act in the company's best interests, with Fynmore describing 'a constant battle ... [going on] almost since the day I took over as chairman'.[12] By late-1991 ADI felt obliged to express concerns at what it regarded as 'pressure within the Public Service for a greater say in the conduct of the Company's affairs'. Fynmore sounded a warning that:

The Board is alarmed about this trend and suggests there is a serious risk of reversing the gains shown ... if management was to be subjected to additional bureaucratic interference.[13]

Particularly deplorable, it seemed to senior company officers, was the tendency within government and the bureaucracy to disregard the advice of the board. Surely, it was argued, ADI's own directors were more competent than officials and others to advise on the company's affairs. If the minister had no faith in the members of the board then he should replace them, but – having made appointments which did enjoy his confidence – there should be no cause for constantly seeking the input of outside consultants.[14]

Of equal concern were constant attempts to reduce the freedom of boards of GBEs like ADI to effectively run their company. The tendency to treat them as just another committee disregarded the personal obligations and liabilities placed on directors by various laws and statutes, as Harris did not hesitate to point out to the joint parliamentary committee of Public Accounts when unsuccessfully opposing the clutch of draft legislation (including the Auditor-General Bill, the Financial Management and Accountability Bill and Commonwealth Authorities and Companies Bill), which was introduced into Parliament in June 1994.[15] The attitude of unwillingness to let go was encountered at many levels, with one GGM in ADI recounting as late as 1998 that:

> Even today we have comments being made by people from the Department of Defence saying 'You should look upon us, mate, as being your head office', as though the company has not one manager but thousands of people there who are looking after ADI. And, goodness me, I thought we looked after ADI! And every year we have meetings with representatives of Defence and Finance to discuss our business plan. This has always seemed a bit strange for me, as someone from a public company, because I am not used to going to the shareholder and baring my soul. I thought talking to the board of directors would be good enough. So there is that element of intrusiveness, when really the whole point behind creating ADI as a company was to break that nexus with government ways of thinking and government ways of doing things.[16]

Predictably, this was an issue on which Harris, too, has been passionate on occasions, suggesting that officials should learn to live in an arms-length relationship with ADI and act like 'customers, not second-guessers':

> That means they have got to sort out clearly what role they are adopting when they are talking to us. The first role is the government as the owner of the company. And I think … the government side needs to say 'How do sensible owners of businesses behave?' and then behave accordingly. The other role is the customer. When the Australian Defence Force talks to us as a major customer of ours, they need to think, speak and behave like a customer. The difficulty in this process of extracting ourselves from the government – and it's a difficulty for them and us – is for all of us … not to mix up the roles.[17]

Others in closer day-to-day contact with the Defence department see the other side of this relationship. As McMahon pointed out in 1994:

> There's a factor that works in a negative way between Defence and ADI, inasmuch as people in the Acquisitions and Logistics area – and to a lesser extent the Resources, Finance and Plans Division – see themselves as advisers to the shareholder. They get pretty irritated when we try to live according to the original philosophy of being a separate legal entity, etc. That is not the way that many elements of the bureaucracy see government-owned companies working, so we're always at loggerheads. Everything that they want us to do, we complain; we don't roll over. At times we use strategic capitulation, but generally speaking we stand up to them every time, whatever it is, and the fight is always on. Now that attitude has led people in Defence and Finance to think that we're just a bunch of intransigent ratbags.[18]

Four years on and McMahon claimed to have observed a marked maturing in the relationship between the company and its principal customer, Defence:

> I think we've reached a plateau now where we've achieved the relationship that we've sought, and our choice of approach to managing it has been vindicated. I don't think it is going to do anything but continue to improve in the months and years ahead. It's probably right to say that of all the achievements that have been made in ADI's short life, it's the turnaround in the relationship between the two organisations that has been more important. It's been a culture change for both of us. In our case we've had to turn our workforce into a customer oriented group, and in their case they have had to recognise that we are no longer the organisation that sold them an ill-fitting shirt or fixed a warship that broke down the next day. … Now ADI is universally acknowledged as a serious competitor for major projects and small ones as well.[19]

This view of the current state of affairs is shared by Garry Jones, the former head of the Defence Acquisitions organisation. He considers that the company has been successful in tendering for major defence projects to an extent 'that surprised the rest of industry', because of the baggage that it carries through its heritage and past associations:

> It gets no special treatment on account of that, but I think many people in ADI realise the perceptions of the company that they have to contend with and put in a much greater effort because of it. They put more work in, to demonstrate that they are different to the past and a truly commercial organisation, and we end up with better offers. They haven't been totally successful in overcoming the ODP legacy, in my opinion, but they have made enormous strides. ADI is

a good strong company with a lot of strengths because of its strong technology base and strong connection with defence issues.

The company has never asked for any favours because of its history either. From the top down, it has always said 'Judge us as we are, as you find us in a commercial sense', which I think has been a very good attitude. With defence projects it is rare to win the trifecta of getting what you want, on time and within budget, because of the complexity and uncertainty of doing things we've never done before. Industry takes a lot of risks, and many companies do well for a while then fall by the wayside. ADI has performed well on our major contracts. Some sub-contracts they've done with others have posed problems, but they are currently sitting in the middle to upper level of defence contractors in Australia. That doesn't mean everything is running smoothly and there aren't any problems, but the company's problems have to be seen in the context of everybody else.[20]

By common consent, therefore – and judged on a range of criteria such as delivery and technical performance, profitability, and so on – the risky experiment undertaken little more than a decade ago with ADI's creation must be judged a resounding success. Australia has gained an efficient economic unit which has served the government and community extraordinarily well within the particular sphere of its activities and operations. As an example of successful micro-economic reform it is both a model and an inspiration. The nation would almost certainly have been worse off, and poorer, without the initiative having been taken to address the serious malaise infecting the organisation which it replaced. Now the company stands on the brink of an unknown future, preparing for a course which will be determined by the business agenda of a new owner. The only certainty is that at last it will have broken free from the shackles which have constrained it since its formation.

Perhaps the ultimate irony of the latest twist in the tale of Australia's defence industry is the curiously cyclical ring which the story has about it. For while the total picture of defence production in this country has changed beyond all recognition from the situation a century ago, the decisions to firstly abandon bureaucratic control in favour of independent commercial management, then to place its ownership in the private sector, have effectively returned this form of activity to where it originated in this country. Another case perhaps of the old French saying: *plus ça change, plus c'est la même chose* – or, loosely translated: the more things change, the more they stay the same.

NOTES

Preface

1. *Australian Financial Review*, 15 May 1995.
2. *Bulletin*, 4 April 1995, p.22.
3. Margaret Thatcher, *The Downing Street Years*, Harper Collins, London, 1993, p.677.
4. B.A. Santamaria, in *Australian*, 11 February 1995.
5. *Economist*, 11 March 1995.
6. Daniel Yergin and Joseph Stanislaw, *The Commanding Heights: The Battle Between Government and the Marketplace That is Remaking the Modern World*, Simon & Schuster, New York, 1998, p.364.
7. *Australian Financial Review*, 9 September 1992, 10 November 1994.
8. John Hyde, in *Australian*, 15 August 1992.
9. Padraic P. McGuinness, in *Sydney Morning Herald*, 6 December 1994.
10. John Hyde, in *Australian*, 15 August 1992.
11. *Australian Financial Review*, 20 December 1994.
12. *Australian Financial Review*, 20 December 1994.
13. Roger Wettenhall, *Public Enterprise and National Development: Selected Essays*, Royal Australian Institute of Public Administration, Canberra, 1987, pp.13, 21; see also his paper 'Corporatised Bodies Old and New: Is Parliament Missing Out?', speech in Senate occasional lecture series, Canberra, 31 May 1993, p.9.

Chapter One

1. The first of these was the schooner *Eliza*, built at the government dockyard at Port Arthur and launched in May 1835. Based at Hobart and used to prevent the escape of convicts, she was a fast vessel of 98 tons and carried two guns. By virtue of this armament, Tasmanians sometimes claim her as Australia's first warship. See C. Jones, *Australian Colonial Navies*, Canberra, 1986, p.11.
2. Jones, p.14; G.J. Odgers, *The Royal Australian Navy: An Illustrated History*, Hornsby, NSW, 1982, p.19.
3. L.L. Barton, *Australians in the Waikato War 1863–64*, Sydney, 1979, p.7; B. Nairn (ed.), *Australian Dictionary of Biography*, vol.6, Melbourne University Press, Carlton, Vic., 1976, p.76.

4. Jones, pp.47, 53–4.

5. Neville Meaney, *The Search for Security in the Pacific, 1901–14*, Sydney University Press, Sydney, 1976, pp.7, 9, 15–16.

6. New South Wales Legislative Council *Journal*, vol.32 (1881), part 1, p.806.

7. The promoter of this scheme was a German-American chemist, Carl Von Bieren, who subsequently converted the business into the Australian Powder and Explosives Manufacturing Company, in which he held one-third of the shares. While there are many conflicting stories about Von Bieren's venture, including fanciful claims that he was an agent of the German government, it seems his initial intentions were honest. Faced with insolvency by the middle of 1885, however, he absconded to England but was arrested on arrival and returned to Sydney to face embezzlement charges in September 1886, which earned him nearly three years in gaol. See P.W. Gledhill, *Manly and Pittwater: Its Beauty and Progress*, Sydney, 1948, p.108; Charles Swancott, *Dee Why to Barrenjoey and Pittwater*, Woy Woy, NSW, 1967, p.93; and material provided by Local History Resource Unit, Pittwater Council, August 1994.

8. G.J.R. Linge, *Industrial Awakening: A Geography of Australian Manufacturing 1788 to 1890*, ANU Press, Canberra, 1979, p.262.

9. Meaney, p.22.

10. T.F.C. Lawrence, 'The Department of Supply: Its Origins and Functions', January 1971, p.3: ODP records held by ADI; J.K. Jensen, Defence Production in Australia to 1941, unpub. ms, ch.1: copy in ADI Maribyrnong records.

11. James Smith (ed.), *The Cyclopedia of Victoria* (3 vols), vol.1, Melbourne, 1903, p.150.

12. *Australian Dictionary of Biography*, vol.6, p.87. Sargood was again Victoria's minister for defence in 1890–92 (by which time he had been knighted), and for three months in 1894.

13. D. Pike (ed.), *Australian Dictionary of Biography*, vol.4, Melbourne University Press, Carlton, Vic., 1972, p.100.

14. Berry to Sargood, 9 July 1886, cited in Jensen, ch.8.

15. *Morning Post* (London), 23 June 1886.

16. Meaney, pp.18–19.

17. A. Deakin, *The Federal Story: The Inner History of the Federal Cause*, Robertson & Mullens, Melbourne, 1944, p.9.

18. *Journals and printed papers of the Federal Council of Australasia*, vol.1, Hobart, 1886, p.38.

19. Pike, *Australian Dictionary of Biography*, vol.4, p.88.

20. C. Kinloch Cooke, *Australian Defences and New Guinea: Compiled from the Papers of the late Major-General Sir Peter Scratchley, RE, KCMG*, London, 1887, p.399.

21. ADI Footscray Facility: an appraisal of the heritage significance, vol.1, p.13: Allom Lovell & Associates report prepared for ADI, 1992.

22. Wettenhall, *Public Enterprise and National Development*, pp.55–6.

23. J.K. Lyons, *The Colonial Ammunition Company (Australia) Ltd. 1888–1926*, privately pub., 1966, p.1.

24. Linge, p.262.

25. *Dictionary of New Zealand Biography*, vol.2, Bridget Williams Books & Department of Internal Affairs, Wellington, 1993, pp.575–6.

26. *Dictionary of New Zealand Biography*, vol.2.

27. Lynn H. Harris, *A Little Further, A Little Faster: A Nostalgic Look at The Colonial Ammunition Company, its History and Cartridges*, New Zealand Cartridge Collectors' Club, Wellington, 1981, p.9.

28. ADI Footscray Facility (Allom Lovell report), p.13. The date of this letter is given in an article by Peter White, in *Australian Cartridge Collectors' Association Journal*, no.55, 1993, p.4.

29. Letter, Witney to Lorimer, 21 July 1887, photographic copy held by ADI Footscray. The certificate incorporating CAC Ltd. is also held in photographic form at Footscray.

30. Linge, p.263.

31. See Victorian *Parliamentary Debates*, 1889, vol.60. The Act, 'to ratify a Lease of certain land granted by the Government of Victoria to the Colonial Ammunition Company Limited for the purposes of an Ammunition Factory', was No.1022.

32. New South Wales Legislative Council *Journal*, vol.46 (1889), p.552.

33. Bob Nicholls, *The Colonial Volunteers: The Defence Forces of the Australian Colonies 1836–1901*, Allen & Unwin, Sydney, 1988, pp.164.

34. D.H. Johnson, *Volunteers at Heart: The Queensland Defence Forces 1860–1901*, University of Queensland Press, St. Lucia, 1975, p.188; Nicholls, pp.157–8.

35. Nicholls, p.164.

36. *Illustrated Australian News* (Melbourne), 8 November 1890, pp.14–15. Broadly, the same claim had also been made in the Legislative Assembly on 2 October 1889: see Victorian *Parliamentary Debates*, vol.61, p.1663.

37. G.C. Craig, *The Federal Defence of Australasia*, William Clowes & Sons, London, 1897, p.343.

38. Craig, pp.346–7.

39. ADI Footscray Facility (Allom Lovell report), p.21.

40. Harris, p.14.

41. Lawrence, p.3; see also *Munitions Diary 1985*, published by Melbourne's Living Museum of the West, Williamstown, Vic.

42. T.R. Frame, *The Garden Island*, Kangaroo Press, Kenthurst, NSW, 1990, p.149.

43. Nicholls, p.172.

44. *Commonwealth Parliamentary Papers*, 1901–02, vol.2, pp.58–9.

45. Letter, Lithgow Progress Association to Cook, 12 February 1903, photographic copy held by ADI Footscray.

46. John Mordike, *An Army for a Nation: A history of Australian Military Developments 1880–1914*, Allen & Unwin, Sydney, 1992, p.179.

47. Mordike, pp.179–80.

48. Mordike, p.184

49. *Commonwealth Parliamentary Debates*, vol.42, pp.7509–36 (see especially p.7530).

50. Department of Supply booklet, 'Small Arms Factory Lithgow 1912–1962': ODP records held by ADI.

51. Department of Supply booklet, 'Small Arms Factory Lithgow 1912–1962': ODP records held by ADI.

52. Olwen Ford & Pamela Lewis, *Maribyrnong: Action in Tranquillity*, Melbourne's Living Museum of the West & Sunshine City Council, 1989, p.31.

53. *Report upon the Department of Defence from the 1st of July, 1914, until the Thirtieth of June, 1917*, Part 1, Government Printer, Melbourne, 1917, pp.431–78.

54. Ernest Scott, *Australia during the War*, vol.11 of *The Official History of Australia in the War of 1914–1918*, Angus & Robertson, Sydney, 1936, p.237.

55. Scott, p.237.

56. *Commonwealth Parliamentary Debates*, vol.77, p.4100. Scott, p.238n, contrasts Cook's remarks with later statements in defence of the government factories – at a time when he held ministerial responsibility for the work of some of them.

57. Wettenhall, *Public Enterprise and National Development*, p.2.

58. John Mortimer, 'HMAS Huon – Australia's first locally constructed destroyer', *Journal of the Australian Naval Institute*, vol.5, no.4, November 1979, pp.10–21.

59. G.L. Macandie, *The Genesis of the Royal Australian Navy*, Government Printer, Sydney, 1949, pp.290–2.

60. Frame, p.168.

61. *Report upon the Department of Defence*, p.432.

62. Scott, p.239. The figure for the total number of enlistees is from L.L. Robson, *The First A.I.F.: A Study of its Recruitment 1914–1918*, Melbourne University Press, Carlton, Vic., 1970, p.202.

63. *Report upon the Department of Defence*, pp.460–74; Scott, p.260, gives revised figures for the number of employees at the factory.

64. *Report upon the Department of Defence*, pp.457–60.

65. *Report upon the Department of Defence*, pp.439–49.

66. *Report upon the Department of Defence*, pp.453–5; also Department of Productivity report, 'Munitions Policy Study', c.1979, p.6: ODP records held by ADI.

67. *Report upon the Department of Defence*, pp.476–7.

68. Lyons, pp.6–7.
69. *Report upon the Department of Defence*, pp.450–52.
70. 'Munitions Policy Study', pp.5–6.
71. *Report upon the Department of Defence*, p.440.
72. *Report upon the Department of Defence*, p.435.
73. *Report upon the Department of Defence*, pp.483–4.
74. *Report upon the Department of Defence*, p.484.
75. Scott, p.240.
76. 'Munitions Policy Study', p.6.
77. *Report upon the Department of Defence*, pp.487–9.
78. *Report upon the Department of Defence*, pp.491–3.
79. *Report upon the Department of Defence*, pp.497–9.
80. Scott, p.246.
81. *Report upon the Department of Defence*, pp.501–2.
82. Jensen, ch.8.
83. *Report upon the Department of Defence*, p.437.
84. *Report upon the Department of Defence*, p.439.
85. Scott, p.276; A.T. Ross, The Arming of Australia: The Politics and Administration of Australia's Self Containment Strategy for Munitions Supply 1901–1945, PhD thesis, University of New South Wales, 1986, pp.23–4, 37–9.
86. *Argus*, 12 April, 28 June 1919.
87. Scott, p.266.
88. Scott, pp.267–71.
89. Ross, The Arming of Australia, pp.49–50, 55.
90. 'Munitions Policy Study', p.10; Lawrence, p.5.

Chapter Two

1. C.E.W. Bean, *The A.I.F. in France: May 1918–The Armistice*, vol.6 of *The Official History of Australia in the War of 1914–1918*, Angus & Robertson, Sydney, 1942, p.485.
2. Scott, p.262.
3. Document titled 'Chronological development and administration: Commonwealth Government munitions factories and establishments', undated, pp.7–9: ODP records held by ADI.
4. 'History of Munitions: Small Arms Factory, Lithgow', departmental history, c.1945, pp.74–5: ODP records held by ADI; 'Chronological development and administration'.
5. Frame, pp.174, 177; R.G. Parker, *Cockatoo Island*, Nelson, Melbourne, 1977, pp.29, 39.
6. Ross, The Arming of Australia, pp.50–51.
7. Ross, The Arming of Australia, p.57; 'Munitions Policy Study', p.7.
8. Ross, The Arming of Australia, pp.55–6.
9. Ross, The Arming of Australia, p.61.
10. Lyons, pp.7–8.
11. (1935) 52 *Commonwealth Law Reports*, pp.533–69.
12. Ross, The Arming of Australia, p.60; ADI Footscray Facility (Allom Lovell report), p.32.
13. Ross, The Arming of Australia, pp.61–2.
14. Ross, The Arming of Australia, pp.63–4.
15. Ross, The Arming of Australia, p.83.
16. Ross, The Arming of Australia, pp.83–4; see also Ross, *Armed and Ready*, pp.50–1.
17. Ross, The Arming of Australia, pp.70, 131–54; see also the article by Ross, 'The economics of rearmament 1933–39', in Australian War Memorial *Journal*, no.7, October 1985, pp.35–43.
18. Ross, The Arming of Australia, pp.84–6.
19. Ross, The Arming of Australia, pp.86–7.
20. *Commonwealth Parliamentary Debates*, vol.99, pp.359–67; 'Chronological development and administration', p.8.

21. Scott, p.205, *Commonwealth Parliamentary Papers*, 1923–24, vol.1, p.295.
22. *Commonwealth Parliamentary Papers*, 1923–24, vol.4, p.293.
23. 'Chronological development and administration', pp.12, 18, 20–21.
24. 'History of Munitions' (SAF Lithgow), p.75; 'Munitions Policy Study', p.10.
25. Ross, *Armed and Ready*, p.59.
26. 'The Origins and History of the Small Arms Factory Lithgow', based on a talk to the Lithgow Historical Society by Mr S.E. Silk, General Manager, p.7: copy in ODP records held by ADI.
27. Lawrence, p.5; 'Chronological development and administration', p.9.
28. See Les McLean, 'The History of Ordnance Factory Maribyrnong 1923–1993', unpub. ms, copy in author's possession; Jensen, ch.8.
29. ADI Footscray Facility (Allom Lovell report), p.33; Lyons, p.10. CAC remained in existence in New Zealand, finally becoming a subsidiary of Imperial Chemical Industries in 1965.
30. D.P. Mellor, *The Role of Science and Industry*, series 4, vol.5, *Australia in the War of 1939–1945*, Australian War Memorial, Canberra, 1958, p.13.
31. 'Munitions Policy Study', p.11; ADI Maribyrnong Facility: an appraisal of the heritage significance, vol.1, p.18, Allom Lovell & Associates report prepared for ADI, 1992.
32. Ross, The Arming of Australia, pp.93–6.
33. Ross, The Arming of Australia, pp.97–8; 'History of Munitions' (SAF Lithgow), p.76.
34. 'Munitions Policy Study', p.10.
35. Mellor, p.25.
36. 'The Origins and History of the Small Arms Factory Lithgow' (Silk talk), pp.7–8; Department of Supply booklet, *Small Arms Factory Lithgow 1912–1962*.
37. Ross, *Armed and Ready*, pp.67–8.
38. Ross, The Arming of Australia, table 2–7, p.99A.
39. Jensen, ch.8.
40. The full text of this letter dated 16 September 1930 is quoted in Jensen, ch.8.
41. Again, full texts are given in Jensen, ch.8.
42. Ross, The Arming of Australia, pp.104–5n.
43. *Commonwealth Parliamentary Papers*, 1920–21, vol.4, p.4.
44. Parker, p.33; Frame, p.179; Wettenhall, *Public Enterprise and National Development*, pp.3, 61.
45. Parker, p.39.
46. Parker, p.39.
47. Senate Select Committee on the Government Clothing and Ordnance Factories, report titled *The Future of the Government Clothing Factory at Coburg*, Australian Government Publishing Service, Canberra, 1982, p.5; (1935) 52 CLR, pp.533–69.
48. Ross, The Arming of Australia, table 2–7, p.99A.
49. Ross, The Arming of Australia, pp.112–22.
50. Ross, The Arming of Australia, p.106.
51. This and subsequent paragraphs draw heavily on Ross, The Arming of Australia, pp.122–8.
52. Ross, The Arming of Australia, pp.99A, 128.
53. Silk talk, p.9.
54. 'Munitions Policy Study', p.13; Jensen, ch.8.
55. Mellor, pp.27–8; Lawrence, p.6.
56. Ross, The Arming of Australia, pp.225–6.
57. Ross, The Arming of Australia, p.227; Mellor, p.28.
58. Ross, The Arming of Australia, pp.232–43; Mellor, pp.28–9.
59. Ross, The Arming of Australia, pp.236–7, 245–7; Mellor, 30–1.
60. Mellor, p.381; N. Parnell & T. Boughton, *Flypast: A Record of Aviation in Australia*, Australian Government Publishing Service, Canberra, 1988, p.143; C.D. Coulthard-Clark, *The Third Brother: The Royal Australian Air Force 1921–39*, Allen & Unwin, Sydney, 1991, pp.273–5; B.L. Hill, *Wirraway to Hornet: A History of the Commonwealth Aircraft Corporation Pty Ltd, 1936 to 1985*, Southern Cross Publications, Bulleen, Vic., 1998, pp.4–8.
61. Parnell & Boughton, pp.118–19; Coulthard-Clark, p.274.

62. Coulthard-Clark, pp.275–9; George Odgers, *The RAAF: An Illustrated History*, 2nd edn, Child & Associates, Frenchs Forest, NSW, 1989, p.52; Hill, pp.9–22.
63. Coulthard-Clark, pp.275–6, 280, 454.
64. Coulthard-Clark, pp.453–4.
65. Odgers, p.52.
66. Parnell & Boughton, p.173; Coulthard-Clark, p.453.
67. Mellor, p.32; Lawrence, p.7; Ross, pp.253, 262, 264.
68. Mellor, pp.35–6; Department of Supply handbook, *An Account of the Purposes, Structure and Functions of the Department* (1955), pp.6–7: ODP records held by ADI.
69. Mellor, p.36.
70. Department of Munitions, 'A Summary of the Development of Munitions Production in Australia, 1940–1945', *Official Year Book of the Commonwealth of Australia*, no.36: 1944–45, p.1037.
71. Mellor, p.45; 'A Summary of … Munitions Production', pp.1039, 1043.
72. Mellor, p.35; Silk talk, p.9.
73. Silk talk, p.9.
74. Silk talk, p.10.
75. 'History of Munitions' (SAF), pp.90–109.
76. 'History of Munitions' (SAF), pp.36–7, 84; see also Silk talk, p.10.
77. ADI Footscray Facility (Allom Lovell report), p.42; Mellor, p.32; 'A Summary of … Munitions Production', pp.1041, 1043, 1053.
78. 'Munitions Policy Study', p.15; 'A Summary of … Munitions Production', p.1053.
79. 'A Summary of … Munitions Production', pp.1043, 1052; 'Munitions Policy Study', p.15; Lawrence, p.10.
80. ADI Maribyrnong Facility (Allom Lovell report), pp.26–7; Senate report on *The Future of Ordnance Factory Bendigo*, Australian Government Publishing Service, Canberra, 1982, p.3.
81. Lawrence, p.10.
82. Senate report on *The Future of the Government Clothing Factory at Coburg*, p.6.
83. Odgers, p.104–5.
84. Lawrence, p.10; Odgers, pp.104–5.
85. Cockatoo Docks & Engineering Co. Pty. Ltd., *Cockatoo Docks, Sydney: War Record 1939–1945* (brochure), undated, p.8: copy held by Australian Defence Force Academy Library, Canberra.
86. Mellor, pp.453–9.
87. Mellor, pp.467–72; Frame, pp.188–91, 193, 199–200.
88. Booklet, *Establishments of the Department of Defence Production* (1956), section on the CGEW, pp.3–4: ODP records held by ADI; Mellor, p.461.
89. Mellor, p.705.

Chapter Three

1. Mellor, pp.673, 692.
2. 'History of Munitions' (SAF), p.109; 'Chronological development and administration', pp.50–4.
3. Department of Productivity booklet, *Australian Government Small Arms Factory, Lithgow* (1979).
4. Senate report on *The Future of Ordnance Factory Bendigo*, p.3.
5. ADI Footscray Facility (Allom Lovell report), pp.53–4, 84; Lyons, pp.10–11.
6. Australian Government Clothing Factory pamphlet (circa 1981); ODP records held by ADI.
7. A.D. Garrisson, 'Australian Aircraft Industry', paper for the Legislative Research Service of the Parliamentary Library, Parliament of Australia, 28 June 1982, p.5: copy in author's possession; Hill, pp.97, 105–7, 109.
8. Mellor, p.692.
9. Ross, The Arming of Australia, pp.404–06.
10. Ross, The Arming of Australia, pp.403–04, 408–09.
11. Mellor, p.693.

12. Department of Post-War Reconstruction booklet, *Wartime Factories with a Peacetime Future: The Story of Industrial Decentralisation* (1949): copy in ODP records held by ADI.
13. Department of Supply handbook (30 September 1955), p.8; Lawrence, p.10.
14. Department of Supply handbook, p.8; Lawrence, p.10.
15. Department of Defence Production booklet, *The Government Munitions and Aircraft Factories* (September 1957), pp.3, 5: ODP records held by ADI.
16. Robert O'Neill, *Australia in the Korean War 1950–53*, vol.1: *Strategy and Diplomacy*, Australian War Memorial and Australian Government Publishing Service, Canberra, 1981, pp.101–104, 196.
17. David Lee, 'The National Security Planning and Defence Preparations of the Menzies Government, 1950–53', *War & Society*, vol.10, no.2, October 1992, pp.119–21.
18. Lee, p.123.
19. Lee, pp.124–8.
20. Australian Archives, MP 1217, Box 1501.
21. Lawrence, p.11.
22. Lee, pp.129–30.
23. Lee, p.133; ADI Maribyrnong Facility (Allom Lovell report), p.28; Senate report on *The Future of Ordnance Factory Bendigo*, p.3.
24. Lee, p.133; Garrisson, p.5; Hill, pp.134–5, 138.
25. 'Establishments of the Department of Defence Production 1956: Outline of History of Establishments', section dealing with Commonwealth Government Aircraft Factories, p.6: ODP records held by ADI; Department of Defence Production booklet, 'The Government Munitions and Aircraft Factories', September 1957, p.4; ODP records held by ADI; Hill, pp.142–3.
26. Garrisson, pp.6–7.
27. Senate report on *The Future of the Government Clothing Factory at Coburg*, p.6; Department of Supply handbook, pp.32–34; Australian Government Clothing Factory pamphlet (c.1981); ODP records held by ADI.
28. Department of Supply booklet, *Small Arms Factory Lithgow 1912–1962*.
29. Department of Supply booklet, *Small Arms Factory Lithgow 1912–1962*.
30. Department of Supply program for official handover of first 7.62 mm rifles manufactured by SAF, 5 March 1959: copy in ODP records held by ADI; ADI Footscray Facility (Allom Lovell report), pp.53–4.
31. Department of Supply booklet, 'Activities and Developments', September 1959, p.12: ODP records held by ADI.
32. Lawrence, p.10.
33. A.E. Fisher, Ammunition Filling – The St. Marys Story over the past forty-five years, paper presented to RAAF Explosives Engineering Seminar, 22 August 1985, pp.9–10; booklet titled 'Munitions Filling Factory St. Marys, N.S.W.: A Brief Description', undated, p.3: copies of both in ODP records held by ADI.
34. ADI Maribyrnong Facility (Allom Lovell report), p.27; Department of Supply booklet, 'Activities and Developments', September 1959, p.14: ODP records held by ADI.
35. ADI Maribyrnong Facility (Allom Lovell report), p.28.
36. Ordnance Factory Bendigo album, 'Photographs of some major projects produced for the B.H.P. Organisation, 1962': ODP records held by ADI.
37. ADI Maribyrnong Facility (Allom Lovell report), p.28.
38. ADI Maribyrnong Facility (Allom Lovell report), p.28.
39. ADI Maribyrnong Facility (Allom Lovell report), p.29.
40. ADI Maribyrnong Facility (Allom Lovell report), pp.29–30.
41. R.H. Bullows, Ordnance Manufacturing Study 1985, unpub. report written for ODP, vol.1, p.7; copy held by ADI.
42. 'The Origins and History of the Small Arms Factory Lithgow' (Silk talk), p.13.
43. 'The Origins and History of the Small Arms Factory Lithgow' (Silk talk), p.13.
44. Department of Productivity booklet, *Australian Government Small Arms Factory, Lithgow* (1979); 'The Origins and History of the Small Arms Factory Lithgow' (Silk talk), p.14.

45. Department of Supply booklet, *Small Arms Factory Lithgow 1912–1962*; Department of Productivity, unpub. ms on SAF Lithgow 'A Brief History of the Factory and a Survey of Production Facilities from 1912' (undated), p.3: ODP records held by ADI.
46. Garrisson, pp.6–7; Hill, pp.153–5, 158–9.
47. Garrisson, pp.6–7; Hill, p.170.
48. Department of Defence Support (DDS) pamphlet on Aircraft Engineering Workshop, c.1983: copy in ODP records held by ADI.
49. Garrisson, pp.9–10; Hill, pp.186–8.
50. Garrisson, p.8.
51. Report dated June 1977, cited in D.H. Eltringham, *Restructuring and Sale of the Defence Production Factories*, 4 February 1981, p.17: copy in ODP records held by ADI.
52. Department of Supply submission to Defence (Industrial) Committee, 'Munitions Manufacturing Policy Review', December 1973, p.2: copy in ODP records held by ADI; 'Munitions Policy Study', p.17.
53. Department of Supply booklet, 'Activities and Developments', September 1959, pp.10–11, 21: ODP records held by ADI.
54. Department of Supply booklet, 'Notes on General Pattern of Organisation', effective July 1967, see introduction: ODP records held by ADI.
55. Department of Supply booklet, 'Notes on General Pattern of Organisation', effective July 1967, see introduction and pp.1, 6.
56. Department of Supply booklet, 'Outline of Organisation and Responsibilities', July 1967, p.3: ODP records held by ADI.
57. Lawrence, p.13.
58. 'Munitions Policy Study', p.17.
59. Janka interview.
60. *Productivity 1977*, pp.33–4.
61. Department of Productivity, *Annual Report, 1981–82*, p.32.
62. *Policies for Development of Manufacturing Industry*, vol.1, October 1975, Canberra, 1975, p.1.
63. Frame, pp.204–5.
64. Frame, pp.205–7.
65. Joint Review of Williamstown Naval Dockyard, final report January 1981; copy in ODP records held by ADI.
66. Report of *Advisory Committee on Management and Operation of Williamstown Naval Dockyard*, June 1981, pp.1–3: copy in ODP records held by ADI.
67. Report of *Advisory Committee on Management and Operation of Williamstown Naval Dockyard*, June 1981, vol.1, pp.102–4: copy in ODP records held by ADI; DDS *Annual Report 1981–1982*, p.5.
68. Munitions Supply Study, p.17.
69. *Australian Defence*, White Paper presented to parliament by D.J. Killen, Minister for Defence, November 1976, p.58.
70. Department of Supply booklet, 'Activities and Developments', September 1959, p.15.
71. Department of Supply booklet, 'Activities and Developments', September 1959, p.15.
72. Department of Supply booklet, 'Small Arms Factory Lithgow 1912–1962'.
73. Targ interview, 28 April 1994.
74. 'The Government Munitions Factories', lecture by R.S. Thompson, Controller of Munitions Supply, Department of Industry & Commerce, 1981, pp.33–4: copy in ODP records held by ADI.
75. Department of Productivity pamphlet, undated but c.1979: copy in ODP records held by ADI.
76. Thompson lecture, p.43.
77. Minute by P.G. Terrill (Controller Munitions Division) on SAF Lithgow, November 1983: ODP records held by ADI.
78. Department of Industry & Commerce, interim report by Internal Audit Section, 'The Role of Standards in Budgeting', April 1982: ODP records held by ADI.
79. Targ interview, 28 April 1994.
80. Targ interview, 28 April 1994.

81. Department of Supply booklet, 'Small Arms Factory Lithgow 1912–1962'.
82. Don Fraser (ed.), *Sydney from Settlement to City. An Engineering History of Sydney*, Engineers Australia, Crows Nest, NSW, 1989, p.148; the section of the book dealing with shipbuilding and repair is acknowledged as drawing on notes provided by Rear-Admiral N.R.B. Berlyn.
83. See, for example, the brochure *GID: Garden Island Dockyard*, produced in 1987–88: copy in ADI records.
84. Department of Supply submission to the Defence (Industrial) Committee, Munitions Manufacturing Policy Review (including rationalisation of the Australian Government Munitions Factories), December 1973, p.1: copy in ODP records held by ADI.
85. Munitions Manufacturing Policy Review, p.16.
86. Report of Committee of Inquiry into Workloads in Government Factories, October 1974, pp.2–4: copy in ODP records held by ADI.
87. Draft report by EFM, Rationalisation of Explosives Factories, 29 April 1976: ODP records held by ADI.
88. Report of interdepartmental committee, Munitions Factories Workload and Employment problems, January 1976: ODP records held by ADI.
89. Department of Manufacturing Industry booklet, *Australian Government Engine Works*, c.1974.
90. Department of Supply booklet, *Commonwealth Government Engine Works*, 1973, and Department of Manufacturing Industry booklet, *Australian Government Engine Works*, c.1974. In July 1974, a seven-cylinder RND90 Sulzer engine weighing 688 tonnes became the biggest diesel marine engine made in Australia. This was handed over to the Botany Bay Tanker Company for installation in a 66,000-ton oil tanker being constructed in Whyalla, South Australia; see *Herald-Sun*, 24 July 1973.
91. Department of Manufacturing Industry booklet, *Australian Government Engine Works*, circa 1974.
92. *Study Report of the Future of the Australian Government Engine Works*, IHI report dated August 1975: ODP records held by ADI.
93. AGEW's financial statements 1978–79: ODP records held by ADI.
94. Department of Supply handbook, 30 September 1955, p.34.
95. Senate report on *The Future of the Government Clothing Factory at Coburg*, pp.6–9.
96. Australian Government Clothing Factory pamphlet (c.1981).
97. Senate report on *The Future of the Government Clothing Factory at Coburg*.
98. Senate report on *The Future of the Ordnance Factory Bendigo*.
99. Parliamentary paper no.225/1977.
100. Parliamentary paper no.260/1979.
101. Janka interview, 30 September 1993.

Chapter Four

1. Eltringham report, *Future Development of the Australian Defence Production Factories*, April 1981, part 1, p.xii.
2. Eltringham report, *Restructuring and Sale of the Defence Production Factories*, pp.41–2.
3. Letter, Blood to Lynch, 19 February 1981, with Cabinet memorandum no.1210 'Review of Commonwealth Functions: Australian Government Clothing Factory' dated 24 February 1981: copy in ODP records held by ADI.
4. *Commonwealth Parliamentary Debates*, vol.HofR 122, p.1831.
5. Senate report on *The Future of the Government Clothing Factory at Coburg*.
6. Factory profile for AGCF, March 1984: copy in ODP records held by ADI.
7. Senate report on *The Future of the Ordnance Factory Bendigo*.
8. DDS press release no.10/82 dated 7 July 1982.
9. *Australian* newspaper, 8–9 May 1982.
10. Interview with Sir William Cole, former Chairman of the Public Service Board 1978–83 and Secretary of the Department of Defence 1983–86, 9 January 1995.
11. DDS *Annual Report 1981–1982*, pp.iii, 4.

12. Ministerial statement on defence industry by K.C. Beazley, Minister for Defence, 10 May 1989.

13. Address by Mr F.N. Bennett on 'Defence Production Policy' to the Joint Services Staff College, 16 September 1985, p.11; copy in ODP records held by ADI.

14. *Defence Report*, 1984–85, pp.60–1.

15. Peter Walsh, *Confessions of a Failed Finance Minister*, Random House, Sydney, 1995, p.79.

16. Draft of Howe's speech to union representatives, 25 March 1983: untitled folder of papers in ODP records held by ADI.

17. Walsh, *Confessions*, p.80.

18. Interview with Rear-Admiral N.R.B. Berlyn, Group General Manager, Development, ADI Corporate Headquarters, 27 April 1994, and letter, Hon. P.A. Walsh (Minister for Finance 1984–90) to author, 10 February 1995.

19. DDS *Annual Report 1981–1982*, Appendix A, pp.58–9.

20. Interview with Hon. P.A. Walsh, 1 April 1995.

21. DDS *Annual Report 1981–1982*, p.2.

22. Interview with Mr A.K. Wrigley, former Deputy Secretary Defence Department 1983–85, 13 December 1994.

23. *Year Book Australia*, no.69, 1985, Australian Bureau of Statistics, Canberra, p.41.

24. Papers relating to DFDC consideration of DDS draft estimates 1984/85, June 1984: folder in ODP records held by ADI.

25. *Sydney Morning Herald*, 15 May 1984.

26. Wrigley interview.

27. Cole interview.

28. Cole interview.

29. Interview with Mr J.E. McMahon, Group General Manager, Defence Liaison & Operations, ADI Corporate Headquarters, 27 April 1994.

30. *Australian*, 12 December 1984.

31. Letter to author from Dr M.K. McIntosh, Chief of Defence Procurement (UK), 10 April 1995.

32. Cole interview.

33. Interview with Mr L.B. Woodward, 5 December 1994.

34. Interview with Mr S. Hickman, Senior Advisor to Minister for Finance, 23 March 1995.

35. Interview with Hon. K.C. Beazley, Minister for Finance, 22 March 1995.

36. Bennett's address on 'Defence Production Policy' to the Joint Services Staff College, 16 September 1985, p.14.

37. Bennett's address on 'Defence Production' to the RAN Staff College, 3 June 1985, p.8: copy in ODP records held by ADI.

38. *Defence Report*, 1984–85, p.59.

39. Woodward interview.

40. Woodward interview.

41. Woodward interview.

42. Ministerial background paper on AEW, prepared by Defence Aerospace Division, 6 March 1985: ODP records held by ADI.

43. Information booklet on ODP/ADI, 1988; see also *Defence Report*, 1984–85, p.62, 1986–87, p.68.

44. Pheasant report, *Review of Explosive Factories*, 2 vols., July 1985: copy in ODP reports held by ADI.

45. *Defence Report*, 1985–86, p.80. Originally the acronym REFA stood for 'Review of Explosive Factories of Australia', but later was often rendered as 'Rationalisation [or Relocation] of Explosive Factories [or Facilities] of Australia', or even 'Relocation of Explosives Factory Albion'.

46. Briefing paper on ODP dated February 1987, p.7.

47. *Defence Report*, 1985–86, pp.79–80; also briefing paper on ODP dated February 1987, pp.6–7: copy in ODP records held by ADI.

48. Press release by Minister for Defence, K.C. Beazley, no.32/86 dated 21 March 1986.

49. Woodward interview; Berlyn interview, 27 April 1994.

50. Woodward interview.

51. Interview with Mr K.A. Harris, Managing Director ADI, 5 August 1993.

52. Briefing paper on ODP dated February 1987, pp.7–8.

53. Harris interview, 5 August 1993.

54. Harris interview, 5 August 1993.

55. Harris interview, 5 August 1993.

56. Minute by Woodward to Beazley dated 24 June 1986: ODP records held by ADI.

57. Hickman interview.

58. Harris interview, 5 August 1993; Briefing paper on ODP dated February 1987, p.8.

59. Briefing paper on ODP dated February 1987, pp.8–9.

60. Briefing paper on ODP dated February 1987, p.9.

61. Woodward interview.

62. Copy of ASTA memorandum and Articles of Association dated 28 November 1986, attached to minute by Harris of 5 December 1986; held by Mr B.F. Conway, General Manager, Planning, Ammunition Division ADI, 1993.

63. Targ interview, 28 April 1994.

64. *Australian*, 15–16, 18 August 1987; *Age*, 19, 20 August 1987.

65. *Defence Report*, 1987–88, p.50; interview with Mr B.F. Conway, 24 August 1993; minute by Harris to Mr P. Walters (senior private secretary to Defence Minister) dated 12 May 1989: copy among papers held by Dr J.R. Barclay, Group General Manager of ADI Ordnance Division.

66. DDS brochure *Williamstown Naval Dockyard* (c.1984): ODP records held by ADI.

67. Frame, pp.209–10.

68. Telephone interview with Dr J.D. White, Transfield Defence Systems, 28 April 1995.

69. Information supplied to author by Transfield Shipbuilding (Vic. Division), February 1995.

70. Text of Berlyn's address on 'Garden Island Dockyard in the 1990s' to Naval Engineering Symposium, 29 November 1988: copy made available by Berlyn.

71. Frame, p.209.

72. Beazley interview.

73. Berlyn interview, 27 April 1994.

74. Information booklet on ODP/ADI, 1988.

75. *The Defence of Australia, 1987* (White Paper), pp.82–3.

76. *The Defence of Australia, 1987*, p.83.

77. *Defence Report*, 1987–88, p.48.

78. Information booklet on ODP/ADI, 1988: copy in ODP records held by ADI.

79. Information booklet on ODP/ADI, 1988.

80. Briefing paper on ODP dated February 1987, p.13.

81. Harris interview, 5 August 1993.

82. On 16 February 1988 Harris wrote to Woods canvassing the options regarding ODP and stating that 'I am at the moment somewhat inclined towards the government Company idea': a copy of this letter is among papers held by Barclay.

83. Harris interview, 5 August 1993.

84. Conway interview, 24 August 1993.

85. Background to the Formation of ADI as a Company, typescript supplied by ADI to Allom Lovell and cited in ADI Footscray Facility (Allom Lovell report), p.57.

86. Harris interview, 5 August 1993.

87. Minute, CDP to Beazley, 7 June 1988: copy in ODP papers held by Mr J.E. McMahon. Not everyone agreed with this analysis. Harris' former boss Woodward, in his role as Head of Defence Logistics, commented that the three options put were those 'most often canvassed' but there was a fourth: amend the Defence Act to provide more commercial freedom, but not such as to turn ODP into a statutory corporation. This course would, Woodward observed, 'leave ODP very much within the Defence family and for that reason it has something going for it'. He also noted that many of the activities it was proposed grouping did not 'sit well' together – ship repair with ammunition production or clothing manufacture – and argued that their disparate nature at least raised the question of whether they should be so linked when setting up such a radically different form of organisation. There had also been no discussion of whether any of the factories should be sold. An incomplete copy of Woodward's response is among the papers held by Barclay.

88. Minute, Secretary of Defence to Beazley, 8 June 1988: copy in papers held by McMahon.
89. Harris interview, 5 August 1993.
90. Beazley interview.

Chapter Five

1. Harris interview, 5 August 1993.
2. *Policy Guidelines for Commonwealth Statutory Authorities and Government Business Enterprises* (issued by the Minister for Finance, Senator P.A. Walsh, October 1987), Australian Government Publishing Service, Canberra, 1987; *Reshaping the Transport and Communications Government Business Enterprises* (issued by the Minister for Transport and Communications, Senator G. Evans, 25 May 1988), Australian Government Publishing Service, Canberra, 1988.
3. Harris interview, 5 August 1993.
4. Notes of 3 July meeting kept by Mr J.E. McMahon.
5. Copy of certificate of incorporation held by Conway; interview with Harris, 5 August 1993, and with Conway, 24 August 1993.
6. *Australian Financial Review*, 31 May 1988; *Canberra Times, Age*, 3 June 1988.
7. Harris interview, 5 August 1993.
8. Harris interview, 5 August 1993.
9. Interview with Dr J.R. Barclay, Group General Manager of ADI Ordnance Division, 18 January 1994.
10. ADI *Newsletter*, October 1988, p.3.
11. Harris interview, 5 August 1993.
12. Harris interview, 5 August 1993, and letter to author from McMahon, 15 June 1993.
13. Interview with Mr W.T. Mitchell, Chief General Manager of ADI Property Division, 26 August 1983.
14. Barclay interview.
15. Letters, Beazley to Hawke, 16 June 1988, and Hawke to Beazley, 29 June 1988: papers held by McMahon.
16. Barclay interview.
17. Conway interview, 24 August 1993.
18. Press release by Minister for Defence, K.C. Beazley, no.146/88 dated 12 August 1988.
19. Harris interview, 5 August 1993.
20. Mitchell interview, 26 August 1993.
21. Interview with Mr K.J. Callinan, General Manager, ADI Employee Development, 30 June 1994.
22. McMahon interview, 27 April 1994.
23. Barclay interview.
24. Minute from Harris to senior ODP officials, 6 January 1988 (in error for 1989): ADI Maribyrnong file 88/226 (3), now held by Australian Archives.
25. Barclay interview.
26. Harris interview, 5 August 1993.
27. Callinan interview.
28. Letters, West to Beazley, 15 November 1988; Walsh to Beazley, 24 November 1988; Beazley to West, 1 December 1988, and Walsh, 13 December 1988: copies in ADI papers held by Barclay.
29. Facsimile letter, Mr P. Walters to author, 8 May 1995; telephone interview with Walters 9 May 1995.
30. Harris interview, 5 August 1993.
31. Beazley interview.
32. McMahon interview, 27 April 1994.
33. Barclay interview.
34. Barclay interview.
35. Letter, Harris to author, 30 November 1998.
36. Summary of correspondence among ADI papers held by Barclay.

37. Telephone interview with Dr J.C. McCorquodale, 11 May 1995.
38. R.W. Taylor, *A Review of the Commercial Viability of Explosives Factory Maribyrnong – With an Emphasis on Corporate Issues of the Office of Defence Production*, September 1988, p.29: copy in ODP records held by ADI.
39. Press release by Minister for Defence, K.C. Beazley, no.34/89 dated 27 February 1989.
40. Minutes of ADI board meeting, 31 October 1988, held by ADI company secretary.
41. Minute by R.W. Taylor, Special Adviser Production ODP, 22 February 1989: ADI Maribyrnong file 88/226 (2).
42. Barclay interview.
43. ADI *Newsletter*, May 1989, p.4.
44. Minute to general managers of ODP factories by Callinan, 10 November 1988: ADI Maribyrnong file 88/226 (2).
45. Callinan interview.
46. ADI *Newsletter*, February 1989, p.2.
47. *Bendigo Advertiser*, 23 February 1989.
48. *Bendigo Advertiser*, 23 February 1989.
49. ADI *Newsletter*, February 1989, pp.1, 2. See also press kit issued to general managers of ODP establishments, 20 January 1989: papers held by Conway. Attachment B to the latter document suggests, however, that ODP head office had already reduced to 197 people.
50. Harris interview, 5 August 1993.
51. Conway interview, 24 August 1993.
52. Minutes of ADI board meetings, held by ADI company secretary.
53. Interview with Mr R.J. Fynmore, Chairman ADI, 28 February 1995.
54. Remuneration Tribunal: *1989 Review*, p.86.
55. Conway interview, 24 August 1993.
56. *Commonwealth Parliamentary Debates*, vol.HofR 163, pp.2408–9, HofR vol.164, p.3758.
57. ADI *Newsletter*, December 1988, p.1, May 1989, p.2.
58. Callinan interview.
59. Harris interview, 5 August 1993.
60. Callinan interview.
61. ADI *Newsletter*, February 1989, p.1.
62. Letter, Beazley to Woods, 3 May 1989: copy with deed of transfer documents held by ADI.
63. Barclay interview.
64. Fynmore interview.
65. Barclay interview.
66. Barclay interview.
67. Barclay interview.
68. Barclay interview.
69. Barclay interview.
70. *Commonwealth Parliamentary Debates*, vol.HofR 166, pp.1820–2, 167, p.3553, vol.S 133, pp.2463–4, 2685–7.
71. Callinan interview.
72. ADI *Newsletter Stop Press*, 11 May 1989, and ADI *Newsletter*, May 1989, p.2.

Chapter Six

1. *Commonwealth Parliamentary Debates*, vol.HofR 166, pp.2343–48; press release by Beazley, no.95/89 dated 10 May 1989.
2. Internal Memorandum from Harris to ADI managers dated 14 June 1989, and Board paper 'Forecast of ADI Financial Position for 1989/90' dated 14 March 1989, p.1: copy in papers held by McMahon.
3. *Commonwealth Parliamentary Debates*, vol.HofR 166, p.2344.
4. Letter, Harris to Beazley, 5 April 1989: copy in papers held by Barclay.

5. Board paper 'Forecast of ADI Financial Position for 1989/90' dated 14 March 1989, p.8.
6. Interview with Mr R.W. Tannahill, 17 April 1998.
7. Letter, Harris to Inglis, 14 March 1989: papers in Barclay's possession.
8. Harris minute MD174/89 dated 3 May 1989: copy in McMahon papers.
9. Harris minute MD173/89 dated 3 May 1989: copy in McMahon papers.
10. *Australian Business*, 29 March 1989, p.64.
11. File note by Barclay dated 27 January 1989: copy in papers held by Barclay.
12. *Defence Report*, 1987–88, pp.49, 51; ADI *Newsletter*, February 1989, p.4.
13. Harris interview, 5 August 1993.
14. ADI *Newsletter*, December 1988, February 1989.
15. ADI *Newsletter*, October 1988, p.4.
16. Harris minute MD213/89 dated 24 May 1989: copy on ADI Maribyrnong file 88/226(10), now held by Australian Archives.
17. Internal memo MD646/89 dated 8 December 1989: copy in McMahon papers.
18. ADI *Newsletter*, February 1989, p.2.
19. Harris minute MD376/89 dated 10 August 1989: on ADI Maribyrnong file 89/0129, now held by Australian Archives; *Australian Defence Report*, 8 February 1990, p.9.
20. Harris minute MD173/89 dated 3 May 1989.
21. *Australian Defence Report*, 8 February 1990, p.9.
22. McMahon interview, 27 April 1994.
23. Telephone interview with McCorquodale; minutes of ADI board meeting, 27 July 1989: held by the company secretary.
24. Minutes of board meeting, 15 October 1990; interview with Mrs P.A. Russell, 26 November 1993.
25. *Australian Defence Report*, 3 May 1990, p.8.
26. Harris interview, 5 August 1993.
27. Minutes of board meeting, 14 February 1989.
28. Letters, Beazley to Woods and Fynmore, both dated 11 April 1989: copies in papers held by Barclay.
29. Fynmore interview.
30. Letters, Beazley to Deighton, 5 May 1989, and Deighton to Beazley, 12 May 1989: copies held by Mrs E. Deighton, Hawthorn Vic.; telephone interview with General P.C. Gration, Queanbeyan NSW, 22 May 1995.
31. Interview with Ms E.B. Bryan, General Manager of Investments, NSW State Superannuation and Investment Management Corporation, 2 March 1995.
32. Minutes of ADI board meeting, 1 September 1989.
33. Minutes of board meetings, 6 November, 7 December 1989, 26 February 1990.
34. *Canberra Times*, 15 January 1990.
35. Interview with Mrs A. Woods, Hawker ACT, 9 May 1995.
36. Harris interview, 5 August 1993.
37. Minutes of board meeting, 26 February 1990.
38. Fynmore interview.
39. Minutes of board meeting, 26 March 1990.
40. *Australian Defence Report*, 3 May 1990, p.8.
41. Minutes of board meetings, 24 April, 31 May 1990.
42. *Age*, 17 April 1991.
43. Telephone interview with Mrs E. Deighton, 15 May 1995.
44. Minutes of board meeting, 18 April 1991.
45. Minutes of board meetings, 21 May, 16 July, 27 August 1991.
46. ADI *Annual Report*, 1992, pp.3, 33.
47. Interview with Mr A. Apted, 7 April 1999.
48. ADI *Annual Report*, 1993, pp.4–5, 41.
49. *Commonwealth Parliamentary Debates*, vol.HofR 166, p.2344.
50. Letter, Woods to Beazley, 8 March 1989: copy in Barclay papers; *Age*, 17 March 1989.
51. Letter, Harris to author, 30 November 1998.

52. Letter, Woods to Walsh, 14 February 1989: copy in McMahon papers.
53. Letter, Walsh to Woods, 28 February 1989. copy in Barclay papers.
54. Letter, Woods to Beazley, 8 March 1989: copy in Barclay papers.
55. Letter, Walsh to Beazley, 11 April 1989: copy in Barclay papers.
56. Letter, Walsh to Woods, 31 July 1989; copy in Barclay papers.
57. Insert to *Pursuit* (ADI newsletter), no.5; ADI *Annual Report*, 1990, p.29.
58. Letters, Woods to Beazley, 20 December 1988 (see Attachment A, p.6), and Harris to Morris, 1 May 1989: copies in Barclay papers.
59. Letter, Harris to Morris, 1 May 1989.
60. Letter, Halley to Harris, 13 April 1989: copy in Barclay papers.
61. Letter, Harris to Halley, 1 May 1989: copy in Barclay papers.
62. Letter, Harris to Morris, 1 May 1989.
63. Letter, Morris to Harris, 23 August 1989: copy in Barclay papers.
64. Harris minute CDP 638/88 dated 2 November 1988: copy in Barclay papers.
65. Minutes of board meeting, 14 February 1989.
66. Woods to Beazley, 14 February 1989: copy in Barclay papers.
67. Letters, Harris to author, 30 November 1998 and 15 July 1999.
68. Letter, Beazley to Woods, 9 March 1989: copy in Barclay papers; Beazley to Walsh, undated: copy in McMahon papers.
69. Letter, Walsh to Beazley, 14 March 1989: copy in Barclay papers.
70. Minute (HDL 53/89), Woodward to Ayers, 3 February 1989; copy in McMahon papers.
71. Letter, Taylor to Hawke, 16 January 1989; copy in Barclay papers.
72. Letter, Hawke to Beazley, 27 February 1989; copy in Barclay papers.
73. Letter, Beazley to Hawke, 11 April 1989: copy in Barclay papers.
74. Minutes of board meeting, 6 April 1989; also letter, Harris to Walsh, 12 September 1989: copy in Barclay papers.
75. Letter (MD372/89), Harris to Mr P. Hamburger (Secretary of Senate Standing Committee), 10 August 1989: copy in Barclay papers.
76. Letter, Harris to Beazley, 12 September 1989: copy in Barclay papers.
77. Minutes of board meeting, 3 October 1989.
78. *Commonwealth Parliamentary Debates*, vol.S 133, pp.2686–7.
79. Minutes of board meeting, 3 October 1989.
80. Letter, Woods to Beazley, 14 February 1989.
81. Letter, Harris to Beazley, 27 November 1989: copy in Barclay papers.
82. The conversion of the company and its incorporation in this form was registered on 2 July 1990. See National Companies and Securities Commission certificate of incorporation on conversion, copy held by company secretary.
83. Internal memo MD646/89 dated 8 December 1989.
84. Letter, E.R. Thorn to R. Divett, General Manager APG, 17 November 1989: copy in Barclay papers.
85. Letter, McMahon to Thorn, 29 November 1989: copy in Barclay papers.
86. Minutes of board meeting, 24 April 1990.
87. Minutes of board meeting, 26 June 1990.
88. Minutes of board meeting, 7 August 1990.
89. Minutes of board meeting, 15 October 1990.
90. Minutes of board meeting, 12 March 1991.
91. Minutes of board meetings, 21 May, 16 July 1991.
92. Minutes of board meeting, 14 October 1991.
93. Minutes of board meeting, 25 November 1991.
94. *Australian Financial Review*, 15, 16 October 1992.
95. *Australian Financial Review*, 21 October 1992.
96. Internal memo (MD777/92) by Harris dated 16 October 1992: copy in ADI Maribyrnong file 89/0256(1), now held by Australian Archives.
97. *Australian Financial Review*, 20 November 1992.

98. Internal memo (MD897/92) by Harris dated 20 November 1992: copy held by Conway.
99. Letter, Woods to Ayers, March 1989: copy in Barclay papers.
100. Letter, Woods to Ayers, March 1989.
101. Letters, Harris to Thorn, 29 March 1989 (MD117/89), and Harris to R.N. McLeod, 2 April 1989 (MD122/89): copies in Barclay papers.
102. Letter, Beazley to Woods, 3 May 1989: copy with deed of transfer documents held by ADI.
103. Letters, Harris to Ayers, 24 August 1989 (MD395/89), Ayers to Woods, 12 December 1989: copies in Barclay papers.
104. Minutes of board meeting, 1 September 1989.
105. Letter, Woods to Ayers, 6 October 1989: copy in Barclay papers.
106. Letter, Ayers to Woods, 12 December 1989.
107. Speech by Harris, 'Financing the Public Sector', 16 October 1991: copy held by ADI Headquarters.
108. Harris speech, 16 October 1991.
109. Letter, Harris to Beazley, 5 April 1989: copy in Barclay papers.
110. Letters, McMahon (acting MD) to Mr A. Uzubalis (Acting Assistant Secretary, Industry Policy and Programs Branch, Defence Department), 3 January 1990, and Harris to Uzubalis, 18 January 1990: copies in Barclay papers.
111. Minute (SEC819/88, CDF649/88) dated 17 August 1988: copy in McMahon papers; Departmental Supply & Support Instruction no.6/88 dated 12 December 1988.
112. Letter, Harris to Ayers, 16 June 1989 (MD248/89): copy in Barclay papers.
113. Press release by Beazley, no.95/89 dated 10 May 1989.

Chapter Seven

1. Harris interview, 5 August 1993.
2. Under the interim award, the public service entitlement of twelve weeks paid leave was continued for all existing employees, but the position for new employees was to be resolved through negotiations over the following twelve months. The issue was taken up by unions keen to set a benchmark which applied to all GBEs, and these succeeded in winning a measure of government public support. At the ACTU congress in September 1989 the Minister for Industrial Relations (Morris) threatened to bring in legislation unless the company arrived at an agreement by 1 November. See *Australian Financial Review*, 1, 2 August, 28 September 1989; *Age*, 2 August 1989; *Canberra Times*, 29 September 1989; *Business Review Weekly*, 1 March 1991, p.68.
3. *Australian Defence Report*, 8 February 1990, p.9; see also *Australian Defence 2000*, March 1990, p.18.
4. Internal memo by Harris (MD173/89) dated 3 May 1989: copy in McMahon papers.
5. *Australian Defence Report*, 8 February 1990, p.9.
6. Callinan interview.
7. Conway interview, 24 August 1993.
8. Harris interview, 5 August 1993.
9. *Defence Industry*, March 1990, pp.5–6.
10. *Defence Industry*, March 1990, pp.5–6.
11. Harris interview, 5 August 1993.
12. Minutes of board meetings, 1 September, 7 December 1989; *Australian Shipyards*, June 1990.
13. Targ interview, 28 April 1994.
14. Minute by Targ, 16 February 1990: ADI Maribyrnong file 89/0129; ADI press release dated 16 March 1990: ADI Maribyrnong file 89/0256(1).
15. Minutes of board meetings, 26 March, 24 April 1990.
16. *Australian Financial Review*, 4 June 1990; *Australian Defence Report*, 14 June 1990; *Directions in Government*, June 1990.
17. Minutes of board meeting, 7 August 1990.
18. Minutes of board meetings, 24 April, 7 August 1990; *Australian Defence Report*, 9 August 1990.
19. Internal memo by Harris (MD462/90) dated 4 September 1990: ADI Maribyrnong file 89/0129.

20. Internal memo by Harris (MD252/91) dated 27 March 1991; ADI Maribyrnong file 89/0120.
21. Internal memo by Harris (MD36/91) dated 11 January 1991: ADI Maribyrnong file 89/0129; *Australian Defence Report*, 7 February 1991, p.4.
22. ADI press release dated 9 April 1991.
23. ADI press release dated 9 May 1991
24. ADI press release dated 9 May 1991; *Australian Financial Review*, 27 May 1991; *Sydney Morning Herald*, 29 October 1992. In the event ADI missed out on the AUSTACSS contract, which was awarded to Nobel/Tech Australia, a subsidiary of the Swedish Nobel Group; see *Sydney Morning Herald*, 11 December 1992.
25. Internal memo by Harris (MD382/91) dated 14 May 1991: ADI Maribyrnong file 89/0129.
26. Minutes of board meeting, 21 May 1991.
27. Minutes of board meeting, 3 March 1992; ADI press release dated 12 November 1992: ADI Maribyrnong file 89/0256(2).
28. *Sun Herald*, 19 July 1992.
29. *Bulletin*, 17 November 1992.
30. Minutes of board meeting, 14 December 1992. The Alan Woods Room was formally dedicated on 2 February 1993 (see minutes of board meeting that date).
31. ADI *Annual Report* 1992, p.9; *Asia-Pacific Defence Reporter*, August–September 1993, p.43.
32. *Defence Industry*, March 1990, p.6.
33. Internal memo by McMahon (DL99/91) dated 4 March 1991: ADI Maribyrnong file 89/0256(1); Navy Public Relations press release dated 28 February 1991.
34. *Australian Financial Review*, 28 May 1991.
35. *Sydney Morning Herald*, *Canberra Times*, 22 August 1991: *Daily Commercial News* (Sydney), 2 September 1991.
36. ADI media release, 1 December 1989; *Defence Industry & Aerospace Report*, 7 December 1989, p.17.
37. Transcript of 2BL news broadcast, 1 December 1989.
38. *Australian*, 28 June 1991; *Australian Defence Report*, 10 July 1991.
39. *Australian Defence Report*, 16 May, 10 July 1991.
40. Commodore G.V. Sloper, 'Personal Experiences in the Gulf', *Journal of the Royal United Services Institute of Australia*, July 1991, p.2.
41. *Asia-Pacific Defence Reporter*, March 1991, p.52.
42. *Australian Financial Review*, 16 January 1991; *Australian Defence Report*, 10 July 1991; George Odgers, *Diggers: The Australian Army, Navy and Air Force in Eleven Wars*, vol.2, Lansdowne Publishing, Sydney, 1994, pp.508, 512.
43. *Navint*, 8 October 1993, p.8.
44. *Sydney Morning Herald*, 25 May 1994; *Daily Commercial News*, 26 May 1994; *Australian Defence Magazine*, June 1994, pp.30–1.
45. *Australian Defence Report*, 13 April 1995, p.12; *Navy News*, 21 April 1995.
46. *Age*, 20 June 1990; *Australian Financial Review*, 21 June 1990.
47. *Australian*, 3 October 1989, 3 July 1990; *Canberra Times*, *Daily Telegraph* (Sydney), 3 July 1990; *Sunday Times*, 24 March 1991; *West Australian*, 25, 26 March 1991.
48. *Sun Herald*, 20 October 1991; *West Australian*, 22 October 1991.
49. *West Australian*, 19 October 1991; *Commonwealth Parliamentary Debates*, vol.S 148, pp.2135–6, 2157–8.
50. McMahon interview, 27 April 1994.
51. Minutes of board meeting, 30 September 1993.
52. Interview with Mr B. Gibson, 24 November 1993.
53. ADI *Annual Report* 1993, p.8; *Pursuit* (ADI newsletter), issue 15, no date (but 1993), p.8.
54. *Sydney Morning Herald*, 2, 3, 5 March 1994.
55. *Australian Financial Review*, *Canberra Times*, 20 September 1991.
56. *Telegraph Mirror* (Sydney), 16 January 1992.
57. Gibson interview.
58. ADI *Annual Report* 1993, p.8.
59. *Sydney Morning Herald*, 22 September 1992; *Telegraph Mirror*, 22 September 1992.

60. *Quality Australia*, June–July 1994, p.32.
61. *Business Review Weekly*, 10 December 1993, p.55; *Australian Financial Review*, 11 May 1994.
62. *Australian Financial Review*, 27 February 1995; *Daily Commercial News* (Sydney), 28 February 1995.
63. *Quality Australia*, June–July 1994, p.33; *Daily Commercial News*, 18 March 1994.
64. *Australian Defence Magazine*, October 1994, p.17.
65. *Sydney Morning Herald*, 18 September 1993.
66. ASC press release dated 26 July 1989; ADI media releases dated July 1989, 9 January 1990, 1 March 1990.
67. *Australian Defence Report*, 16 May 1991; *Australian*, 27 August 1993; *Pursuit* (ADI newsletter), issue 32, no date (but end 1997), p.8.
68. ASC press release dated 9 March 1990.
69. *Defence Industry & Aerospace Report*, 22 May 1992; *Australian*, 23 May 1992; *Daily Commercial News*, 4 June 1992.
70. ADI news release dated 26 November 1992.
71. The various other equipments making up AMASS were progressively adopted by the RAN in 1992–93. In March 1993 a small team under Donohue (based at ADI's Barton offices but forming part of Development Group) began marketing the system. In September 1994 this team moved across to ADI Minehunter, and by mid-1995 had secured contracts for sales of AMASS to the USA and Indonesia. Letter, Donohue to author, 20 June 1995; *Asian Military Review*, August–September 1993, pp.38–9; *Australian*, 29 October 1993.
72. Snowy Mountains Hydro-electric Authority press release dated 27 March 1991; *Australian Defence Report*, 2 May 1991.
73. *Australian Financial Review*, 4 November 1992; *Electrical Engineer*, December 1992, p.26; *West Australian*, 16 January 1995.
74. *Australian*, 15 December 1992, 10 May 1994.
75. *Bendigo Advertiser*, 21 February 1991.
76. *Bendigo Advertiser*, 26 February 1992.
77. *Bendigo Advertiser*, 26 January, 7 February 1991.
78. *Sydney Morning Herald*, 12 December 1992; *Australian Financial Review*, 15 December 1992.
79. ADI news release dated 26 November 1992; *Quality Australia*, June–July 1994, p.32; *Bendigo Advertiser*, 20 December 1994.
80. *Bendigo Advertiser*, 15, 16 May 1995.
81. *Australian Defence Report*, 18 October 1990, p.7; *Asian Defence Journal*, May 1990; *Courier-Mail* (Brisbane), 23 June 1990.
82. *Asia-Pacific Defence Reporter*, June–July 1994, p.39.
83. Defence news release 41/95 dated May 1995.
84. *Australian Defence Report*, 18 October 1990, p.6.
85. *Evening Post* (Wellington), 18 September 1991; *Army News* (NZ), 11 August 1993, p.3.
86. *Business Review Weekly*, 10 December 1993, p.55.
87. *Canberra Times*, 20 August 1991.
88. *Australian Financial Review*, 6 February, 20 March 1991; *Herald-Sun*, 26 February 1991.
89. *Herald-Sun*, 23 April 1992.
90. *Sydney Morning Herald*, 13 August 1994; *Canberra Times*, 15, 16, 18 August 1994; *Australian*, 16, 18 August, 11, 14, 15 November 1994; *West Australian*, 17 August, 10 November 1994.
91. *Australian*, 17, 18, 19, 24 January 1995; *Courier-Mail*, 18 January 1995; Indonesian embassy, Canberra, press release 02/PR/I/95 dated 23 January 1995; *Commonwealth Parliamentary Debates*, vol.S 169, pp.409–10.
92. *Lithgow Mercury*, 14 April 1994, 2 March 1995.
93. *Age*, 26 July 1990; *Canberra Times*, *Age*, 2 December 1993; *Herald-Sun*, 15 December 1993; Targ interview, 28 April 1994.
94. *Business Review Weekly*, 10 December 1993, p.55.
95. Transcript Albury Prime news, 24 June 1994.
96. *Border Mail* (Albury), 9 December 1993.

97. Minutes of board meetings, 21 October 1992, 1 September 1993; ADI *Annual Report 1993*, p 14.
98. *International Defense Review*, October 1991, *Defence News*, 25 November 1991.
99. *Ashfield Courier*, December 1992.
100. *West Australian*, 26 August 1992.
101. *Business Review Weekly*, 10 December 1993.
102. Minutes of board meeting, 28 November 1994.
103. *Australian Defence Report*, 9 February 1995, p.7; AAP report dated 18 April 1995.
104. News releases by ADI and the Office of the Minister for Energy & Minerals, dated 9 March 1995.
105. *Age*, 21 July 1992.
106. Defence news release DPR 243/92 dated 28 October 1992; *Australian*, 3 November 1992; *Defence Industry & Aerospace Report*, 6 November 1992, p.12; *Sunday Times*, 8 November 1992.
107. *West Australian*, 23 July 1993.
108. *Defence Industry & Aerospace Report*, 22 October 1993, p.7.
109. Defence news release DPR 143/93 dated 13 December 1993.
110. *Australian Defence Report*, 2 September 1993, p.14, 9 February 1995, p.6; *Australian Defence Intelligencer*, September 1994, pp.2–3, November 1994, p.4.
111. *Australian Defence Report*, 13 October 1994, p.4; *Defence Industry & Aerospace Report*, 28 October 1994; *Jane's Defence Contracts*, October 1994, p.12.
112. Defence news release DPR 20/94 dated 18 February 1994.
113. *Australian Defence Report*, 8 July 1993, p.11; *Asian Military Review*, August–September 1993, p.66.
114. *Australian*, 30 March, 27 May, 14 December 1994; news release by Senator R. Ray (Min78/94) dated 29 July 1994.
115. *Asian Defence Journal*, July 1991, p.29.
116. ADI news release dated 6 April 1992.
117. *Border Mail* (Albury), 8 July 1992.
118. Minutes of board meeting, 4 May 1992.
119. *Border Mail* (Albury), 29 February 1992, 24 May 1995.
120. Interview with Dr R.E. Babbage, CGM Consulting, ADI Services, 1 July 1995.
121. The papers delivered at this gathering were later published in Ross Babbage & Sam Bateman (eds), *Maritime Change: Issues for Asia*, Allen & Unwin, Sydney, 1993.
122. *Telegraph Mirror* (Sydney), 29 February 1992.
123. Defence news release DPR 176/92 dated 28 July 1992.
124. Defence news release DPR 241/92 dated 28 October 1992.
125. ADI news release, 17 August 1993.
126. ADI news release, 11 October 1993; *Canberra Times*, 12 October 1993; *Army News*, 2 June 1994.
127. *Advertiser* (Adelaide), 5 December 1989; *Military Technology*, July 1990.
128. *Canberra Times*, 15 July 1991.
129. *Australian Financial Review*, 15 July 1991; ADI *Annual Report 1990*, p.8.
130. ADI news release dated 26 July 1990.
131. *Herald-Sun*, 8 December 1991; transcript of ABV2 News, 6 December 1991.
132. *Bendigo Advertiser*, 3 August 1991.
133. *Bendigo Advertiser*, 18 November 1992; *Herald-Sun*, 18 November 1992.
134. *Pursuit*, issue 16, p.3.
135. *Australian Defence Report*, 19 August 1993, p.11; *Business Queensland*, 15 November 1993.
136. *Bendigo Advertiser*, 22 November 1993.
137. *Business Review Weekly*, 3 December 1993; Brisbane *Courier-Mail*, 2 November 1993; *Government Officers Magazine*, December 1993; *Manufacturers' Monthly*, February 1994.
138. Letter, Mr M. Church (CGM ADI Minehunter) to author, 23 May 1995.
139. Minutes of board meeting, 11 February 1992.
140. Letter, Harris to author, 15 July 1999.
141. Minutes of board meeting, 2 April 1992; *Daily Commercial News*, 24 June 1992.
142. Letter, Harris to author, 30 November 1998.
143. Letter, Commodore H. Donohue (GM Mine Countermeasures, ADI) to author, 9 June 1995; *Defence*

Industry & Aerospace Report, 8 May 1992, p.7; *Bulletin* (Sydney), 10 November 1992, p.3.

144. *Australian Defence Report*, 8, 22 July 1993; *Australian Defence Intelligencer*, July 1993, p.7.

145. *Newcastle Herald*, 13 November 1993; *Australian Defence News*, 12 November 1993.

146. *Newcastle Herald*, 23 December 1993.

147. *Defence Industry & Aerospace Report*, 11 March 1994, p.8.

148. *Newcastle Herald*, 15 January, 5 February 1994; *Australian Financial Review*, 31 May 1994; *Daily Commercial News*, 1 June 1994.

149. *Newcastle Herald*, 31 May, 3 June 1994.

150. *Defence Industry & Aerospace Report*, 11 March 1994, p.8.

151. News release by Minister for Defence, MIN 59/94 dated 2 June 1994.

152. ADI news release dated 12 August 1994.

153. Transcript NBN3 (Newcastle) news, 29 August 1994. Permanent accommodation at Carrington for 100 ADI project management and engineering personnel was officially opened during the first week of May 1995; see *Newcastle Herald*, 2 May 1995, and *Newcastle Star*, 10 May 1995.

154. ADI news release dated 30 November 1994.

155. *Newcastle Herald*, 28 December 1994; ADI news release dated 14 March 1995.

156. *Navint*, 24 February 1995, p.8; *Jane's Defence Contracts*, March 1995, p.12.

157. ADI *Annual Report* 1993, p.8; *Defense News* (Springfield, Virginia, USA), 20–26 December 1993, p.22.

158. McCorquodale interview.

159. Letter, Harris to author, 30 November 1998.

160. Minutes of board meeting, 11 February 1992.

161. Internal memo by Harris (MD252/91) dated 27 March 1991.

162. *Bendigo Advertiser*, 9 September 1992, quoting Mr Harry Bullows, former manufacturing manager and deputy general manager of the old Ordnance Factory Bendigo.

163. Fynmore interview.

164. Harris interview, 5 August 1993.

Chapter Eight

1. Harris to Beazley (MD136/89) dated 5 April 1989: copy in Barclay papers.

2. Harris interview, 5 August 1993.

3. Barclay interview. Probably also in the back of his mind was the British experience. The London *Daily Mail* of 23 June 1989 carried a report that, when the Royal Ordnance factories were privatised three years earlier, the British Aerospace company had paid £13.6 million for three sites which later brought £462 million on redevelopment. A copy of the article was sent to Ron Taylor (then with the Project REFA team), who passed it on to Barclay.

4. Barclay interview.

5. Harris interview, 5 August 1993; also interview with Harris reported in *Defense News*, 20–26 December 1993, p.22.

6. Harris interview, 5 August 1993.

7. McCorquodale interview.

8. Barclay interview; Mitchell interview, 26 August 1993.

9. Barclay interview.

10. Internal memo by Harris (MD487/90) dated 31 August 1990: ADI Headquarters records.

11. Paper titled 'The State of the Business and Options for Restructuring', August 1990: ADI Headquarters records.

12. The fall in Defence ammunition orders had already caused 120 retrenchments at Footscray: see minutes of board meeting, 31 May 1990.

13. Minutes of board meeting, 21 November 1990.

14. *Age*, 1 December 1990.

15. Barclay memo (MPG JB 379/91) dated 11 February 1991: ADI Maribyrnong file 89/0129.

16. See Beazley's speech of 10 May 1989 in *Commonwealth Parliamentary Debates*, vol. H of R 166, p.2344.

17. Internal memo by Harris (MD401/91) dated 14 May 1991: ADI Headquarters records.
18. Harris interview, 5 August 1993.
19. Internal memo by Harris (MD652/91) dated 29 July 1991: ADI headquarters records.
20. *Business Review Weekly*, 1 March 1991, p.68.
21. Harris interview, 5 August 1993.
22. Interview with Mr J. Pettifer, General Manager, ADI St. Marys, 25 November 1993.
23. *Australian Defence Report*, 13 December 1990.
24. *Community News* (Essendon, Vic.), 5 December 1990.
25. Transcript of ATV10 news, 30 November 1993.
26. *Pursuit*, issue 17, no date (but 1993), p.12.
27. *Age*, 2 December 1990.
28. *Sunday Sun* (Melbourne), 2 December 1990.
29. *Commonwealth Parliamentary Debates*, vol.S 142, p.4866.
30. Pettifer interview.
31. Pettifer interview.
32. St. Marys facility, Performance Achievement newsletters, July, October, December 1992, February, March–April 1993.
33. *Pursuit*, issue 19, no date (but 1993), p.4.
34. *Pursuit*, issue 19, p.4.
35. *Australian*, 31 May 1994; *Army Magazine*, 16 June 1994.
36. Janka interview.
37. Janka interview; *Pursuit*, issue 16, p.9; ADI *Annual Report* 1993, p.8.
38. Janka interview.
39. Barclay interview.
40. Janka interview.
41. *Telegraph Mirror* (Sydney), 20 September 1991; *Mt. Druitt–St. Marys Standard*, 25 September 1991.
42. *Australian Financial Review*, 4 June 1992.
43. Letter, Mr R. Maclellan (Victorian Minister for Planning) to Mitchell, 10 November 1993: ADI records.
44. *Age, Herald-Sun*, 1 December 1993.
45. Pamphlet, 'ADI St Marys Redevelopment Project Update', no.1, December 1992.
46. *Sydney Morning Herald*, 26 October 1991.
47. News release by Yabsley dated 14 February 1992.
48. *Sydney Morning Herald*, 14 March 1992.
49. *Border Mail* (Albury), 24 March 1992.
50. *Australian Financial Review*, 7 August 1992.
51. *Australian Financial Review*, 28 March 1994.
52. *Age*, 13 November 1993.
53. Letter, Harris to author, 30 November 1998.
54. Mitchell interview, 26 August 1993.
55. *Mt. Druitt–St. Marys Standard*, 26 November 1991; *Penrith Press*, 17 December 1991; *Australian Financial Review*, 7 August 1992; *Blacktown City Guardian*, 5 August 1993.
56. *Blacktown Advocate*, 15 December 1993.
57. Minutes of board meeting, 11 February 1992.
58. Mitchell interview, 26 August 1993. For an example of antagonism based on such a perception, see the questioning of Defence Minister Ray by Senator Dee Margetts in the Senate Estimates Committee on 15 February 1995.
59. *Sydney Morning Herald*, 10 May 1995.
60. *Penrith Press*, 15 February, 22 March 1994: *Blacktown Advocate*, 23 February, 20 April, 11 May 1994; *Blacktown City Guardian*, 20 April, 11 May 1994.
61. *Penrith City Star*, 18 October 1994.
62. *Mt. Druitt–St. Marys Standard, Blacktown Advocate*, 29 March 1995.
63. *Australian Financial Review*, 9 March 1995; *Sydney Morning Herald*, 11 March 1995.

64. Barclay interview. Prior awareness of the contamination problem at St. Marys is confirmed by Barclay's minute to R. Divett, General Manager of Australian Property Group (Department of Administrative Services), 12 April 1989: copy in Barclay papers.
65. *Australian*, 22 May 1992.
66. ADI Ordnance background paper titled 'Restructuring ADI's Ammunition Business', 1994, p.4: ADI records.
67. Minutes of board meeting, 12 March 1991.
68. ADI news release dated 6 September 1991.
69. *Border Mail* (Albury), 26 November 1991.
70. Minutes of board meeting, 16 July 1991.
71. Minutes of board meeting, 11 February 1992.
72. *Defence Industry & Aerospace Report*, 21 February 1992, p.11.
73. Letter, Barclay to Babbage (Ref: JB980101nf), 30 June 1998: copy held by author.
74. *Proposed Ammunition Manufacturing Facility: Benalla, Victoria*, p.9; ADI news release dated 17 November 1992.
75. Minutes of board meeting, 14 December 1992.
76. Minutes of board meeting, 30 March 1993.
77. *Benalla Ensign*, 16 June 1993.
78. Interview with Mr A.S. Podger, Secretary of the Department of Housing and Regional Development, 23 May 1995.
79. ADI paper 'Restructuring ADI's Ammunition Business', pp.3–4.
80. Podger interview.
81. Minutes of board meetings, 23 April, 31 May 1993.
82. ADI news release dated 7 September 1993.
83. ADI news release dated 11 October 1993.

Chapter Nine

1. Harris minute (MD573/93) dated 21 July 1993: copy in ADI Corporate Headquarters records.
2. ADI *Annual Report* 1990, pp.2, 6.
3. ADI *Annual Report* 1991, pp.2, 5.
4. ADI *Annual Report* 1992, pp.2, 4.
5. ADI *Annual Report* 1993, p.6.
6. ADI *Annual Report* 1994, pp.2–3, 6.
7. ADI *Annual Report* 1994, p.4.
8. Harris interview, 5 August 1993.
9. ADI *Annual Report* 1995, p.3.
10. ADI *Annual Report* 1994, p.8.
11. ADI *Annual Report* 1998, p.6.
12. Callinan interview.
13. Harris interview, 15 January 1998.
14. Harris interview, 5 August 1993.
15. *Commonwealth Parliamentary Debates*, vol.HofR 166, pp.2349–50.
16. *Business Weekly Review*, 15 February 1991, p.26.
17. *Daily Commercial News*, 18 November 1994.
18. *Commonwealth Parliamentary Debates*, vol.S 167, p.1604.
19. ADI *Annual Report* 1994, p.10.
20. *Australian*, 27 May 1994.
21. Targ interview, 28 April 1994.
22. *Australian*, 11 October 1994.
23. ADI *Annual Report* 1994, p.10.
24. *Defence Industry & Aerospace Report*, 16 December 1994, p.12; *Australian Business Monthly*, April 1995.

25. Transcript of 2DAY news (Sydney), 29 January 1992.
26. *Herald-Sun, Daily Telegraph-Mirror*, 26 July 1993.
27. Transcript 2BL news, 18 April 1995.
28. *Age, Herald-Sun*, 17 April 1995.
29. Harris interview, 15 January 1998.
30. Babbage interview, 27 march 1998.
31. *Australian Defence Report*, 26 May 1994, p.12; *Defence Industry & Aerospace Report*, 27 May 1994, p.10.
32. *Australian Defence Report*, 21 July 1994, p.10.
33. Internal memo by Kelaher to CGMs of ADI Services dated 15 June 1994, p.7.
34. Minutes of board meeting, 20 July 1992; *Australian Defence Report*, 6 August 1992.
35. Minutes of board meeting, 27 July 1993.
36. Minutes of board meetings, 1, 30 September, 26 October 1993.
37. *Pursuit*, issue 20, no date (but late 1993), p.8.
38. Minutes of board meeting, 23 November 1993.
39. *Pursuit*, issue 21, no date (but early 1994), p.9.
40. Minutes of board meeting, 22 March 1994.
41. Minutes of board meetings, 31 May, 31 October 1994.
42. Minutes of board meetings, 21 July, 22 September, 20 October 1995; *Australian Financial Review*, 31 October 1995.
43. Minutes of board meetings, 16 December 1993, 10 February 1994.
44. *Pursuit*, issue 27, pp.1–2, issue 26, p.10.
45. Harris interview, 15 January 1998.
46. *Pursuit*, issue 31, p.8.
47. Minutes of board meeting, 21 July 1995.
48. Internal memo by Harris (MD576/95ab) dated 7 December 1995: copy held by Corporate Headquarters.
49. Harris interview, 15 January 1998.
50. Minutes of board meeting, 31 October 1996; see also *Pursuit*, issue 32, p.2.
51. *Pursuit*, issue 32, p.9.
52. Minutes of board meeting, 31 October 1996.
53. *Pursuit*, issue 26, p.9.
54. Mitchell interview, 29 September 1998.
55. *Pursuit*, issue 38, p.4; issue 39, p.9.
56. Minutes of board meeting, 22 September 1995.
57. Conway interview, 16 January 1998.
58. Interview with Mr M. Diedrichs, General Manager, Engineering, Bendigo, 15 October 1998.
59. *Pursuit*, issue 25, p.4.
60. *Pursuit*, issue 35, p.3, issue 38, pp.1–2.
61. *Pursuit*, issue 28, p.5.
62. *Australian Financial Review*, 8 October 1997.
63. Defence news release (DPR 47/95) dated 2 June 1995; *Canberra Times*, 4 June 1995.
64. Interview with Mr K. de Wet, General Manager, Military & Specialist Vehicles, Bendigo, 15 October 1998.
65. Tunny interview, 23 April 1999.
66. ADI news releases, 12, 31 July 1996.
67. *Pursuit*, issue 31, pp.1, 3.
68. *Pursuit*, issue 32, p.2.
69. Berlyn interview, 17 April 1998.
70. *Canberra Times*, 5 September 1997; *Australian Financial Review*, 1 December 1997.
71. *Sydney Morning Herald, Canberra Times*, 15 November 1995.
72. *Australian*, 17 July 1998; *Daily Commercial News*, 22 July 1998.
73. *Australian, Canberra Times*, 11 August 1998.
74. *West Australian*, 22 June 1999.

75. Minutes of board meetings, 20 October 1995, 2 May 1997.
76. See *Pursuit*, issue 25, p.2; issue 28, p.2; issue 32, p.1; issue 34, pp.1–2.

Chapter Ten

1. *Age*, 13 May 1998, 12 May 1999; *Sydney Morning Herald*, 12 May 1999.
2. *Australian Financial Review*, 11 May 1989.
3. *Australian Financial Review*, 18 August 1993.
4. News release by Senator Ray (MIN145/93) dated 17 December 1993.
5. *Australian*, 14 October 1994.
6. *Australian Financial Review*, 2, 8 February 1995.
7. Media release 14/95 by Minister for Finance, K.C. Beazley, dated 18 April 1995.
8. Hill, *Wirraway to Hornet*, p.238.
9. Letter, P.A. Walsh to author, 10 February 1995, and interview, 1 April 1995.
10. ADI *Annual Report* 1993, p.4.
11. *Defence Industry & Aerospace Report*, 8 October 1993, p.13.
12. *Business Review Weekly*, 28 March 1994, p.33.
13. *Business Review Weekly*, 4 April 1994, p.98.
14. Barclay interview.
15. Fynmore interview.
16. *Bendigo Advertiser*, 23 April 1994.
17. *Age*, 9 May 1994.
18. *Border Mail*, 28 September 1994.
19. Beazley was quoted by the *Bendigo Advertiser*, 20 May 1995, during a visit to that city.
20. Beazley interview.
21. *Australian*, 28 June 1995.
22. ADI *Annual Report* 1996, pp.6, 29.
23. Targ interview, 14 May 1999.
24. Apted interview.
25. Harris interview, 14 May 1999.
26. Letter, Fynmore to McLachlan (MD031/97), 12 February 1997: copy in ADI Corporate Headquarters records.
27. Telephone interview with Hon. I.M. McLachlan, 19 April 1999.
28. *Commonwealth Parliamentary Debates*, vol.HofR 211, pp.1576.
29. Budget Paper No.1, *Budget Strategy and Outlook 1997–98*, p.4–116.
30. *Australian, Sydney Morning Herald*, 15 May 1997.
31. Media release 35/97 by Minister for Finance, J. Fahey, dated 1 July 1997.
32. Minutes of board meeting, 11 July 1997.
33. Apted interview.
34. Harris interview, 14 May 1999.
35. Targ interviews, 30 September 1998, 14 May 1999.
36. Minutes of board meeting, 3 July 1998.
37. Targ interview, 14 May 1999. By mid-1999 the number of formal questions from bidders totalled more than 2000.
38. ADI *Annual Report* 1997, pp.3, 6.
39. Media release by Minister for Defence, I.M. McLachlan, dated 2 September 1997.
40. Letter, Fynmore to Fahey and McLachlan (MD473/97jk), 26 November 1997: copy in ADI Corporate Headquarters records.
41. *Australian*, 16 September 1997.
42. *Australian Financial Review, Age*, 12 November 1997.
43. *Defense News*, 24–30 November 1997.
44. *Australian Financial Review*, 13 November 1997.

45. *Australian Financial Review*, 17 November 1997.
46. *Australian Financial Review, Australian*, 20 November 1997.
47. Media release 83/97 by Minister for Finance and Minister for Defence, dated 9 December 1997.
48. McLachlan interview.
49. *Australian Financial Review*, 7, 14 March 1998.
50. Media release MIN219/98 by Minister for Defence J. Moore, dated 13 November 1998.
51. *Sydney Morning Herald, Age*, 16 April 1998.
52. *Australian Financial Review*, 23 April 1998.
53. *Jane's Defence Weekly*, 29 April 1998.
54. Minutes of board meeting, 27 March 1998.
55. Harris interview, 14 May 1999; see also ADI paper titled 'Major issues being considered by the Department of Defence during the pre-sale phase of ADI's privatisation' dated 11 March 1998: copy held by ADI Headquarters.
56. Media release 55/98 by Minister for Finance and Minister for Defence, dated 12 June 1998; *Australian Financial Review*, 12 June 1998.
57. Media release 72/98 by Minister for Finance and Minister for Defence, dated 31 July 1998.
58. *Australian Defence Business Review*, 31 July 1998.
59. *Australian Financial Review*, 19 September 1998; *Australian*, 29 September 1998.
60. Harris interview, 30 September 1998.
61. ADI *Annual Report* 1996, p.3.
62. *Australian Financial Review*, 7 November 1998.
63. *Australian Financial Review*, 14 November 1998.
64. *Australian Defence Business Review*, 26 March 1999; *Australian Defence Report*, 1 April 1999.
65. *Asian Military Review*, May 1979, p.46.
66. SECA press release dated 10 May 1999.
67. *Australian Financial Review*, 14 May 1999.
68. *Sydney Morning Herald*, 27 February 1999; *Australian Financial Review*, 1 March 1999.
69. Speech by Harris at launch of Minehunter *Norman*, 3 May 1999.
70. Excerpt from press conference with the Minister for Finance and Managing Director of ADI, 3 May 1999: copy held by ADI Corporate Headquarters.
71. *Australian, Australian Financial Review, Sydney Morning Herald, Bendigo Advertiser*, 2 June 1999.
72. Joint media release by Ministers Fahey and Moore, no.34/99, dated 1 July 1999.
73. *Australian Defence Report*, 22 July 1999; *Sydney Morning Herald*, 9 August 1999.
74. *Australian Financial Review*, 9 August 1999.
75. *Australian Financial Review*, 30 June, 13 July 1999.
76. *Age*, 26 June 1999; *Australian Financial Review*, 22 July 1999.
77. *Australian Defence Report*, 27 May 1999
78. *Australian*, 2 August 1999.
79. ADI statement to employees dated 4 August 1999; this was quoted in *Australian Financial Review* the next day, but as a footnote to another story regarding the alleged problems of the sale.
80. *Australian Financial Review*, 5 August 1999.
81. *Australian Financial Review*, 6 August 1999.
82. Joint media release by Ministers Fahey and Moore, no.42/99, dated 17 August 1999.
83. ADI news release dated 17 August 1999.

Chapter Eleven

1. Harris interview, 15 January 1998.
2. Beazley interview.
3. Woods' speaking notes for the opening ceremony, 27 July 1989: in possesion of Mrs A. Woods.
4. Harris interview, 5 August 1993.
5. Harris interview, 5 August 1993.

6. Beazley interview.
7. Harris interview, 15 January 1998.
8. Fynmore interview.
9. Russell interview.
10. Harris interview, 5 August 1993.
11. Wettenhall, 'Corporatised Bodies Old and New', p.17.
12. *Australian Financial Review*, 5 July 1991.
13. ADI *Annual Report* 1991, p.3.
14. Fynmore, Harris (5 August 1993) and Barclay interviews.
15. Harris' letter (MD518/94) to Mr G. Harrison (Secretary of the JCPA) dated 11 July 1984: ADI Corporate Headquarters records; see also *Newcastle Herald*, 28 July 1994; *Australian Financial Review*, 29 August 1994.
16. Tannahill interview.
17. *Directions in Government*, March 1990, pp.44–6. So concerned was the company regarding this question that the report 'The State of the Business and Options for Restructuring', delivered to Defence Minister Ray in August 1990, contained an annex attempting to define what ADI's relationship with its owner should be (see pp.59–64).
18. McMahon interview, 27 April 1994.
19. McMahon interview, 18 February 1998.
20. Interview with Mr G. Jones, Deputy Secretary Acquisitions, Department of Defence, 11 May 1999.

BIBLIOGRAPHY

ADI company records

Current working, policy and correspondence files at ADI Corporate Headquarters were used little in researching this study, although originals of minutes and internal memorandums cited can be found there. Primary source material of the greatest historical worth, for example in tracing the activities of the transition team, was found to be held still by the individuals who were principally involved at the time. Major collections of papers are in the possession of Dr J.R. Barclay (now head of ADI's Systems Group, Sydney) and Mr J.E. McMahon (now head of Government Relations Group at Canberra), while another useful batch are in the custody of the first company secretary, Mr B.F. Conway (now General Manager Business Development within the Operations Group, also in Sydney). Other company documents of particular use are listed below.

ADI Footscray Facility: an appraisal of the heritage significance, 2 vols., Allom Lovell & Associates report prepared for ADI, 1992.

ADI Maribyrnong Facility: an appraisal of the heritage significance, 2 vols., Allom Lovell & Associates report prepared for ADI, 1992.

ADI Ordnance background paper titled 'Restructuring ADI's Ammunition Business', 1994.

'ADI St Marys Redevelopment Project Update', pamphlet, no.1, December 1992.

Annual Report, 1990, 1991, 1992, 1993, 1994, 1995, 1996, 1997, 1998.

Minutes of board meetings, 1988–99, held by Company Secretary.

Newsletter, August, October, November, December 1988, February, May 1989.

Newsletter Stop Press, 11 May 1989.

Proposed Ammunition Manufacturing Facility: Benalla, Victoria, comprehensive environmental report, September 1992.

Pursuit (newsletter), issues 1–42; covering period from March–April 1990 to April 1999, but not dated between issue 9 (December 1991/January 1992) and issue 33 (March 1997).

'The State of the Business and Options for Restructuring', paper, August 1990.

Visits to individual facilities established that, in general, the records held at this level were too detailed and localised for the study being attempted. Nonetheless, some useful material was identified and has been used.

Footscray
Historical photographic collection.

Maribyrnong
(files since transferred to Australian Archives' regional office in Victoria)

88/226 (2), (3), (10); 89/0129; 89/0256 (1), (2).

St. Marys
Performance Achievement newsletters, July, October, December 1992, February, March–April 1993.

Unpublished manuscripts and papers

Berlyn, N.R.B., 'Garden Island Dockyard in the 1990s', address to Naval Engineering Symposium, 29 November 1988, copy in author's possession.

Garrisson, A.D., 'Australian Aircraft Industry', paper for the Legislative Research Service of the Parliamentary Library, Parliament of Australia, 28 June 1982, copy in author's possession.

Jensen, J.K., Defence Production in Australia to 1941, chaps.1, 8, formerly held at ADI Maribyrnong.

McLean, Les, 'The History of Ordnance Factory Maribyrnong 1923–1993', copy in author's possession.

Ross, A.T., The Arming of Australia: The Politics and Administration of Australia's Self Containment Strategy for Munitions Supply 1901–1945, Ph.D. thesis, University of New South Wales, 1986.

Wettenhall, R., 'Corporatised Bodies Old and New: Is Parliament Missing Out?', speech in Senate occasional lecture series, Canberra, 31 May 1993, copy in author's possession.

Woods, A.J., speaking notes for opening of ADI Corporate Headquarters ceremony, 27 July 1989, in possesion of Mrs A. Woods.

ODP records held by ADI

As the successor to ODP, ADI inherited a large collection of records of historical value, including reports, pamphlets, promotional and pictorial material. These are held at the company's former headquarters in Barton, Canberra. They remain unsorted and uncatalogued, and present a valuable but largely fragmentary view of the activities of ODP and predecessor organisations back to the Department of Supply. The documents of principle use for this study are listed below.

Advisory Committee on Management and Operation of Williamstown Naval Dockyard, report, June 1981, vol.1.

Aircraft Engineering Workshops, ministerial background paper prepared by Defence Aerospace Division, 6 March 1985.

Australian Government Clothing Factory, pamphlet, c.1981.

——, Factory profile, March 1984.

Australian Government Engine Works, financial statements 1978–79.

Bennett, F.N., 'Defence Production', address to the RAN Staff College, 3 June 1985.

——, 'Defence Production Policy', address to the Joint Services Staff College, 16 September 1985.

Bullows, R.H., Ordnance Manufacturing Study 1985, unpub. report, vol.1.

'Chronological development and administration: Commonwealth Government munitions factories and establishments', undated document, originator unknown.

Briefing paper on ODP, February 1987.

Defence Production, Department of, *Establishments of the Department of Defence Production*, 1956.

——, *The Government Munitions and Aircraft Factories*, booklet, September 1957.

Defence Support, Department of, Aircraft Engineering Workshop, pamphlet, c.1983.

——, *Williamstown Naval Dockyard*, brochure, c.1984.

Eltringham, D.H., *Restructuring and Sale of the Defence Production Factories*, report, 4 February 1981.

——, *Future Development of the Australian Defence Production Factories*, April 1981, part 1.

Explosives Factory Maribyrnong, Rationalisation of Explosives Factories, draft report, 29 April 1976.

Fisher, A.E., 'Ammunition Filling – The St Marys Story over the past forty-five years', paper presented to RAAF Explosives Engineering Seminar, 22 August 1985.

GID: Garden Island Dockyard, brochure, c.1987.

Industry & Commerce, Department of, 'The Role of Standards in Budgeting', interim report by Internal Audit Section, April 1982.

IHI, *Study Report of the Future of the Australian Government Engine Works*, report, August 1975.

Joint Review of Williamstown Naval Dockyard, final report, January 1981.

Lawrence, T.F.C., `The Department of Supply: Its Origins and Functions', printed paper, January 1971.

Manufacturing Industry, Department of, *Australian Government Engine Works*, booklet, c.1974.

Munitions, Department of, `History of Munitions: Small Arms Factory, Lithgow', booklet, c.1945.

——, 'A Summary of the Development of Munitions Production in Australia, 1940–1945', reprinted from the *Official Year Book of the Commonwealth of Australia*, no.36: 1944–45, Canberra, undated.

'Munitions Factories Workload and Employment problems', report of inter- departmental committee, January 1976.

'Munitions Filling Factory St. Marys, N.S.W.: A Brief Description', undated booklet.

Ordnance Factory Bendigo, album, 'Photographs of some major projects produced for the B.H.P. Organisation, 1962'.

Pheasant, W.F., *Review of Explosive Factories*, report, 2 vols., July 1985.

Post-War Reconstruction, Department of, *Wartime Factories with a Peacetime Future: The Story of Industrial Decentralisation*, booklet, 1949.

Productivity, Department of, *Productivity 1977*.

——, *Australian Government Small Arms Factory, Lithgow*, booklet, 1979.

——, 'Munitions Policy Study', report, c.1979.

——, pamphlet, undated but c.1979.

——, unpub. ms on SAF Lithgow 'A Brief History of the Factory and a Survey of Production Facilities from 1912' (undated).

Report of Committee of Inquiry into Workloads in Government Factories, October 1974.

'Review of Commonwealth Functions: Australian Government Clothing Factory', Cabinet memorandum no.1210 dated 24 February 1981.

Silk, S.E., 'The Origins and History of the Small Arms Factory Lithgow', based on a talk to the Lithgow Historical Society, undated.

Supply, Department of, *An Account of the Purposes, Structure and Functions of the Department*, 1955.

——, *Handbook*, 30 September 1955.

——, program for official handover of first 7.62 mm rifles manufactured by SAF, 5 March 1959.

——, 'Activities and Developments', booklet, September 1959.

——, *Small Arms Factory Lithgow 1912–1962* (booklet).

——, 'Notes on General Pattern of Organisation', booklet, effective July 1967.

——, 'Outline of Organisation and Responsibilities', booklet, July 1967.

——, 'Munitions Manufacturing Policy Review (including rationalisation of the Australian Government Munitions Factories)', submission to Defence (Industrial) Committee, December 1973.

——, *Commonwealth Government Engine Works*, booklet, 1973.

Taylor, R.W., *A Review of the Commercial Viability of Explosives Factory Maribyrnong – with an Emphasis on Corporate Issues of the Office of Defence Production*, September 1988.

Thompson, R.S., 'The Government Munitions Factories', lecture by Controller of Munitions Supply, Department of Industry & Commerce, 1981.

Official publications

Australian Defence (1976 White Paper).

Commonwealth Parliamentary Debates: vols 42, 77, 99; vols. HofR (House of Representatives) 122, 163, 164, 166, 167; vols S (Senate) 133, 142, 148, 167, 168, 169

Commonwealth Parliamentary Papers, 1901–02, vol.2; 1920–21, vol.4; 1923–24, vol.4; paper no.225/1977; paper no.260/1979.

Defence of Australia (1987 White Paper).

Defence Report, 1984–85, 1985–86, 1986–87, 1987–88.

Defence Support, Department of, *Annual Report 1981–1982*.

Defending Australia (1994 White Paper).

Journals and Printed Papers of the Federal Council of Australasia, vol.1, Hobart, 1886.

New South Wales Legislative Council, *Journal*, vol.32 (1881), part 1. vol.46 (1889).

Policies for Development of Manufacturing Industry, October 1975, vol.1, Canberra, 1975.

Policy Guidelines for Commonwealth Statutory Authorities and Government Business Enterprises (issued by the Minister for Finance, Senator P. Walsh, October 1987), Australian Government Publishing Service, Canberra, 1987.

Remuneration Tribunal: *1989 Review.*

Report upon the Department of Defence from the 1st of July, 1914, until the Thirtieth of June, 1917, Part 1, Government Printer, Melbourne, 1917.

Reshaping the Transport and Communications Government Business Enterprises (issued by the Minister for Transport and Communications, Senator G. Evans, 25 May 1988), Australian Government Publishing Service, Canberra, 1988.

Senate Select Committee on the Government Clothing and Ordnance Factories, *The Future of Ordnance Factory Bendigo*, Australian Government Publishing Service, Canberra, 1982.

Senate Select Committee on the Government Clothing and Ordnance Factories, *The Future of the Government Clothing Factory at Coburg*, Australian Government Publishing Service, Canberra, 1982.

Year Book Australia, no.69, 1985, Australian Bureau of Statistics, Canberra.

Other published references

Australian Dictionary of Biography, Melbourne University Press, Carlton, Vic. vol.4, (D. Pike, ed.), 1972. vol.6, (B. Nairn, ed.), 1976.

Commonwealth Law Reports, 1935, vol.52.

Dictionary of New Zealand Biography, vol.2, Bridget Williams Books & Department of Internal Affairs, Wellington, 1993.

Published books & articles

Babbage, R.E., & Bateman, W.S.G. (eds), *Maritime Change: Issues for Asia*, Allen & Unwin, Sydney, 1993.

Cockatoo Docks & Engineering Co. Pty. Ltd., *Cockatoo Docks, Sydney: War Record 1939–1945*, brochure, undated, copy held by Australian Defence Force Academy Library, Canberra.

Cooke, C.K., *Australian Defences and New Guinea: Compiled from the Papers of the Late Major-General Sir Peter Scratchley, RE, KCMG*, London, 1887.

Coulthard-Clark, C.D., *The Third Brother: The Royal Australian Air Force 1921–39*, Allen & Unwin, Sydney, 1991.

Craig, G.C., *The Federal Defence of Australasia*, William Clowes & Sons, London, 1897.

Deakin, A., *The Federal Story: The Inner History of the Federal Cause*, Robertson & Mullens, Melbourne, 1944.

Ford, O., & Lewis, P., *Maribyrnong: Action in Tranquillity*, Melbourne's Living Museum of the West & Sunshine City Council, 1989.

Frame, T.R., *The Garden Island*, Kangaroo Press, Kenthurst, NSW, 1990.

Fraser, D. (ed.), *Sydney, from Settlement to City: An Engineering History of Sydney*, Engineers Australia, Crows Nest, NSW, 1989.

Harris, L.H., *A Little Further, A Little Faster: A Nostalgic Look at the Colonial Ammunition Company, its History and Cartridges*, New Zealand Cartridge Collectors' Club, Wellington, 1981.

Hill, B.L., *Wirraway to Hornet: A History of the Commonwealth Aircraft Corporation Pty Ltd, 1936 to 1985*, Southern Cross Publications, Bulleen, Vic., 1998.

Johnson, D.H., *Volunteers at Heart: The Queensland Defence Forces 1860–1901*, University of Queensland Press, St. Lucia, 1975.

Lee, D., 'The National Security Planning and Defence Preparations of the Menzies Government, 1950–53', *War & Society*, vol.10, no.2, October 1992.

Linge, G.J.R., *Industrial Awakening: A Geography of Australian Manufacturing 1788 to 1890*, ANU Press, Canberra, 1979.

Lyons, J.K., *The Colonial Ammunition Company (Australia) Ltd. 1888–1926*, privately pub., 1966.

Macandie, G.L., *The Genesis of the Royal Australian Navy*, Government Printer, Sydney, 1949.

Meaney, N.K., *The Search for Security in the Pacific, 1901–14*, Sydney University Press, Sydney, 1976.

Mellor, D.P., *The Role of Science and Industry*, series 4, vol.5, *Australia in the War of 1939–1945*, Australian War Memorial, Canberra, 1958.

Mordike, J., *An Army for a Nation: A History of Australian Military Developments 1880–1914*, Allen & Unwin, Sydney, 1992.

Munitions Diary 1985, Melbourne's Living Museum of the West, Williamstown, Vic., 1985.

Nicholls, R., *The Colonial Volunteers: The Defence Forces of the Australian Colonies 1836–1901*, Allen & Unwin, Sydney, 1988.

Odgers, G.J., *The RAAF: An Illustrated History*, 2nd edn, Child & Associates, Frenchs Forest, NSW, 1989.

——, *Diggers: The Australian Army, Navy and Air Force in Eleven Wars*, vol.2, Lansdowne Publishing, Sydney, 1994.

Parker, R.G., *Cockatoo Island*, Nelson, Melbourne, 1977.

Parnell, N. & Boughton, T., *Flypast: A Record of Aviation in Australia*, Australian Government Publishing Service, Canberra, 1988.

Ross, A.T., 'The economics of rearmament 1933–39', in Australian War Memorial *Journal*, no.7, October 1985.

——, *Armed and Ready: The Industrial Development and Defence of Australia 1900–1945*, Turton & Armstrong, Sydney, 1995

Scott, E., *Australia During the War*, vol.11 of *The Official History of Australia in the War of 1914–1918*, Angus & Robertson, Sydney, 1936.

Sloper, G.V., 'Personal Experiences in the Gulf', *Journal of the Royal United Services Institute of Australia*, July 1991.

Thatcher, M., *The Downing Street Years*, Harper Collins, London, 1993.

Walsh, P.A., *Confessions of a Failed Finance Minister*, Random House, Sydney, 1995.

Wettenhall, R., *Public Enterprise and National Development: Selected Essays*, Royal Australian Institute of Public Administration, Canberra, 1987.

Yergin, D., & Stanislaw, J., *The Commanding Heights: The Battle Between Government and the Marketplace That is Remaking the Modern World*, Simon & Schuster, New York, 1998.

Interviews & correspondence

Apted, Mr A., 7 April 1999.
Babbage, Dr R.E., 1 July 1995, 27 March 1998.
Barclay, Dr J.R., 18 January 1994.

Beazley, Hon. K.C., 22 March 1995.
Berlyn, Rear Admiral N.R.B., 27 April 1994, 17 April 1998.
Bryan, Ms E.B., 2 March 1995.
Callinan, Mr K.J., 30 June 1994.
Church, Mr M., 23 May 1995 (facsimile letter).
Cole, Sir William, 9 January 1995.
Conway, Mr B.F., 24 August 1993, 16 January 1998.
De Wet, Mr K., 15 October 1998.
Deighton, Mrs E., 15 May 1995 (telephone).
Diedrichs, Mr M., 15 October 1998.
Donohue, Commodore H., 9, 20 June 1995 (facsimile letters).
Fynmore, Mr R.J., 28 February 1995.
Gibson, Mr B., 24 November 1993.
Gration, General P.C., 22 May 1995 (telephone).
Harris, Mr K.A., 5 August 1993, 15 January, 30 September 1998, 30 November 1998 (letter), 14 May 1999, 15 July 1999 (letter).
Hickman, Mr S., 23 March 1995.
Janka, Mr Z., 30 September 1993.
Jones, Mr G., 11 May 1999.
McCorquodale, Dr J.C., 11 May 1995 (telephone).
McIntosh, Dr M.K., 10 April 1995 (facsimile letter).
McLachlan, Hon. I.M., 19 April 1999 (telephone).
McMahon, Mr J.E., 27 April 1994, 18 February 1998.
Mitchell, Mr W.T., 26 August 1993, 29 September 1998.
Pettifer, Mr J., 25 November 1993.
Podger, Mr A.S., 23 May 1995.
Russell, Mrs P.A., 26 November 1993.
Tannahill, Mr R.W., 17 April 1998.
Targ, L.M., 28 April 1994, 30 September 1998, 14 May 1999.
Tunny, Mr G., 23 April 1999.
Walsh, Hon. P.A., 1 April 1995.
Walters, Mr P., 9 May 1995 (telephone).
White, Dr J.D., 28 April 1995 (telephone).
Woods, Mrs A., 9 May 1995.
Woodward, Mr L.B., 5 December 1994.
Wrigley, Mr A.K., 13 December 1994.

Newspapers, periodicals, radio & TV reports

The Corporate Relations branch at ADI Headquarters has maintained a record of all media items regarding the company since its inception. This includes press releases, radio and television items monitored, and clippings from newspapers and major periodical publications in Australia and overseas. This has made possible a detailed scanning of a wide range of material from this source. Among the publications used were the following:

Advertiser (Adelaide), 5 December 1989.

Age (Melbourne), 19, 20 August 1987; 3 June 1988; 17 March, 2 August 1989; 20 June, 26 July, 1, 2 December 1990; 17 April 1991; 21 July 1992; 13 November, 1, 2 December 1993; 9 May 1994; 17, 19 April 1995; 26 June 1999.

Argus (Melbourne), 12 April, 28 June 1919.

Army Magazine, 16 June 1994.

Army News (Australia), 2 June 1994.

Army News (New Zealand), 11 August 1993.

Ashfield Courier, December 1992.

Asia-Pacific Defence Reporter, March 1991; August–September 1993; February–March, June–July 1994.

Asian Defence Journal, May 1990; July 1991.

Asian Military Review, August–September 1993.

Australian (Sydney), 8–9 May 1982; 12 December 1984; 15–16, 18 August 1987; 3 October 1989; 3 July 1990; 28 June 1991; 22, 23 May, 15 August, 3, 18 November, 15 December 1992; 27 August, 29 October 1993; 30 March, 10, 27, 31 May, 16, 18 August, 11, 14 October, 1, 11, 14, 15 November, 14 December 1994; 17, 18, 19, 24 January, 11 February, 19 April, 28 June 1995; 15 May 1997; 17 July, 11 August 1998; 2 August 1999.

Australian Business, 29 March 1989.

Australian Business Monthly, April 1995.

Australian Defence 2000, March 1990.

Australian Defence Intelligencer, July 1993; September, November 1994.

Australian Defence Magazine, June, October 1994.

Australian Defence News, 25 November 1991; 12 November 1993.

Australian Defence Report, 8 February, 3 May, 14 June, 9 August, 18 October, 13 December 1990; 7 February, 2, 16 May, 10 July 1991; 6 August 1992; 8, 22 July, 19 August, 2 September 1993; 3 February, 26 May, 21 July, 13 October 1994; 9 February, 13 April 1995; 27 May, 22 July 1999.

Australian Financial Review, 31 May 1988; 11 May, 1, 2, 4 August, 28 September 1989; 4, 21 June 1990; 16 January, 6 February, 20 March, 27, 28 May, 5, 15 July, 20 September 1991; 4 June, 7 August, 9 September, 15, 16, 21 October, 4, 20 November, 15 December 1992; 18, 19 August 1993; 28 March, 31 May, 29 August, 20 December 1994; 2, 8, 27 February, 9 March, 19 April, 15 May 1995; 31 October 1995; 8 October, 1 December 1997; 30 June, 13, 22 July, 5, 6, 9 August 1999.

Australian Shipyards, June 1990.

Benalla Ensign, 16 June 1993.

Bendigo Advertiser, 23 February 1989; 26 January, 7, 21 February, 3 August 1991; 26 February, 9 September, 18 November 1992; 22 November 1993; 23 April, 20 December 1994; 15, 16, 20 May 1995.

Blacktown Advocate, 15 December 1993; 23 February, 20 April, 11 May 1994; 29 March 1995.

Blacktown City Guardian, 5 August 1993; 20 April, 11 May 1994.

Border Mail (Albury), 26 November 1991; 29 February, 24 March, 8 July 1992; 9 December 1993; 28 September 1994; 24 May 1995.

Bulletin (Sydney), 10, 17 November 1992, 4 April 1995.

Business Queensland, 15 November 1993.

Business Review Weekly, 15 February, 1 March 1991; 3, 10 December 1993; 28 March, 4 April 1994.

Canberra Times, 3 June 1988; 29 September 1989; 15 January, 3 July 1990; 15 July, 20, 22 August, 20 September 1991; 12 October, 2 December 1993; 15, 16, 18 August 1994; 4 June, 15 November 1995; 5 September 1997.

Community News (Essendon, Vic.), 5 December 1990.

Courier-Mail (Brisbane), 23 June 1990; 2 November 1993; 18 January 1995.

Daily Commercial News (Sydney), 2 September 1991; 4, 24 June 1992; 10 February, 18 March, 26 May, 1 June, 18 November 1994; 28 February 1995; 22 July 1998.

Daily Telegraph (Sydney), 3 July 1990.

Defence Industry, March 1990.

Defence Industry & Aerospace Report, 7 December 1989; 21 February, 8, 22 May, 6 November 1992; 8, 22 October 1993; 11 March, 27 May, 28 October, 16 December 1994; 21 April 1995.

Defense News (Springfield, Va., USA), 20–26 December 1993.

Directions in Government, March, June 1990.

Economist (London), 11 March 1995.

Electrical Engineer, December 1992.

Evening Post (Wellington, NZ), 18 September 1991.

Government Officers Magazine, December 1993.

Herald-Sun (Melbourne), 2 December 1990; 26 February, 8 December 1991; 23 April, 18 November 1992; 26 July, 1, 15 December 1993; 17 April 1995.

International Defence Review, October 1991.

Jane's Defence Contracts, October 1994; March 1995.

Lithgow Mercury, 14 April 1994; 2 March 1995.

Manufacturers' Monthly, February 1994.

Military Technology, July 1990.

Mt. Druitt–St. Marys Standard, 25 September, 26 November 1991; 29 March 1995.

Navint, 8 October 1993; 24 February 1995.

Navy News, 21 April 1995.

Newcastle Herald, 13 November, 23 December 1993; 15 January, 5 February, 31 May, 3 June, 28 July, 28 December 1994; 2 May 1995.

Newcastle Star, 10 May 1995.

Penrith City Star, 18 October 1994.

Penrith Press, 17 December 1991; 15 February, 22 March 1994.

Sun (Melbourne), 24 July 1973.

Sun Herald (Sydney), 20 October 1991; 19 July 1992.

Sunday Times (Perth), 24 March 1991; 8 November 1992.

Sydney Morning Herald, 15 May 1984; 22 August, 26 October 1991; 14 March, 22 September, 29 October, 11, 12 December 1992; 18 September 1993; 2, 3, 5 March, 25 May, 13 August, 6 December 1994; 11 March, 19 April, 10 May 1995; 15 November 1995; 15 May 1997: 9 August 1999.

Telegraph Mirror (Sydney), 20 September, 16 January, 29 February, 22 September 1992; 26 July 1993.

West Australian (Perth), 25, 26 March, 19, 22 October 1991; 26 August 1992; 23 July 1993; 17 August, 10 November 1994; 16 January 1995; 22 June 1999.

Appendix 1 ADI Statistics

Profit before tax and abnormals 1989/90–1997/98 ($ million)

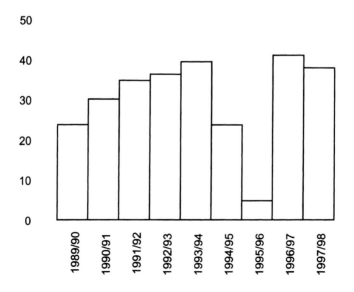

Total sales 1989/90–1997/98 ($ million)

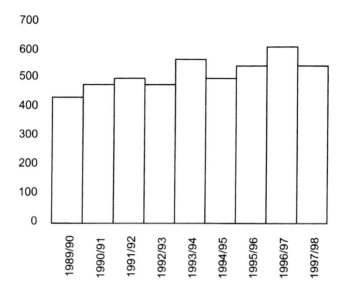

Sales per employee and employee numbers 1989/90–1997/98

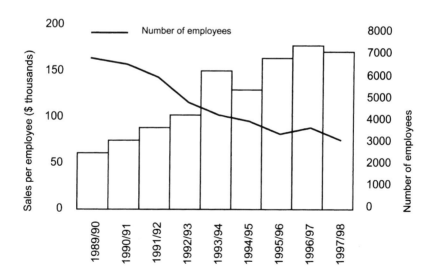

Defence production: impact on government outlays 1984–1994

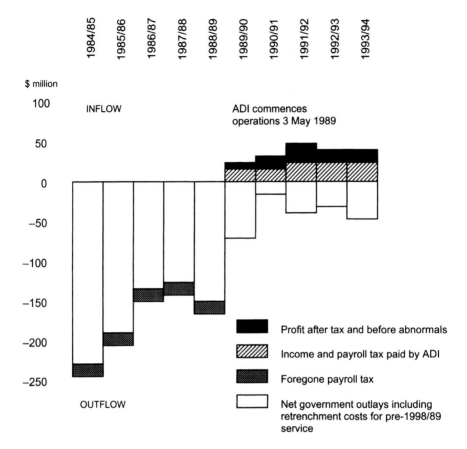

Appendix 2 ADI Corporate Structure

1989

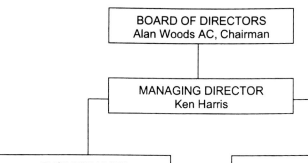

BOARD OF DIRECTORS
Alan Woods AC, Chairman

MANAGING DIRECTOR
Ken Harris

BUSINESS UNITS
SYDNEY &
MELBOURNE

Ammunition & Missiles Division
Chief General Manager
Bryan Padman

Clothing Division
Chief General Manager
Brian Lanigan

Naval Engineering Division
Chief General Manager
Nigel Berlyn

Weapons & Engineering Division
Chief General Manager
Graeme Phipps

CORPORATE
HEADQUARTERS
CANBERRA

Defence Liaison
Group General Manager
John McMahon

Development
Group General Manager
John Barclay

Finance
Group General Manager
Les Massey

Company Secretary/Legal
Counsel
John McCorquodale

1990

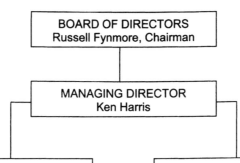

BOARD OF DIRECTORS
Russell Fynmore, Chairman

MANAGING DIRECTOR
Ken Harris

BUSINESS UNITS SYDNEY, CANBERRA & MELBOURNE	CORPORATE HEADQUARTERS CANBERRA

BUSINESS UNITS SYDNEY, CANBERRA & MELBOURNE

Ammunition & Missiles Division
Chief General Manager
Bryan Padman

Clothing Division
Chief General Manager
Brian Lanigan

Consulting Division
Chief General Manager
Ross Babbage

Electronics Division
Chief General Manager
Graham Shepherd

Industrial Decontamination
Division
Chief General Manager
Ron Taylor

International Marketing Division
Chief General Manager
Les Targ

Logistic Support Division
Chief General Manager
Peter Badman

Naval Engineering Division
Chief General Manager
Bryan Gibson

Training Systems Division
Chief General Manager
Neville Rogers

Weapons & Engineering Division
Chief General Manager
Graeme Phipps

CORPORATE HEADQUARTERS CANBERRA

Defence Liaison & Operations
Group General Manager
John McMahon

Development
Group General Manager
Nigel Berlyn

Finance
Group General Manager
Les Massey

Major Projects
Group General Manager
John Barclay

Corporate Relations
Group General Manager
Leigh Funston

Company Secretary/Legal
Counsel
John McCorquodale

1993

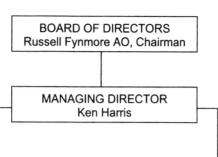

BOARD OF DIRECTORS
Russell Fynmore AO, Chairman

MANAGING DIRECTOR
Ken Harris

**BUSINESS UNITS
SYDNEY, CANBERRA &
MELBOURNE**

Ammunition Division
Chief General Manager
John Barclay

Clothing Division
Chief General Manager
James Kelaher

Consulting Division
Chief General Manager
Ross Babbage

Electronics Division
Chief General Manager
Graham Shepherd

Industrial Decontamination
Division
Chief General Manager
Ron Taylor

Logistic Support Division
Chief General Manager
Peter Badman

Minehunter Project Division
Chief General Manager
Merv Church

Naval Engineering Division
Chief General Manager
Bryan Gibson

Property Division
Chief General Manager
Bill Mitchell

Training Systems Division
Chief General Manager
Neville Rogers

Weapons & Engineering Division
Chief General Manager
Graeme Phipps

**CORPORATE
HEADQUARTERS
SYDNEY**

Defence Liaison & Operations
Group General Manager
John McMahon

Development
Group General Manager
Nigel Berlyn AO

Finance
Group General Manager
Rob Tannahill

International Business
Group General Manager
Les Targ

Corporate Relations
Group Manager
Leigh Funston

Company Secretary
Trish Russell

CANBERRA OFFICE

Defence Requirements
General Manager
Jack Byrnes

1994

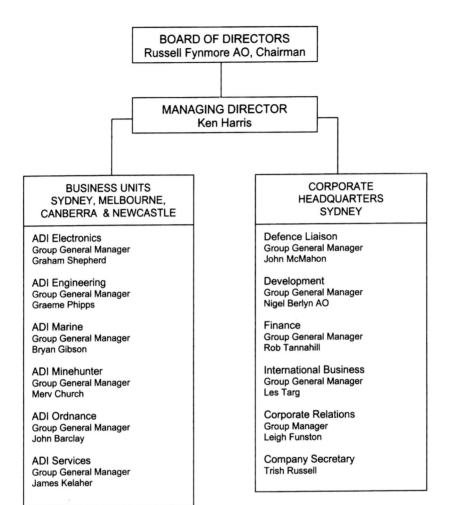

BOARD OF DIRECTORS
Russell Fynmore AO, Chairman

MANAGING DIRECTOR
Ken Harris

BUSINESS UNITS
SYDNEY, MELBOURNE,
CANBERRA & NEWCASTLE

ADI Electronics
Group General Manager
Graham Shepherd

ADI Engineering
Group General Manager
Graeme Phipps

ADI Marine
Group General Manager
Bryan Gibson

ADI Minehunter
Group General Manager
Merv Church

ADI Ordnance
Group General Manager
John Barclay

ADI Services
Group General Manager
James Kelaher

CORPORATE
HEADQUARTERS
SYDNEY

Defence Liaison
Group General Manager
John McMahon

Development
Group General Manager
Nigel Berlyn AO

Finance
Group General Manager
Rob Tannahill

International Business
Group General Manager
Les Targ

Corporate Relations
Group Manager
Leigh Funston

Company Secretary
Trish Russell

1995

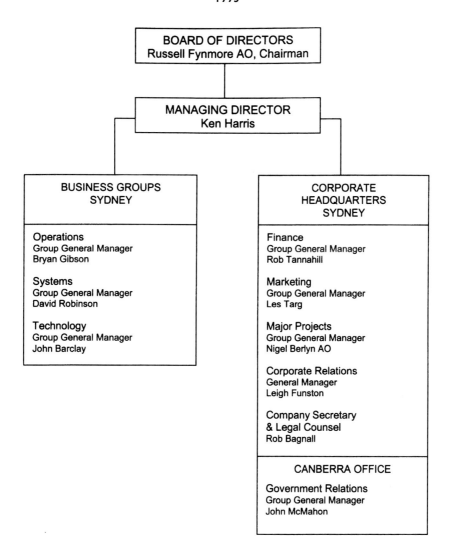

1998

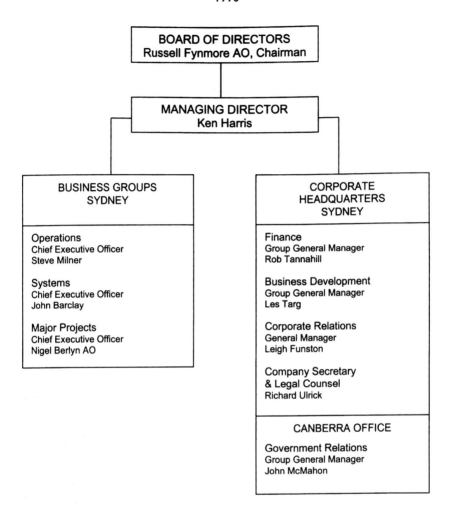

BOARD OF DIRECTORS
Russell Fynmore AO, Chairman

MANAGING DIRECTOR
Ken Harris

**BUSINESS GROUPS
SYDNEY**

Operations
Chief Executive Officer
Steve Milner

Systems
Chief Executive Officer
John Barclay

Major Projects
Chief Executive Officer
Nigel Berlyn AO

**CORPORATE
HEADQUARTERS
SYDNEY**

Finance
Group General Manager
Rob Tannahill

Business Development
Group General Manager
Les Targ

Corporate Relations
General Manager
Leigh Funston

Company Secretary
& Legal Counsel
Richard Ulrick

CANBERRA OFFICE

Government Relations
Group General Manager
John McMahon

INDEX